The Guaraní and Their Missions

The Guaraní and Their Missions

A Socioeconomic History

Julia J. S. Sarreal

STANFORD UNIVERSITY PRESS

STANFORD, CALIFORNIA

Stanford University Press
Stanford, California

Map 1 originally appeared as Map 8 in David J. Weber's *Bárbaros: Spaniards and Their Savages in the Age of Enlightenment*, published in 2005 by Yale University Press. © Yale University Press. Reprinted by permission.

The Institute for Humanities Research and the Center for Critical Inquiry and Cultural Studies at Arizona State University provided subsidies toward the publication of this book.

Printed in the United States of America on acid-free, archival-quality paper

Library of Congress Cataloging-in-Publication Data

Sarreal, Julia J. S., author.

The Guaraní and their missions : a socioeconomic history / Julia J.S. Sarreal.

pages cm

Includes bibliographical references and index.

ISBN 978-0-8047-8597-6 (cloth : alk. paper)

1. Guarani Indians—Missions—Rio de la Plata Region (Argentina and Uruguay)—History—18th century. 2. Guarani Indians—Rio de la Plata Region (Argentina and Uruguay)—Economic conditions—18th century. 3. Missions—Economic aspects—Rio de la Plata Region (Argentina and Uruguay)—History—18th century. 4. Jesuits—Missions—Rio de la Plata Region (Argentina and Uruguay)—History—18th century. 5. Rio de la Plata Region (Argentina and Uruguay)—Economic conditions—18th century. 6. Rio de la Plata Region (Argentina and Uruguay)—History—18th century. I. Title.

F2230.2.G72S27 2014

916.3'68—dc23

2013049707

ISBN 978-0-8047-9122-9 (electronic)

Typeset by Newgen in 10/12 Sabon

In memory of my mother, Leah K. Rose

Contents

Illustrations

TABLES

Acknowledgments

I am grateful for the invaluable support of numerous individuals and institutions that have helped me throughout the process of researching and writing this book. In addition to the names listed below, many other scholars, colleagues, institutions, family members, and friends made this book possible with their generous assistance and encouragement.

I first learned of the Guaraní missions as a Peace Corps volunteer in Curuguaty, Paraguay. For two years, the family of Melchor and Elisea Velázquez, the members of the Almacen de Consumo of Santa Rosa Cue, and many other Paraguayans welcomed me into their lives and taught me about the joys and struggles associated with being a campesino. Such experiences enriched my life and continue to subtly influence my understanding of the Guaraní and their missions. Upon returning to the United States, graduate studies at Harvard University provided the tools and resources necessary to develop this passion into a scholarly project. I am grateful to John Coatsworth for giving me both the freedom to pursue my interests and invaluable guidance about framing my research in a compelling manner. I thank John Womack for his unwavering support, generosity with his time, and wide breadth of knowledge. I always left our brainstorming sessions with new ideas and a sense of direction. Jeffrey Williamson and Stuart Schwartz also provided help in the early stages of this project. Fellow graduate students at Harvard and members of graduate student writing groups at Stanford and UC Berkeley gave valuable advice, encouragement, and camaraderie.

Access to a wealth of resources at various archives and libraries was crucial to this project. The staff at the Archivo General de la Nación in Buenos Aires welcomed me during numerous research trips and shared the archive's vast array of documents related to the Guaraní and their missions. My project would not have been possible without their generosity. The project also benefited from resources at the Archivo Nacional de Asunción, the Archivum Romanum Societatis Iesu in Rome, the Archivo

Histórico Nacional de Madrid, the Biblioteca Nacional de España, and the Real Academia de la Historia in Madrid. As a graduate student at Harvard, a visiting scholar at Stanford, and an assistant professor at Arizona State University, I had the privilege of using these institutions' extensive library holdings.

I am grateful for the warm welcome that fellow scholars gave me during research trips. In Argentina, I received the help and advice of various scholars, including Guillermo Wilde, Julio Djenderedjian, Norberto Levinton, Lía Quarleri, Mercedes Avellaneda, Juan Carlos Garavaglia, and Jorge Gelman. During my first research trip, Ernesto Maeder and Alfredo Poenitz generously offered their time and books. Both Rafael Carbonell de Masy and Martín Morales introduced me to the Jesuit archive in Rome.

As the project matured, senior colleagues generously provided mentorship. Susan Socolow, Lyman Johnson, Cynthia Radding, Thomas Whigham, and Jerry Cooney gave valuable advice and encouragement throughout the process. Erick Langer, Jeremy Baskes, and Barbara Ganson have also been supportive. I am grateful to my colleagues at Arizona State University for their insights and feedback on different parts of the manuscript. Tatiana Seijas provided useful input at a key point in the manuscript's development. Herbert Klein and three anonymous readers provided lengthy comments and suggestions that have greatly improved the manuscript. I alone am responsible for any mistakes.

The staff at Stanford University Press have been kind, prompt, and accommodating. They have made the publishing process as pleasant as possible. I am especially grateful to Norris Pope, who was extremely helpful and understanding during the early stages of the publishing process, and to Stacy Wagner, who brought this project to fruition. Fran Andersen professionally ushered the book through the production process.

This book was made possible by various fellowships and awards. Subventions from both the Center for Critical Inquiry and Cultural Studies and the Institute for Humanities Research at Arizona State University helped fund publication. A Fulbright-Hays research fellowship and a Frederick Sheldon Traveling Fellowship funded a year of research in Argentine and Paraguayan archives. Arizona State University, the David Rockefeller Center for Latin American Studies at Harvard University, the Mellon Foundation, and the Real Colegio Complutense funded summer research in Argentina, Paraguay, Spain, and Italy. Foreign Language and Area Studies Fellowships, Mellon Fellowships in Latin American History, an appointment as visiting scholar at Stanford University, a fellowship from Harvard University, and a semester's research leave from Arizona State University generously supported my research and writing.

Most of all, this project would not have been possible without the support of my family. I owe my greatest debt to my husband, John. His unending love, flexibility, and encouragement over the years make this book a shared accomplishment. My sons, Félix and Benicio, make the frenetic experience of juggling a career and family worthwhile. My favorite research trips are the ones when they both accompany me. Lastly, I am forever indebted to my mother and friend, Leah Rose. With her unconditional love, she encouraged me to stretch my wings and follow my dreams. I miss her dearly.

Abbreviations

AGI: Archivo de las Indias, Seville

AGN: Archivo General de la Nación, Buenos Aires

ACAL: Archivo y Colección de Andrés Lamas

CBN: Colección Biblioteca Nacional

AHN: Archivo Histórico Nacional, Madrid

ANA: Archivo Nacional de Asunción

NE: Sección Nueva Encuadernación

SH: Sección Histórica

ARSI: Archivum Romanum Societatus Iesu, Rome

AS: Archivo General de Simancas

BANH: Biblioteca de la Real Academia de la Historia, Madrid

BNM: Biblioteca Nacional, Madrid

BNP: Bibliothèque Nationale de France, Paris

The Guaraní and Their Missions

Introduction

During the colonial period, hundreds of thousands of Indians from frontier regions of Latin America joined Catholic missions. They left small, dispersed, and mobile communities to live in large, settled mission towns with Catholic priests. Many turned to missions as a way to protect themselves and their communities from pressures associated with Spanish imperialism. In contrast, the Spanish Crown envisioned missions as a tool for incorporating these peoples and their lands into its empire. Under such a mandate, the Crown contracted Jesuits, Franciscans, Dominicans, and Mercedarians to bring together dispersed groups of indigenous peoples to live together in single mission towns, where missionaries taught them Catholicism and instructed them in settled agriculture and European cultural practices. By 1767, over 265,000 Native Americans resided in more than two hundred Jesuit missions throughout the Americas (see Map 1).[1]

Of all the missions in the Americas, the Guaraní missions of the Río de la Plata region of South America are widely believed to have been the most successful in terms of the number of indigenous inhabitants, economic prosperity, and historical importance. The Jesuit historical dictionary claims the Guaraní missions to have been the order's most famous achievement in Spanish America.[2] From their founding in 1609, the Guaraní missions grew to over 140,000 inhabitants at their peak in 1732—an average of over 4,500 Indians per mission.[3] The two Jesuits assigned to each mission could not force hundreds or thousands of Indians either to join or to stay. Rather, the Guaraní chose to join and remain in the missions in the face of Spanish and Portuguese colonialism.

By the eighteenth century, the majority of mission Guaraní had been residing in the missions for generations, and as a result, mission culture—biological, technological, organizational, and theological systems that incorporated aspects of both native and Jesuit-inspired customs and

Map 1. *Jesuit missions in Spanish America, 1766*
SOURCE: Weber, *Bárbaros*, 111. Reprinted by permission of Yale University Press.

practices—developed among the Guaraní.[4] Growth through natural re-production rather than immigration allowed the Jesuits to move beyond baptism and intensify their efforts at such wide-ranging cultural change.[5] Other missions in Spanish America never reached this stage; mission populations elsewhere only grew with the addition of new converts.[6] Given the extended period of population growth without new immigrants, mission culture developed more deeply and broadly among the Guaraní than among other mission populations.

The Guaraní missions were significant population centers for seventeenth- and eighteenth-century Río de la Plata. In 1745, the number of Guaraní residing in a single mission—Mission Yapeyú—equaled more than half the total population of Buenos Aires a year earlier.[7] The missions also contained a large portion of the entire region's population. Between 1680 and 1682, the twenty-two Guaraní missions accounted for over half of the entire Río de la Plata population, and by 1759 the number of Guaraní residing in the thirteen missions of the province of Paraguay outnumbered all other inhabitants of the province combined.[8] The large numbers of inhabitants meant that the mission labor force enabled high levels of economic activity.

The Guaraní missions played an important role in the economy of the Río de la Plata region. Extensive territory and a diversity of productive assets made the missions into a regional economic powerhouse. The missions' main trade good—*yerba maté* (Paraguayan tea that continues to be popular in the Southern Cone)—supplied the local and regional markets as far away as Potosí and Chile. The missions reinvested a significant portion of the proceeds from such sales to develop mission towns and build grand religious structures. Scholars of mission art and architecture attest to the missions' affluence, as evident in the façade of the Mission San Miguel church (see Figure 1).[9]

In the second half of the eighteenth century, political restructuring and competition undermined the missions' favorable position. The institution

Figure 1. Catholic church at Mission San Miguel
SOURCE: Julia Sarreal, 2005.

could not withstand reforms that gave a greater role to both the Crown and the market economy. Regional economic growth further undermined the institution. As a result of these changes, the missions became bankrupt. By 1800, Crown officials decided that the Guaraní missions were beyond repair and formally began to dismantle them.

This book argues that the Guaraní people built the structural foundations for the economic success of the thirty Jesuit missions between 1609 and 1768 and subsequently continued to shape their social development. As such, it provides a context for understanding indigenous agency in the borderlands of Spanish America. Although the Spanish Crown's reforms and intervention led to the missions' economic decline, the Guaraní missions continued to endure until the end of the colonial period. This book explores the economic foundations for the missions' success as well as ultimate deterioration and emphasizes Guaraní participation in these processes.

Given their importance, the Guaraní missions have attracted the attention of numerous scholars.[10] While many important works have been written on the subject, my discussion will be limited to those most relevant to the topics at hand. In the past, scholars tended to describe missions on the basis of Spanish sources without addressing the authors' biases or underlying motivations. In recent years, mission scholarship has become more critical of sources and shifted its focus to the Indians' experience and Indian agency.[11] In addition to re-examining Jesuit sources, scholars use Guaraní letters as a means of drawing out Guaraní voices.[12] This book extends such methodology by highlighting the Guaraní perspective and the economic actions of Guaraní communities as recorded in quantitative sources such as accounting books and censuses.

Much of the recent scholarship on the Guaraní and their missions has been cultural history.[13] These works primarily explore Guaraní identity—how the Guaraní viewed themselves and the world around them. This book takes a different approach to ethnohistory (the interdisciplinary study of indigenous, diasporic, and minority peoples). While I use documents written by the Guaraní to shed light on their experiences with and perception of the mission economy, my goal is not to describe their entire mission experience. Instead, this study is the first to focus on the missions' socio-economic structure. Such analysis leads to a fuller understanding of how the Guaraní experienced the missions. The Guaraní spent much of their time working in the mission economy as laborers and received regular distributions from the mission's communal supplies; thus the mission economy directly affected their standard of living. Equally important, the mission economy provided the funding that made the mission enterprise possible.

Scholars have explored how the Guaraní fit into the political and social structures that organized the mission population.[14] A complex administrative structure emerged to organize and manage the large mission population. This book contributes to such discussion by characterizing native leadership in the missions as either charismatic, coercive, or organizational. Charismatic leaders possessed traits that fit with Guaraní concepts of leadership; coercive leaders exercised authority based on the threat of punishment; organizational leaders divided the mission population into smaller units. Such analysis demonstrates that while native elites without charismatic leadership qualities had difficulty exercising power, the governing structure's flexibility allowed non-elites with such traits to access leadership positions. In contrast to earlier studies, this book also underscores how during the post-Jesuit period Guaraní *cabildos* (town councils) gained substantial new powers and became increasingly important as compared to Spanish officials and other Guaraní leaders.[15]

The mission economy, which funded operations and sustained the population, also shaped mission history. Scholars, however, have not focused ample attention on this important aspect of Guaraní history.[16] This book is the first economic history of the Guaraní missions from their peak through their decline. It employs mission account books, letters, and other archival materials to trace the Guaraní mission work regime and to examine how the Guaraní shaped the mission economy. It also describes the missions' larger importance in the Río de la Plata region by highlighting the interplay among the missions, their Guaraní inhabitants, and the regional economy.

Tracking changes in the mission population is one of the best measures of the missions' vitality. Most demographic studies calculate the size of the mission population over time and divide the inhabitants into categories based on gender, age, and marital status.[17] Such studies provide some anecdotal information about mortality rates and flight. In contrast, this study quantifies population numbers over time and explores the relative importance of mortality versus flight during the post-Jesuit years.

While the missions underwent definitive decline after the Jesuit expulsion in 1768, events in the 1750s foreshadowed such problems. In 1750, the Treaty of Madrid awarded the seven easternmost missions to the Portuguese in return for Colonia del Sacramento. In response to the treaty, mission Guaraní fought Portuguese and Spanish troops in defense of their land in the Guaraní War. Although the terms of the treaty were officially rescinded in 1761, the missions never fully recovered. While earlier scholarship focuses on the Treaty of Madrid and how the war affected the Jesuits, more recent scholarship focuses on the actions taken by the Guaraní.[18] This work adds to the existing literature by showing how contemporary descriptions of Jesuit activity among the Guaraní were among the most effective means employed both to promote and defend the expulsion of the Jesuits from Portuguese (1759), French (1762), and Spanish territory (1767).

Between 1768 and 1800, the mission population fell by almost half, and the economy became insolvent. Scholarship on the Guaraní missions generally overlooks this important period.[19] Conventional accounts attribute the missions' decline to the expulsion of the Jesuits, first from territory ceded to Portugal in 1750 (as depicted in the film *The Mission*) and then from all of Spanish America in 1767. Mission historiography highlights the role of corruption and poor administration while also addressing other contributing factors.[20] Much of this analysis relies on reports by mission administrators and fails to provide a coherent and comprehensive explanation for the missions' decline. In contrast, this book provides an integrated explanation of the various causal factors that led to that decline. In addition, it highlights how the Guaraní contributed to and experienced this process.

The missions' prosperity and importance in the region led contemporaries to form strong opinions either in support of or in opposition to the institution; such conflicting views continue to be apparent today. On one hand, proponents of the missions highlight that the Jesuits protected the Indians from exploitation and preserved the Guaraní language and other aspects of indigenous culture.[21] On the other hand, opponents emphasize that the Jesuits took away the Indians' freedom, forced them to radically change their lifestyle, physically abused them, and subjected them to disease.[22]

My intent is not to pass moral judgment on the missions. It is a given that contact with Europeans decimated indigenous populations and irrevocably changed the Guaraní way of life.[23] The missions were a function of their time and clearly had both negative and positive repercussions for the Guaraní. My goal is rather to provide a better understanding of the mission experience from the Guaraní perspective. Why did the Guaraní join the missions? Why did many opt to stay after the Jesuits left? How did the Guaraní influence daily life in the missions and how did they contribute to the missions' decline? This study takes a new approach by combining economic and social analysis to understand the Indians' daily life and living standards in the missions. The result is a richer and more complex understanding of the changes that mission Indians experienced during the colonial period.

The Guaraní were exposed and reacted to Spanish imperialism in two distinct stages. First, from 1609 to 1768 the Jesuits introduced the Guaraní to certain aspects of Spanish culture and practices. The Guaraní adopted some of these changes, resisted others, and made their own mark on the missions. Mission culture reflected such negotiation between the Guaraní and the Jesuits. During this period the Jesuits exposed the Guaraní to settled agriculture and the Catholic religion in addition to European cultural norms while simultaneously trying to limit Guaraní exposure to behaviors that contradicted Catholic teachings. The missionaries tried to restrict outside influences on the Guaraní by limiting the Indians' absences from the missions and contact with outsiders. Despite such efforts, activities such as hunting cattle, gathering yerba maté, transporting goods, and participating in military engagements took the Indians outside of the mission. The Guaraní also left the mission without Jesuit approval. Still, mission Guaraní were more isolated than other mission Indians. Sonoran, Nueva Vizcayan, and Californian Indians regularly left the missions in order to labor in presidios and mines.[24] Such competition over labor and other productive resources at least partly explains why these missions never achieved demographic and financial success equivalent to that of the Guaraní missions.

A communal structure of collective labor, shared ownership, and redistribution of mission property formed the basis of the mission economy. Mission Guaraní generally did not engage in paid labor, commerce, or the ownership of private property. Instead, they worked both collectively and independently, and they relied primarily on provisions supplied from communal supplies. While private property existed, communal property played a much more significant role in the missions. Such communal culture did not make the missions proto-socialist societies as some have argued.[25] Although not dramatic, inequalities existed among Indians in terms of power, status, and the receipt of material goods.

During the Jesuit period, the missions prospered as a result of this communal culture, but they were not efficient. The missions' prosperity depended on subsidies from the Jesuit order, special protection and privileges from the Crown, and the lack of competition. These factors enabled the missions to use their productive resources inefficiently yet still flourish financially. The inefficiency of the Jesuit missions contrasts with earlier studies that highlight the productivity of rural enterprises operated by the Jesuits in Spanish America.[26]

In the second half of the eighteenth century, Bourbon reforms exposed the missions' inefficiency. The missions lost both their subsidy from the Jesuit order and their special protection and privileges from the Crown. Furthermore, regional economic growth led to competition over the missions' productive resources. As a result of these changes, the missions found that they could no longer either defend their property rights or inefficiently use productive resources.

With the Jesuit expulsion, the Guaraní were suddenly thrown into the second stage of exposure to Spanish imperialism. Crown officials replaced Jesuit missionaries with priests from other religious orders to oversee the missions' religious affairs and government-appointed officials to oversee all nonreligious affairs. In addition, mission reforms promoted private property and commerce. In response, acculturation and assimilation intensified as individual Guaraní increasingly engaged in the market economy.

In contrast to earlier scholars, I downplay the importance of corruption in explaining the missions' decline. Royal officials instituted a system of checks and balances that limited, though failed to eliminate, corruption. To maintain accountability at the highest level of mission management, the general administrator in charge of the mission economy provided a substantial deposit before assuming his position. Additionally, oversight by the Guaraní, higher-level officials in the mission bureaucracy, and priests increased accountability and prevented Spanish administrators from acting autocratically at the individual mission level.

The Guaraní cabildo in the post-Jesuit era played a much larger formal role in mission management than before. During the Jesuit period, Guaraní scribes and secretaries recorded information related to mission management, but there is no indication that they gave their signed consent or approval to trade documents, audited account records, or had high-level decision-making power.[27] In contrast, post-Jesuit reforms mandated that the administrator consult with the cabildo when making decisions and that the cabildo approve—with their signatures—all transactions related to mission property. At least as early as 1770, Guaraní leaders started signing receipts for their mission's trade and summaries of their mission's accounting records; hundreds of mission receipts, inventories, and summaries of inflows and outflows of goods contain such signatures.[28] These written records created an intricate paper trail for documenting and tracing all transactions. Accounting records included signed receipts at all stages of a transaction, while various debit-and-credit books summarized transactions. Cabildo members almost always signed these documents, and every two to three years the principal accounts office (Tribunal Mayor de Cuentas) for the Viceroyalty of the Río de la Plata audited these account records.

Even though cabildo members regularly signed their mission's accounting documents, Guaraní leaders generally lacked the knowledge and training to take full advantage of formal inclusion in their mission's management decisions. The Jesuits had not prepared the Guaraní for such oversight responsibilities. For over 150 years, the missionaries had made all of the high-level decisions, signed all contracts, managed trade, and arranged business outside of the missions on behalf of the Guaraní. Although post-Jesuit reformers nobly empowered the Guaraní to oversee and manage their mission's resources, on-the-job training generally did not provide the requisite skills. Cabildo members' signatures did not mean that the signatories understood the numerous receipts with an immense amount of detail and the complex accounting books with many pages of information.

At least some cabildo members could not read the documents that they were charged with signing, owing to inadequate literacy skills. Signature patterns suggest that some Guaraní leaders were illiterate or semiliterate. Generally only a few cabildo members signed a document, and frequently one member explicitly signed on behalf of those who could not sign their own name. Furthermore, many Guaraní leaders who signed their names often did so with a rough hand. Those who struggled with signing their name likely also had difficulty in reading the documents.

The use of the Spanish language was a further obstacle for some Guaraní leaders. All of the accounting documents—except for some occasional information written by Guaraní leaders—were in Spanish. While a literate but non-Spanish-speaking Indian could probably decipher written numbers and names of people and items, descriptive text written in Spanish would be more difficult to understand. Even though post-Jesuit reformers promoted educating mission Guaraní in Spanish, the Guaraní language still prevailed. Throughout the post-Jesuit period Guaraní leaders almost always continued to conduct their written correspondence with mission or viceregal officials in Guaraní. This preference suggests that at least some Guaraní leaders felt uncomfortable with or had difficulty writing in Spanish.

While the signatures do not prove that the Guaraní leaders actually participated in or understood the transactions described in the documents, the process itself provided them with the opportunity to influence mission management. Signatures by cabildo members are found in hundreds of mission accounting documents from the post-Jesuit period. Signing the documents required exposure to descriptions of their mission's economic transactions and financial condition. If cabildo members did not agree with this information or wanted to make life difficult for the Spanish administrator, they could withhold their signatures. Given that receipts and account books almost always contained various signatures by cabildo members, a lack thereof would be a red flag for the higher-level bureaucrats who inspected these accounting documents. Thus, even if the Guaraní did not understand everything that they signed, their signature of consent was still a powerful tool for both empowering the Guaraní cabildo and keeping the administrator in check.

Both mission and regional reforms spurred economic growth in the Río de la Plata region and thereby also led to the missions' decline. Crown officials thought such reforms would bring prosperity to the missions and the Guaraní. The reforms succeeded in increasing private property, commerce, and wage labor among the Guaraní, but not in the way that Spanish reformers expected. Guaraní engagement in the market economy undermined the communal foundation that defined the missions.

The mission economy never underwent a resurgence during the post-Jesuit period.[29] While gross revenue (total revenue before expenses) was significantly higher during the first two decades after the Jesuit expulsion, this does not mean that the thirty missions enjoyed a period of economic recovery.[30] Rather, the boom in revenues resulted from one mission's (Mission Yapeyú) sale of cattle hides. Not including Yapeyú (an anomaly among the missions and discussed in its own chapter), average yearly sales revenue for the remaining twenty-nine missions during these post-Jesuit years did not exceed the average for the Jesuit period.

While the Guaraní were pressured to produce trade goods for the market economy, the Guaraní found ways to mediate labor demands. Higher quantities of yerba maté sold during the first decades after the Jesuit expulsion erroneously imply increased exploitation of Guaraní workers.[31] In fact, almost all of this yerba maté was of inferior quality as compared to the Jesuit period and thus required significantly less labor to produce. Its lower quality was reflected in a much lower price, and although the quantity of yerba maté substantially increased during the post-Jesuit period, gross revenues did not. Furthermore, the missions disinvested—as they did with most of their productive assets.[32] By no longer maintaining and replanting many of the missions' domesticated yerba maté trees, the Guaraní reduced their labor demands. In effect, such purposeful depletion of assets prolonged the missions' decline.

Post-Jesuit reforms thus made the missions unsustainable. The market-based ideology of private property and commerce clashed with the communal culture of collective labor, shared ownership, and redistribution of mission property. Furthermore, the separation of the religious and secular aspects of mission management, combined with regional economic growth, undermined the missions' financial viability. The missions were no longer receiving subsidies from the Jesuit order at the same time that expenses ballooned as a result of the market wages paid to new secular officials. The expanding regional economy led to competition over resources such as Guaraní labor, land, cattle, and yerba maté trees. By 1801 the mission population had fallen by two-thirds from its peak in 1732 and the missions were struggling to maintain their very existence. This decline was caused by official efforts to develop the Río de la Plata region and modernize the missions and their Indian inhabitants by pushing them into the taxable world economy.

The market-based reforms created both winners and losers among the Guaraní. Many took advantage of opportunities offered by the rapidly growing regional economy. Skilled Guaraní had the most to gain and easily found employment elsewhere. Working-age males, and to a lesser degree females, also left the missions at a high rate. Still, a considerable number of Guaraní remained in the missions. These Guaraní received fewer goods overall from communal supplies than before and now had to find alternate ways to procure necessities. Many began to buy and sell goods on their own behalf—something that did not occur under the Jesuits. Inequality also increased. While Guaraní leaders clearly did not become as wealthy as native leaders elsewhere in Spanish America, some benefited from mission reforms that encouraged distinctions and privileges based on status. Cabildo members, especially the *corregidor* (head of the cabildo), were best positioned to take advantage of these changes. They had significantly more control and access to mission resources than during the Jesuit period. Some individuals used their connections to engage in market exchanges for their own benefit and/or diverted mission resources for their own use. The biggest losers were widows, orphans, and others who had difficulty supporting themselves; the missions no longer set aside material resources as a safety net to help such individuals. This change points to the breakdown of the missions' social fabric; those in need could no longer rely on distributions of food, clothing, or other items for subsistence.

There were also winners and losers among the missions; those with access to goods in high demand from the booming regional economy had the most to gain. A few missions (primarily Yapeyú and San Miguel) had rights to massive quantities of cattle, which gave them a tremendous advantage, given the high demand for cattle hides (the primary regional export during this period). The benefit to these missions, however, was short-lived. High production costs consumed much of the revenues, and the missions could not continue to use productive resources inefficiently or defend their property rights.

Although some aspects are unique to this particular institution, studying the Guaraní missions also offers new insights into the broader relationship between European colonists and native peoples. The history of colonial Latin America is the extension of Spanish and Portuguese rule—or failure thereof—over indigenous peoples and their territory. In the past, this has been a story of how Spaniards and Portuguese (conquistadors, missionaries, and settlers) forced their rule upon Indians.[33] As attention has shifted from the colonial state to Indians and their communities, many scholars have highlighted Indian resistance to European imperialism and the devastation of native societies.[34]

This study of the Guaraní adds to such work by highlighting Indians' ability to consciously manipulate the institutions of European imperialism. Indigenous peoples adopted aspects of Iberian culture and worked within the new political system in an effort to maintain and revitalize their own communities.[35] Both individually and collectively, Indians used the colonial structure—especially the legal system—to protect and advance their interests.[36] Some Indians found roles as intermediaries, purposefully building alliances with Europeans for their own benefit or that of their community.[37] Even in places where both the state and the Catholic Church made few inroads, scholars have found that indigenous intermediaries still participated in and manipulated Iberian imperialism. As in other places in Spanish America, indigenous communities maintained a degree of autonomy by engaging with colonial authorities.[38]

This book does not aspire to provide a comprehensive history of the Guaraní missions but rather traces the process by which the Guaraní responded to political changes during the late colonial period, and how they became increasingly integrated into the Spanish Empire and the broader Atlantic world. Detailing the entire lifespan of the missions is likewise beyond the scope of this book: the development of the missions during the seventeenth century falls outside of the goals of this project, and ample literature about this period already exists.[39] Moreover, accounting records—foundational to this study—have not been located for the seventeenth century. This study is also limited in that it focuses only on the missions founded by the Jesuits and not on the Franciscan missions as well.[40] Finally, Missions San Joaquín and San Estanislao are not included because they were founded later and followed a different trajectory from the thirty Guaraní missions.[41] Specifically, then, this study focuses on the thirty missions that bordered the Paraná and Uruguay Rivers and their eighteenth-century peak and decline.

A brief clarification of terminology is necessary before proceeding. I rely heavily on terms used in source documents. Unless otherwise noted, the terms "Guaraní" and "Indian" refer to the inhabitants or former inhabitants of the Guaraní missions. "Guaraní" is an oversimplification given that various ethnic groups inhabited the missions, and the term "Indian" is clearly problematic. Source documents refer to mission inhabitants as Guaraní, *Indios*, or *naturales*. I have chosen to use the first two terms, since *naturales* (natives) translates poorly into English. Likewise, I follow the primary sources by using "Spaniard" and "Portuguese" for all Hispanicized peoples regardless of their place of birth or racial composition. Such classifications are necessary, but the reader should keep in mind that these artificially constructed categories obscure social and cultural complexities. Within the text, I use the term "pueblo" when referring to a mission's urban center—the housing, church, storerooms, and workshops—as opposed to all of a mission's territory. I use "governor" in reference to the Spanish governor of Río de la Plata, Buenos Aires, or Paraguay and "gobernador" for the Spanish governor of the thirty missions. Before the creation of the Viceroyalty of Río de la Plata in 1776, the most important Crown official in the region was the governor. After the creation of the viceroyalty, governors continued to exist but were subordinate to the viceroy. Likewise, the most important Spanish official overseeing the thirty missions was also called governor. The use of either "governor" or "gobernador" should limit any confusion between the two. Other Spanish or Guaraní terms are explained within the text or glossary.

The book is grounded in archival research: its descriptions and conclusions are based on a variety of primary sources. The discussion of the Jesuit period relies heavily on the writings of Jesuit missionaries, censuses of the mission population, and accounting records from the mission trading centers in Buenos Aires and Santa Fe.[42] Many Jesuits wrote detailed accounts of mission life. Although the biases of the authors must be taken into account, these writings provide a great deal of information about the missions.

Discussion of the post-Jesuit period is based on both quantitative and qualitative sources. Mission reformers instituted a complex record-keeping and oversight apparatus. Tens of thousands of pages of receipts, accounting records, summary reports, and audits are found in Buenos Aires at the Archivo General de la Nación (AGN). This study uses the centralized mission accounting records of the Buenos Aires general administration to track the overall health of the mission system and the mission-level account records to track Guaraní living standards and the performance of individual missions.

Even though they contain a tremendous amount of information, accounting records cannot be taken at face value. Record keepers sometimes wrote down the wrong numbers, forgot to record something, incorrectly added or subtracted, or omitted or distorted information. Various levels of checks and balances limited but did not correct all mistakes or prevent all abuses. The various signatories of receipts and/or account books likely did not always understand what they were signing. Furthermore, at least some merchants, Spanish officials, and Guaraní leaders were either willingly involved in corrupt activities or were threatened or bribed into compliance. Such shortcomings do not mean that the data are meaningless. By observing trends in the data rather than relying on individual cases, we can avoid various pitfalls. I use qualitative documents to give context to the accounting records. Given the deteriorating conditions in the missions, both Guaraní and Spaniards wrote letters and reports describing their experiences and suggesting reforms. As with Jesuit writings, the authors' biases must be taken into account. Most of the authors were interested parties who had something to gain. With all of the primary sources, I pay particular attention to drawing out Guaraní voices. While most authors were Spanish, mission Guaraní also left a paper trail. In addition to their letters and signatures, individual Guaraní also appeared in account records when they purchased something from or sold something to the mission. As best as the sources allow, such Guaraní experience both frames and shapes my analysis.

The book is organized both chronologically and thematically. The chronological organization results in a deeper understanding of how native peoples experienced as well as shaped mission life in its various stages. The thematic approach provides a comprehensive explanation for the missions' decline. The first section contains four chapters explaining the life cycle of the missions under the Jesuits. The second section contains five chapters exploring the reasons for the Guaraní missions' decline. Chapter 1 examines Guaraní and Jesuit motivations behind the missions and provides background about the founding of the institution and its early years in the Río de la Plata region. Chapters 2 and 3 focus on the peak period of the missions during the first half of the eighteenth century. Chapter 2 explains the urban design of the mission pueblos, the Guaraní populations living in these towns, and the governing structure. Chapter 3 describes the economy that funded the missions and Guaraní participation in it. Chapter 4 explores how events related to the Guaraní missions contributed to the Jesuit expulsion from Portuguese, French, and Spanish territory in the second half of the eighteenth century.

Chapters 5 through 8—the central part of the book—explain why the missions declined. Chapter 5 looks at how mission reforms bankrupted the coordinated enterprise of the thirty missions. Chapter 6 both explores why the Guaraní opted either to remain in or to abandon their mission and analyzes the impact of the declining number of mission inhabitants. Chapter 7 examines the living standards of the Guaraní who opted to stay in the missions and how they met their basic needs. Chapter 8 looks at how the expanding regional economy offered a unique financial opportunity for Missions Yapeyú and San Miguel and why these two missions and their inhabitants failed to prosper. The final chapter explains how the communal structure of collective labor, shared ownership, and distribution of mission supplies endured for over three decades after the Jesuit expulsion and the factors that led to its ultimate collapse.

In addition to providing a comprehensive explanation of the ways in which Crown reforms made the missions unsustainable, this book is the first to explain how actions taken by mission administrators and the Guaraní prolonged the missions' history for over three decades. The study's most significant contribution relates to the missions' decline and the integration of the Guaraní into the market economy. Such an understanding, however, requires an explanation of the sociopolitical structures that underlay the missions' success. The book, overall, provides this long-term analysis, focusing at all times on the Guaraní and their unique contributions to the construction, maintenance, and ultimate end of the missions as a colonial institution.

CHAPTER I

Founding and Early Years

The Guaraní and Jesuits underwent great hardship and sacrifice in order to lay the foundations for the missions' later success. During their initial encounters, the world as they knew it turned almost entirely upside down for both parties. The Guaraní abandoned their homes and relocated to large, compact towns shared with various other groups of Guaraní. They had to live with new people and submit to new authorities. They gave up much of their former freedom, encountered strange new rules, and were compelled to restructure many aspects of their daily life. The Jesuits tried to force foreign and incomprehensible cultural practices upon them, and many of their longstanding beliefs and customs came under attack. Underlying all of these changes was a new hierarchy, in which the Jesuits envisioned an inferior and subordinate role for the Guaraní. In the face of such pressures, nonetheless, the Guaraní also exerted influence and shaped the missions by maintaining various aspects of their precontact practices and beliefs.

While in many respects the missionaries gained the upper hand in implementing their vision for the missions, the first Jesuits experienced great difficulty, danger, and uncertainty. Early missionaries left the relative familiarity, security, and comfort of their colleges and residences for the unknown. Many even left their country of origin. They traveled for extended periods through difficult and dangerous terrain filled with venomous snakes, jaguars, and other unfamiliar and frightening creatures. The missionaries did not know if the Indians would be friendly or kill them. Even after founding a mission, the Jesuits wondered if the Indians would turn against them. In addition to facing hunger, deprivation, and poverty, the missionaries also had to adopt new cultural practices. They learned a new language or languages and ate foods that they found to be foreign and strange. At least as frustrating to the missionaries, the Jesuits found that even with their religious zeal they could not stop all of the Indian practices that they found to be sinful and immoral.

Why did the initial missionaries seek to establish missions, given the great risks and personal discomfort? Why did the Guaraní agree to join the missions if they had to sacrifice so much? This chapter seeks to answer these questions. The missionaries' motivations can be explained by the founding principles of the Jesuit order; their religious zeal played a key role in spurring them to make such sacrifices. The reasons why the Guaraní joined the missions were more varied and complex. Even before the Jesuits' arrival, contact with Europeans had radically altered life for the Guaraní. Disease, kidnapping, slavery, and coerced labor threatened the Indians' way of life. Given these upheavals, many Guaraní saw the mission as a place for survival. For many, material goods and the ability to shape mission life, both with and without the Jesuits' consent, made the missions tolerable.

THE GUARANÍ

At the time of European contact, the Guaraní numbered some two million or more and lived in the region stretching from the Paraguay, Uruguay, and Paraná Rivers to the Patos Lagoon on the Atlantic Ocean.[1] The Guaraní sustained themselves through agriculture, hunting, fishing, and gathering. They were a semisedentary people who moved every couple of years as soil fertility declined.[2] They planted corn, manioc, legumes, peanuts, squash, and sweet potatoes and sometimes grew a few tobacco and cotton plants for ceremonial purposes.[3] Forest products supplemented cultivation; they often consumed heart of palm in October, when there was little manioc and corn.[4] Subgroups of Guaraní often followed subsistence patterns in accordance with their particular environment. For example, Jesuit missionaries frequently commented about how the Guaraní living in the Guairá region (roughly the same as the present-day Brazilian state of Paraná) consumed tubers—manioc, potato, squash, and the like. In contrast, missionaries highlighted the cultivation of corn, beans, and manioc by the Guaraní closer to the Paraná River. Furthermore, the Paranaguaýs and others who lived close to rivers depended more on fishing than did inland subgroups, who focused more on hunting. The characteristics of each natural environment largely explain these differences.[5]

The Guaraní organized their labor primarily on the basis of gender.[6] Men cleared the fields for planting, while the women did the rest of the agricultural work. All of the farming was done by hand with a digging stick. In addition to the day-to-day agricultural tasks of planting, caring for, and harvesting crops, women did domestic chores—preparing food and caring for the children. They also raised ducks, transported water, made pottery, spun cotton, and wove baskets and hammocks, and they collected wild fruit, roots, grubs, and honey in the forest.[7]

Most of the men's work entailed leaving the village. According to the Jesuit missionary José Sanchez Labrador, Guaraní men trapped boars and a large animal called *borebí* by digging and then concealing deep holes. They caught rabbits and similar animals in smaller traps and placed lassos in trees to catch birds. They fished using strong wooden hooks with worms or insects on the end.[8] Men also left the village to engage in warfare. The Guaraní held masculine activities in high esteem because of the danger associated with them; warriors faced threatening enemies and hunters faced mysterious, malicious forces that lived in the forest.[9]

The Guaraní did not seek to maximize production. Instead, as Marshall Sahlins argues for primitive societies in general, they tried to meet their needs rather than produce a surplus.[10] They valued leisure and frequently interrupted productive activity with nonproductive activities such as ceremonies, entertainment, social activities, and rest. They did not try to accumulate goods for later use; they accepted that, just as in nature, there would be periods of plenty followed by periods of scarcity. Nor did they equate status with the accumulation of material goods; they valued reciprocity and generosity, and leaders shared what they had instead of accumulating personal wealth.[11]

Guaraní agricultural practices and religious beliefs meant that they were a mobile people. Slash-and-burn agriculture (also known as shifting cultivation or swidden agriculture) caused soil fertility to decline after a couple of years, and so the Guaraní had to search for new land every two to six years. They also migrated in search of a place they called "a land without evil." In this earthly paradise, people did not die and did not have to work but spent their time drinking, feasting, and dancing. At various times before European contact, as well as throughout the colonial period and even into the twentieth century, groups of Guaraní abandoned their homes and followed a shaman in search of this land without evil. These migrations sometimes involved large-scale and far-reaching population movements and occurred most frequently during periods of crisis. The wide dispersion of Tupí-Guaraní tribes suggests numerous pre-Columbian migrations. Furthermore, the high degree of cultural and linguistic uniformity implies that such dispersion occurred relatively recently.[12]

Before European contact, the Guaraní lived in extended families or lineage groups called *teýy*s. Headed by a *teýy-ru* (father of the teýy), the ten to sixty or more nuclear families that made up the teýy lived together in one large communal house.[13] Constructed from tree branches and thatch, these long houses varied in size depending on the availability of materials and the number of members in the teýy. In general, they tended to measure about 165 feet by 16 to 20 feet.[14] The long houses did not have inside walls; vertical posts that supported the roof acted as dividers to separate family units. The shared living arrangements and close proximity created a high degree of interdependence among nuclear families. As a result, nuclear families were subordinate to the teýy. The teýy was the most important organizational unit for the Guaraní; each teýy exercised a high degree of autonomy and functioned as a single political and economic unit.[15]

In an effort to collectively protect themselves against their enemies, a group of teýys sometimes joined together to form a village, or *amundá*. Each settlement consisted of a plaza surrounded by five or six long houses with stockades and moats surrounding the village for defense. The next level of organization—the *teko'a*—consisted of either a village or a group of villages and was not easily distinguishable from an amundá. The highest level of organization—a group of teko'a—formed a *guará*. These larger groupings of Guaraní occurred infrequently and lasted for only a short period of time. Special circumstances such as group warfare or large celebrations created conditions suitable for their formation. After accomplishing their intended goal, these larger formations often broke apart owing to the proclivity for autonomy at the lower levels of social organization, especially at the level of the teýy. Every successive organizational unit above the teýy experienced greater instability and likelihood of fissure.[16]

According to anthropologists, each level of social organization had its own leader. A teýy-ru led the teýy, a *tuvichá* led the amundá and the teko'a, and a *mburuvichá* led the guará.[17] The teýy-ru exercised the most authority; he organized both the production and consumption of goods, and the teýy functioned as a single economic unit. As the head of the teýy, the teýy-ru assigned plots of lands to individual families, directed collective labor projects, and distributed the goods. Together teýy members worked collectively in agriculture, gathering forest products, hunting, and making war.[18] Within the teýy, the teýy-ru resolved disputes and cultivated unity; externally, he maintained relations with other teýys through warfare and diplomacy.[19]

Guaraní leaders used marriage alliances to build social relations. Often female children married adult males. Marriage with a cross cousin—a cousin from a parent's opposite-sex sibling—was encouraged. In contrast, marriage with a parallel cousin—a cousin from a parent's same-sex sibling—was considered incest by some Guaraní.[20] The Guaraní practiced polygamy for diplomatic purposes and as a sign of prestige. A teÿy-ru built connections with other teÿys by having multiple wives: uxorilocal tradition meant that a wife remained a part of her parents' teÿy while living in her husband's teko'a.[21]

Like other Indian chieftains, Guaraní leadership exhibited fluidity and flexibility.[22] A man could become a teÿy-ru by uniting approximately forty males related to him through blood or marriage ties.[23] Leaders could either gain prestige and authority by attracting new followers or lose prestige and authority by losing followers. Loosely based on lineage, leadership positions were generally hereditary but they did not necessarily pass from father to biological son. The Guaraní did not interpret hereditary succession in a strictly vertical sense; a position could legitimately pass to a son or a nephew. The successor not only had to belong to his predecessor's lineage, he also needed to possess personal characteristics such as eloquence, generosity, and prestige gained through warfare.[24] Jesuit missionary Antonio Ruiz de Montoya acknowledged that many Guaraní leaders inherited their position, but many also acquired such status through the eloquence of their speech.[25]

Within Guaraní society, teÿy-rus shared power with shamans. Rather than competing for power, each generally served a different function. While a teÿy-ru maintained human relations, a shaman was responsible for relations with the spiritual world. Shamans were thought to have magical, healing, and weather-forecasting powers. They performed ceremonial rituals, preserved oral history, and communicated with spirits. Shamans were very influential in Guaraní society. Sometimes the distinction between a shaman and a teÿy-ru blurred: a teÿy-ru could become a shaman and vice versa. Such a combination of spiritual and temporal powers depended on the ability to successfully build networks and attract followers.[26]

CONTACT WITH EUROPEANS

For many Guaraní, their way of life had already been disrupted well before they came in contact with Jesuit missionaries. Europeans began infiltrating the region almost a century before the founding of the first Jesuit mission. Even though the first explorers did not establish permanent settlements among the Guaraní, contact between the two peoples definitely occurred. The first European to reach Paraguay was the Portuguese explorer Aleixo Garcia and his men. After being shipwrecked in southern Brazil in 1516, Garcia and several shipmates traveled west with several friendly Indians to Paraguay in 1524. There, they joined with a large army of Guaraní allies and made their way to the outskirts of the Inca Empire. Upon returning to the shores of the Paraguay River with Inca treasure, the Indians killed Garcia but spared his mestizo son.[27] Over a decade later, Europeans began settling in Paraguay permanently; in 1537, Europeans founded the city of Asunción.

Many Guaraní hoped that an alliance with Europeans and access to European weaponry could give them an edge against their rivals, but they soon found the costs of such an alliance too great.[28] According to Guaraní practices, Indian women cemented alliances. From Guaraní wives and concubines the Spaniards not only received sexual pleasure but also gained Guaraní labor; women did most of the agricultural labor among the Guaraní. Spaniards took advantage of this practice to accumulate a large labor force. In most cases, a Spaniard did not limit himself to a relationship with one Guaraní woman; the first Spanish governor, Domingo Martínez de Irala, had at least seven Indian concubines.[29]

The Guaraní expected that such ties would lead to kinship, but the Spaniards did not act as the Guaraní anticipated. Even though relationships between Guaraní women and Spanish men often resulted in mixed-race children, the Spaniards did not treat the Guaraní as relatives or friends. Instead, they capitalized on these associations to make excessive labor demands upon the Guaraní. Moreover, the Spaniards did not respect Guaraní gender roles: they wanted Guaraní males to work in agriculture, performing tasks that the Guaraní considered women's work.[30]

In the eyes of the Guaraní, the Spaniards did not treat them as allies but as slaves. Within several years, some Guaraní began to refer to the Spaniards not as relatives but as thieves, adulterers, and scoundrels.[31] Yet despite such complaints, relationships between Spanish men and Guaraní women continued. In 1541, the first Spanish governor, Domingo Martínez de Irala claimed that seven hundred Guaraní women served the Spanish population.[32] Even in the late sixteenth and early seventeenth centuries, the fact that women outnumbered men by about ten-to-one in Asunción suggests that settler men continued to have multiple Guaraní concubines.[33]

Further eroding collegial relations between the settlers and the Guaraní, royal officials issued *encomienda* grants to Spanish settlers. The encomienda was a coercive labor structure that entitled the recipient of an encomienda (an *encomendero*) to collect tribute in the form of labor or goods from the Indians assigned to him. In return, the encomendero was obligated to teach the Indians Spanish and Catholicism. According to Governor Martínez de Irala, in 1556 he divided an estimated 20,000 Guaraní among 320 or more Spaniards.[34] These Indians had to work for their encomenderos for several months each year. Many encomenderos took advantage of and overworked their Indian charges: Guaraní males often had to work longer than the allotted period of time, and women, children, and the elderly often also had to participate even if they were formally exempted from encomienda labor obligations.[35] Royal officials issued various ordinances to moderate these and other abuses; the repetition of such regulatory efforts suggests their ineffectiveness and that abuses by encomenderos continued.[36]

The encomienda was only one form of forced labor; the Guaraní also faced outright slavery. Spanish settlers enslaved Indians under the pretext that the Indians had mounted or were about to mount an armed attack.[37] More frequently, the perpetrators were Portuguese adventurers accompanied by mestizos, Tupí Indians, and Africans.[38] Originating from São Paulo, these *Paulistas* or *bandeirantes* conducted slave raids that reached far into Spanish territory and took thousands of Indians as captives.[39] The bandeirantes then sold the Guaraní into slavery for agricultural, domestic, and plantation labor in Portuguese territory.[40] These slave raids flourished and continued to threaten the Guaraní during the first half of the seventeenth century.

Even for those Guaraní who successfully avoided encomienda and slavery, life did not remain the same. Guaraní communities did not exist in isolation. Certainly most were aware of the Europeans or at least heard rumors of their activities. In an effort to maintain their freedom, the Guaraní turned to such strategies as greater mobility, relocation, restructured communities, and new alliances—changes that altered their way of life.[41]

The introduction of new diseases to which the Indians did not have immunity also had huge repercussions for the Guaraní. Such diseases not only affected Indians in direct contact with Europeans but followed Indian-to-Indian trajectories as well. Daniel T. Reff estimates that as a result of European illnesses, native populations declined 30 to 50 percent before they encountered Jesuit missionaries.[42] Within a generation after the settlement of Asunción, if not sooner, disease afflicted the Guaraní. Two epidemics in 1558 or 1560 and 1605–1606 killed great numbers of Indians. By 1611, encomenderos were complaining about declining numbers of Indians.[43] Disease radically altered native communities and their social structure; numerous individuals died, including leaders, elders, and other individuals who held the community together. There were additional far-reaching consequences. A large percentage of the population were too ill too work during an epidemic. Individuals infected with smallpox—one of the main European diseases to attack Native American populations—were sick for about three weeks. While an individual might feel better and perform easy tasks during some of this period, the ill depended heavily on others for water, food, and basic care.[44] As a result, those who were moderately well or not sick had to care for the ill. If severe enough, disruptions in labor patterns threatened the Indians' food supply. Such upheaval caused by the arrival of Europeans forced the Guaraní to seek new ways of protecting themselves and their communities. Missions offered one such option.

THE JESUITS

From its inception in 1540 until its suppression in the second half of the eighteenth century, the Society of Jesus developed into one of the most powerful as well as controversial religious orders.[45] The Jesuits' wide-ranging activities brought them into close contact with both the wealthy and poor around the globe and led to both veneration and scorn. Their role as missionaries, together with that of teachers, was among the Jesuits' most prominent and controversial activities. The order prioritized the promulgation of Catholicism among foreign peoples.[46] Such initiatives, combined with both royal and papal support, led to the Jesuits' rise to prominence in the missionary fields of Latin America, Asia, and Africa.

The Jesuits sent missionaries to the Americas significantly later than other religious orders. The Dominicans, Franciscans, and Augustinians had already sent missionaries to Latin America when Pope Paul III issued the papal bull that founded the Society of Jesus. In part because of this delayed start, Jesuit missionary activity flourished. Founded about three centuries after the three other religious orders, the Jesuits conceived of the world and the challenges facing the Catholic Church differently. Events and the environment of the early sixteenth century shaped the Society of Jesus and made it especially suited for missionary work.

In the sixteenth century, Catholicism encountered new opportunities and challenges. The expulsion of Muslim rulers from the Iberian Peninsula in 1492 ushered in the age of conquest, and in the Americas Spain encountered a large population unfamiliar with Catholicism. Concurrently, the Protestant Reformation threatened Catholicism's supremacy in Europe. The desire to promulgate the faith to potential new converts and defend the faith against alternate interpretations of Christianity thus shaped the Jesuit order.[47]

The Society of Jesus's founding principles reflected the above-mentioned forces and set the stage for successful missionary activity. According to Ignatius of Loyola's autobiography, he and the other founders of the Jesuit order initially wanted to dedicate their lives to advancing Catholicism in Jerusalem. Not able to achieve this goal, they instead offered

themselves to the pope for whatever he deemed to be "for the greater
glory of God and the good of souls," and in 1539 Ignatius and ten companions proposed a new religious order to Pope Paul III.[48] The proposal,
known as the "formula of the Institute," set out the basic principles and
practices for the new order. The pope agreed, and in the following year
he issued a papal bull officially approving the formation of the Society
of Jesus. In the papal bull, the pope included the formula proposed by
Ignatius and his companions.[49]

Although the formula did not specifically mention the establishment of
missions among indigenous peoples, such activity clearly met the order's
goals as stated in the document. The formula specified that the Jesuit
order was "a Society founded chiefly for this purpose: to strive especially for the progress of souls in Christian life and doctrine and for the
propagation of the faith."[50] In 1550, an expanded version of the formula
specified that the Jesuits should work in "the education of children and
unlettered persons in Christianity."[51] By teaching Catholic practices to Indians unfamiliar with Catholicism, missions clearly fulfilled this require-
ment. Among the unbelievers to whom the Jesuits should minister, the
formula specified "even those who live in the region called the Indies."[52]
In sum, the formula clearly established that missions fit within the basic
principles of and guidelines for the Society of Jesus.

The formula not only emphasized the importance of propagating the
faith among unbelievers but encouraged social assistance of the kind promoted in the missions as well. "This Society should show itself no less
useful . . . in performing any other works of charity, according to what
will seem expedient for the glory of God and the common good."[53] This
clause mandated that Jesuits undertake activities for charitable, not just
evangelical, purposes.[54]

John W. O'Malley convincingly argues that such an explicit articula-
tion of charitable acts set the Jesuits apart from other religious orders.
The founding principles of the other orders did not include so overt and
specified a commitment to bettering the world. This secondary goal of
the Jesuits fit well with a key component of the missions—feeding and
clothing the Indians. According to O'Malley, the written instruction "to
help souls" did not encompass only ministering to the spirit; when referring to "soul" Jesuits considered all aspects of a person and not just the
religious. Helping souls thus also included providing food for the body
and learning for the mind.[55]

The missions offered an opportunity to fulfill such goals. By teaching
Indians the Catholic faith, the Jesuits propagated their religious beliefs
among persons unlettered in Christianity. By protecting the Indians and
providing material succor, the Jesuits performed works of charity for the

common good. For anyone drawn to the Society of Jesus, the missions clearly fit well with such mandates. Hundreds of Spanish, French, and other European Jesuits volunteered for missions in the Americas, Asia, and Africa.[56]

Despite the order's emphasis on propagating the faith and performing charitable acts, however, few early novitiates joined the Jesuit order out of a desire to become a missionary. Based on questionnaires and auto-biographies of sixteenth-century Jesuits, T. V. Cohen found that most joined the order not to advance Catholicism or help others but for personal reasons.[57] Novitiates wanted to escape the temptations, uncertainty, and vanity associated with the outside world rather than to transform it. For Jesuits in the Iberian provinces of Portugal, Castile, Andalucía, and Aragon between 1561 and 1562, a call "to serve man" ranked sixth (5 percent) as a motive for entering the order. The opportunity "to serve God" ranked first (38 percent) and "to leave the world" ranked second (24 percent).[58] Other motivations also came into play but were of less importance.[59] Many novitiates likely joined the order because of their experience as students in Jesuit schools.[60]

How did the Jesuits develop such a strong missionary presence if few novitiates identified missions as a primary motivation for joining the order? Likely, many of the novitiates who wanted to withdraw from the world either changed their views or left the order. According to their testimonies, most of the individuals who sought to leave the order shared a tendency to view efforts to help others as a distraction from their primary goal of saving their own souls. Those who remained in the order probably did not exchange their pursuit of personal salvation for the salvation of others; rather, they envisioned missionary service as a way to advance their own salvation by serving God.[61]

Jesuit leadership promoted missionary work as a way to pursue God. In a guide for German missionaries to the Americas, Franz Xavier Amrhyn explained that a missionary followed God's calling. The primary goal of a missionary should not be to save either his own soul or Indians' souls but rather to serve God.[62] This vision of missionary work fit well with the most frequently cited motivation of Iberian Jesuits—the opportunity to serve God.[63]

Unlike other orders, the Jesuits rarely lacked volunteers for missions. Most came from Europe. Between 1550 and 1749, nearly three-quarters of the Jesuits in the Río de la Plata region were European born.[64] In 1768, only eleven of the seventy-eight Jesuits expelled from the Guaraní missions were born in the Americas.[65] Writings by missionaries in the field attracted new volunteers. Accounts of their experiences and the people and environment they encountered sparked missionary enthusiasm. The

Jesuits also crafted texts specifically for recruiting new missionaries. A *procurador* (agent or representative) sent to Europe on behalf of a Jesuit province served as the primary agent for recruiting these volunteers. In addition to procuring supplies and informing Jesuits in Europe, the Crown, and/or the papacy about conditions in the province, procuradors often sought new missionaries.[66] Procuradors from the Jesuit province of Paraguay frequently returned with new Jesuits from Europe.[67]

THE SPANISH CROWN AND THE FRONTIER

The Crown wanted not only to pacify and incorporate Indians and their land into the Spanish Empire, but to convert native peoples to Catholicism. Both the Crown and the Church believed that the saving of Indian souls justified Spanish rule. To that end, Catholic priests—primarily those belonging to religious orders—became a major force in the conversion effort. In frontier regions, Catholicism converged with other efforts to Europeanize native peoples. Friars were not satisfied with baptizing the Indians; they wanted to make sure that Indians behaved as Christians and ceased practicing polygamy, infanticide, adultery, and all vestiges of idolatry.[68] The priests promoted what they considered upright Christian behavior. They tried to alter the Indians' work ethic and put an end to what they perceived as indolence. Such changes included replacing hunting, gathering, and slash-and-burn agricultural practices with a regimented work schedule associated with living in a permanent community based on cultivated agriculture. In essence, the priests tried to enforce idealized forms of Spanish culture as part of the conversion process.

In frontier regions, missions became the primary mechanism for introducing Indians to Catholicism and European practices. Each mission brought various dispersed Indian groups together into a large settlement under the oversight of one or several Catholic priests. Reducing, that is, concentrating many small Indian groups into a single large community,[69] played a key part in the strategy behind the missions; these condensed settlements enabled priests to have more regular contact with the Indians than the less permanent, smaller, and more geographically dispersed communities where the Indians lived previously. The rationale was that more regular contact with the Indians enabled the priests to more effectively teach Spanish economic, cultural, and religious practices and to better police Indian actions and behavior. With missions, the Crown found an economical way to achieve its dual goals of expanding the Spanish Empire and spreading Catholicism. By passing this immense task to religious orders, the Crown effectively outsourced a significant portion of the expense.[70] This convergence of multiple interests of the Crown and the Church made the missions the primary agency for extending Spanish rule, language, laws, and traditions in the frontier.[71]

Missions proliferated in frontier regions throughout Spanish America. Over their lifespan, these missions affected hundreds of thousands of Indians. The flagship of all the missions was the thirty Guaraní missions in the Río de la Plata region. These were the most populous and financially prosperous of all the Catholic missions in the frontiers of Spanish America.

JESUIT BACKGROUND IN THE RÍO
DE LA PLATA REGION

In 1607 Diego de Torres Bollo became the first *provincial* (head) of the newly created Jesuit province of Paraguay. Centered in Córdoba, the vast territory included present-day Paraguay, Argentina, Uruguay, and parts of Bolivia, Chile, and Brazil. Accompanied by a dozen missionaries, Torres established a network of colleges in Spanish population centers. The colleges served both as educational institutions and as bases for missionary work. While still building this foundation, the Jesuits simultaneously formulated plans for and embarked on missionary work.

The Jesuits received permission to establish missions in Paraguay as part of a strategy for advancing and securing Spanish territory. During his three terms as governor of Río de la Plata and Paraguay, Hernandarias (Hernando Arias) de Saavedra actively tried to expand Spanish territory from Asunción southeast to include most of the three southernmost Brazilian states (Paraná, Santa Catalina, and Rio Grande do Sul).[72] This territory attracted not only Hernandarias and the Spanish but slave raiders from São Paulo as well. In the early seventeenth century, groups of bandeirantes kidnapped and sold large numbers of Indians from this region in the lucrative São Paulo slave market.[73] Recognizing this threat to both royal authority and the welfare of the Indians, Hernandarias argued in a 1607 letter to Philip III that Spanish expansion emanating from Asunción would repel the Portuguese and protect Indians from enslavement. Hernandarias did not believe Spanish settlers could conquer or pacify an estimated 150,000 Indians and therefore requested missionaries for the Guairá region to help achieve his goal. In response, Philip III ordered that Jesuits recently sent from Spain to Paraguay initiate missionary activity in Guairá. Furthermore, he asserted that even if the Spaniards had sufficient force, only Catholic doctrine should be used to conquer the Indians.[74] The following year, Governor Hernandarias and the bishop of Asunción,

Reginaldo Lizárraga, assigned Jesuit provincial Torres the task of sending missionaries not only to the Guaraní of Guairá but also to the Guaraní of Paraná (in the vicinity of the Paraná and Uruguay Rivers) and the Guaycurú of the Chaco. Torres promptly sent two missionaries to each zone even though the Jesuits and royal officials would not formally agree on the structure of the missions for another year.

The Jesuit missions in Paraguay resembled missions elsewhere but with a few key differences. Torres negotiated important concessions for the Guaraní missions. Well informed about Paraguayan encomenderos' abuse of Indian labor, Torres understood encomienda service as a potential threat to missionary efforts. During encomienda service, Indians would not be under the Jesuits' watchful care, and the missionaries could not proselytize, police the Indians' behavior, or protect them from abuse. Armed with a royal dispatch, Torres took a strong stand against the encomienda. He negotiated a ten-year exemption from encomienda labor service and tribute payments for Indians converted by the Jesuits who peacefully agreed to become subjects of the king of Spain. Such concessions stood in stark contrast to the Indians in the Franciscan missions of Paraguay, who were not exempt from encomienda labor.[75]

While Torres was busy negotiating with the governor and other royal officials, Jesuit missionaries actively worked among the Indians. In late 1609, the rector of the Jesuit college in Asunción, Marciel de Lorenzana, and his Jesuit companion, Francisco de San Martín, set out for the Paraná region. They did not go alone: the priest from the Franciscan Guaraní mission Yaguarón, Hernando de la Cueva, and some *caciques* (leaders of native lineages) from this pueblo accompanied them and facilitated communication. The party went some forty leagues southeast of Asunción to meet cacique Arapizandú, who had recently requested missionaries as part of peace negotiations with Governor Hernandarias. On December 29, 1609, they founded the first Jesuit mission among the Guaraní—Mission San Ignacio Guazú in the Paraná region.[76] In July 1610, two Jesuit missionaries convinced other Guaraní to form Missions Loreto and San Ignacio Miní in the Guairá region. Other missions followed.

Unlike the two other regions, the Jesuits had little success in the Chaco. While the Guaycurú tolerated the Jesuits for some years, they did not join missions. A band of Guaycurú experimented with mission life for almost two decades but ultimately opted for a seminomadic lifestyle instead. The Guaycurú did not adapt well to the missions in part because before European contact they were a mobile people very minimally acquainted with cultivated agriculture.[77] They scorned settled agriculture and a sedentary lifestyle. In 1612, a Jesuit wrote to his superior in Rome, "In this manner the mission has been left futile; because they cannot find it within themselves to leave the natural inclination to hunt and fish, nor to give themselves over to the work of laboring."[78] Throughout the seventeenth century, the Guaycurú maintained a nomadic and subsistence lifestyle by raiding and trading with Spanish settlements.[79] The Chaco Indians' bellicosity and lack of interest in the missions led the Jesuits to focus their evangelization efforts on more receptive populations until the middle of the eighteenth century.[80]

Some Guaraní also resisted the missions. In the early seventeenth century, Guaraní opponents killed four Jesuits who tried to establish missions.[81] In his account of the founding and early years of the missions, Ruiz de Montoya described Guaraní who were receptive and unreceptive. Some, like cacique Miguel Artiguaye, first opposed the missionaries but then changed their minds. According to Ruiz de Montoya, cacique Artiguaye initially accused the missionaries: "You are no priests sent from God to aid our misery; you are devils from hell, sent by their ruler for our destruction. What teaching have you brought us? What peace and happiness? Our ancestors lived in liberty."[82] After losing a dispute with Indians allied with the missionaries, however, Artiguaye recanted and sought protection with the Jesuits. According to Ruiz de Montoya, Artiguaye pleaded, "For the love of Jesus Christ and St. Ignatius, I implore you to forgive my stupid insolence towards you. . . . I beg you to shield and defend me, for I have good reason to fear that these people will kill me."[83]

In the first two decades after the founding of the first Guaraní mission, the Jesuits rapidly established a number of missions in Paraná and Guairá. The missions covered a lot of territory. From Asunción, the Paraná missions advanced in a southeast trajectory (see Map 2). Many of them bordered either the Paraná or Uruguay River, but the latter missions especially reached much further east. Between 1614 and 1628, Roque González de Santa Cruz led the advance from the proximity of the Paraná River. The murder of this missionary and two other priests by a Guaraní cacique and his followers did not stop the spread of the missions.[84] Twelve missions founded in the 1630s extended south and east from the Uruguay River toward the Atlantic Ocean and Patos Lagoon in a region called Tape.

Despite initial success in attracting the Guaraní to missions in the Guairá region, the Jesuits soon encountered problems. Within five years after founding the first two Guairá missions—Loreto and San Ignacio Miní—the Jesuit provincial optimistically estimated a mission population of five thousand.[85] During the same period, the Jesuits founded—and then abandoned—an additional three missions in the region.[86] The Jesuits

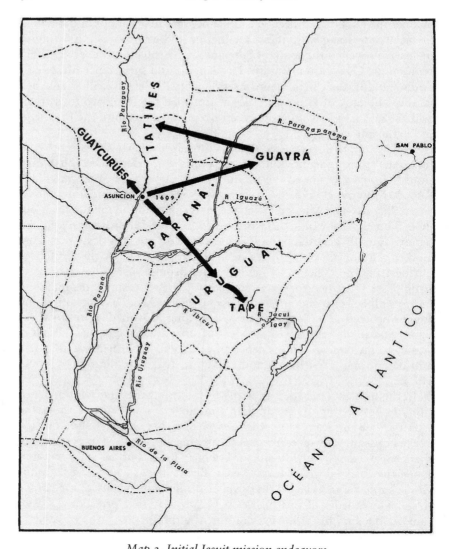

Map 2. Initial Jesuit mission endeavors
SOURCE: Bruno, *Historia de la Iglesia en la Argentina*, 2:211. Reprinted by permission of Editorial
Don Bosco, Edebé, S.A.

did not establish any new missions for another decade. A lack of priests
partly explains the delay: in addition to the two Jesuits originally sent to
the region, only two more arrived to oversee San Ignacio Miní. Hostilities
between the Jesuits and the Spanish settlers of the region also influenced
the decision not to send more priests. Decades earlier, Spanish settlers

had founded the cities of Ciudad Real (1554) and Villa Rica (1576) in the Guairá region, and the Crown awarded the settlers Indian inhabitants to serve as encomienda laborers.[87] The settlers' dependence on encomienda labor for their livelihood—primarily the harvest and processing of yerba maté—put them in direct conflict with the Jesuits, who lobbied to exempt mission Indians from the encomienda. The settlers contested the 1611 decree that exempted Indians peacefully converted by the Jesuits. They appealed to the governing judicial body of the Audiencia of Charcas, which in turn declared itself unqualified to resolve the issue. In 1618, with some modifications, the central government confirmed the decree and maintained the ten-year exemption from encomienda labor for mission Guaraní peacefully converted by the Jesuits.[88] With the encomienda dispute temporarily resolved, the Jesuits expanded mission operations in Guairá. Between 1622 and 1629, Antonio Ruiz de Montoya founded eleven missions south of the original two and distant from Spanish settlements.[89] According to Jesuit accounts, these missions grew rapidly. The Jesuit provincial optimistically claimed that more than forty thousand Indians had joined these eleven Guairá missions before their destruction.[90]

Despite this rapid advance, the Guairá missions did not have time to fully stabilize and mature. In 1627, Jesuits in São Paulo informed their brethren in Paraguay that bandeirantes were planning an armed raid on the Guairá missions. In 1628, four groups of bandeirantes with nine hundred Paulistas and two thousand Tupí Indians departed for Guairá and took thousands of Indians captive.[91] By 1631, all of the Guairá missions had been destroyed except for the two oldest—Loreto and San Ignacio Miní. The residents of the other missions were either enslaved or had fled.[92] The Jesuits recognized that they could not stop such slave raids; instead, they opted to abandon the Guairá region and relocate the two remaining missions southwest into Spanish territory.

In 1631, Antonio Ruiz de Montoya and more than ten thousand Guaraní left Loreto and San Ignacio Miní for new settlements near the early Paraná missions.[93] Although approximately only a quarter of the mission Indians joined Ruiz de Montoya, the number was significant. These individuals abandoned their homes and joined the exodus knowing that the journey would be long and arduous and that they would face great hardship during the relocation and reestablishment of their mission. Ruiz de Montoya estimated the distance between their point of departure and destination to be more than one hundred leagues (approximately six hundred miles). Before leaving, the Guaraní rapidly constructed some seven hundred canoes or rafts for travel on the Paraná River. The huge Guairá waterfalls forced them to abandon the rafts and take an overland detour of eight days.[94] To travel the rest of the way along the Paraná River, the refugees built new rafts supplemented by canoes sent by the Paraná missions. By the end of the journey, the group had lost a large number of its original members, many of whom died, while others abandoned the journey. In addition to the difficulties associated with travel, migrants suffered from illness and a lack of food. They also faced the emotional toll of abandoning their homes, fear of attack by their enemies, and an unknown future.

The migrants' troubles did not end with their journey; many Guaraní died or abandoned the missions during the rebuilding process. In order to facilitate assistance from other Jesuit missions, the migrants rebuilt Loreto and San Ignacio Miní close to the first Paraná missions. Despite provisions of food and other necessities, the new arrivals continued to experience hunger. According to Ruiz de Montoya, the Indians ate only enough—mostly beef rations from more than forty thousand cattle donated by a Spanish settler in Corrientes—to postpone death. In addition to severe food shortages, an epidemic killed some two thousand of the new arrivals.[95] The missions struggled for survival. Three years after the exodus, only an estimated four thousand of the original twelve thousand Guaraní remained in the two missions.[96]

Bandeirante raids not only led the Guaraní to abandon the Guairá missions, they also led Spanish settlers to abandon the region. A year after the mission exodus from Guairá, Spanish settlers evacuated Villa Rica and Ciudad Real—the two main towns in the region.[97] Clearly the missions had not fulfilled Governor Hernandarias's hopes for expanding and defending Spanish territory from Portuguese advancement.

In 1631, the Jesuits advanced into Itatín (a region west of Guairá, part of the present-day Brazilian state of Mato Grosso do Sul) in response to both caciques' requests for missions and bandeirante raids. Ruiz de Montoya erroneously thought that such missions could serve as refuges for Guaraní fleeing bandeirante attacks in Guairá. Within less than a year, the Jesuits and some Guaraní founded four missions with an estimated two hundred to four hundred families each. The missions were quickly destroyed. In 1632, bandeirantes again attacked. Most of the mission inhabitants either fled or were enslaved. Food shortages and an epidemic plagued those who remained. Again, some Guaraní opted to flee the region with the Jesuits. After first moving closer to Asunción, the refugees and other Guaraní eventually formed Mission Santiago in the Paraná region.[98]

The bandeirantes forced the Jesuits to relocate not only their eastern and northern missions (Guairá and Itatín) but also their southern missions (Tape). In 1636 and 1637, bandeirantes attacked the Tape missions, in response to which the Jesuits abandoned the easternmost missions. At this point, the Jesuits became more proactive in defending the missions against the bandeirantes.

In 1637, the Jesuit provincial of Paraguay sent Ruiz de Montoya to Spain to lobby the king for support in stopping bandeirante raids, and Ruiz de Montoya's efforts yielded results. In 1639, the viceroy, the audiencia, and the governors received *cedulas* mandating action to prevent bandeirante incursions into Spanish territory. Ruiz de Montoya also sought permission to arm mission Indians, but this matter was not decided for another decade.[99]

The Jesuits not only pursued diplomatic channels, they also took direct action. Although lacking official authorization, they started training and arming the Guaraní to defend their missions. The missionaries purchased muskets and started producing firearms and gunpowder in the missions. Lay brothers taught the Indians how to use the firearms. As a result, mission Guaraní defeated the bandeirantes in Caazapá Guazú in 1639 and again in Mbororé in 1641.[100] In the latter battle, the Guaraní defeated a group of some four hundred Paulistas and more than one thousand Tupí in a long and bloody battle.[101] Official authorization for arming the Guaraní came a decade after mission militias first defeated the bandeirantes.

Guaraní militias were controversial. Many Paraguayans strongly opposed arming the Guaraní. They claimed that as Indians the Guaraní were unreliable allies, and they feared that the Guaraní would use their weapons and military training against them. Despite such opposition, the Jesuits and their allies successfully lobbied the Crown and Crown officials. In 1647, the viceroy in Lima sent firearms to the Jesuits. Two years later, after much debate and some supportive preliminary rulings, Guaraní militias officially became the king's militias.[102]

The 1649 ruling clarified both the missions' rights and duties to the Crown. The missions received permission to form armed troops of Guaraní; in return they had the obligation of defending Spanish territory against Portuguese incursions. The ruling also finally resolved the issue of encomienda labor service. Up until this point, the Jesuits had successfully lobbied for extensions to the ten-year exemption from encomienda labor for Guaraní from all of the missions except San Ignacio Guazú and Loreto. The 1649 ruling confirmed that Guaraní inhabitants of the Jesuit missions did not have to perform encomienda labor. Instead, the missions had to pay tribute equivalent to one peso per year for each male between the ages of eighteen and fifty.[103] Caciques, their first sons, a few church officials, and the disabled were exempted. The Crown did not receive all of the tribute money: the priests' stipends (466 pesos 5 reales per mission regardless of the number of missionaries) were deducted from this amount.

This agreement was advantageous to both the Guaraní missions and the Crown. Not only did the Indians avoid coerced labor outside of the missions, but the agreed-upon tribute of one peso per year was exceptionally low.[104] In comparison, nonmission Indians in Paraguay legally had to pay six pesos in tribute according to the Ordenanzas de Alfaro, ratified in 1618.[105] Crown officials recognized the cost-saving benefits of Guaraní militias. A royal cedula issued in 1716 acknowledged that Guaraní militias were the only force with horses and weaponry that could rapidly be assembled to fight a frontier attack without the Crown incurring great financial costs.[106] When in service to the Crown, Guaraní soldiers often fought together with Spanish settlers.[107] Arming Indians was not unique to the Guaraní missions; Indian militias existed elsewhere in the Spanish Empire, but they served only as auxiliary soldiers. In contrast, the Río de la Plata region did not have any regular troops, and thus the mission militias served as the Crown's primary military force.[108]

With the bandeirante threat largely under control and the relationship with the Crown resolved, the Jesuits focused on consolidating and developing the missions. By the 1640s, the territory of the thirty Guaraní missions along the Paraná and Uruguay Rivers had taken its final form. Twenty-three missions existed, with some forty thousand inhabitants.[109] Descendants of mission inhabitants founded six of the last seven Guaraní missions; the final mission was founded in 1707. Located on the eastern shores of the Uruguay River, these last seven missions also served to secure Spanish territory from Portuguese westward advancement (see Map 3).[110]

REASONS FOR JOINING THE MISSIONS

Why did the Guaraní join the missions? As mentioned earlier, residing in the missions meant great change for the Guaraní residents. Given the large number of Guaraní and small number of Jesuits, force cannot explain why the Guaraní gave up many cultural practices, radically changed their daily lives and living conditions, and subjected themselves to Jesuit authority. Without strong military backing, the Jesuits could not force the Guaraní to join the missions against their will. The deleterious impact of Spanish contact and settlement described earlier in the chapter played a large role in convincing the Guaraní to join the missions.

The world in which the Guaraní lived had changed, and in this context the missions were an appealing option. Epidemics, enslavement, and forced labor threatened the very underpinnings of Guaraní society. Family members died or disappeared, and authority structures broke down. Such calamities disrupted native society, political structure, economy, and family life. As a result, the Guaraní became more receptive to accepting change and radically altering their way of life in order to survive.

Map 3. Thirty Guaraní missions

SOURCE: Bruno, *Historia de la Iglesia en la Argentina*, 2:314. Reprinted by permission of Editorial Don Bosco, Edebé, S.A.

In joining the missions, many Guaraní perceived a way for both self-preservation and the partial defense and reconstruction of their weakened and threatened society. Material goods provided succor, new political structure filled voids, and Catholic beliefs and rituals possibly offered some form of comfort. The Guaraní approached the missions as an adaptive strategy to reconstitute and defend their ravaged community.

Guaraní leaders took an active role in negotiating mission settlement as a means of protection. A group of Guaraní leaders made this clear when they specified that they would only let Jesuit missionaries enter their territory if the missionaries guaranteed that they were "vassals of the King and would not have any obligation to serve any Spaniard; that [they were] like free Spaniards without forced service or *mita*; and that nobody [would] take [their] territory from [them]."[111] These leaders consciously used the missions as a way to protect themselves and their communities from external threats of violence and exploitation.[112] They saw the Jesuits as "go-betweens" who could help them negotiate the Spanish bureaucracy and lobby on their behalf.[113]

The Guaraní also found the missionaries' gifts of material goods—food, tools, and trinkets—attractive. In a deliberate effort to entice Indians to join the missions, the Jesuits offered them gifts.[114] In one instance, Ruiz de Montoya overtly acknowledged that "in this way I succeeded in attracting some of them to visit me," and in another instance, he recognized that after distributing such items the Indians "grew more fond of my words."[115] Gifts served a variety of purposes—productive (scissors, knives, fishhooks, needles, and axes), religious (rosaries and crosses), and adornment (glass beads, clothing, and mirrors)—and influenced native life in many ways. Food supplemented the native diet, tools lessened the Indians' workload, and religious and adornment items offered prestige and status. The Guaraní especially appreciated tools for productive purposes; according to Ruiz de Montoya, the Indians found iron axes the most useful and prized them above other gifts.[116]

Guaraní influence on the missions also made the institution more attractive. While the Laws of the Indies provided specifications for building Indian towns, Guaraní leaders participated in selecting the location of a mission.[117] The first Jesuit provincial of Paraguay advocated including the Guaraní in such decisions: "Before founding the mission, [you] should strongly believe that the location [is] suitable for many Indians, of good weather, good water, appropriate for sustenance, with farms, fish, and hunting: in [all] this, the same Indians should deliberately acquaint [you]."[118] Basically, according to Torres's guidelines, the Indians determined the suitability of a site.

Despite radical changes promoted by the Jesuits, many aspects of day-to-day life remained the same for Guaraní in the missions. For the most part, the Indians continued to eat the same food, speak the same language, and maintain their membership in a native lineage group.[119] The continuance of Guaraní practices occurred both with and without Jesuit support—even religion was a negotiation between Catholic and Guaraní spiritual realms.[120]

The missionaries integrated native practices as a way to facilitate the adoption of Catholicism and other European cultural practices. As Gauvin Alexander Bailey argues, "And just as the Jesuits adopted Guaraní economic, political, and ritual traditions when founding the reductions [i.e., missions], they tacitly allowed indigenous style and even symbols to pervade mission art."[121] Guaraní artisans used their own artistic preferences and worldview in depicting Christian figures and symbols. The Jesuits hoped that such integration of Guaraní culture would create linkages to help the Guaraní to understand Catholic beliefs.

Even when a link to Catholic practices was nonexistent or negligible, the Guaraní still incorporated aspects of their precontact lifestyle into the missions. For example, despite early opposition to yerba maté, the missionaries allowed its consumption to be a cornerstone of daily life and made its production and sale a key part of the mission economy. Ruiz de Montoya initially argued that yerba maté "deserves condemnation because of the abuse made of it, the hardship involved in its cultivation, the high esteem it enjoys, its sustaining and stimulating effect on workers, the high prices it commands . . . its superstitious employment in sorcery, and even for its odor and taste."[122] Despite such opinions, the Jesuits did not stop the Guaraní from consuming yerba maté; instead, its consumption was so pervasive that later missionaries defended the practice by claiming it helped the missions achieve their goals: "Its use and abundance has totally banished the drunkenness and intoxication so innate in the Indians."[123]

Other native practices continued in the missions despite Jesuit opposition. The Jesuits strongly condemned and vehemently tried to suppress anything that clashed with Catholic beliefs. They persecuted Guaraní shamans and actively punished adultery and polygamy.[124] Despite such pressure and coercion, individual Indians found ways to continue such practices.[125] Although shamans had lost most of their power by the second half of the eighteenth century, activities labeled as witchcraft by Europeans still occurred in the missions.[126] For example, Joseph Antonio Papá, a cacique from Mission Corpus Christi, was accused of sorcery (*hechicerías*) in 1781—over 150 years after the founding of the mission.[127] Likewise, polygamy and adultery continued.[128] A mission official asserted in 1784 that without proper supervision, married Guaraní had no qualms about separating and falsely claiming to be single or a widow/widower in order to marry someone else.[129]

As these examples reveal, the Guaraní actively participated in shaping the missions and maintaining their precontact cultural practices both with and without the missionaries' consent. Although the Guaraní had to adapt to mission life, the changes were not as drastic as the Jesuits' idealized version. Still, the incorporation of Guaraní beliefs and practices should not be overstated. The missions were far from a utopia based on harmonious and egalitarian relations between the Guaraní and the Jesuits. Although the Guaraní greatly outnumbered the missionaries, the Jesuits had a more powerful position within the colonial structure.

CONCLUSION

The mission project among the Guaraní succeeded as a result of the particulars of its time and place. Crown officials hoped that missions would expand and secure Spanish territory against Portuguese advancement. While the missions failed to accomplish this goal in the Guairá, Itatín, and Tape regions, they succeeded around the Paraná and Uruguay Rivers. Both the Jesuits and the Guaraní joined the missions for protection. The Jesuits became missionaries in order to find God and ensure their own salvation. Secondarily they sought to "help souls" by introducing the Indians to Catholicism and European practices. In contrast, the Guaraní turned to the missions for protection in this life. Attacked by devastating new illnesses and threatened with enslavement and other forms of forced labor, many Guaraní turned to the missions to protect themselves, their families, and their communities. By joining a mission, the Guaraní received material goods and varying degrees of protection from enslavement and exploitative labor practices. Furthermore, they preserved aspects of their culture both with and without the Jesuits' consent. And they continued to exert such influence throughout the life of the missions. The next two chapters describe this influence and the Guaraní experience during the missions' peak in the first half of the eighteenth century.

CHAPTER 2

Urban Towns on the Frontier

Hundreds, often several thousands, of Guaraní resided together and shared a single mission pueblo. What was it like to live in such a place? Since this chapter cannot hope to address all aspects of mission life, it will focus on the urban design of mission towns and their governing structure during the missions' peak in the first half of the eighteenth century.

The Jesuits envisioned a mission as a permanent, compact, and urban town.[1] In the layout of the pueblo and position of the buildings, missions followed a standard design. All Guaraní mission towns looked alike, and they shared many similarities with other missions in Latin America. Their layout not only reflected European views as to how a civilized town should look but was designed to maximize missionary influence and control over the Indians as well.

Large numbers of Guaraní inhabited these pueblos. With an average population of over 4,700 per mission at their peak in 1732, the Guaraní missions were the most populous of all the missions in Spanish America.[2] Sustaining several thousand Indians in a single mission required a complex management system. While the Jesuits desired to be the ultimate decision makers, they also recognized that the two missionaries—the priest and the priest's companion—assigned to a mission could not control everything. Native leaders played a key part in managing and organizing the mission population. Guaraní lineage groups and the associated leadership position—renamed *cacicazgo* and *cacique*, respectively, by the Spaniards—continued in the missions.[3] While cacicazgos played an important role in organizing a mission, census data call into question both the leadership role of caciques and cacicazgo stability. Caciques lost authority under the Jesuits, and important new leadership positions for the Guaraní developed in the missions. The Spanish-style Guaraní cabildo acted both as the highest native governing body and as an intermediary between the Jesuits and the Guaraní population. In addition, Guaraní *alcaldes* (overseers) oversaw almost all aspects of mission life. While hereditary elite received preference, individuals with other leadership qualities also had access to these and other leadership positions. This complex and hierarchical structure enabled a mission to maintain a population numbering in the hundreds or even thousands.

PHYSICAL STRUCTURE OF THE MISSION

In contrast to the small, semipermanent communities of the pre-European contact period, mission Guaraní lived in large, densely populated towns. Mission sites stretched about one mile in both directions, with thousands of Guaraní living in compact housing units that resembled orderly city blocks.[4] In 1735, an average of 3,677 Indians resided in each mission. Mission Santa Rosa had the smallest population (1,780 inhabitants) and Mission San Nicolás the largest (6,986 inhabitants).[5]

In 1753, the Jesuit provincial of Paraguay sent a diagram of Mission San Juan Bautista to the Jesuit confessor of Ferdinand VI (see Figure 2).[6] This diagram provides a general but idealized image of a mission pueblo.[7] It portrays the pueblo's urban design but seriously understates the population density. In 1735, San Juan Bautista had 1,056 nuclear families with a male head of household and 4,595 individuals—more than double the number represented by the housing units in this image.[8] All but the three least populated missions required more housing units in 1735 than depicted in this diagram.[9]

Despite its significant underestimate of Guaraní housing, the diagram provides a good representation of the urban layout common to all mission pueblos. From the beginning, the Jesuits had a clear idea of how they thought a mission town should look. In the first instructions issued to missionaries leaving for the field, Jesuit provincial Diego de Torres Bollo specified that the pueblos should reproduce the format used in Peru.[10] Each adult male with his nuclear family should have his own dwelling, and four of these dwellings should form a block. Streets should divide these blocks. The church, the priests' quarters, and the cemetery should be attached to each other and adjoin the central plaza. Recognizing that such infrastructure could not be built overnight, Torres instructed the missionaries to construct buildings gradually and to the Indians' liking. The Indians' houses, a small house for the missionary, and an arbor for saying mass were essential; the rest could wait.[11]

The diagram of San Juan Bautista includes all of the components of a mission pueblo described by Torres and much more. Following Luiz Antônio Bolcato Custódio's innovative example, I use the San Juan Bautista

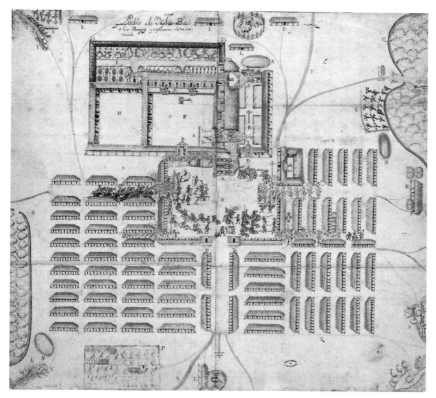

Figure 2. Diagram of Mission San Juan Bautista, ca. 1750
SOURCE: Plano de San Juan Bautista, Archivo de Simancas, Estado 7381-71.

diagram to show the layout of the mission pueblos.[12] In each town, a central plaza separated the Indians' residences from the church and the priests' quarters. The plaza was large—the length of each side was generally greater than that of an American football field.[13] It had to be large enough to accommodate the mission population for various civic, religious, cultural, sporting, and military activities. Under Jesuit oversight, Guaraní alcaldes or corregidores punished Indians found guilty of breaking mission rules at the cross in the center of the plaza. The Jesuits hoped that such public punishment would discourage future infractions.[14] On Sundays Guaraní militias trained and drilled in the plaza, and throughout the year the Indians celebrated various holidays in the plaza with processions, military activities, and dance performances.[15] Such a celebration is depicted in the diagram of San Juan Bautista (see Figure 3): a crowd of women and children watch from in front of the priests' quarters (upper

Figure 3. Procession and central plaza of Mission San Juan Bautista, ca. 1750
SOURCE: Plano de San Juan Bautista, Archivo de Simancas, Estado 7381-71.

left corner of the plaza) and musicians play music (upper right corner of the plaza) while a procession of standard-bearers, cavalry armed with swords and lances, a few artillery men, and archers converge on and circle the plaza.

Facing the center of the plaza, the church dominated the mission landscape. Comparable in size to Spanish cathedrals, the church was always the largest building in a mission pueblo (see Figure 4).[16] Church construction evolved in stages; by the 1730s mission churches were designed by first-rate Jesuit architects.[17] Today, visitors to mission ruins and museums can get an idea of the impressive size, architectural sophistication, and ornate decoration of this latter stage (see Figure 1).[18] The Jesuits laid out the pueblo in such a way as to further draw attention to the church. Three principal roads fed into the mission plaza at ninety-degree angles; in place of a fourth road, the church opened to the middle of the plaza and the principal road leading out of the pueblo.[19]

On one side of the church, two patios formed the priests' residence and the mission's educational facilities, storerooms, and workshops (see Figure 5). Both patios measured between 160 and 230 feet on each side. The first patio, with direct access to both the church and the plaza, was the cloister, or the priests' quarters (F in the diagram of San Juan Bautista). In the rooms surrounding the patio, the Jesuits had bedrooms, a salon, a kitchen, and a dining room (G). Sometimes, a cellar under the kitchen conserved foodstuffs.[20] Also called the *colegio*, this first patio and the surrounding structures included much more than just the priests' private quarters. Some of the rooms served as the mission school, where Guaraní males chosen to learn reading, writing, music, and/or dance studied. This section also included the armory and storerooms for textiles, clothing, and other items.[21]

Figure 4. Mission San Juan Bautista church, ca. 1750
SOURCE: Plano de San Juan Bautista, Archivo de Simancas, Estado 7381-71.

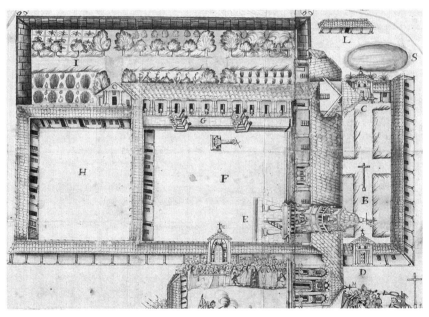

Figure 5. Church compound at Mission San Juan Bautista, ca. 1750
SOURCE: Plano de San Juan Bautista, Archivo de Simancas, Estado 7381-71.

The second patio (H) contained rooms for productive activities and storerooms to sustain the mission. All sorts of Guaraní artisans—carpenters, sculptors, artists, metalworkers, and weavers—worked in the workshops located in the rooms surrounding this patio. Some of the rooms served as storerooms for agricultural products such as yerba maté, corn, beans, and cotton that the Indians produced and consumed. In another section, other Guaraní butchered cattle for beef rations.[22]

Two other structures formed the church compound. A garden (I), located behind the two patios described above, contained fruit trees, vegetables, and flowers for both communal consumption and the Jesuits' use. A cemetery (E) generally was situated on the opposite side of the church and frequently had a chapel (C) associated with it.

Bordering the other three sides of the central plaza were the Indians' residences (see Figure 6). The Jesuits encouraged the Guaraní to transition from sharing a house with other members of their lineage to each nuclear family having its own house. The diagram of San Juan Bautista depicts such nuclear-family housing units. Each unit was uniform in size and design, measuring approximately nineteen feet on all four sides and having a door and a window in both the front and the back. Inside, Indians sometimes hung woven mats or cattle hides to separate sleeping quarters. Except for sleeping and possibly cooking, the Guaraní spent much of their time outdoors. The covered porches that extended along

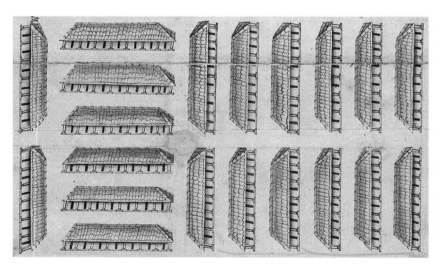

Figure 6. Guaraní housing at Mission San Juan Bautista, ca. 1750
SOURCE: Plano de San Juan Bautista, Archivo de Simancas, Estado 7381-71.

the front and back of the housing units provided protection from both the sun and rain. Given the rectilinear positioning of the housing units, these porches formed covered passageways about fifteen feet wide that bordered the roads in the residential part of the pueblo.[23]

Guaraní housing—like other mission buildings—evolved over time. During the founding of a mission—approximately the first fifteen or twenty years—the Guaraní lived in buildings that the Spaniards viewed as basic and humble. The structures were built of thatch and had dirt floors. During the consolidation period in the mid-seventeenth century, Indian houses generally had adobe walls but still continued to have thatched roofs and dirt floors. In the peak years of the early eighteenth century, stone walls took the place of adobe and tiles replaced the thatched roofs and dirt floors.[24] All of this construction fell into disrepair in the second half of the eighteenth century, as the post-Jesuit administration failed to repair and maintain mission buildings. The changes in Guaraní housing reflect the missions' development, growing prosperity, and decline.

According to missionary accounts, each nuclear family had its own house. The only exception was when a newly married wife did not know how to manage a household; in such cases, the newlyweds resided with the husband's family until the bride learned the necessary domestic skills. At the end of the seventeenth century, orders issued by the general of the Jesuit order suggest that nuclear families still did not always live in separate quarters. Thereafter, the missionaries reinforced efforts to ensure that separations divided nuclear-family housing units. This transition from shared housing to separate nuclear-family housing took at least a century.[25]

Not all Guaraní resided in nuclear-family housing units. The Jesuits did not trust women to live without the protection of their father or husband. Hence, the missionaries created a separate dormitory called the *cotiguazú* (M in Figure 2) to protect female honor and virginity. Widows, female orphans, and women whose husbands were absent from the pueblo resided in the cotiguazú. These women were not free to come and go as they pleased. The cotiguazú was locked and had only one entrance; the women and girls could only leave the building together to attend religious celebrations.[26] This lack of freedom was oppressive, and such confinement was a new experience for Guaraní women.[27]

The diagram of San Juan Bautista highlights a number of other important structures and locations outside of the center of the mission pueblo: ponds for reserving water and washing clothes, a corral for livestock, and agricultural fields. Although a key for deciphering all of the structures and images has not been found, the diagram likely also includes a hospital, jail, and *tambo* (housing for visitors, travelers, and merchants).

The Jesuits structured the mission pueblo to restrict the Indians' contact with outsiders and to facilitate their control over mission inhabitants. On one hand, the Jesuits feared that without close supervision, the Guaraní would learn behaviors from outsiders that conflicted with Jesuit ideals. Because of these concerns, the Jesuits sought to prevent such contact as much as possible. They instituted strict regulations as to when, for how long, and under what conditions non-Indian outsiders could visit the missions. Legally, travelers, visitors, or merchants could only stay in a mission for a maximum of three days, during which time their accommodations in the tambo kept them separate from the Indians.[28]

On the other hand, the Jesuits feared that the Guaraní would continue heathen practices if left to their own devices. They believed that the compact urban design of the mission pueblos facilitated the teaching and enforcement of their ideals, and therefore they endeavored to prevent the Indians from leaving the pueblo. Legally, a mission inhabitant could not leave her mission without the Spanish governor's written permission.[29] Nonetheless, although in many respects the Jesuits insulated the Guaraní from contact with outsiders, they could not eliminate it entirely. The missions were much more permeable than the regulations seem to imply.

The Jesuits sent mission Guaraní outside of the pueblo on mission business. The environment immediately surrounding the pueblo could not sustain thousands of Indian residents. Guaraní inhabitants sometimes had to travel hundreds of miles to procure goods needed by the mission. For most of the seventeenth century, the missions got their yerba maté from the distant *yerbales silvestres* (wild growths of yerba maté trees) of Maracayú located northeast of Asunción. To harvest the yerba maté, a mission sent fifty or more Indians some four to five hundred miles to Maracayú. By the end of the expedition, the Indians had been away from the mission for two to three months.[30] Even after the Jesuits learned how to domesticate yerba maté trees in the early eighteenth century, many missions continued to send groups of Indians to harvest yerba maté at a distance from their pueblo.[31]

Similarly, missions restocked their *estancias* (livestock ranches) by sending Indians to round up wild cattle. Such expeditions took Indians away from the pueblo for several months.[32] In the eighteenth century, the Jesuits promoted the domestication of cattle in estancias in order reduce the missions' reliance on wild herds. Raising cattle did not eliminate the absence of Guaraní from the pueblo, however. The estancias were large and not always located close to the pueblo. In the case of Missions Yapeyú and San Miguel, the mission inhabitants who worked as cowboys and peons had houses on the estancia and resided there. Not only did these

Indians live apart from the mission pueblo, they also came in regular contact with outsiders. In 1735, the Jesuit provincial of Paraguay issued permission for the missions to hire some Spaniards or other "people of intelligence and caution" to work on the estancias.[33] Based on iconography, Bolcato Custódio believes that blacks may also have lived and worked on San Miguel's estancias.[34] Many of the estancias had chapels so that the Guaraní could continue Catholic practices. The Jesuits also sent a priest and an assistant to live among the Indians on the Yapayú estancia;[35] the same was likely true for San Miguel.

Mission inhabitants resided outside of the pueblo during periods of intense agricultural labor. The Guaraní constructed thatched-roof houses on their agricultural plots.[36] Given that the fields were not very distant from the pueblo, the Guaraní likely used such structures for protection from the sun and rain when they took breaks from their work, as do present-day campesinos in Paraguay.[37] During planting and harvesting, the Guaraní slept in these houses and only returned to their mission on Sundays and festival days.[38]

Although a mission independently produced much of what it needed, each pueblo was far from insular. In addition to hunting, gathering, raising livestock, and cultivating products at a distance from the pueblo, a mission engaged with surrounding missions and with other institutions and individuals. The Jesuits regularly sent Guaraní outside of the pueblo as envoys or messengers on official mission business. Such envoys regularly went to other missions to seek assistance, trade, or share information. Messengers also transported goods to trading centers in Buenos Aires and Santa Fe on behalf of the mission. Traveling by river and land, such trips would take months to complete.[39]

Service to the Crown also took Guaraní outside of the pueblos. Many Guaraní left their pueblo as members of mission militias. Royal officials readily called these Guaraní militias for service, using them to put down uprisings and defend Spanish settlements and territory against the Portuguese, other foreign powers, and Indians they considered to be hostile. There were fifty-eight requests for assistance from the Guaraní militias over the period between 1637 and 1735, resulting in Guaraní militias leaving their pueblos more than once every other year on average to perform military service for the Crown. The duration of service and the number of Indians required varied, but overall a large number of Indians were affected; the Jesuits calculated that over 45,000 Indians had to leave their pueblos to provide such services.[40] In addition to military service, royal officials called on mission Guaraní to labor on public works projects in Montevideo, Santa Fe, and Buenos Aires. The building and rebuilding of forts, defensive walls, and other structures sometimes took years to complete and thus kept Guaraní laborers away from their pueblos for extended periods.[41]

In addition to the variety of excused absences, some Guaraní also left the missions without official permission. With an average of two missionaries and hundreds or thousands of Indians in each mission, the Jesuits clearly could not force the Guaraní to stay.

Even though the missions were not hermetic environments sealed off from external influences, the Guaraní had far less exposure to outsiders than mission Indians elsewhere. The Guaraní missions possessed an expansive amount of territory, and so the nonmission population generally resided at some distance from the pueblos. Furthermore, the weak regional economy meant there was limited demand for mission Indians to labor outside of the missions. Only under exceptional circumstances did the Guaraní labor outside of the mission other than in service to the Crown.

MISSION POPULATION

The large number of Indian inhabitants set the Guaraní missions apart from other missions in Spanish America. While populations in other missions sometimes reached a couple of thousand, they did not approach the size of the Guaraní mission population.[42] Under Jesuit oversight in the eighteenth century, the population of each mission averaged between 2,500 and 4,700 inhabitants, and only on very rare occasions did the population of a mission fall below 1,000.[43]

As the missions matured between the 1640s and 1730s, the total population of the thirty missions almost quadrupled. In 1732, it reached its maximum with 141,182 Indians (see Figure 7). This quantity not only exceeded mission populations elsewhere; it accounted for a large portion of the entire population of Guaraní. Pierre Clastres has estimated that over 85 percent of all Guaraní resided in the missions as of the 1730s.[44]

New converts cannot explain the population growth of the Guaraní missions. New Christians made up a large portion of the initial population in only one of the seven Guaraní missions established after the mid-seventeenth century. All of the other missions began primarily as offshoots of older missions.[45] Censuses from 1735 confirm that few Indians had joined the missions within the preceding twenty years. Eighteen of the thirty missions did not have anyone who had converted within the previous twenty years; the remaining twelve missions had only a few converts—on average five families.[46]

Figure 7. Total mission population, 1647–1767
SOURCE: 1647–1670, Maeder, "La población de las misiones," 64–65; 1671–1767, Maeder and Bolsi, "La población guaraní de las misiones," 42–44.

By the eighteenth century, the Jesuits only sporadically tried to proselytize to Indians outside of the missions. They lacked the manpower for such campaigns. Jesuit reports constantly complained about the lack of priests and requested new recruits from Europe. For example, the Jesuit provincial of Paraguay informed the king in 1712 that the Jesuits did not have the capacity to convert Indians who expressed interest in missions owing to a shortage of missionaries and the dispersion and remoteness of the potential converts: "The province suffers from an extreme necessity for operatives [missionaries] who can satisfy the obligation to maintain the converted Christians that are in its care; and even more so to further the conversion of the many heathens willing and desiring to receive the Holy Baptism." He followed this with an appeal to the king for at least another sixty missionaries.[47] In the 1740s, the Jesuits founded two missions among the Tarumá and one among the Mbayá, but these did not have time to mature and thus are not included in this analysis.[48]

Most of the increase in the missions' population resulted from a high birth rate that would quickly make up for a few years of population decline.[49] Mission Guaraní had a lot of children, in part because they married young. In order to prevent what they viewed as sexual promiscuity, the Jesuits tried to compel males at the age of seventeen and girls at the age of fifteen to marry.[50] Some married even younger; in 1735 all but a couple of missions had a few married males under the age of seventeen. Despite pressure from the Jesuits, however, some males still remained unmarried at the age of eighteen in all but one, or possibly two, of the missions as of 1735. These men did not stay single long; rarely were there bachelors over the age of twenty in the missions. Widowers also rarely remained single; a mission seldom had more than ten widowers. Widows did not remarry at the same rate; hundreds of widows in a single mission were not uncommon. The Jesuits did not formally allow widows or any other women to head their own households. Instead, they lived in the cotiguazú with female orphans and other females whom the Jesuits deemed in need of protection. In the censuses, a widower appeared as a head of household with his children under his care. In contrast, widows had their own category and their children appeared as orphans.[51]

Except in the rare case of a widower, each household contained a male head of household, his wife, and all of his unmarried children. While a family had on average four to five members, this figure disguises a large range in household sizes.[52] In 1735 and 1759, the most frequent household size for Mission Santa Ana was two members (see Figure 8). Thereafter, as family size increased, the number of families declined; only three families had the maximum of nine members.[53] Given that married children no longer appeared in the census as part of their parents' family, household size significantly undercounts mission Guaraní fertility rates. Massimo Livi-Bacci and Ernesto J. Maeder estimate that on average, mission Guaraní women had 7.7 children.[54]

The high birth rate and the population growth over time should, however, not be overstated. As elsewhere among Native Americans, epidemics regularly cycled through the mission population with devastating consequences. Before the arrival of Europeans and Africans, diseases such as smallpox, measles, and typhus did not exist. Huge numbers of native peoples sickened and died from European diseases, since only individuals who had previously contracted such an illness had immunity. Estimates of the decline in the native population—primarily from these illnesses—reach as high as 95 percent of the precontact population.[55] This decline lasted for at least the first century and a half following European contact.[56]

The overall upward trend in the mission population obscures devastating periods of decline. When an epidemic hit, a huge portion of the mission population became ill and many died. Generally, during an epidemic the number of people who died exceeded the number born, and as a result mission population declined; at other times, the mission population fell as the result of flight or a combination of these two factors. After several years of such decline, the mission population would begin to recover. For example, in the 1730s the Guaraní missions suffered a series of calamities—epidemics, extended military service, drought, and upheaval associated with the Comunero Revolt in Asunción; in the 1740s the mission population began to recover.[57]

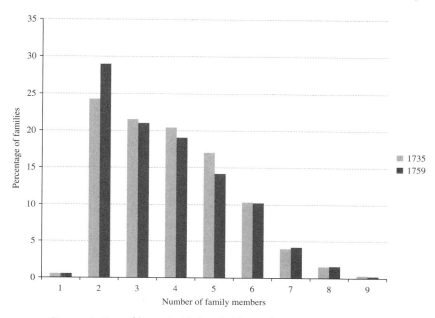

Figure 8. Size of households headed by males, Mission Santa Ana
SOURCE: 1735 Census of Mission Santa Ana, AGN, IX 18-8-2; 1759 Census of Mission Santa Ana, AGN, IX 17-3-6.

Smallpox and measles ranked as the most prevalent and deadliest diseases in the missions. Of the two, smallpox caused the most deaths. Smallpox was also the leading cause of death in eighteenth-century Europe, accounting for 5–10 percent of all deaths.[58] The death toll among Native Americans was much higher. In eighteenth-century Europe, approximately 15 percent of those infected with the disease died, while reports for the Americas indicate a death rate of often 50 and even as much as 90 percent.[59] The age structure of the population affected the death rate: fatality rates for smallpox are high in infancy, decline to a low point between the ages of five and fourteen, and increase again thereafter.[60] The likelihood of death also varied depending on the strain of smallpox; the more virulent variants—those with a higher mortality rate—cycled repeatedly through the New World and thus also the Guaraní missions.[61]

Even those who did not die during epidemics still experienced adverse effects due to the disease. Many Indians who did not die still became very ill. With smallpox, infected individuals would experience a rash, fever, chills, headache, nausea, vomiting, and severe muscle aches. Symptoms lasted for twenty to twenty-four days, with periods of varying intensity.

The long duration meant that many people would be sick during over-lapping periods. Even though measles lasted for a shorter time—seven to ten days—people were more likely to be sick at the same time with the disease.[62] During their illness, these people could do little if any work. Healthy individuals thus had to nurse the sick and work more to com-pensate for those who could not.

The missionaries and the Indians could not easily prevent smallpox and measles from turning into epidemics. Both diseases are airborne—transmitted by breathing droplets or dust particles carrying the virus. Contact with an infected person, non-Indian or Indian, quickly spread the disease. Expeditions to gather yerba maté, hunt cattle, trade mis-sion goods, visit other missions, or defend Spanish territory put mission inhabitants in contact with outsiders, some of whom carried diseases. Once a mission inhabitant became infected with smallpox or measles, it was almost impossible to prevent an epidemic. The Jesuits often tried to isolate the sick in hospitals, but contagion still spread. Containment was impeded by the urban structure of the missions. In their small, apartment-like housing units, mission inhabitants lived very close to one another and thus came in contact frequently.[63] Such close proximity made it hard for individuals to avoid breathing the virus and contracting the illness. Sleeping in the same room also efficiently exposed susceptible individuals to disease.[64]

After infecting one mission, a disease frequently spread to neighbor-ing missions. Robert H. Jackson's case study of the 1764–1765 smallpox epidemic reveals that the virus spread through almost all of the thirty missions. Following several geographic trajectories, the virus moved from one mission to the next. By the end of two years, smallpox had claimed the lives of over twelve thousand mission inhabitants.[65]

Diseases did not infect and kill the mission population only once; they cycled through missions approximately every generation. The disease would die off after an epidemic because, once exposed, an individual gains immunity to the disease. With a large enough population—several hundred thousand—a disease becomes endemic, that is, it does not die out but remains continuously active, affecting a small portion of the pop-ulation. The number of infected individuals does not increase exponen-tially, nor do a large proportion of the population fall ill at the same time. Thus, even though an endemic disease continually causes sickness and death, it does not result in the devastation that occurs from an epidemic. But the population of an individual mission—less than ten thousand—never approached the threshold for a disease to become endemic, that is, to remain continuously active from generation to generation. Without an adequate supply of hosts, a disease would die off after an epidemic. Then, a generation or so later, an infected person would bring the virus back to the mission to wreak havoc on a heretofore unexposed population. On average, between 1690 and 1767 a smallpox epidemic struck the missions every fifteen years.[66]

GOVERNING STRUCTURE

A mission needed a complex governing structure to manage all of the requisite activities to sustain thousands of Indian inhabitants, and thus a variety of different leadership positions developed. Native leadership in the missions can be categorized as coercive (exercised by bureaucratic authorities such as cabildo members and overseers), organizational (exercised at the level of the cacicazgo or *parcialidad*), or charismatic (based on Guaraní concepts of leadership). A leader might possess any or all of these traits.

Instituted in municipalities throughout the Americas and introduced into the missions by the Jesuits, the cabildo, or town council, became the most powerful Guaraní authority. Ideally, the cabildo consisted of a corregidor; a lieutenant corregidor, who assisted the corregidor; two *alcaldes ordinarios* (municipal magistrates); four *regidores* (secondary officers); an *alcalde de hermandad* (lower-ranking military officer); an *alférez real* (royal ensign); an *alguacil mayor* (constable); a *mayordomo* (steward); and a secretary.[67] Each cabildo member received an object that symbolized his leadership role.[68]

Mission regulations specified that cabildo membership change each year. Although in theory outgoing cabildo members named incoming members, the Jesuits intervened in elections. Outgoing cabildo members could not freely choose their successors. They elected a candidate to fill each position but had to submit the results to the priest for his approval. If the priest did not like a candidate, he could veto the outgoing cabildo members' choice and order the substitution of another candidate. Once the priest found the list of new members to his liking, he forwarded it to the secular governor of the region for his approval.[69] The priest's vetting of candidates resulted in cabildo members who generally worked with rather than against the Jesuits. Such a relationship meant that cabildo members exercised a coercive form of leadership: they encouraged compliance and enforced their leadership powers with policing and punishment backed by the missionaries.

While the Jesuits wanted to manage, direct, and oversee all aspects of mission operations, they granted significant power to Guaraní cabildo members. In his idealized account, Jesuit missionary José Cardiel described the Guaraní leaders as completely dependent on the Jesuits for instruction: "The corregidor, alcaldes, etc. neither punish, nor send on a trip, nor assign a task, without the order of the Priest; and no more."[70] In practice, of course, Guaraní leaders had much more power. While Cardiel emphasized the central role of the Jesuit missionary, elsewhere he acknowledged the important roles played by the Guaraní corregidor and mayordomo. He likened a mission's governing structure to a Jesuit college: the priest was the rector, the corregidor was the minister or manager, and the mayordomo was the procurador. While still an important figure in the mission, the priest's companion did not involve himself in secular matters but instead assisted with spiritual affairs.[71] In this vision of governance, the priest and the rector held ultimate authority over all the affairs of their respective institutions. Like a rector in a college, the priest's duties in a mission included maintaining spiritual welfare, establishing the rules and making sure they were followed, appointing and supervising everyone else in the hierarchy, presiding over all activities, and maintaining relationships with Jesuit superiors, other Jesuit institutions, and civil authorities.[72]

The corregidor in a mission (like the minister in a college) occupied the next rung in Cardiel's idealized representation of the mission's governing hierarchy. The position dealt primarily with management and economic affairs rather than religious matters. The Jesuits delegated a great deal of responsibility to this individual but still expected him to defer to the priest. Like a minister with the staff of a college, the corregidor supervised other Guaraní in mission leadership positions. He also kept inventories and other records.[73] Of all the Guaraní leaders in a mission, the Jesuits awarded the corregidor the largest role. He was the head of both the cabildo and his mission's militia unit.[74] *Corregidor* in Guaraní (*poroquaitara*) means "he who arranges that which has to be done."[75]

According to Cardiel, the mayordomo in a mission (like the procurador in a college) had the next most important role in the governing structure. In a college, the procurador was responsible both for managing the inflow and outflow of funds and for keeping financial and legal records.[76] In contrast, since a mission did not conduct many monetary transactions, the mayordomo did not manage money so much as oversee the inflows and outflows of mission goods. As a symbol of this role, the mayordomo received keys to his mission's storerooms when he took office.[77]

While Cardiel sought to show the priest as the ultimate decision maker in a mission's governing structure, his description reveals that Guaraní leaders had substantial power. As the primary intermediary between the Jesuits and the Guaraní, the corregidor exercised a great deal of authority and influence. Similarly, given the large scale of mission operations, the mayordomo also exercised important management powers. By equating a mission to a college, Cardiel overstated the discipline and autocracy of the mission's governing structure. Guaraní leaders were not Jesuits, and they did not act with the same degree of obedience and deference as Jesuits in a college.

In a similar vein, Jesuit missionary Juan de Escandón's description of the daily governance practices in a mission emphasized the priest's role as the ultimate decision maker in a mission while also acknowledging indirectly that cabildo members acted independently or even in conflict with the Jesuits. According to Escandón, cabildo members met each day with the mission priest to discuss judicial and economic matters. First, cabildo members informed the priest as to who had been sent to the mission jail or the women's dormitory. Without identifying the arbiter, Escandón explained that a decision was made whether to punish or liberate the individual. Next, the priest told cabildo members what work the mission population should accomplish during that day. All of this, Escandón stated, "is executed in the same manner as is done in a well-governed family where each day [the family] executes what the father of the family commands."[78] While Escandón presented the priest as the ultimate decision maker, in his account cabildo members also had a significant amount of power. For example, when explaining that cabildo members communicated the plan for planting crops to the rest of the mission population, he acknowledged that they and the priest had come to an agreement.[79] In addition to influencing the priest during such meetings, as Escandón also acknowledged, cabildo members sometimes altered the priest's instructions when repeating this information to the rest of the mission population. He indirectly alluded to cabildo members putting their own twist on the Jesuits' instructions, talks, and sermons by reinterpreting or revising them. When they were asked to repeat a sermon, he admitted, cabildo members usually communicated only part of the essence of the speech and only rarely the entire speech.[80] If cabildo members shortened Jesuit speeches, they likely also changed or omitted information not to their liking.

In addition to the cabildo, the Jesuits created a variety of other new leadership positions in the missions. An overseer was named to supervise almost every mission activity. Sacristans helped the missionaries with the administration of sacraments and other religious and church-related functions.[81] A separate leader was named for each of the artisan trades and almost every type of work project.[82] For example, a *zoorerequadra* (someone who cares for the meat) oversaw the slaughter of cattle and distribution of the meat.[83] Separate Guaraní leaders also oversaw the affairs of the women, boys, and girls.[84]

At the microlevel, the Jesuits sought the assistance of caciques in managing the members of their cacicazgos. The position of cacique and cacicazgo membership played an important role throughout the lifespan of the missions. Guaraní generally joined a mission as part of a cacicazgo led by a cacique. The few who joined independently were added to a pre-existing cacicazgo.[85] Although some cacicazgos disappeared, many continued, and their roots could be traced to when they joined the mission.[86]

The Jesuits cultivated the caciques' leadership role and paid them respect as minor nobility with vassals.[87] In recognition of their status, caciques used the title "Don" and wore distinctive clothing during mission festivities.[88] They also received preference for other leadership positions in their mission. In 1697 and again in 1725 the Crown reinforced and formalized caciques' special status and privileges with royal cedulas that officially declared caciques noblemen of Castile.[89]

Although the Spanish Crown promoted the use of caciques as intermediaries between the state and indigenous peoples throughout Latin America, the obligations and privileges associated with being a cacique in a Guaraní mission were somewhat different than elsewhere in the Americas.[90] Guaraní caciques were not responsible for collecting tribute from cacicazgo members; instead, a mission used its trade revenues to pay all of the tribute accrued by its inhabitants. Furthermore, even though caciques and their first sons were exempt from tribute, as elsewhere, this privilege had little practical effect for the caciques, given that the mission paid tribute on behalf of all its inhabitants. Another striking difference is that cacicazgos did not own land or other property in the Guaraní missions, and thus caciques did not have an entail over cacicazgo property. Instead, the mission population collectively owned the land and property. While a cacique might distribute plots of land for farming to each nuclear family in his cacicazgo, the land belonged to the mission rather than the cacique or cacicazgo.[91] Additionally, while cacicazgo members might help a cacique with his house or fields, they did not pay tribute or service to their cacique, and caciques were not exempt from agricultural or other labor.[92]

Mission Indians spent a lot of time with other members of their cacicazgo, and cacicazgo membership structured mission life. Cacicazgos formed separate residential neighborhoods, with members of a single cacicazgo inhabiting the same row or rows of houses.[93] Adult Guaraní males received plots of land for farming based on cacicazgo membership, and cacicazgo members often worked together on communal work projects.[94] Furthermore, the mission population was divided into cacicazgos whenever the Indians had to be counted. For example, men and women went into the plaza after religious services and were separated by cacicazgo in order to facilitate the identification of those not in attendance.[95] The Guaraní also received goods distributed from mission supplies on the basis of their lineage group.[96] Such frequent and regular separation into cacicazgos in all probability reinforced an Indian's sense of identity as being part of a particular cacicazgo.

While the Guaraní likely felt ties to their cacicazgos at least in part because of their precontact traditions, the Jesuits encouraged such associations because they facilitated governance. With the average population of a mission ranging between 2,500 and 4,700 inhabitants over the course of the eighteenth century, cacicazgos divided mission inhabitants into smaller and more manageable groups.[97]

As heads of the cacicazgos, caciques could be either necessary or superfluous to the governing structure of the Guaraní missions. While some actively exercised leadership roles, hereditary birthright did not necessarily bestow legitimacy as a leader. Sometimes caciques functioned more as placeholders or figureheads for dividing the mission population into smaller, more manageable subsets, functioning only as organizational leaders.

Primogeniture succession led to the appointment of some caciques who did not have the respect of their followers. The Guaraní looked for qualities such as eloquence and generosity in their leaders, in addition to bloodline. Cacique succession in the missions, however, did not allow for such flexibility. Male primogeniture succession limited the successor to being the eldest son regardless of his personal attributes. In cases where there was no son, the successor tended to be the closest living relative. Cacique succession in the missions rarely took into account any leadership qualities other than descent, and as Guillermo Wilde has highlighted, the Guaraní sometimes contested such successions.[98]

If the cacique left no adult male heir, the first option was to give the position to the eldest underage son. In the missions, a male was considered an adult at the age of eighteen for tribute purposes and seventeen for marriage purposes. In 1735, 15 percent of all of the caciques in the thirty missions (170 out of 1,102) were males under the age of eighteen (see Table 1).[99] Minors, especially young children, would generally not have the ability to command respect and actively lead their cacicazgo.

If a cacique left no male heirs, the second option was to pass the position to either a daughter or son-in-law. This happened less frequently; in 1735, only 3 percent of all cacicazgos (34 out of 1,102) had passed to the daughter of a cacique. In such cases, it would not always be clear who acted as cacique. When the daughter was an unmarried child (the Jesuits tried to enforce marriage for females at the age of fifteen), the census frequently specified that the cacicazgo passed to her; for example, in Mission San Cosme, the cacicazgo of don Christobal Taruima inherited the only daughter of the deceased cacique, named Maria Magdalena Apora. When the daughter was an adult, the census was often more ambiguous

TABLE I. *Caciques of the thirty Guaraní missions, 1735*

Mission	Males 18+ years of age	Males <18 years of age	Females	Fugitives	No cacique	Total
Ana	42	4		1		47
Angel	25	2				27
Apóstoles	31	3		3	1	38
Bautista	18	5				
Borja	23	3	1		4	31
Candelaria	23	2	2	1		28
Carlos	28	2				30
Concepción	23	3	2			28
Corpus	33	8	3			44
Cosme	19	2	1	2	1	25
Cruz	20	3	1	1		25
Ignacio Guazú	13	9	1	7	1	31
Ignacio Miní	77	8			8	93
Itapúa	38	10	4	2	1	55
Jesús	23	7		2		32
José	28	6	3	2		39
Lorenzo	38	2				40
Loreto	65	14	5	1		85
Luis	33	8	2			43
María la Mayor	14	8	2		2	26
Mártires	25	9	2		2	38
Miguel	18	2		2		22
Nicolás	40	6				46
Rosa	15	4				19
Santa Fe	15	8				23
Santiago	21	6				27
Tomé	14	5	1	2	2	24
Trinidad	19	5				24
Xavier	22	6	1	1		30
Yapeyú	45	10	3	1		59
All missions	848	170	34	28	22	1,102
Percentage of total	77%	15%	3%	3%	2%	

SOURCE: Reprinted with the permission of the *Colonial Latin American Review* from Sarreal, "Caciques as Placeholders in the Guaraní Missions of Eighteenth Century Paraguay," forthcoming 2014.

about who assumed the leadership role. For example, in Mission Concepción, the cacicazgo of don Poti simply listed the first family as thirty-six-year-old Christobal Guari and his wife, Maria Rosa Cuyabe, daughter of the deceased cacique; the entry did not include "don" or "doña" to specify who was cacique—the daughter, the son-in-law, or both.

The relatively high number of child caciques, and possibly the female caciques as well, challenges the notion that the cacique exercised the most power within a cacicazgo and raises questions about the leadership capabilities of such individuals. In Mission Santo Tomé, did the ninety-three cacicazgo members follow the orders of cacique Damaso Maragua, a three-year-old toddler? Could a three-year-old assign plots of land for agriculture and direct his followers in their labors? Likewise, given the strict gender roles taught by the Jesuits and the precontact Guaraní preference for male caciques, how much power did a female cacique have? In Mission Itapúa, did the forty-two families belonging to the cacicazgo of don Guirapici listen to and obey Bibiana Marta, the daughter who inherited the cacicazgo after her father's death?

A cacique might be unable or unwilling to assume the responsibilities of managing a cacicazgo, owing to a disability, an accident, or an assortment of other reasons. For example, the census of Mission Candelaria identified forty-five-year-old cacique Pasqual Curapiu as chronically infirm for two years; it seems likely that such illness or disability would have prevented don Curapiu from fulfilling his duties as a cacique.

The question of who led a cacicazgo is even more pronounced in cases where a cacique fled the mission or was absent for an extended period of time. An Indian could legally leave a mission only with the Spanish governor's written authorization; any unauthorized absence was officially illegal.[100] But Guaraní fled the missions during difficult times. Rates of flight intensified in the 1730s because of the aforementioned series of hardships: military conflict, disease, and drought. Ernesto Maeder and Alfredo Bolsi estimate that over seventeen thousand Guaraní left the missions between 1733 and 1740.[101] Some of the fugitives were native elite; the 1735 census listed 3 percent (28 out of 1,102) of the caciques as fugitives. One cacique had been absent for less than a year, while the rest had been away for between one and three years. As fugitives, these caciques could hardly have fulfilled the leadership duties associated with their position.

In the most extreme cases, a cacicazgo did not have a cacique. For 2 percent (22 out of 1,102) of the cacicazgos, the cacique had died without an heir and a replacement cacique had not been named. Who was in charge of the cacicazgo in such cases? One possibility is that a Guaraní administrator either formally or informally assumed responsibility. But there is little direct reference to such individuals; in the 1735 census, only two missions identify administrators in charge of cacicazgos.

In the place on the census form for Mission Santa María la Mayor where the cacique was normally identified, the census taker listed administrators as the heads of nine cacicazgos. All of the administrators were older males, aged thirty-four to forty-five. Given that six of the nine had the same surname as the cacicazgo, most were probably brothers or other relatives of the deceased caciques. An administrator was listed for each of the two cacicazgos without a cacique—those of don Cañarima and don Tiariya. One of the two cacicazgos inherited by a daughter of the deceased cacique also had an administrator: Lazaro Araguira, aged forty, served as administrator of the cacicazago inherited by Rosalia Mboiri, the unmarried legitimate daughter of don Aretumba. This cacicazgo had an administrator because Rosalia Mboiri was likely a child (if an adult, she would have been either married or widowed and not listed as single; censuses never identified any single adult females). In contrast, the cacicazgo inherited by Roselia Cuñaete, the married daughter of don Apuribiyu, did not have an administrator. For her cacicazgo, it is unclear who was in charge. Neither Rosalia Cuñaete nor her nineteen-year-old husband, Sebastian Tiariya, was identified as either the cacique or the administrator of the cacicazgo. Six of the eight cacicazgos with male caciques under the age of eighteen had administrators. The two exceptions were a married seventeen-year-old cacique (who was probably capable of managing the cacicazgo himself) and an unmarried twelve-year-old cacique. Although the census of Mission Santa María la Mayor only mentioned administrators when there was no cacique or the cacique was too young to govern by himself, other circumstances, such as a cacique who was a fugitive, chronically ill, or otherwise incapable of exercising a leadership role, might also have required that someone like an administrator take charge of a cacicazgo.

The only other mission census to explicitly identify an administrator in 1735, Santos Mártires, did so under unique circumstances: Marcos Moncado, identified as the administrator of the Yrama cacicazgo, was a free mulatto. According to the body of laws relating to Spanish territory in the Americas and the Philippines issued by Charles II in 1680, no Spaniard, negro, mestizo, or mulatto could reside in a mission.[102] While formally acknowledging that the king's orders forbade mulattos from living in the missions, Jesuit missionary José Cardiel, who worked in the Guaraní missions from 1731 to 1743 and from 1749 to 1768, wrote that a mulatto did reside in a Guaraní mission and had incorporated himself into a cacicazgo. According to Cardiel, in contrast to what would have been expected, the unnamed mulatto had married a Guaraní woman who was the daughter of a cacique and heir to a cacicazgo. Cardiel claimed that this mulatto commanded respect from the members of the cacicazgo and had risen to a position of power in the mission.[103]

Even though only two mission censuses in 1735 identified administrators as being in charge of cacicazgos, the relatively small number of documented cases does not necessarily mean that it was a rare practice. Given that an administrator was not exempt from tribute and that calculation of the mission's total tribute obligation was the purpose of the census, there would have been no motivation to identify administrators in a census. Thus, administrators might have existed even though they did not appear in a census. Furthermore, given that administrators seem often to have functioned as regents for underage caciques, they likely continued to exercise influence if not leadership powers once the cacique came of age.

In addition to dealing with ineffective caciques, the mission regime also had to find ways to compensate for excessively small cacicazgos. In the 1735 census, cacicazgos consisted of an average of twenty-six families, but this average disguises wide variations among the missions.[104] Mission San Ignacio Miní averaged only eight families in each of its cacicazgos, while Mission Concepción averaged forty-six families. Some cacicazgos consisted only of the cacique and his nuclear family, while at least several cacicazgos comprised close to one hundred families. A cacicazgo with only a few members meant that the cacique had few people to lead; in contrast, a cacicazgo with one hundred or more families (approximately 450 people) potentially stretched a cacique's leadership abilities. One way that the missions dealt with cacicazgos that had few members was to consolidate such cacicazgos into larger groups. Cardiel called these larger groups *tribus* or *parcialidades*.

According to Cardiel, a parcialidad comprised four to six cacicazgos and a mission had up to eight or ten parcialidades; the exact number varied depending on the size of the pueblo. Parcialidades not only were a way of combining small cacicazgos into more effective units for organizational purposes but they also created leadership opportunities for non-caciques. According to Cardiel, a cabildo member served as boss or supervisor of the parcialidad, and overseers policed the caciques and cacicazgo members during the agricultural season.[105]

While Jesuit missionary Antonio Sepp mentioned caciques and their vassals when discussing agricultural labor, in his description of how Indians should be distributed in all mission labor projects, he did not even mention caciques:

For governing the Indians in temporal matters, the experience that I have had over many years and in many missions has taught me that the only way is to always divide them into crews [*en quadrilla*]. In each crew there cannot be more, and preferably less, than ten according to their labor. Each crew should have an overseer or secretary who has written their names in a leather book, in the same way that the musicians [Guaraní assistants in the church] count who is missing from Mass on Sunday.[106]

Jesuit writings highlighted the caciques' noble status and the importance of the cacicazgos in organizing the mission population, but they focused far less attention on the caciques' actual leadership activities. In fact, they often expressed concern that caciques were not exercising enough of a leadership role. In 1742, the provincial of the Jesuit province of Paraguay, Antonio Machoni, provided specific instructions for the missionaries to cultivate caciques as native leaders. In his guidelines, Machoni admitted that the Guaraní did not always respect or obey their caciques. He explicitly instructed the missionaries as follows:

> Show some more respect to all of the caciques and honor their person so that their vassals respect them and venerate them. And for all those who are capable and show good behavior, give them an office in the cabildo and in the functions of the church. Give them all a seat in the benches, after the military leaders. Do this because some are seen as debased and are not at all esteemed by their vassals and are without the spirit to govern them because of the poverty in which they find themselves. The priest will help them with the necessary and decent clothing appropriate to their status and for their wives and children. Pay special attention to [their children] in their upbringing, putting them in the school so that they learn to read and write even if they do not become singers.[107]

Machoni suggested that the cacicazgo members' lack of respect for their caciques derived from the caciques' lack of charisma ("some are seen as debased . . . and are without the spirit to govern"). His assessment points to problems arising from the missions' strict adherence to male primogeniture succession; such a practice solely prioritized father-to-eldest-son lineage. It did not consider other leadership qualities and thus could not guarantee that a cacique would be a capable and motivated leader respected by fellow Guaraní.

A cacique without leadership skills served more as a placeholder than an actual leader. He or she was needed as a figurehead for the cacicazgo, an important unit for organizing the mission population: the cacicazgos divided the hundreds or thousands of Indian residents into smaller, more manageable groups. When such a cacique lacked leadership skills, other members of the cacicazgo with leadership skills compensated for this shortcoming.

Since strict adherence to hereditary succession meant that not all caciques were effective leaders, many active leadership positions went to non-caciques. For example, the head of the Guaraní troops during much of the Guaraní War, Sepé (José Tiarayú), was a cabildo member but not a cacique of Mission San Miguel.[108] Additionally, the fact that the missions had permission to exempt church officials and the corregidor from tribute suggests that these leaders were often not caciques:[109] if they had been caciques, there would have been no reason for this exemption, since caciques and their first-born sons were already exempt from tribute. Most noteworthy is that the corregidor—the most powerful Guaraní leader in the Jesuits' political hierarchy—was not always a cacique. In describing corregidors, Cardiel referred to leadership qualities without referring to the preference given to caciques: "Sometimes, when the governor is informed of the notable qualities and merits of a particular Indian, he confers to him a lifelong appointment as corregidor."[110] Escandón's acknowledgment that preference was given to caciques for the position of corregidor suggests that this was often not the case. Rather, other leadership qualities were valued more in such a decision: "[A corregidor] is generally one of the most rational and an authority among the Indians. And because of that, if among all of the leaders there are two or more equal candidates, the one that is a cacique is elected."[111]

Both the lack of respect shown some caciques and the high value placed on nonlineage leadership qualities for the position of corregidor likely reflects at least in part Guaraní ideals of leadership. The Guaraní did not conceive of leadership ability as determined only by primogeniture succession. When describing who attended a mission school, Cardiel identified not only caciques but also an assortment of other leaders and he did not differentiate between the respect the Guaraní gave to caciques as opposed to non-cacique leaders. "The children of the caciques, of the cabildo members, musicians, sacristans, overseers, and master artisans go to school; all are esteemed like nobility."[112] This description indicates that popular legitimacy was not based merely on heredity.

To be effective, a leader had to be able to lead the Guaraní, and to do so he needed respect. Such leaders gained the respect of their followers by exhibiting leadership qualities valued by the Guaraní. These leaders can be characterized as charismatic, as exemplified by Don Ignacio Abierú. In describing why Don Abierú was chosen as a Guaraní military leader in 1659, a missionary highlighted that he was "an Indian of valor who had distinguished himself among other Indians in the service of the two majesties and of his homeland during the occasions when the Portuguese of São Paulo infested the said missions and was loved and feared and respected among all of the Indians."[113]

An array of leadership opportunities open to individuals who possessed leadership qualities but fell outside of the hereditary line of caciques provided flexibility in compensating for the deficiencies of caciques without such qualities. Hence, individuals who exhibited traits that fulfilled Guaraní concepts of leadership might become charismatic leaders. Another route to power was gaining the missionaries' trust. Cabildo members, overseers, and other leaders could use their relationships with the missionaries to become coercive leaders. While caciques could be charismatic or coercive leaders, the inheritance of this position did not guarantee the exercise of power. A cacique with no other leadership trait than lineage would serve more as a placeholder (an organizational leader for identifying cacicazgo members). As this analysis shows, leadership was not the exclusive domain of caciques or even of the cabildo;

rather, a complex assortment of native leadership positions supported the mission.

CONCLUSION

A mission's governing structure supported hundreds, and more frequently several thousands, of Indians. The Guaraní missions became the most populous of all the missions in colonial Latin America. While the mission population grew over the long run, the Indians suffered from periods of high mortality due to diseases and other hardships. When an epidemic struck, the mission population would decline for several years and then begin to grow again. Population growth in the eighteenth century resulted primarily from high birth rates. Few newly converted Indians joined the missions in this period. During this extended period of maturity, the Jesuits and the Guaraní focused on developing the missions. The pueblos became compact, urban towns based on a standardized design.

The large number of Guaraní inhabitants in each mission required a multilevel governing structure. To organize and direct the mission population, the Jesuits instituted a hierarchical governing structure similar to that used for Jesuit colleges. They envisioned the priest and his companion at the top level, followed by several layers of Guaraní leaders, and then the rest of the mission population. While the missionaries tried to be the ultimate decision makers, Guaraní leaders took a proactive role as go-betweens who shaped the missions both with and without the missionaries' consent. Hereditary leaders of native lineages divided the large mission population into more manageable subsets for governance. While some caciques played an active leadership role, the Jesuits' adherence to male primogeniture succession meant that sometimes caciques lacked the charismatic qualities necessary to lead the members of their cacicazgos, and thus they served primarily as figureheads of their respective cacicazgos. A variety of other Guaraní leadership positions supported the missions. While caciques received preference, these positions were open to individuals with coercive powers derived from Jesuit backing and/or charismatic leadership traits valued by the Guaraní. The next chapter looks at the economy that sustained the thousands of mission inhabitants and structured their daily life.

The Mission Economy

> When the Indians of our pueblos have enough to support
> themselves, even if little, the Fathers pay little or no attention to
> temporal matters, as occurs in some pueblos of Mexico and Peru.
> All attention is given to the spiritual. When the [mission] economy
> is something, but not sufficient, [the Jesuits] pay much more
> attention to acts of bodily compassion: caring for their estates,
> communal property, etc., directing them in their business dealings,
> [and] teaching them all [of the duties of] the elected offices. If it is
> not done like this, there will be no attendance at the church and
> to the Christian obligations. They flee to the backcountry, forests,
> and countryside for hunting and wild fruit, and to the livestock
> estancias.
>
> Cardiel, *Declaración de la verdad*

> If they want to make us pay more tribute, we will return to living
> like our grandparents.
>
> Opinion of an elderly Guaraní man,
> as represented by a Jesuit missionary[1]

The Guaraní forced the Jesuits to attend to the mission economy and
the Indians' material condition before trying to effect cultural change.
The above quotations point to the importance of the mission economy.
As José Cardiel, a Jesuit priest who worked in the Guaraní missions for
almost thirty years, explained, the Jesuits could not hope to convince the
Guaraní to change their religious practices or beliefs unless the mission
adequately provisioned the Indians with food and other material goods.
Cardiel also recognized that when the mission economy failed to meet the
Indians' temporal needs, the Guaraní fled.

The Guaraní forced the Jesuits to be cautious about how they procured
the goods for sustaining the missions. The mission economy depended on

Guaraní labor. While the Indians produced the goods that supported the economy, they limited the amount of labor that could be demanded of them. As the elderly Guaraní man above made clear, the Guaraní did not acquiesce to all of the labor demands made of them. If asked to pay more tribute—either by cutting back on consumption or producing more trade goods—he and his fellow Guaraní would likely flee the mission.

This chapter begins with a discussion of how the economy shaped daily life. Jesuit sources describe a strictly regimented work schedule that lasted from morning until late afternoon six days of the week. While much of the mission inhabitants' day revolved around this work schedule, the Guaraní tempered the rigor with evasion. As a result, the missionaries failed to achieve their goal of forming the Guaraní into what they perceived as a diligent and industrious workforce.

What became of the goods produced by or acquired with Guaraní labor? Ostensibly, the Indians were the beneficiaries. The Guaraní collectively owned all mission lands, buildings, and goods. While the Guaraní produced some things for themselves, they relied heavily on distributions from mission supplies.

The mission economy did not function in isolation. The missions could not produce everything that they needed or wanted; they had to obtain some items elsewhere. They also had to pay tribute and other expenses. To generate income, the missions sold goods produced by the Indians. As major landowners with access to a huge labor force, the missions became a regional economic powerhouse. A full understanding of the mission economy remains incomplete without discussing its connections and ties to the regional economy.

DAILY LIFE AND THE ECONOMY

The following description of daily life in the missions is based primarily on the writings of Jesuit missionaries José Cardiel, Juan de Escandón, and Jaime Oliver.[2] It is the missionaries' vision of the workday and workweek, which they succeeded in imposing upon the Guaraní only to a degree. These missionaries wrote their accounts between 1758 and 1779—at a time when the Jesuit order was under severe attack. As described in the following chapter, between 1759 and 1767 the Portuguese, French, and Spanish kings expelled the Jesuits from their respective territories, and in 1773 Pope Clement XIV suppressed the Jesuit order. Cardiel, Escandón, and Oliver lived through these events, which were in part motivated by negative sentiment toward the Guaraní missions.[3] Given the circumstances, these Jesuit authors clearly had an agenda: to defend and lobby in favor of their order and its activities in Paraguay.

In their writings, the missionaries asserted two seemingly opposite points: first, that the Jesuits achieved the Crown's goals for the missions, but second, that the mission enterprise required the continuation of Jesuit management. The missionaries' descriptions of a strictly regimented work schedule suggested that the Guaraní had become a settled, reliable workforce and thus had become civilized under the missionaries' care. But despite this achievement, the Jesuits argued, the Guaraní and the missions needed their continued assistance. Even though the Guaraní body grew and aged, asserted Cardiel, the Guaraní intellect never developed beyond that of a child of eight or nine; therefore the Guaraní needed the Jesuits just as children need parents, and with such guidance and discipline the Guaraní and their missions flourished.[4] Likewise, Escandón claimed, "You can see [the Guaraní] are incapable of governing themselves."[5] By contrasting Guaraní incapacity with the Indians' achievements under Jesuit direction, both authors hoped to show that the missions required Jesuit management. Nevertheless, despite such biases in their descriptions, Jesuit writings should not be completely discounted; they reveal the vision that the missionaries tried to impose in the missions.

The Indians' day began at dawn (between 4:00 a.m. and 5:00 a.m., depending on the season) with the beating of drums in the central plaza and a respected, older Guaraní man crying out in the streets, "Brothers, the day already desires to brighten; may God guard you and help all. Wake your sons and daughters so that they come to pray and praise God, hear the holy mass, and after, go to work. Do not hold back. Do not be lazy. Do not delay. Behold that already [they] are playing the drums . . ."[6] In response, parents sent their adolescent children to the church, where they prayed, recited the catechism, and sang. The entire mission population then joined them to hear mass.

After mass on Mondays through Saturdays, cabildo members met the priest at the door to his rooms. They kissed his hand and he gave them instructions about the tasks that the people should engage in for the day. The adult males received their ration of yerba maté for the morning. At the sound of drums or tambourines, those capable of work gathered. The cabildo members assigned tasks so that each person knew where to work and what to do. The Guaraní workers then left for the fields or workshops in a hierarchical procession behind the image of a saint—generally St. Isidro Labrador, to whom the Indians had a particular devotion—and to the sound of the drums or tambourines. By having them accompanied by music and the image of a saint, the Jesuits wanted these tasks to acquire religious meaning. The image of the saint was placed near the work site, and the Guaraní labored at their assigned tasks through the morning without interruption. They ate lunch midday near the image of the saint and then returned to work.

In the middle of the afternoon, the church bell rang, calling the Guaraní back to the church. The laborers returned from the work site in the same hierarchical procession following the image of the saint. In the church, they prayed, recited the catechism, listened to the priest explain a point of Christian doctrine for a quarter hour, and recited the rosary. After the religious activities concluded, Guaraní leaders informed the priest about the outcome of the day's work, and mission inhabitants received their afternoon yerba maté ration and, when available, a meat ration. The women prepared the dinner meal at home. The husbands ate first, then the women ate what remained. The children frequently did not eat at home, having eaten breakfast, lunch, and dinner together under the Jesuits' supervision.[7]

The Jesuits split the six workdays into four days for *amambaé* (man's possession) and two days for *tupambaé* (God's possession). Tuesday through Friday, the Indians worked on amambaé projects, intended for their family's well-being. In these plots, the Guaraní primarily cultivated the foodstuffs that they had grown before joining the missions—corn, manioc, sweet potato, beans, squash, and peanuts. Some mission Guaraní also planted melons, sugarcane, wheat, barley, and/or cotton for clothing. Outsiders, such as the bishop of Paraguay, Manuel Antonio de la Torre, expressed surprise at the Jesuits' mix of European and American agricultural techniques.[8]

While the Jesuits taught the Guaraní to cultivate barley and wheat—which the missionaries especially prized for bread—they had difficulty in persuading the Guaraní to cultivate and consume such European foodstuffs. Cardiel reported that even though many Guaraní knew how to make bread (since they took turns baking it for the missionaries), none made it for themselves except during the festival of the patron saint.[9] Not only were native crops more palatable to native tastes, they were also better suited than European crops to the missions' semitropical environment.

Manioc—a mainstay of the Guaraní diet—required a minimal amount of labor. Unlike wheat or barley, manioc did not have to be harvested at a specific time, separated from the chaff, and properly stored for protection from spoilage or pests. Six months after planting, the root of the manioc plant matured and then remained in the soil where it had been planted for up to three years. Whenever Indians wanted to eat manioc, they simply dug up the roots and cooked them.[10]

On Mondays and Saturdays, the Guaraní worked on tupambaé projects, intended for the well-being of their community and church.[11] For half of the year—from June to December—most adult males worked on communal agriculture plots for these two days a week. In addition to corn, beans, rice, wheat, other grains, cotton, sugarcane, and tobacco, communal gardens contained cultigens such as melons, watermelons, peaches, and oranges. Unlike individual amambaé plots, however, not all adult males worked on communal agriculture projects. The Jesuits trained a significant number of Guaraní as artisans and tradesmen so that they did not need to hire outsiders for such work. According to the Jesuit Antonio Betschon, there was not a skill or trade that was not practiced in the missions.[12] These individuals were exempt from working in communal agriculture; instead, they worked in the missions' workshops at their particular trade, for example, weaving, blacksmithing, carpentry, metalworking, painting, or carving.

For the remaining six months of the year—December through May—when collective labor was not focused on agriculture, the Guaraní worked in a variety of other communal activities necessary to maintain the mission. These tasks included collecting and processing yerba maté, herding cattle, gathering wood from the forest, transporting trade goods, and repairing and constructing mission buildings and infrastructure.

Guaraní women were not exempt from collective labor; they spun cotton into thread for communal supplies. Twice a week—on Saturdays and Wednesdays—each woman received half a pound of cotton to spin into thread. The women had three workdays to remove the seeds and spin the cotton into thread.[13] On the fourth workday, the women brought the thread in front of the priests' quarters, where Guaraní alcaldes inspected and weighed it, recording their observations for the priest. If the thread was too thick or poorly made, the woman received a penance as punishment. In addition to making thread and performing their domestic duties, Guaraní women also continued to help plant and harvest crops.[14]

A variety of factors interfered with the enforcement of the rigorous labor schedule just described. First, service to the Crown took Guaraní away from the missions and their regular work schedule. Crown officials used Guaraní militias to put down uprisings and defend Spanish territory against the Portuguese, hostile Indians, and others.[15] Royal officials also called on mission Guaraní to work on public works projects.[16] Second, epidemics and illnesses cycled through the missions, removing Indians from the labor force temporarily and sometimes permanently.[17] The sick could not work, and other Indians had to care for them rather than following the schedule described above; others fled the missions out of fear of contagion. Third, the Jesuits' work schedule could be interrupted by weather. Every few years, droughts, floods, locusts, or other pestilences wreaked havoc on a mission's crops.[18] Even during a normal year, inclement weather such as heavy rainstorms likely kept the Guaraní from their fields, just as such weather interferes with present-day farmers' work outdoors. Fourth, a variety of Catholic holidays interrupted the work schedule: the mission's patron saint's day, Christmas, Three Kings, Easter, Corpus Christi, Assumption, Annunciation, and several other saint's days. The missions also celebrated the king's name day and visits by special guests such as the bishop, governor, or other Jesuits. For each holiday, the festivities and their preparation took several days, thus disrupting the work schedule and reducing agricultural yield.[19]

The work schedule was also not as rigorous as the Jesuits intended because the Guaraní resisted the labor demands made of them. They simply refused to exert the effort desired by the missionaries. According to the Jesuit missionary Antonio Sepp, "It is true that no Indian works all day at any chore."[20] Examples of evasion by the Indians abound. Many missionaries asked questions like Juan de Escandón's: "Who would believe the indolence, sluggishness, extreme carelessness, and lack of frugality of the [Guaraní]?"[21] It is likely that the Jesuits made such assertions in part to justify their continued presence in the missions, but despite such ulterior motives, they were not incorrect in their assessment that the Guaraní did not apply themselves wholeheartedly to the daily work schedule.

Many Guaraní did not place the same value on maximizing production or storing food for times of scarcity as the Jesuits did, and thus the Jesuits' rigid work schedule did not make sense to them. Instead, the Guaraní continued to value leisure highly and accepted that there would be periods of plenty followed by periods of scarcity. Barbara Ganson suggests that the Guaraní may also have resisted work in protest of changes in gender roles.[22]

Those Guaraní who adopted European ideas about property accumulation found that they had little to gain by adhering to the Jesuits' work schedule. A mission inhabitant did not benefit from working harder at agricultural tasks and producing more than his or her peers. The Indians did not receive wages; they worked two days a week on communal projects for the benefit of their community and in return received distributions from communal supplies. Cabildo members, certain artisans, and individuals sent on arduous trips might receive additional distributions from communal supplies, but this reflected higher degrees of responsibility and skill and did not affect agricultural laborers.[23] During the four days a week when an Indian worked on his family plot, how hard he worked should in theory have determined his remuneration. In reality, while the Jesuits said that they promoted the concept of private property, a laborer could not do as he pleased with his harvest. The laborer could only keep what he and his family needed for two or three months; everything else was stored in the communal storeroom. The missionary labeled the laborer's harvest and gave him more only when his family had finished their two or three months' supply.[24] Hence, a laborer had little control over his harvest. Cardiel further acknowledged that some priests did not even permit the Guaraní to have family plots; rather, on the days allotted to amambaé labor, these priests had the Indians work together as a cacicazgo or tribe (parcialidad) in a particular field.[25]

A mission inhabitant did not have additional free time after meeting the Jesuits' labor expectations. The Jesuits' goal was not to maximize production but rather to produce enough to sustain the mission enterprise while keeping the Indians occupied with what the missionaries perceived as godly activities.[26] The Jesuits valued a regimented daily schedule filled with work and religious devotion. They did not want the Indians to have much free time lest they engage in non-Catholic behavior. On holidays and Sundays—the Indians' one day free from work—the Jesuits scheduled the Indians' day. Religious obligations filled the mornings and planned diversions overseen by the Jesuits filled the afternoons. During workdays, the priests even occupied the time of children too young to work. Instead of allowing them to play under the care of their parents, the Jesuits forced them to attend religious education in both the morning and afternoon.[27] Given the Jesuits' zealous efforts to schedule almost every hour of the mission inhabitants' day, shirking labor obligations was one of the few ways for Indians to gain some control over their time.

The Jesuits tried with limited success to force compliance by policing and punishing infractions. According to Oliver, "[The Guaraní] are by nature so lazy that they would be without food because of not working. It is necessary that the priest see that in the same [fields] they are flogged for not having planted enough for the year or for not having hoed. And [the priest] must return again and again until they do it."[28] Such efforts to force compliance often failed to accomplish the intended goal. Cardiel observed that "only when the priest is present, [a Guaraní] works diligently; and it is impossible that the priest can always be present."[29] The missionaries could not police all of the Indians all of the time, since they were far outnumbered by the Indians.[30]

The missionaries relied on native elite—cabildo members, caciques, and other Guaraní leaders—as intermediaries, but with mixed results. The native elite's interests and those of the missionaries did not always coincide. The native elite often helped fellow Indians avoid labor demands. In the post-Jesuit era, a Spanish administrator in the missions complained: "[A] large number of people remain idle. At the least, they are more than one-third [of the mission population], if not one-half. Some are employed in things that are not necessary in the colegio, others feign sickness, others are hidden and freed from communal labor by the corregidor and members of the cabildo."[31] Mission Indians found a variety of ways to resist labor demands, and if the demands and punishments became excessive, they could flee the missions relatively easily. For this reason, the Jesuits could not have strictly enforced the stringent labor schedule described above.

Agricultural yields confirm this conclusion. Cardiel reported that while the soil in mission territory was so fertile that four weeks of work would yield enough to last the entire year, Guaraní laziness forced the missions to allot over six times that much to agricultural labor.[32] This casts some doubt on the missionaries' description of the rigid work schedule. Moreover, even four days a week of labor on familial plots over six months did not yield enough to feed the Guaraní and their families. The bishop of Buenos Aires found that the Guaraní produced enough on their familial plots to sustain themselves for only two-thirds of the year.[33] According to another Jesuit: "With total certainty, I can confirm that in none of the missions are there more than twelve families that either gather from their harvest or acquire by their individual industry enough to consume and clothe themselves, but instead their priest helps them with goods belonging to the community."[34] Given such low yields, labor requirements could not have been as onerous as implied by the missionaries' schedule; the Guaraní could not have labored on their familial plots from dawn to late afternoon for four days a week over a six-month period and still not produce enough to feed their families.

MISSION PROPERTY

The Jesuits instituted amambaé in order to encourage the development of individual labor and private property, but the Guaraní did not show an interest in individually accumulating wealth according to European norms. As stated by Jesuit Antonio Betschon, the Guaraní "do not think about wealth, nor do they yearn for it. With only a bridle, spur, or a knife, a man is wealthy, and even this he dispenses with easily."[35] The Jesuits reported that the Guaraní did not make wills because they hardly had any possessions; instead, almost everything belonged to the mission community.[36] Furthermore, they repeatedly complained that the Guaraní squandered anything in their possession—grain, animals, or money. According to Cardiel, the Guaraní consumed grain or livestock without concern for future consumption; if they did not eat an animal immediately, they let it wander off or failed to care for it properly. To further reinforce his point, Cardiel reported that even after living twenty, thirty, or more years among Spaniards, a nonmission Guaraní did not save any of the wages he earned.[37]

In order to better control how the Indians managed their property, the missionaries treated amambaé property in the same way as the rest of mission property. While each family had rights to a plot of land and the fruit of their amambaé labor, an Indian did not have full ownership rights over either of these. Individual Guaraní did not own specific plots of land; the mission, and thus the Indians as a collective body, owned all of the land. Each cacique had an allotment of land that he then divided and distributed among the members of his cacicazgo as he deemed appropriate.[38] The recipient only had usufruct privileges with respect to the land; he could not sell the plot or pass it on to his children.[39]

The recipient had not only the right but an obligation to work the land. As described above, the Jesuits involved themselves in how the Indians worked their amambaé plots and managed their amambaé property. The Jesuit missionary Juan Joseph Rico justified such interference as being like the action taken by a father who makes sure that his son does not squander his possessions.[40]

The Jesuits followed the same principles in managing the mission's communal property—tupambaé. Each mission had a communal herd of oxen, for example, because the Jesuits did not believe the Indians to be capable of maintaining their own animals. When it was time to plow the fields, the Jesuits ordered that six to eight hundred oxen be brought from the estancia to an enclosure next to the pueblo. A Guaraní secretary made note of who borrowed oxen and informed the priest if anyone did not return the animals at the end of the day.[41]

Tupambaé production played a key role in compensating for shortfalls in amambaé production. Tupambaé both served as a safety net and provisioned the general mission population. It sustained the general mission population when families ran out of supplies from their amambaé production and helped mission Guaraní when in need. Tupambaé provided for those who could not produce for themselves (the widows, orphans, sick, and disabled), provisioned Indians traveling outside of the mission or otherwise working on behalf of the communal good, fed outsiders who visited the mission, and provided seed for the following year. The general mission population also relied on regular distributions of a variety of goods from communal supplies.[42]

Although often viewed as models of socialism or communism, the Guaraní missions were not egalitarian.[43] Despite the communal structure of collective labor and shared ownership, social and economic distinctions still existed in the missions. Cardiel openly acknowledged that caciques, cabildo members, musicians, sacristans, overseers, and skilled artisans were esteemed like nobles.[44] As members of the native elite, caciques used the honorific "don," and cabildo members carried symbols pertaining to their office. Cabildo members and military leaders also sat in their own pews at the front of the church, and wore distinctive clothing and played special roles in mission festivities.[45]

Guaraní leaders not only received respect and special privileges reflective of their elite status, they also received larger rations and special items from communal supplies. According to Cardiel, cabildo members and other leaders received double rations of beef, and musicians, sacristans, cabildo members, and caciques received delicate striped cloth for ponchos.[46]

Guaraní leaders were not the only ones to receive special compensation. Both Escandón and Cardiel stated that weavers received a premium for each completed textile. Cardiel added that the mother of a family often gave a weaver a small gift when he wove cotton that her family had produced on their own plot. According to Escandón, only weavers received such a premium, because their work "has the reputation of being the most difficult"; other artisans did not receive such a premium.[47]

While Cardiel repeatedly asserted that mission Guaraní did not work for wages, he acknowledged obliquely that "those who work harder than the rest are remunerated more from communal property."[48] Elsewhere he more clearly explained that missionaries gave gifts when an Indian's work required more labor (such as someone traveling outside of the mission) or when an Indian accomplished an assignment with unusual care or utility. Such gifts included rosaries, glass beads for the Indian or his wife, cloth, knives, spurs, bridles, axes, and wedges.[49]

Of all the items that mission Guaraní received from communal supplies, beef rations were likely the most important. According to Cardiel, "because the expansive countryside that extends from the pueblos to the sea was full of cattle without owners," the Jesuits did not put much effort into the seedbeds until the 1720s.[50] While farming (or pretending to farm) amambaé and tupambaé plots took up much of the Guaraní workday, the harvest accounted for only a portion of the Guaraní diet; beef was also a mainstay of the Guaraní diet. Depending on the size of its herd, each mission distributed meat rations either daily or several times a week.[51]

The Guaraní received their rations after the afternoon rosary—usually about an hour before the sun went down. To oversee the slaughter of cattle and distribution of the meat, the Jesuits named an Indian whom they assessed to be one of the most capable to serve as *zoorerequadra* (someone who cares for the meat). In one of the patios or corrals connected to the Jesuits' quarters, and under Jesuit direction, the zoorerequadra and his assistants killed the animals and cut the meat into pieces. When it was ready for distribution, the sound of a drum called the women. A Guaraní secretary read from a list of all the mission's inhabitants, calling out the name of each family in a cacicazgo before proceeding to the next cacicazgo. When a woman heard her family's name, she collected her ration and then returned to her house to prepare the evening meal.[52]

Mission Guaraní consumed huge quantities of beef. According to Cardiel, each family—about four to five people—received a ration of four pounds.[53] Likely, adults consumed a little more than a pound while children ate less than a pound. Over a year, this quantity ranged between 100 and 365 pounds per person, depending on whether the Indians received rations three times a week or daily. Regardless of frequency, mission Guaraní consumed significantly more than people in the United States consume today; in the 1990s, for example, Americans consumed an average of 67 pounds of beef per year.[54]

Beef consumption rose even higher during times of hardship. From their early years the missions relied on beef rations for sustenance during periods of difficulty. Just over two decades after the founding of the first mission, beef rations helped Missions Loreto and San Ignacio Guazú recover from one of the most challenging events faced by the missions— the relocation of an estimated twelve thousand Guaraní in response to Paulista slave raids.[55] The trip down the Paraná River and deeper into Spanish territory subjected the Indians to extreme hardship, and many died or fled. The missions continued to face difficulties during their recovery, including an extreme shortage of food. Ruiz de Montoya explained that beef rations helped mission inhabitants survive: "Initially, twelve to fourteen cows [cattle] were slaughtered daily in each of the two missions, Loreto and San Ignacio [Guazú]. This provided each person with a portion so small that it just sufficed to keep life going and postpone death."[56] According to Ruiz de Montoya's estimate, the missions consumed about 13,000 head of cattle in the course of their recovery.[57]

Throughout their lifespan, the missions continued to depend upon beef rations for succor. Every few years, droughts, floods, locusts, or other pestilences destroyed a mission's crops; as agricultural output fell, the mission would turn to beef rations to feed the population. At other times, epidemics, military service, or other work for the Spanish Crown took Guaraní away from work in the fields, causing agricultural output to fall and the mission again to turn to beef rations to make up the difference. The Jesuits recognized the importance of beef rations during such crises: according to Cardiel, "When it does not rain—something that can happen for three or four years in a row—it is vital that beef make up for the lack of food."[58]

The missions slaughtered large numbers of cattle to feed the Guaraní. On the low end, Cardiel estimated that a mission of one thousand families killed ten head of cattle three times a week for beef rations. Based on Cardiel's estimate and the population of the thirty missions at the time of the Jesuit expulsion, three distributions of beef per week would have resulted in the slaughter of almost 31,000 cattle per year.[59] On the high end, Jesuit missionary Martin Dobrizhoffer estimated that a mission with seven thousand Indians killed at least forty cattle for one day's rations. Based on Dobrizhoffer's estimate and the 1767 population, the thirty missions would have killed over 79,000 cattle to distribute beef rations three times a week.[60] The number of cattle killed by the missions overall fell somewhere within this range, depending on the level of succor needed and the amount of cattle in mission estancias.[61]

Beef rations were also important simply because the Guaraní liked meat. Although cattle were not native to South America, the Guaraní acquired a taste for beef. In his description of early Guaraní encounters with beef, Provincial of Paraguay Francisco Vázquez Trujillo stated that the Indians prized the meat exceedingly.[62] Years later Cardiel asserted, "Even during the bad times when the harvest is lost, here is refuge for all: the Indian is very fond of meat, especially beef, and having this, he has everything."[63] This was true throughout the region, as observed by Martin Dobrizhoffer:

Beef is the principal, daily, and almost only food of the lower orders in Paraguay. Moreover that quantity of meat which would overload the stomach of a European is scarce sufficient to satisfy the appetite of an American. A Guarany, after fasting but a very few hours, will devour a young calf. An Indian, before he lies down to sleep, places a piece of meat to roast at the fire, that he may eat immediately when he wakes. Place food before him, and the rising and setting sun will behold him with his jaws at work and his mouth full, but with an appetite still unsatisfied.[64]

The Guaraní often consumed their beef nearly raw, which led to health problems such as parasites.[65]

The Jesuits recognized the value of providing the Guaraní with an ample supply of beef: "From the beginning, the missionaries knew that people of such little economy could not be maintained without cattle."[66] Cardiel also stated that Guaraní who did not receive beef rations on a daily basis had a greater tendency to run away to the back country to hunt and gather wild fruit than Guaraní who received daily beef rations.[67] Cardiel took a strong stand on the importance of cattle: "The good or bad of the mission in temporal and spiritual [matters] depends on the good state of these [livestock] ranches."[68] In 1740, after instability in Asunción, epidemics, and drought devastated the missions, the provincial of Paraguay found Cardiel's views to be accurate. Antonio Machoni claimed the lofty goal of the "restoration of the missions, and for the good of the Indians" when introducing his instructions for rebuilding the missions' cattle herds.[69]

Almost a century earlier, the Jesuit provincial recognized the importance of regular access to cattle and ordered each mission to establish its own estancia. Three decades later, each mission had at least one estancia.[70] These estancias were located at a distance from the mission pueblo, sometimes as far as a hundred miles (see Map 4).[71] They served not only as reserves for cattle but also as places to domesticate and raise a variety of livestock.[72] In addition to beef rations, cattle provided the oxen needed as work animals and the dairy cows needed for milk.[73] The estancias also contained other livestock, including sheep, horses, burros, mules, and donkeys. An estancia generally had several *puestos* (areas enclosed by natural barricades such as rivers and streams), each of which specialized in a distinct type of livestock.

To operate these estancias, the Jesuits selected some Guaraní whom they deemed most capable. These individuals resided on the estancia and worked as cowboys and peons. Sometimes the Jesuits entrusted day-to-day management of an estancia to Indians and only inspected the estancia themselves twice a year, but they also hired Spaniards as managers.[74] Most estancias had chapels to encourage Catholic practices.[75]

Although the estancias contained huge numbers of cattle, the missions also relied heavily on hunting. Cattle introduced by Spaniards in the sixteenth century proliferated in the region. Whenever an estancia needed to replenish its cattle supplies, between fifty and sixty Indians with five horses each and a small herd of tame cows went on a hunting expedition (*vaquería*).[76] Once the Indians encountered wild cattle, they positioned their small herd of cows on a hill where they could be seen. Thirty to forty Indians on horseback encircled the herd at a convenient distance. Also on horseback, the remaining Indians went after the wild cattle that approached the tame herd. The Indians carefully maintained their encirclement of the cattle because the animals would scatter if hemmed in too tightly. At night, the Indians made bonfires on all sides to keep the cattle from fleeing. Within two to three months, they would gather and transport five to six thousand cattle one hundred leagues (323 miles) to their mission's estancia.[77]

Beginning in the 1670s, the missions regularly hunted wild cattle (*cimarron*) outside of mission territory in southeastern Uruguay. The Jesuits

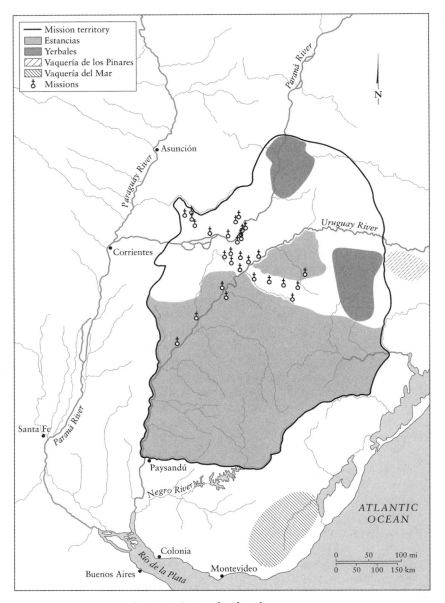

Map 4. Mission land and resources

SOURCE: Adapted from Maeder and Gutiérrez, *Atlas histórico del nordeste argentino*, 65 and 67.

called this location the Vaquería del Mar (see Map 4) and asserted that the vast wild herds descended from cattle abandoned by the missions in the 1630s.[78] Cardiel estimated that this territory supported millions of cattle and that the thirty missions gathered several hundred thousand cattle per year from it without depleting the herd.[79] Such quantities of wild cattle attracted the attention of other inhabitants of the Río de la Plata region, and by the early 1700s, the missions faced increasing competition over the herds of the Vaquería del Mar.

Driven by the growing demand for cattle and cattle products, inhabitants of Santa Fe and Buenos Aires legally contested the missions' rights to the Vaquería del Mar. To resolve the dispute, a series of accords in the 1720s permitted the missions, on one hand, to continue taking only as many cattle as were needed to sustain the Indians and the inhabitants of Santa Fe and Buenos Aires, on the other hand, to take no more than fifty thousand cattle to their respective cities and countryside.

In 1719, Betschon expressed concern about the effects of such competition. He speculated that the missions' policy of hunting large droves of wild cattle to replenish their herds "will with time lead to shortages because not only the Indians and the Brazilians, but also even the Spanish, Portuguese, Dutchmen, Englishmen, and maybe even the French kill an immense quantity of cattle."[80]

The Jesuits blamed the growing export market in cattle hides (*cueros*) for depleting the region's wild herds. Looking back on the situation, the representative of the Jesuits in Spain wrote that in the Río de la Plata region,

the almost innumerable multitude of [cattle] that were admired in this fertile countryside during the last century are now almost completely consumed. Those that come from there are witnesses of this. The cause is some years of continual drought, but even more influential is the Spaniards' greed. Without more to gain than lard for personal use and the hides to sell and supply to all of Europe, they have extinguished even the hope of rebuilding in many years this abundance.[81]

Concerned about the continued viability of the Vaquería del Mar, the Jesuits established an alternate cattle reserve for the missions—the Vaquería de los Pinares—in what is now the northern part of the Brazilian state Rio Grande do Sul (see Map 4).[82] In establishing this reserve, the Jesuits looked for an unowned expanse of at least sixty leagues (about 200 miles) that was about eighty leagues (250 miles) from the missions. Following Jesuit instructions, in 1701 the Guaraní started rounding up some eighty thousand cattle to stock Vaquería de los Pinares. They left the cattle to multiply, protected by the mountains and thick forests surrounding it. The Jesuits mistakenly believed that this location could be successfully defended against invasions by the Portuguese and hostile Indians: the Vaquería de los Pinares lasted less than three decades. In the late 1720s, Portuguese Americans and hostile Indians hunted these cattle in earnest.[83]

Recognizing the threats to cattle outside of mission territory, the Jesuits sought to gain greater control over wild herds by relocating them inside mission territory. In the 1730s, the Jesuits created two large cattle reserves for the thirty missions within the extensive estancias of Missions Yapeyú and San Miguel. Not only were Yapeyú's and Miguel's estancias huge—measuring fifty by thirty leagues and forty by twenty leagues (over 15,600 and 8,300 square miles), respectively, according to Cardiel—they were better suited for livestock than the other missions' estancias.[84] After much discussion, in 1737 the Jesuit provincial in charge of the Jesuit province of Paraguay, Jaime Aguilar, established guidelines for these two communal reserves. He ordered the selection of ample land suitable for forty thousand cattle, with good pasture, watering holes, and natural enclosure. He also ordered cattle to be gathered from Yapeyú's and San Miguel's estancias for these reserves.[85]

While Aguilar emphasized the importance of leaving these animals to procreate, the strong wording of his mandate suggests that he thought it likely to be violated: "For the first two years after the cattle arrive in the designated pasture, do not remove for anybody, or for any reason, any cow." Aguilar instructed that, after these two years, the Jesuit superior of the missions could authorize the removal of offspring of the original herd, depending on the needs of the thirty missions.[86]

In response to growing competition over wild herds, the Jesuits also intensified their efforts to domesticate cattle.[87] In his instructions, Aguilar specified that the cattle in the two reserves be *de rodeo* (trained to be rounded up) rather than cimarron.[88] Aguilar gave specific instructions for taming the cattle: the animals should by divided into groups of five to six thousand and separated in areas enclosed on all sides by streams, swamps, or ditches. Every morning, the cattle should be brought into a large corral made of sticks in order to be trained not to wander away. After several weeks, when the cattle became more docile, they would only have to be gathered twice a week.

The missions never fully transitioned to domesticated livestock.[89] Instructions issued by Aguilar's successor as Jesuit provincial, Antonio Machoni, reveal that the missions did not have the time necessary to complete the desired reforms. Five years after Aguilar issued his instructions, Machoni investigated compliance. He found that Yapeyú had brought forty thousand cattle into its reserve but that San Miguel had failed to do so. Even more disturbing, Machoni found the Yapeyú and San Miguel estancias in an alarming state. The excessive number of cattle—up to forty thousand cattle each year—sent to sustain other missions threatened to deplete these reserves within a few years. Thus, in 1742 Machoni extended for another eight to ten years the prohibition on removing cattle from the communal reserves without the express orders of the father superior in charge of the missions. In addition to redoubling efforts for the communal reserve, Machoni ordered that the missions "create with great care, large seedbeds so that the Indians become accustomed to maintaining themselves for most of the year with their harvests, ceasing little by little to give them meat."[90]

In the 1750s, geopolitical events further hindered the Jesuits' efforts to domesticate cattle and develop mission estancias. Under the Treaty of Madrid (1750), the missions temporarily lost valuable cattle territory—seven missions, including San Miguel, and four other missions' estancias—to the Portuguese. Nusdorffer estimated that this territory contained more than one million cattle before the treaty; most of these cattle were lost by the missions. The governor of Buenos Aires only allowed the Guaraní to drive into Spanish territory the number of cattle that they needed to survive. Spanish and Portuguese troops charged with implementing the treaty confiscated and consumed much of the remaining cattle. Missions not directly affected by the treaty also lost cattle. The Jesuits estimated that Yapeyú lost 24,000 cattle to these troops and that much of Yapeyú's tamed cattle dispersed and became *alzado* (undomesticated).[91] In 1761, a new Spanish king—Charles III—annulled the Treaty of Madrid, but neither the missions nor their cattle herds completely recovered.

When describing the missions' cattle management practices, Cardiel asserted that the Treaty of Madrid "ended everything."[92] As the result of this upheaval, according to his account, only three missions (Santa Rosa, San Ignacio, and Yapeyú) were self-sufficient in cattle as of 1752,[93] and furthermore, only six or eight missions could distribute beef rations daily—generally a necessity during the six months after a drought—without diminishing their herds.[94] While events prevented the missions from developing a reliable supply of domesticated cattle, other factors were at work as well.

The transition to domesticated cattle also failed because the Guaraní did not value the domestication of livestock as the Jesuits did. The Guaraní preferred hunting, which required less work than animal husbandry and much less work than cultivated agriculture. Cultural factors also played at least as big a role. The Guaraní did not think of hunting merely as an activity for procuring beef; they enjoyed it and valued it as a pleasurable activity.[95] Hunting also fit better with Guaraní ideas about gendered tasks and prestige. Before European contact, Guaraní men cultivated prestige by showing valor during a hunt; they did no agricultural labor other than clearing the fields for planting. Mission Guaraní found that hunting cattle fit better with these gender roles than either domesticating cattle or farming.

The Jesuits repeatedly wrote about how the Indians refused to properly care for cattle and other livestock. According to Cardiel, "When we give them a pair of cows with offspring so that they can have milk, [the cattle] roam in their agricultural fields. Out of pure laziness they do not milk them and sometimes with voracity they eat the calf. The same happens with oxen that we give to them for plowing. Either [the Indians] lose them or they kill and eat them."[96] Betschon described a similar occurrence:

When night comes, and with the idea that now they do not need the ox, many [Guaraní] after having worked all day are capable of killing it. If they lack firewood they use the plow to make a fire and with it roast the victim and devour it in only one gluttonous feast. Their night feasts frequently last all night, during which they cut one piece of meat after another and after passing it several times over the fire, bloody and still semiraw, they scarf it down. For better digestion, they fling themselves in a circle around the fire and with its heat build an appetite. If they sleep, the stomach has some respite, but quickly they wake up and begin to roast and eat until they have finished off the animal. In this manner a few Indians completely devour an ox in a very short time, passing the night in eating and sleeping.[97]

According to the modern scholar Maxime Haubert, the most capable Guaraní confessed that even though they were judicious in other things, they could not be so with cattle.[98]

What the Jesuits saw as irrational behavior seemed rational to the Indians. Owing to the plentiful existence of wild cattle, the Guaraní most likely never saw value in domesticating and caring for large livestock. The work required in raising cattle would have seemed unnecessary when animals could easily be hunted or obtained from communal supplies. With mission herds numbering up to one million head or more, supply likely seemed endless.[99] In contrast, the Jesuits predicted that the Indians' practice of hunting cattle was not sustainable.[100] Despite this foresight, the perception of a need for the missions to transition to domesticated livestock was premature.[101] Competition for wild cattle had not yet grown acute; wild cattle continued to roam until the last years of the eighteenth century. With so many wild cattle readily available, shifting to a model of cattle management based on domestication did not make sense.

Yerba maté—likewise distributed to mission Guaraní from communal supplies—also played an important part in mission life. Every day the Guaraní received yerba maté rations, and twice a day they brewed a handful of the leaves and drank it communally, as described in Chapter 1. Such regular consumption meant that the Guaraní drank great quantities of yerba maté and valued it highly. The drink had both addictive properties and strong cultural meaning. The Guaraní told early missionaries that yerba maté lightened their workload, sustained them when without food, purged their stomachs of phlegm, awakened their senses, and dispelled drowsiness.[102] According to Cardiel, yerba maté consumption was such an important part of Guaraní daily life that it was like bread and wine in Spain or tea in China.[103] Another missionary underscored that a Guaraní always needed to have yerba maté among his provisions.[104]

The missions produced two types of yerba maté—*caaminí* and *de palos*. Caaminí was finer and of higher quality than de palos and producing it required more time and labor.[105] Caaminí included only the yerba maté leaves; in producing caaminí, the Indians sifted the yerba maté and removed all of the small stems, as well as the dirt and sticks from the canoe or pit where they ground the yerba maté. In contrast, the Indians did not sift the yerba maté when producing de palos; they removed the large branches but left the smaller stems. According to Cardiel's description, they also did not clean the place where they ground the yerba maté, and so dirt mixed with the yerba maté.[106] While the missions were most famous for caaminí, they also produced de palos.

Initially, the Guaraní harvested yerba maté found in yerbales silvestres distant from the missions. The Indians of the seven missions bordering the right bank of the Uruguay River traveled to yerbales silvestres by land with wagons and provisions of live cattle. The remaining twenty-three missions faced intervening mountain ranges that hindered travel by land. Instead, these Guaraní traveled along the Uruguay and Paraná Rivers in rafts made of canoes. Since yerba maté trees were located inland, the Indians transported the yerba maté on their shoulders back to the raft. After harvesting, toasting, and grinding the yerba maté, each Indian made two trips carrying six or more *arrobas* (150 pounds) of yerba maté in bags made of cow hide along a very bad pathway for six or more leagues (nineteen miles).[107]

The Jesuits did not like that this enterprise took the Guaraní away from the missions for several months at a time. During the two to three months that the Indians worked in the yerbales silvestres, the Jesuits did not have direct oversight over them and could not push their religious agenda. In order to end such prolonged absences "without spiritual succor, and so much work for the poor Indians," the Jesuits applied themselves to establishing yerba maté plantations in the missions.[108] After much experimentation, the missionaries figured out how to cultivate yerba maté trees.[109]

In 1701, Jesuit missionary José Arce recommended that the missions plant their own yerba maté trees.[110] As of 1704, the Jesuits had taken steps—with varying levels of success—for each mission to establish its own *yerbal*. Cardiel likely overstated the missions' reliance on domesticated yerba maté when he claimed that the Jesuits "have made yerbales so large in all of the missions that it is not necessary for the poor Indians to go with such toil to the forests."[111] In contrast, according to Escandón: "All of the seven pueblos east of the Uruguay River have (or had) those plantings, or communal yerbales, and they worked on them and treated them like olive trees. The other twenty-three pueblos have tried to make similar plantings, but since the tree does not grow in all types of land, very few [missions] have achieved [plantings], neither in the Uruguay nor in the Paraná. For this reason, they need to go to look for the said yerba maté in the backcountry."[112] Mission inventories done at the time of the Jesuit expulsion listed each mission with its own yerbal(es), but not all of the yerbales contained domesticated yerba maté trees or were close to their respective pueblos.[113]

Another stimulant—tobacco—played a less important role in mission life. After mass on Sundays, the Guaraní received weekly rations of tobacco. The Indians chewed their tobacco; they said it gave them strength to work, especially during cold weather. A few Indians planted their own tobacco plants, but most of the tobacco consumed in the missions came from plants grown in communal fields.[114]

If a mission had enough salt, the Guaraní also received salt rations. The Jesuits recognized that the Guaraní liked salt, but they did not give them salt all of the time because the missions could not produce it themselves. As Escandón explained: "Since [salt] is expensive, and [the Guaraní] are many, it is not possible to give it to everyone every day, and barely on all of the festival days. For this reason, they ordinarily eat without salt."[115]

The Indians also got most of the cloth for clothing from distributions of communal supplies. Their regular attire included a cotton shirt either white or dyed another color, long trousers, underwear, a cotton or wool poncho depending on the season, a hat, and sandals for work or celebrations.[116] To make these clothes, the Indians received cotton cloth twice a year from the mission's communal supplies—twice a year for children and once a year for adults. On the specified day, each boy received fifteen feet or more of cotton cloth based on his size. On separate days, girls, men, and women received their pieces of cotton cloth. Each man received a piece of cloth measuring twenty-four feet or more and each woman received a piece of the same size or larger.[117] A family generally produced thirty feet of their own cloth—less than a third of the total they consumed in a year.[118]

At the beginning of winter and sometimes again later in the year, each Indian received a piece of wool cloth (*bechara*). A prosperous mission gave each Indian a piece of wool cloth measuring fifteen feet; more often, the Indians received about five feet of wool cloth.[119] Even though Cardiel felt that winters in the mission region did not get very cold—there was frost only a couple of times in the three months of winter—he believed that the Indians needed wool. According to his account, the Indians were very sensitive to the cold and became unable to work; as a result, "there is not a thing that [the Guaraní] esteem as much as a little bit of wool cloth to keep warm."[120] The Indians received coarse wool cloth, like a horse's blanket, differentiated only by the colored striped cloth that the musicians, sacristans, cabildo members, and caciques received for ponchos.[121]

The missions obtained wool from sheep in their estancias, and much of the cotton came from communal plantings. Guaraní women grew a small amount of cotton but not enough to meet all of their family's needs. Cardiel complained that, initially, much of the cotton grown by individual production was lost. Cotton matured over a period of three months and needed to be harvested every day, but instead of gathering all of the cotton as it matured, a Guaraní woman only gathered the cotton that she needed for the day, or sometimes a little more for later. She never harvested all that she needed for the entire year. According to Cardiel, she left the rest to go to waste in the field. Some of the Jesuits responded by incorporating these cotton plants into communal property.[122]

The missions not only distributed communal property to the Indians, they also sent mission goods to Buenos Aires, Santa Fe, and other cities for trade. Through such exchanges, a mission obtained access to goods that the missionaries or Indians either needed or wanted. In addition, proceeds from these sales generated the revenues needed to fund mission operations and pay tribute.

MISSION TRADE

A mission did not operate in isolation. Missions worked together extensively and with the larger Jesuit network to advance their interests. Just as mission Guaraní relied on communal supplies to supplement and diversify their individual production and for succor during emergencies, each mission relied on the larger mission network.

The missions needed to generate revenues to cover their expenses. One such expense was the *sínodo* (stipend) that the Jesuits received for feeding and clothing themselves. The stipend amounted to 466 pesos 5 reales per mission, regardless of its size. In total, the Jesuits received 13,999 pesos for all thirty missions. The order received no other financial support from the Crown for additional missionaries, their companions, upper management, artisans, tradesmen, or other Jesuit officials.[123]

Unlike other missions, the Guaraní missions generated the funds to pay these stipends by means of the taxes they paid to the Crown.[124] With few exceptions, the missions paid tribute of 1 peso per adult Guaraní male to the Crown; the Crown then deducted money from these tribute payments to cover the missionaries' stipends. The yearly tribute of 1 peso per male between the ages of eighteen and fifty (caciques, their first-born sons, twelve Indians who worked for the priests, the chronically infirm, and long-term fugitives were exempted) amounted to 19,116 pesos for the thirty missions at the time of the Jesuit expulsion. In addition, the missions had to pay 100 pesos per mission in *diezmos* (tithes). In 1768 the missions' yearly taxes totaled 22,116 pesos;[125] of this amount, 13,999 pesos went to pay the Jesuits' stipend.

The missions also purchased tools and luxury goods for the Indians using revenues generated from trade. At least once a year, every Guaraní man received a multipurpose knife and an ax for such tasks as cutting firewood. The Guaraní also received large and small needles, and if available an assortment of other items, including medallions, locks, scissors, and strings of glass beads. The Jesuits claimed that Guaraní women valued these beads like pearls and diamonds. In addition to goods distributed directly to the Indians for their personal use, the proceeds from trade also purchased firearms for Guaraní militias, raw materials and tools for Guaraní tradesmen, adornments and implements for the mission church, and ornate clothing for religious festivals. As Cardiel explained, the missions purchased "thousands of other things that were needed at any given time and place."[126]

A mission not only looked externally for trade but also sought assistance from the outside during periods of hardship or need. In such cases, a mission might receive assistance from other missions, nonmission Jesuit entities, or non-Jesuit individuals. This network provided a mission with stability and succor. If a mission had a shortfall for some reason or lacked something it needed, the missionaries turned to one of the other twenty-nine missions or the larger Jesuit network for help in the form of trade or a loan. The mission *oficios* (trade centers) in Buenos Aires and Santa Fe served as one of the most important structures for facilitating both mutual assistance and connections with non-Jesuit institutions and individuals.[127]

The two oficios officially managed the missions' economic affairs, and the missions conducted trade primarily through these entities. At least once a year on average, each mission sent trade goods with as many as two dozen Guaraní boatmen to one or the other oficio. The boatmen took the goods down the Paraná and Uruguay Rivers on rafts made of two dugout tree trunks lashed together, with a floor of bamboo. The rafts ranged from forty-eight to eighty feet in length and six to eight feet in width and had a straw cabin lined with cowhide that accommodated up to four people.[128] The boatmen transported hundreds, even thousands, of kilos of merchandise between their mission and the oficio. While they generally traveled unaccompanied by a Jesuit, the missionaries remained in charge of the transported goods even at a distance. Not trusting the Guaraní, the Jesuits made sure to include two separate lists—one in Guaraní and one in Spanish (written by the priest)—of the goods sent from the mission and the goods requested by the mission. The boatmen were held accountable for the items on the list and so could not dispose of any of the trade goods themselves. On the return trip, silks, knives, bells, and other small items were sent in locked chests with the keys inside the letter sent to the mission priest. According to Cardiel, the missionaries did this because "the Indians are very inclined to steal these things. They do not know how this [trade] occurs, nor are they capable of it."[129] Thus, even though the missionaries did not transport or trade the goods themselves, they tried to maintain firm control over all transactions.

The missions benefited from better terms of trade by selling and buying goods through the Buenos Aires and Santa Fe oficios. Mission products—such as yerba maté and textiles—sold at a higher price and imported goods sold at a lower price in these cities than in Asunción. Cardiel stated that merchants in Asunción charged four times more for European goods than in Buenos Aires. Transportation-related expenses account for only a portion of such a higher price. The oficios covered transportation expenses by charging the missions 25 percent more than the Buenos Aires price.[130]

The only years for which there are consistent sales data for both oficios—1731 to 1745—cover a tumultuous period for the missions. During this time, the total mission population reached both its eighteenth-century apex and nadir under the Jesuits—141,182 and 73,910, respectively—as the missions faced war, epidemics, and drought. These hardships affected mission production, but given that the period also included the largest population numbers and trade goods were produced prior to the sales date, the sales figures are within reason and should not be discounted.

Account records for the Buenos Aires and Santa Fe oficios reveal that the thirty missions sold on average about 12,000 arrobas (309,000 pounds) of yerba maté, 24,000 varas (71,000 feet) of cloth, and 700 arrobas (19,000 pounds) of tobacco per year between 1731 and 1745 (see Table 2). Trading on such a scale made the missions a major actor

TABLE 2. *Average yearly mission sales quantities and gross revenue, 1731–1745*

Item	Measurement	1731–1735	1736–1737	1738–1739	1740–1742	1743–1744	1745	Average
Yerba	Revenue	44,924	42,340	68,110	49,693	44,461	46,397	49,321
	Quantity (lb)	259,150	214,169	381,406	331,835	317,973	352,157	309,448[a]
Textiles	Revenue	14,054	14,055	16,860	15,870	10,077	8,116	13,172
	Quantity (ft)	73,099	48,907	80,653	122,325	55,673	45,038	70,949
Tobacco	Revenue	3,921	6,772	2,155	3,034	4,531	2,976	3,898
	Quantity (lb)	26,178	22,257	7,690	19,106	26,374	9,949	18,592
Thread	Revenue	1,348	1,432	2,889	1,375	585	349	1,330
	Quantity (lb)	2,476	2,530	4,538	2,486	1,097	644	2,295
Sugar	Revenue	605	1,526	1,157	585	1,532	—	901
	Quantity (lb)	3,309	4,833	6,460	3,284	7,698	—	4,264
Furniture	Revenue	449	37	59	44	34	—	104
	Quantity (unit)	3	2	2	1	1	—	1
Livestock	Revenue	211	—	31	9	—	—	42
	Quantity (unit)	552	—	3	9	—	—	94
Cotton	Revenue	—	252	192	—	—	—	74
	Quantity (lb)	—	3,149	2,402	—	—	—	925
Wood	Revenue	3	102	85	4	106	—	50
Honey	Revenue	31	149	38	7	—	—	37
Cattle Hides	Revenue	—	20	—	—	—	—	3
	Quantity (unit)	—	7	—	—	—	—	1
Miscellaneous	Revenue	158	74	36	88	26	233	103
Yearly Revenue		65,704	66,759	91,613	70,709	61,351	58,072	69,035

SOURCE: "Oficio de Santa Fe, 1730–1745, Misiones cuentas con los pueblos, colegios y oficios . . . ," AGN, XIII 47-3-5; "Oficio de Buenos Aires, Libro de las visitas que hacen los padres provinciales . . . ," 1731–1767, AGN, XIII 47-3-7.

NOTE: Time periods are based on the periods listed in the oficio accounting books. The time period 1745 includes the second half of 1744 and the first half of 1745.

[a]The missions could legally sell 12,000 arrobas (300,000 pounds) per year. The Jesuit accounting periods are not divided into 12-month periods. The average over the entire period is within 3 percent of 300,000 pounds.

in the regional economy. Based on the quantities that the missions sent to the Buenos Aires and Santa Fe oficios in 1731–1745 and 1751–1756, Juan Carlos Garavaglia has estimated that mission sales accounted for 15–25 percent of all the yerba maté, 60–70 percent of all the cotton textiles, 15–30 percent of all the tobacco, and 30–60 percent of all the sugar sold in Santa Fe and Buenos Aires.[131]

Such quantities generated huge amounts of revenue for the missions. Total mission sales in a single year averaged 69,035 pesos in revenue between 1730 and 1745: an impressive figure considering that between 1728 and 1744 in all of the Río de la Plata region—including modern-day Argentina, Uruguay, and Paraguay—the royal treasury collected an average of 405,527 pesos per year.[132] In relation to the size of the mission population, however, the amount of total revenue is not as impressive: revenue per mission inhabitant was generally less than 1 peso.

Yerba maté was the principal trade item, but the missions also sold significant quantities of textiles and tobacco. The revenues that the missions received from yerba maté—an average of 49,321 pesos per year between 1731 and 1745—far surpassed the revenues from any other good. Yerba maté sales accounted for over 70 percent of total revenue for the thirty missions. Textiles generated less than a third of that amount, and tobacco generated far less. Jesuit records show the sale of an assortment of other goods including cotton, honey/sugar, furniture, and thread; a mission sold any tradable item that it had in excess of its own needs.

The first records of yerba maté sales by the missions date from the 1620s. Yerba maté reached Potosí (in present-day Bolivia)—the center of silver mining in the Andes—in the 1630s. By the 1660s yerba maté was the principal Paraguayan good traded in this regional market. Spanish Paraguayans complained about competition from the Guaraní missions; as a compromise, in 1664 authorities in Buenos Aires limited the missions' yerba maté sales to twelve thousand arrobas (300,000 pounds) per year.[133] Despite the ceiling on mission sales, increases in overall yerba maté sales from all sources put downward pressure on yerba maté prices throughout most of the first half of the eighteenth century.[134] But the ceiling on mission yerba maté sales prevented the missions from selling more yerba maté as prices fell.

The missions probably sold mostly caaminí yerba maté as a way to compensate for the price ceiling. The higher-quality caaminí required significantly more labor, but the Andean market preferred it and was willing to pay double the price of the lower-quality de palos.[135] From 1730 to 1745, between 63 and 89 percent of the yerba maté sold by the missions was caaminí.[136] In contrast, Spanish Paraguayans produced and sold the lower-grade, and lower-priced, de palos.

In the mid-eighteenth century, Yapeyú—a mission rich in cattle—expanded into a new market. Capitalizing on the growing trade in cattle hides, in 1745 Yapeyú began selling significant quantities of cattle hides. In 1745–1746, Yapeyú sold 4,344 hides through the Buenos Aires oficio; thereafter, Yapeyú sold almost nothing but hides at the Buenos Aires oficio.[137] Jesuit writings paid scant attention to hide sales despite their growing importance to Yapeyú. One of Cardiel's treatises asserted there were no hide sales by the missions, with only some minor exceptions: "There is neither trade nor sale of hides, rather of yerba maté, textiles, and cotton, as I already explained. Maybe occasionally the mission of Yapeyú has made a contract of bull hides with those of Buenos Aires, sending for this [purpose] the stubborn and stray livestock to the estancia for the killing of bulls that cause more damage than benefit to the estancia: and that [happens] maybe one time in many years."[138]

Instead of selling hides, Cardiel argued, the missions used all of the hundreds of thousands of hides that they produced. They made leather rope and string for the Indians' daily use and for borders for seedbeds; they shaped cattle hides into bags for storing corn, beans, and yerba maté; they produced boxes and chests to transport goods; and they adorned their floors with hide rugs. Considering all of these various uses, Cardiel concluded that a mission with one thousand families could easily consume fifteen hundred hides in a year—the hides of all of the cattle slaughtered for beef rations in the same year.[139] Clearly, the Jesuits had not yet shifted the focus of mission trade to hides.

After receiving a mission's trade goods in the Buenos Aires or Santa Fe oficio, the Jesuit procurador (agent) most often either sold the goods to merchants or sent them to other Jesuit oficios in places such as Potosí or Santiago, Chile. By tapping into the larger Jesuit network, procuradors captured better prices for mission goods. For example, the missions sold their yerba maté at an average of four pesos per arroba, while the going rate in Asunción was generally half that amount—two pesos per arroba.[140] Likewise, the missions paid significantly less for the goods that they purchased through mission oficios than the going rate in Asunción.[141]

The strength of the Jesuit network was especially evident during difficult periods such as the 1730s. As of January 1, 1737, the Buenos Aires oficio was extremely short of funds (see Table 3). Its liabilities totaled 261,710 pesos, while its assets totaled only 97,491 pesos—a shortfall of 164,219 pesos. All of the 261,710 pesos in liabilities were monies owed by the oficio, and since the oficio operated on behalf of the thirty missions, the missions were liable for this money. Notably, only a small amount—24,870 pesos—was loaned within the Jesuit order; the oficio owed the remaining 236,840 pesos to non-Jesuit parties. The missions

TABLE 3. *Financial status of the Buenos Aires oficio, January 1, 1737*

Net Assets	Pesos
Monies owed by the thirty Guaraní missions	5,654
Monies owed by the Jesuit colleges	4,327
Inventory at the oficio	84,890
Monies owed by non-Jesuits	2,618
Total Net Assets	97,491
Net Liabilities	
Monies owed within the Jesuit order	24,870
Monies owed to non-Jesuits with interest	66,991
Monies owed to non-Jesuits without interest	101,872
Other monies owed to non-Jesuits	67,977
Total Net Liabilities	261,710
Assets less Liabilities	(164,219)

SOURCE: "Resumen general y liquidación de cuentas de Este Oficio de Misiones de Buenos Aires . . . ," Jan. 1, 1737, AGN, IX 6-9-7.

incurred these huge debts to rebuild infrastructure and restock supplies after the difficulties of the early 1730s. In 1738, the oficio assessed each of the thirty missions 5,474 pesos, totaling 164,220 pesos (the amount of the 1737 shortfall), "for the expenses of the building/repair of the *rancherías* (small hamlets), store-rooms, and arrears that the oficio is in."[142] In effect, the oficio transferred its debt to the thirty missions, and they gradually repaid it through the sale of trade goods. The large quantity owed to non-Jesuit parties demonstrates that the missions were very active in the regional economy, and this extended network provided invaluable assistance that allowed the missions to withstand periods of extreme hardship.

CONCLUSION

By the early eighteenth century, the missions were well prepared to face various hardships that arose. Despite outbreaks of epidemics every generation or so, the mission population gradually grew to a peak of over 140,000 Indians. While missionaries described a rigid work schedule based on cultivated agriculture, the Guaraní found ways to resist. This flexible system provided the Guaraní with sufficient material goods without making excessive labor demands. The communal structure of collective labor, shared ownership, and distribution of mission supplies enabled the missions to produce large quantities of goods to both provision the

Indians and trade for income. Regular beef and yerba maté rations were most important, but the missions also distributed tobacco, textiles, salt, tools, and trinkets to the Indians.

As part of a larger network, the system of mutual aid and coordinated trade both provided insurance during periods of hardship such as the 1730s and enabled the missions to generate large amounts of revenue to cover their expenses and pay off debts. Yerba maté sales generated the most revenue, but the missions also sold textiles and an assortment of other goods. Large sales revenues made the missions a major economic player in the region and sustained the institution. The Jesuits realized that they had to prioritize the mission economy if they wanted to advance their religious agenda. As the bishop of Paraguay noted in 1761, the Indians' temporal conveniences "were no less than the spiritual ones, [and] inasmuch a principal objective of the apostolic fervor of these Fathers."[143]

After the middle of the eighteenth century, however, conditions changed, and the future of the Guaraní missions became uncertain. The Jesuits' privileged position of power came under attack, and they lost their ability to effectively lobby the Crown on behalf of the Guaraní missions. Events associated with the Guaraní missions turned public opinion against the Jesuits and contributed to the order's expulsion. The next chapter explores these changes and their relation to the Guaraní missions.

CHAPTER 4

End of an Era

The Jesuit order was a power to be reckoned with at the end of the seventeenth century. Jesuit priests were valued friends and advisors to kings, princes, and other important people, and such relations gave the order great influence and power. The situation changed drastically in the middle of the eighteenth century. No longer in a privileged position, the Jesuits now struggled to preserve their order's existence. As opposition to the Jesuits grew, the Portuguese, French, and Spanish Crowns expelled the Jesuits from their respective territories. Anti-Jesuit sentiment culminated in Pope Clement XIV's suppression of the order in 1773.

The Guaraní missions played an important role in the Jesuits' fall from power. Events involving the Guaraní missions turned people against the Jesuits and served as useful propaganda for the anti-Jesuit lobby. Although each of the three expulsion decrees ultimately had more to do with imperial policies and court intrigues, complaints about the Jesuits almost always referred to the order's activities related to the Guaraní missions.

In order to better comprehend why the Jesuits fell from power, one must understand how the Jesuits came to power. A glimpse into imperial politics provides the backdrop for understanding the reasons for the Jesuit expulsion. Threats to the Jesuit order accelerated after the Spanish and Portuguese Crowns signed the Treaty of Madrid (1750), under which Spain agreed to give Portugal land that included seven of the Guaraní mission pueblos and extensive mission territory. Jesuit lobbying efforts against the treaty and efforts by the Guaraní to defend their land proved counterproductive. The ensuing Guaraní War between Indians who opposed the treaty and combined Spanish and Portuguese troops not only failed to halt the implementation of the treaty but also served as excellent fodder for cultivating anti-Jesuit sentiment. The Treaty of Madrid and the Guaraní War drew critical attention to Jesuit activities related to the

Guaraní missions. Opponents of the order used Jesuit opposition to the treaty and Guaraní armed resistance as examples of Jesuit disobedience and treachery against the Crown. Furthermore, they claimed that Jesuit management of the missions went against the Crown's political and financial interests. Such discourse played an important part in anti-Jesuit propaganda, which ultimately contributed to the expulsion of the Jesuits from all Spanish territory—including the Guaraní missions—in 1767.

The Treaty of Madrid and the Guaraní War not only changed the relationship between European leaders and the Jesuits; these events also changed Guaraní-Jesuit relations. The Guaraní recognized that Jesuit missionaries had lobbied the Crown unsuccessfully to either negate or significantly amend the treaty in their favor and that high-level Jesuit officials had ignored their pleas for support. As a result, the Guaraní lost confidence in the Jesuits' ability to protect them and defend their interests. They realized that the Jesuits no longer served as effective go-betweens for helping to negotiate the Spanish bureaucracy. When the Crown removed the Jesuits from the missions, the Guaraní did not rebel and few complained.

THE ASCENT OF THE JESUITS

For two hundred years—from the founding of their order in 1534 through the early eighteenth century—Jesuit power and wealth grew until the order became one of the most important power brokers in all of Europe. As H. M. Scott describes, "At [the] mid-[eighteenth] century, the Jesuits appeared unassailable: they provided confessors, often highly influential, to Catholic rulers, princes, and statesmen; dominated education in both the schools and universities; and exercised influence and, to a degree, power not only in Rome but also throughout Catholic Europe."[1]

While they were clearly influential, the rise of the Jesuits did not exclude other religious orders from the halls of power. Although a Spaniard (Ignatius of Loyola) founded the Jesuits and the order closely identified with Spain, the older Dominican and Franciscan orders remained vigorous and influential. Unlike most other Catholic European monarchs, Spanish kings generally continued the tradition of naming Dominican confessors during the Habsburg period. As a result, the Jesuits never achieved the same level of influence in Spain as they did in Germany and France.[2] When the Bourbons assumed the Spanish Crown at the beginning of the eighteenth century, they joined other European monarchs in choosing Jesuit confessors. As confessors, the Jesuits had the ear of the king and his court, which gave them the ability to influence and shape imperial politics.

Their role as educators provided the Jesuits with the opportunity to directly shape an even broader group of powerful and wealthy individuals. Less than two decades after the founding of the order, the Jesuits took up educational work. They intended such activities for the common good, in addition to the glory of God. Around 1750, Jesuit writings reveal a shift away from viewing themselves as itinerant preachers focused solely on advancing the Christian faith to seeing themselves as resident schoolmasters and missionaries who also performed works of charity for the common good.[3] The Jesuits' goal was to educate the children of the elite in preparation for their future roles in society. According to Juan Alfonso de Polanco, an important Jesuit and confidant to Ignatius, "Those who are now only students will grow up to be pastors, civic officials, administrators of justice, and will fill other important posts to everybody's profit and advantage."[4] In furthering this goal, the Jesuits established colleges (secondary schools) and universities throughout the Spanish empire. In contrast to monastery schools for educating the religious, these secondary schools focused on providing a general education to the children of local elites. At the date of the expulsion, the Jesuits operated 117 colleges in Spain and 2 of the most distinguished institutions for educating the nobility—the Colegio Imperial and the Seminario de Nobles in Madrid.[5] More than any other religious order, the Jesuits educated the sons of elite families; and by educating these youths, the Jesuits shaped their knowledge and influenced their views.

Just as in Spain, the Jesuits maintained and cultivated connections with local elites in Spanish America. Between 1600 and 1767, the Jesuits educated over 500,000 students in Spanish America. At the date of the expulsion, the order operated seventy-one colleges in Spanish America, thirteen of which were in the Río de la Plata region.[6] In addition to educating the upper crust of Spanish American society, the Jesuits also crossed paths with the economic elite in their business dealings. The Jesuits owned many of the most prosperous rural estates in Spanish America.[7] While other religious orders tended to loan capital to generate interest income, the Jesuits more frequently invested capital in properties, which they operated as productive enterprises.[8] These operations primarily funded Jesuit colleges.[9] Like other religious orders, the Jesuits also owned urban and rural land and served as landlords and bankers to the elite. Often, Jesuit colleges owed considerable sums of money to high-level Crown officials and wealthy private citizens.[10] The Jesuits also loaned money to private individuals. As of May 1, 1739, laymen owed the Guaraní mission oficio in Buenos Aires a total of 23,502 pesos, incurred in forty-four separate transactions.[11] On one hand, such business relations often led to friendships with the local elite, who then became benefactors and/or advocates of the Jesuits. On the other hand, such business enterprises angered other individuals who felt threatened by the Jesuits' economic activities.

Jealous of the prosperity and special privileges enjoyed by the Guaraní missions, many Paraguayan settlers strongly disliked the Jesuits. At a far distance from commercial centers, most of the inhabitants of Asunción and the surrounding region lived at close to subsistence level. In contrast to their humble existence, rumors circulated about the Jesuits hiding treasures and operating secret mines in Guaraní mission territory. In addition to these rumors, Paraguayans who sought to rise above subsistence level by selling their goods often faced competition from the Guaraní missions in the marketplace. The missions sold large quantities of the marketable goods produced in the region. The missions not only did not have to pay sales tax and customs duties, they also had abundant Indian labor to produce goods at a low cost. Like the missions, the Paraguayans relied heavily on Indian labor. As great numbers of Indians died and miscegenation increased, settlers complained about a labor shortage. To remedy this problem, settlers wanted Indians from the Guaraní missions as laborers. But, as described in preceding chapters, the Jesuits zealously protected mission Guaraní from encomienda labor and other work for private citizens.

Animosity toward the Jesuits exploded in Paraguay during the Comunero Revolt (1721–1732), but the Jesuits successfully rallied their powerful allies to win this power struggle.[12] In the lead-up to the rebellion, the Jesuits strongly influenced and directed the actions of the governor of Paraguay, Diego de los Reyes Balmaceda. In 1717, the Jesuits convinced the governor to ignore a peace treaty and attack the Payaguá Indians. Reyes's troops captured seventy Payaguás, whom he sent to the Jesuit missions instead of awarding them to the settlers as encomienda laborers. Such pro-Jesuit policies and other actions by Reyes angered Paraguayan settlers, who complained to the Audiencia of Charcas. The audiencia judges sent José de Antequera y Castro to Paraguay to investigate. If he found Reyes guilty, the audiencia instructed Antequera to arrest Reyes and open a sealed document that gave him the power to take over the governorship of Paraguay until the Crown appointed a new governor. After some initial investigations, Antequera removed Reyes from office, placed him under house arrest, and assumed the governorship. As governor, Antequera took a strong stand against the Jesuits because of what he perceived as their discriminatory economic activities and arrogant political behavior. Such actions appealed to many Paraguayans who complained that the Guaraní missions took all of the profits generated in the region while they remained impoverished.

Jesuit opposition to Antequera and their continued support of Reyes sparked the Comunero Revolt. In clear violation of Antequera's authority, the Jesuits helped Reyes escape imprisonment—the Jesuits did not shy away from proactive involvement in the conflict. In response, an open cabildo assembly of Paraguayan leaders vowed never to submit to the authority of Reyes or any other Jesuit supporter. Such intransigence led Paraguayan settlers to rise up in arms to support Antequera, while the Jesuits called upon Guaraní militias to defend Reyes. After being expelled from their college in Asunción and having their property in and around Asunción expropriated, the Jesuits ultimately won the struggle for power.

In this conflict, the Jesuits and their allies successfully lobbied against Antequera and the comuneros. Soon after Antequera arrived in Paraguay, friends of Reyes lobbied the viceroy of Peru, Diego Morcillo Rubio de Auñón, in support of the Jesuits and against Antequera. In response, Morcillo issued various orders reinstating Reyes as the legitimate governor of Paraguay. Morcillo's successor, the marqués de Castelfuerte, continued this stance by ordering an end to the uprising in Paraguay and demanding that the audiencia not interfere again. In 1725, Antequera fled Asunción, believing that the Audiencia of Charcas would exonerate him. In Charcas, Antequera was imprisoned and after a five-year trial sentenced to execution for treason. Throughout the conflict, the Jesuits successfully used their friendship with important Crown officials to win the power struggle. A little over a century later, the Jesuits again forcefully lobbied to protect their interests in the region. But by that time, the Jesuits had lost the support of powerful individuals and the outcome was very different.

UNDER ATTACK

The Catholic Church began to feel its power recede in Spain with the ascent of the Bourbon family to the Spanish Crown. The Bourbons believed that the papacy impeded their attempt to strengthen and revitalize the Spanish Empire. In this effort, the Bourbon kings instituted a series of reforms—known as the Bourbon Reforms—to consolidate and centralize power in the hands of the monarch by increasing efficiency, reducing corruption, and improving administration. This strengthening of royal power came at a cost to other institutions and individuals. The Catholic Church was a major target of such reforms. The Bourbons saw the

Catholic Church as a competitor and threat to the monarch's power; they wanted the monarch rather than the papacy to oversee church operations and the religious activity of both the clergy and the laity. In turn, Spanish clergy would be quasi agents of the state.[13]

Even though the Jesuits theoretically had a stronger connection to the papacy than other religious orders, the Bourbons' efforts to distance themselves from the papacy did not initially translate into a commensurate decrease in Jesuit influence. In addition to the standard three vows of poverty, chastity, and obedience, Jesuit priests took final vows that included special obedience to the pope regarding missions.[14] This vow meant that the Jesuits owed their allegiance first to the pope and then to the monarch. Such loyalty and commitment to the papacy clashed with the prerogatives of Bourbon absolutism. Despite such conflicts, the Jesuits initially benefited from absolutist trends.

Unlike the Habsburgs, both Philip V and his son, Ferdinand VI, had Jesuit confessors. In addition, both monarchs appointed either Jesuits or laymen favorable to the order as government ministers. These individuals actively enacted reforms that institutionalized absolutism. Jesuit officials did not see any conflict between such measures and loyalty to the papacy. Rather, they believed that by reducing the Roman curia's power, they limited abuses. In their eyes, they would best implement the pope's wishes because they were the most loyal and obedient followers of the pope. Furthermore, they believed that because of their close relationship with the Bourbon monarchy, they could better defend the papacy's interests.[15]

In the process of consolidating power in the hands of the king, the Jesuits engaged in intrigues that created many enemies. Actions taken by Francisco Rávago, Ferdinand VI's Jesuit confessor, especially aggravated other religious orders. In 1747, under Jesuit influence, the Spanish Inquisition banned the writings of authors revered by the Dominicans and Augustinians. The pope then intervened on behalf of the authors, but Rávago took advantage of his close relationship with the king to maintain the prohibition. Such clearly partisan action intensified rifts between the Jesuits and the Dominicans and Augustinians. Nevertheless, despite growing animosity toward their order, the Jesuits felt secure as valued and powerful advisors to the king. Such confidence proved to be ill founded.

In part, the Jesuits' fall from power resulted from the responses of the Jesuits and the Guaraní to the Treaty of Madrid. On January 13, 1750, the Spanish and Portuguese Crowns signed this treaty in an attempt to settle South American boundary conflicts. Up to this point, the greatly outdated Treaty of Tordesillas (1494) provided the legal dividing line between Spanish and Portuguese territory in the Americas. While most of the land in the Americas, based on the terms of the Treaty of Tordesillas, officially belonged to Spain, the Portuguese had advanced far into Spanish territory. By 1750, the Portuguese had achieved de facto sovereignty over almost half of the continent. They had outposts in the Amazon basin and settlements in the Banda Oriental. The town of Colonia del Sacramento—directly across the Río de la Plata from Buenos Aires—was especially in contention. The Portuguese insisted that the line of demarcation extended to the Río de la Plata and that part of the Banda Oriental fell in Portuguese territory. In contrast, the Spanish contended that the Treaty of Tordesillas reached Rio de Janeiro. In territorial struggles over the Banda Oriental, Colonia del Sacramento changed hands between the Spanish and Portuguese Crowns five times between 1680 and 1750.[16] Such conflicts rendered the Treaty of Tordesillas dividing line outdated and meaningless.

Ferdinand VI's ascension to the Spanish Crown in 1746 seemed like the ideal time to settle this dispute. Relations between the Spanish and Portuguese Crowns had improved, in large part owing to the influence of Ferdinand VI's wife, María Bárbara. She was the daughter of John V (king of Portugal, 1706–1750) and sister of Joseph I (king of Portugal, 1750–1777). After her marriage, María Bárbara maintained strong ties with Portugal. She strongly supported a territorial agreement between the two Crowns and lobbied her husband on its behalf.

With the Treaty of Madrid, both the Portuguese and Spanish Crowns sought to secure their positions in South America. In return for recognizing the western advance of the Portuguese, the Spanish tightened their control over the Río de la Plata estuary. The new dividing line generally followed clear topographical landmarks such as rivers as well as the idea of *uti possidetis* (as you possessed, you shall possess henceforth). The two major exceptions to the principle of occupation—Colonia del Sacramento and territory belonging to the Guaraní missions—were also the most controversial. The Portuguese agreed to give Colonia to the Spaniards in return for Spanish territory between the Uruguay and Ibicuí Rivers.[17] This territory included seven Guaraní missions (San Borja, San Nicolás, San Luis, San Lorenzo, San Ángel, San Miguel, and San Juan Bautista); estancias replete with cattle belonging to Santo Tomé and La Cruz; and yerbales belonging to Santa María la Mayor and San Xavier (see Map 5). In addition, the territory included access to the cattle reserves of Yapeyú, Concepción, and Apóstoles.[18]

Both Crowns had geopolitical and strategic reasons for signing the treaty. Spain wanted to maintain peace with Portugal in order to prevent a foreign invasion into the Río de la Plata region. Furthermore, Spain hoped that control of Colonia del Sacramento would limit contraband, especially of Andean silver. While the loss of Colonia del Sacramento hurt

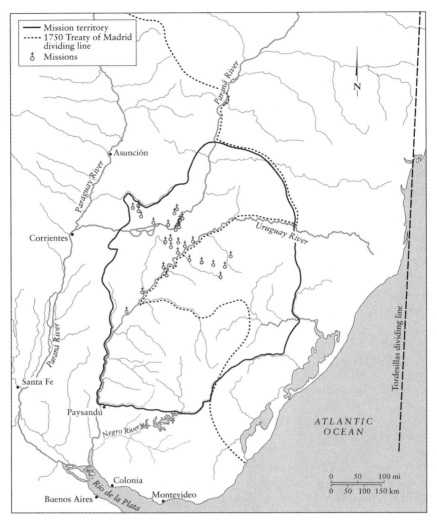

Map 5. Spanish-Portuguese border

SOURCE: Adapted from Maeder and Gutiérrez, *Atlas histórico del nordeste argentino*, 71 and 73; Mansuy-Diniz Silva, "Portugal and Brazil," 473.

Portugal's pride, the territorial exchange justified the loss. Distant as it was from the rest of Portuguese territory, maintaining Colonia was costly. Furthermore, the Portuguese Crown received minimal tax revenue from the contraband trade. In contrast, the area that included the Guaraní missions better advanced the Portuguese Crown's territorial interests. This territory would secure Portuguese colonization and access to land in Río Grande do Sul and the Amazon.[19]

Everyone understood that carrying out the treaty would be difficult, especially with respect to the Guaraní missions. Under the terms of the treaty, the Guaraní missions had no more than one year to relocate from the eastern side to the western side of the Uruguay River. The Jesuits had to leave and take all of their furniture and personal belongings. The Guaraní could choose to leave and rebuild their missions in Spanish territory or remain and become Portuguese subjects. The Guaraní who relocated to Spanish territory could take all of their belongings. Everything remaining after a year reverted to the Portuguese Crown.[20] Relocating approximately thirty thousand Guaraní, their belongings, and approximately one million livestock within a year seemed an impossible task.[21]

Recognizing the possibility of opposition to the treaty, Ferdinand VI emphasized that he wanted the Guaraní to vacate the mission territory affected by the treaty. He had given his word that the Jesuits and their Guaraní charges would meet the terms of the agreement. Even before the treaty became official, the king clarified that if the Guaraní resisted, a combined troop of Spanish and Portuguese soldiers would enforce the turnover of the mission lands to the Portuguese. In the hope of avoiding such an outcome, he instructed the marqués de Valdelirios (the Spanish envoy in charge of enforcing the exchange of territory in the Río de la Plata region) to communicate this information to the Jesuit provincial in Paraguay.[22]

Ferdinand VI had good reason to emphasize that the Guaraní missions must follow the terms of the treaty. Many doubted that the Jesuits would ever comply. Even before his appointment as the Portuguese envoy charged with enforcing the treaty in the Río de la Plata region, Gomes Freire de Andrada voiced multiple concerns about the Jesuits in correspondence to Crown officials in Lisbon. He expressed surprise that the Jesuits in Madrid had not prevented the signing of the treaty. Even so, he predicted that the Jesuits in Paraguay would not willingly give up their control of the Guaraní missions affected by the treaty. He believed they would create obstacles to its enforcement, just as they had endeavored to turn Amerindians against the Portuguese in Brazil. Furthermore, he reported that the Jesuits in Paraguay claimed that the Guaraní missions did not belong to the king but rather had been acquired by Jesuit sweat.[23]

Such commentary promoted suppositions of potential Jesuit disobedience and fed into the concerns of the most powerful individual in the Portuguese court, Sebastião José de Carvalho e Melo, otherwise known as the marquês de Pombal.[24] About six months after the signing of the treaty, Pombal took office as secretary of state for foreign affairs and war.

As a Crown official, he officially had to support the treaty, but he was reluctant to give Colonia to the Spanish. In a secret letter, Pombal told Freire de Andrada to maintain control of Colonia until the Guaraní missions were in Portuguese possession.[25]

The Jesuit hierarchy in Europe recognized that they, and the rest of their order, had to support and comply with the treaty in order to demonstrate their loyalty to the Spanish Crown. Even before the treaty was signed, Ferdinand VI's Jesuit confessor urged Franz Retz, the superior general of the Jesuit order, to make sure that the Jesuits in Paraguay evacuated the seven missions and complied with all of the terms. Six days before the treaty was signed, Retz wrote to the Jesuit provincial in charge of Paraguay, recommending that he begin evacuating the missions that would be affected by the treaty.[26]

The rest of the order was not united in its response to the treaty. Initially, a clear divide arose between the Jesuit hierarchy in Europe, who believed that the terms of the treaty had to be enforced, and the Jesuits in Paraguay, who actively lobbied against it. Upon hearing rumors about the treaty in September 1750, the Jesuit provincial of Paraguay called all of his counselors to discuss and strategize a response. After official confirmation of the treaty arrived in February of 1751, the Jesuits in Paraguay initiated a lobbying effort in opposition to it. They wrote long and detailed appeals to influential Spanish officials, including José Antonio Manso de Velasco (viceroy of Peru), José de Carvajal (the Spanish foreign minister who signed the Treaty of Madrid), Francisco de Rávago (the Jesuit confessor to Ferdinand VI), and the superior general of the Jesuit order. In addition to such letters, Juan José Quesada, the Jesuit priest in charge of the province of Paraguay, sent three Jesuits—Pedro de Logu, Carlos Gervasoni, and Pedro Arroyo—to Madrid to personally lobby for modification of the Treaty of Madrid.[27]

In their appeals, the Jesuits in Paraguay argued that the treaty was highly detrimental to the Guaraní, the missions, and the Spanish Empire. Some were so surprised by the terms that they wondered if Ferdinand VI had been tricked or poorly advised into signing it.[28] Many Jesuits in Paraguay believed that the treaty would lead to deleterious moral, economic, religious, and strategic results. They argued that by taking land and property that the Crown had given to the Guaraní, the treaty betrayed the Indians and threatened the conversion process. The Guaraní might become more suspicious of the missionaries and the Catholic faith. Relocating almost thirty thousand Guaraní not only would affect the inhabitants of the seven missions, but the rest of the missions and their Guaraní inhabitants would feel the impact as well. During the transition and until their productive infrastructure was rebuilt, the occupants of the seven missions would have to rely on support from the other missions. Relocating was a daunting task.

The financial costs related to such a move were great. Bernardo Nusdorffer, a former head of the Guaraní missions, estimated that the missions would lose over 3.5 million pesos as the result of relocation. This considerable sum included cattle herds worth 999,999 pesos, buildings worth 960,000 pesos, yerbales worth 763,800 pesos, agricultural fields worth 600,000 pesos, cotton fields worth 35,000 pesos, and orchards and gardens worth 27,000 pesos. The Jesuits argued that by destroying the missions' economic foundation, the relocation threatened not only their ability to provide for their Guaraní charges but also their ability to pay tribute to the Crown.[29] In compensation for the furnishings and other goods that could not be relocated within the allotted time, the Jesuit envoy charged with enforcing the treaty promised that the Portuguese would reimburse the missions based on a just price.[30] The missionaries argued that such a price would fall far short of the true value of the mission lands and property. To help defray the relocation costs and compensate for lost land and property, the Crown promised each mission 4,000 pesos and exempted the Indians from taxes for ten years.[31] This amount totaled 28,000 pesos—much less than the 3,522,167 pesos estimated by Nusdorffer.

Despite such objections, Ferdinand VI continued to support the treaty and the Jesuit hierarchy continued to demand compliance. After Franz Retz died, the Spanish foreign minister, José de Carvajal, immediately pressured the new superior general of the Jesuit order, Ignacio Visconti, about the treaty. On July 21, 1751—seventeen days after his election as superior general—Visconti wrote letters to the provincial of Paraguay and the superior of the missions. He explained that the Jesuits had to obey the king and demanded that they do nothing to hinder the treaty's implementation; instead, they should do everything they could to support it. In order to ensure the evacuation of the seven missions, Visconti sent a Jesuit envoy, Lope Luis Altamirano, to the Río de la Plata region. Visconti charged Altamirano with making sure that the Jesuits and the Guaraní complied with the treaty. If the Guaraní resisted, Visconti ordered Altamirano to have the Jesuits abandon the missions. Visconti felt so strongly about the Jesuit response to the Treaty of Madrid that he was willing to remove all Jesuit ministries from the Americas in order to prove the order's loyalty to the king.[32]

On February 20, 1752, Altamirano and the Spanish and Portuguese envoys sent to enforce the southern demarcations arrived in Buenos Aires. When the Jesuits in the Río de la Plata region learned of the intransigence of both the Spanish Crown and the Jesuit hierarchy regarding the treaty, they reacted in various ways. Outwardly, most took steps to obey the treaty; accompanied by some Guaraní, missionaries began looking for suitable areas for rebuilding the missions.

Some Jesuits pleaded with the Guaraní to comply with the treaty, while others remained passive as the Guaraní opposition organized itself. A few Jesuits persisted in taking action against the treaty. José Cardiel and Giacomo Passino continued writing letters in opposition to the treaty.[33] After the fact, some Guaraní caciques blamed Jesuits Tadeo Henis and Miguel de Soto for fomenting Guaraní rebellion.[34] In contrast, Guaraní caciques under investigation by the governor of Buenos Aires claimed the contrary—that the Jesuits "had never ceased to insist with them, begging them to obey, and that the rebellion would be the act, deed and fault of themselves (the Indians)."[35]

The Treaty of Madrid generated conflict among the Guaraní. Initially, it seemed as if they would comply with the treaty. Caciques and cabildos from six of the seven missions agreed to relocate. Only Mission San Nicolás disobeyed from the beginning, but even so there was not complete consensus among the Guaraní of that mission. The priest of San Nicolás blamed Cristobal Paicá, a Guaraní born in Mission Santos Mártires, for convincing forty-one of the forty-five caciques not to abandon their land.[36]

The other six missions initially sent out parties of Guaraní to find new mission sites in compliance with the treaty. Between June and October of 1752, groups of one to two hundred families from each mission set out to relocate. These families accounted for only a minority of the population of their respective missions. Most of the Jesuits also remained behind to organize subsequent departures. Of the six groups that went in search of new mission sites, only two (San Lorenzo and San Borja) reached their final destination, and only Indians from the latter mission remained for an extended period of time.[37]

Guaraní opposition to the treaty grew as the Indians became convinced that there was not enough suitable uninhabited land for rebuilding their missions. The territory to the south did not have the right climate for growing essential crops, and other Guaraní missions already occupied the territory to the west.[38] As the Guaraní realized their options were limited, many became unwilling to sacrifice their existing missions and property in order to comply with the treaty.

Overall, Guaraní from San Nicolás and San Miguel opposed the treaty more vigorously than Guaraní from the other missions. The Guaraní from San Nicolás resisted because their mission had already undergone multiple relocations and had finally returned to the land of their ancestors. For the Guaraní from San Miguel, the threat to their immense livestock holdings and their reputation as valiant warriors led them to take a leadership role in opposing the treaty. Guaraní from the other missions showed more ambivalence. On two occasions, the priests and corregidors of San Juan Bautista, San Ángel, San Luis, and San Lorenzo convinced Guaraní from their missions to send relocation parties. But such compliance with the treaty did not last long; the resistance movement soon convinced Indians from these missions to join the opposition.[39]

Divisions also arose within missions between those willing to comply with the treaty and those who refused. Even in San Nicolás and San Miguel, only some of the mission population participated in the first uprisings.[40] Frequently, the corregidor's close relationship with the missionaries led him to advocate for compliance with the treaty. But as the opposition gained momentum, corregidors often lost their leadership positions. The Guaraní who opposed the treaty overthrew and replaced the Guaraní corregidors of San Nicolás, San Miguel, San Lorenzo, and San Juan Bautista who supported acquiescence.[41] By the end of 1752, rebellion against the treaty began to seem likely.

Tensions grew as an increasing number of mission inhabitants refused to leave their land and opposition organized across missions. Guaraní opponents of the treaty voiced their unwillingness to comply to Jesuit missionaries, and rebel caciques began taking concrete action. In order to prevent the relocation of mission goods, some Indians burned carts, gathered horses and oxen, and took control of mission supplies and munitions.[42] The Guaraní opposition was now ready to use force to stop the treaty's enforcement. In early 1753, some six hundred armed Guaraní advanced on Mission Santo Tomé, where Altamirano was staying. Angered by Altamirano's support of the treaty, the Guaraní intended to kill him. In response, Altamirano fled the missions in February 1753.[43] In the same month, a hundred or so Guaraní with some weapons and horses refused to let the combined Spanish-Portuguese boundary commission enter Santa Tecla (Mission San Miguel's estancia). José Tiarayú (a member of San Miguel's cabildo) threatened to assemble an army of nine thousand Guaraní. In response, the boundary commission retreated.[44]

In another effort to elicit compliance with the treaty, José de Andonaegui, the governor of Buenos Aires, turned to written correspondence with the rebels. In May 1753, he sent a letter addressed to the rebels of the seven missions that were required to relocate according to the terms of the treaty. He demanded they leave their lands and buildings. In July, caciques and cabildo members from six of the seven missions sent letters in response; only San Borja did not. In addition to these six missions, the corregidor of Mission Concepción—Nicolás Ñeenguirú—also sent a letter to the governor. Employing both pleading, religious language and a bellicose tone, the seven letters articulated their authors' opposition to the treaty and questioned its validity. The authors cited their rights to the land and couched their claims in references to both God and the king. Their arguments shed light on the Guaraní elite's understanding of the relationship between their people and the Crown: God gave them the land and they would fight to defend it. Moreover, they argued, they were loyal vassals of the Spanish king; their enemies must have tricked the king into signing the treaty.[45] In the face of such opposition, commissioners Valdelirios and Freire de Andrada met with Governor Andonaegui on July 15, 1753. They declared the Guaraní to be in rebellion and began preparing for war.[46]

The Guaraní opposition also prepared for war. They recruited Guaraní soldiers from other missions, but gaining such support was not easy. In most of the missions, the Jesuits tried to prevent the Guaraní from joining the opposition, and the Guaraní themselves were divided about defying Crown officials.[47] In addition to mission soldiers, the opposition also sought the assistance of nonmission Indians. They built on kinship relations between mission Guaraní and nonmission Guenoas, Charrúas, and Minuanes and offered gifts to solicit their support.[48]

Written communication played an important role in the rebels' strategy. As the seven letters to the governor of Buenos Aires reveal, the rebels used writing as a tool of diplomacy. Even more important, Guaraní rebels used notes to correspond among themselves. During the buildup to the war, the Jesuit priest from San Lorenzo reported that the caciques sent "papers" to each other day and night.[49] Such communication was rapid and facilitated the transfer of information needed to mobilize and unite the inhabitants of different missions throughout the conflict.[50] The rebels also intercepted their opponents' letters in order to obtain information about their adversaries' location and movements.[51]

Given their experience in the mission militias, Guaraní soldiers were relatively well trained for battle. For over one hundred years, the Crown had regularly called on the Guaraní militias for assistance. Under normal circumstances, the missionaries directed the Guaraní militias, but in this case the Guaraní could not rely on Jesuit leadership. Instead, individual Guaraní rose to take leadership positions and to unite and direct Indian soldiers from different missions.

The two best-known Guaraní rebel leaders were José Tiarayú (otherwise known as Sepé), a cabildo member but not a cacique of Mission San Miguel, and Nicolás Ñeenguirú, a cacique and the corregidor of Mission Concepción.[52] Sepé initially led the Guaraní rebels, and then Ñeenguirú assumed the position after Sepé's death. Recent scholarship has brought to light additional Guaraní rebel leaders.[53]

The impending rebellion by the Guaraní came at a bad time for the Jesuits. In 1753, the Jesuit and pro-Jesuit advisors negotiated an agreement—the Concordat—between the papacy and the Spanish Crown. The Concordat drastically reduced the pope's role in Spanish affairs. Under the Concordat, the king and the pope exchanged roles in relation to the temporal affairs of the Catholic Church in Spain. The pope lost and the king gained the rights over church appointments and income. In addition, church lands in Spain were no longer exempt from taxes. While reconciliation came at a great cost, the papacy agreed to such terms in order to restore relations with the Spanish Crown. The two powers had not had diplomatic relations since the Bourbons came to power in Spain at the beginning of the eighteenth century. For their part, the Jesuits hoped that their role as intermediaries in this reconciliation would help to maintain their position in Spain.

A year after the Concordat, relations between the Spanish monarchy and the Jesuits seriously faltered. In 1754, palace intrigues led to the arrest and forced resignation of the pro-Jesuit minister of finance and navy, the marqués de Ensenada. In addition to losing a valuable ally, the Jesuits also lost their influential position as confessor to the king; the Jesuit priest Francisco Rávago was removed as the king's confessor. His replacement, Manuel Quintano Bonifaz, was a secular, not a Jesuit, priest; Rávago was the last Jesuit confessor at the Spanish Court.

Back in Buenos Aires, Altamirano recognized that the Jesuits were acquiring a bad name at the royal court. He understood that the Jesuit order had to do everything possible to demonstrate its loyalty to the Spanish Crown. Hence, he wanted to ensure that Jesuit missionaries had nothing to do with a possible Guaraní uprising. To make this clear to the missionaries, Altamirano decreed that accompanying the rebels would be a mortal sin and ordered that no Jesuit should advise, direct, or support the rebels.[54]

Jesuit opposition, however, did not prevent Guaraní rebellion. Armed confrontations began in 1754, when Guaraní soldiers twice attacked Portuguese settlements. In the same year, Andonaegui and Freire de Andrada tried to occupy the seven missions. While approaching the first mission, Andonaegui encountered fierce Guaraní resistance. After 260 casualties and the loss of many livestock, he retreated. Likewise, Freire de Andrada withdrew after his army of one thousand encountered two thousand Guaraní soldiers from five of the missions.[55]

During the next year, Spanish and Portuguese officials prepared for a major campaign against the Guaraní insurgents. They gathered more than three thousand troops to fight approximately thirteen hundred Guaraní soldiers. In late 1755, combined Spanish and Portuguese troops advanced toward the disputed territory, and in February 1756 they defeated the Guaraní insurgents in two battles.[56] The rebel leader, Sepé, was injured in the first battle. As punishment, he was burned to death and decapitated, with his head and body buried separately.[57] Ñeengirú subsequently assumed the role of commander, and three days later, the Guaraní rebels were defeated at Caaíbaté. In this battle, the governor of Buenos Aires claimed that 154 Guaraní were taken prisoner and 1,511 died on the battlefield, while only 3 Spanish soldiers and 1 Portuguese soldier died.[58]

Over the course of the war, almost 1,800 Guaraní died.[59] These deaths represented Guaraní soldiers from half of the thirty missions; the other half did not send any soldiers to battle. For those missions that did participate, only a minority of their adult males generally decided to join the fight. On average, between one hundred and three hundred out of a pool of approximately fifteen hundred potential soldiers joined the rebellion.[60]

At the end of the war, Governor Andonaegui showed clemency to most of the Guaraní insurgents. They had to turn over all of their weapons within fifteen days, and no leaders were executed. Spanish officials and the Jesuits showed leniency to Ñeengirú. They banished him from his native mission of Concepción and sent him to live in exile at Mission Trinidad.[61]

Even though the Spanish and Portuguese troops defeated the Guaraní soldiers, not all Guaraní complied with the Treaty of Madrid. On October 7, 1758, Pedro Antonio de Cevallos wrote to authorities in Spain that 26,686 Guaraní had relocated to the other side of the Guaraní River—12,402 during his almost-two-year tenure as governor of Buenos Aires and 14,284 before then. In addition, he estimated that 2,000 Guaraní remained in what was now Portuguese territory.[62]

The Guaraní-Jesuit relationship changed as a result of the events surrounding the Treaty of Madrid. During the conflict, rebel leaders verbally threatened the Jesuits and rejected their role as political leaders.[63] The Guaraní realized that the Jesuits no longer had the ability to effectively lobby on their behalf; the missionaries could no longer defend and protect them or obtain special concessions from Crown officials. During previous conflicts, such as the Comunero Revolt, the Jesuits had successfully stood up to their opponents—including Crown officials such as Antequera—and convinced the Crown to follow their advice. With the Treaty of Madrid, the Jesuits had no such success. Despite their best efforts, they could not make the Crown change its mind; the Crown did not revoke the treaty, delay its enforcement, or amend its terms. As a result, the Jesuits lost prestige and status in the eyes of the Guaraní.

Rumors of Jesuit betrayal circulated among the Guaraní. A story spread that the Jesuits had secretly sold the land to the Portuguese.[64]

Such rumors further discredited the Jesuits and fostered animosity toward them. The Jesuits who followed instructions from their superiors and urged mission inhabitants to relocate across the Uruguay River were perceived as betraying the Guaraní.

After the war, investigations into the rebellion further ruptured the relationship between the Guaraní and the Jesuits. Officials who interrogated the Guaraní about the rebellion asked pointed questions and directed their witnesses to blame the Jesuits. The Guaraní frequently responded with what their interrogators wanted to hear.[65] Such questions revealed the authorities' animosity toward the Jesuits and promoted further anti-Jesuit sentiment among the Guaraní.

Life outside the missions increasingly came to be seen as an appealing option by many Guaraní after these events. By this time, few Guaraní who left the missions came under the threat of coercive labor regimes such as the encomienda and Portuguese enslavement. Instead, Spaniards employed fugitives in both the countryside and cities.[66] Many fugitives sought such employment. Jesuit Domingo Muriel considered these fugitives fools because they left the missions to earn half a peso. This small amount, opined Muriel, "opens more the eyes of a fool, than that security [of the missions]."[67] The protection offered by the missions—which initially attracted the Guaraní—became less of an attraction as opportunities for greater freedom and wage labor developed outside of the missions and the Jesuits lost their ability to effectively lobby on behalf of the Guaraní.

Even though the Treaty of Madrid was revoked in 1761, the missions never fully recovered from the upheaval. By 1764, the seven missions located in the disputed region had regained about two-thirds of their population—21,209 inhabitants—but another 6,519 Guaraní never returned.[68] The total population of the thirty missions never again reached its 1755 level.[69]

CONSEQUENCES FOR THE JESUITS

Both the failure to comply with the Treaty of Madrid and the Guaraní War created long-lasting problems for the Jesuits. Starting in 1752, Freire de Andrada and other officials associated with enforcing the terms of the treaty in both the Amazon basin and the Río de la Plata region regularly sent the marquês de Pombal reports that were highly critical of the Jesuits. These officials complained that the Jesuits were deliberately blocking the treaty. Such actions, they believed, merited a strong response by the Portuguese Crown: the order should be sharply disciplined, if not eliminated entirely. For many, the Guaraní War provided conclusive evidence of Jesuit sedition. They believed that the Jesuits maintained strict control over the Guaraní and that the Indians could not act of their own volition. Hence, when the Guaraní took up arms, Freire de Andrada informed Pombal that the Jesuits must have instigated such defiance. Most of the Spanish authorities involved, with the exception of Andonaegui, also blamed the Jesuits for the Guaraní rebellion.[70]

By 1755, Pombal concluded that the Jesuit order constituted a potential threat to the king's absolute power and thus had to be eliminated.[71] He viewed both the Crown and the Guaraní as victims of the Jesuits. In Pombal's opinion, the Jesuits' roles as educators and confessors gave them too much power and autonomy in Europe, and in his view, Paraguay served as a prime example of Jesuit excesses. One of his main accusations was that the Jesuits openly defied royal authority by actively opposing the Treaty of Madrid. He blamed the order for preventing the stipulated territorial exchanges and therefore for the treaty's failure. Pombal's accusations, moreover, extended beyond events associated with the Treaty of Madrid. He also claimed that the Jesuits kept the Guaraní in conditions of slavery and that the missionaries had created a state within a state independent of Crown authority.

The most prominent minister in the Portuguese government between 1750 and 1777, Pombal became the main instigator of growing anti-Jesuit sentiment. He cultivated opposition to the Jesuits in Portugal and throughout Europe by adroitly mixing facts and unsubstantiated accusations concerning the Treaty of Madrid and the Guaraní War. Starting in 1757, Pombal and the Portuguese government published a series of glaringly anti-Jesuit documents. The first, "A Short Account of the Republic Which the Jesuits Have Established in the Spanish and Portuguese Dominions of the World," accused the Jesuits of a variety of abuses, based on both fact and rumor. The document not only alleged that the Jesuits had mobilized large indigenous armies in opposition to the treaty, but also described the thirty Guaraní missions as an autonomous Jesuit state that oppressed the Indians. The document reached a wide readership; translated into Italian, French, German, and English, an estimated twenty thousand copies were distributed throughout Europe. With its incriminating descriptions of Jesuit defiance and misdeeds, opponents used this document and other similar propaganda to call for the expulsion and suppression of the order.[72]

In 1759 Pombal succeeded in expelling the Jesuits from Portuguese territory. Prior to this date, he was able to arrest and exile individual Jesuits, but he did not have a strong enough case to expel the Jesuits from the Portuguese Empire. An assassination attempt against Joseph I in 1758 provided the opportunity that Pombal was looking for; accusations of Jesuit complicity in such treachery justified the expulsion of the Jesuit order from Portuguese territory.[73]

Pombal's anti-Jesuit propaganda had effect not only in Portugal but throughout Europe. Philosophes and government ministers published numerous works sharply criticizing the Jesuits. These documents crossed borders and influenced important individuals. After the Jesuits' expulsion from Portuguese territory, the French philosopher Voltaire published at least two works highly critical of Jesuit activity in the Guaraní missions.[74]

In a chapter of *Short Studies in English and American Subjects* dedicated to the Jesuits in Paraguay, Voltaire both mirrored and built on Pombal's complaints about the Jesuits. Like Pombal, Voltaire asserted that the Jesuits deprived the Guaraní of their liberty and made them work as slaves for the missionaries' benefit.[75] In his opinion, the Jesuits could act this way because "they have made themselves absolute sovereigns" with "an absolute government over the people they organized."[76] As a result, he argued, the Crown did not exercise either civil or religious authority over the Jesuits' "empire in Paraguay."[77]

Voltaire's popular novelette *Candide* was also highly critical of the Jesuits' involvement in the Guaraní missions. When Candide asks Cacambo if he has been to Paraguay, Cacambo answers, "There the Fathers possess all, and the people nothing; it is a masterpiece of reason and justice. For my part I see nothing so divine as the Fathers who here make war upon the kings of Spain and Portugal, and in Europe confess those kings; who here kill Spaniards, and in Madrid send them to heaven."[78] This satirical account highlights the two main controversial points raised in the debates about the Jesuits' activities among the Guaraní. First, the Jesuits' autonomy and dominion over the missions came to be interpreted as both a threat to the Crown's sovereignty and forced servitude for the Indians. Second, Jesuit opposition to the Treaty of Madrid and the ensuing Guaraní War demonstrated Jesuit insubordination to the Crown. Opponents saw the Jesuits as responsible for Guaraní armed opposition. As a result of these beliefs, many important government officials and intellectuals became more critical of Jesuit activities. Thus, the first point drawn out in *Candide*—the criticism of Jesuit management of the Guaraní missions—resulted in large part from the second—Jesuit opposition to the Treaty of Madrid and the Guaraní War.

Voltaire's writings played into growing anti-Jesuit sentiment in France, where such opinions culminated in Louis XV expelling the Jesuits three years after Joseph I. As in Portugal, opposition to the Jesuits involved much more than the order's activities in Paraguay. Theological disputes had festered since the seventeenth century. Jansenism, which began in

France, conflicted with the Jesuits' theology on several key points.[79] The Jesuits' efforts to suppress the Jansenists and other opponents spurred further anti-Jesuit sentiment.[80] In the end, a financial dispute involving a Jesuit priest in the West Indies proved pivotal to the Jesuit expulsion from French territory in 1762.[81]

At the same time as the Jesuits were under attack in Portugal and France, their position also deteriorated in Spain. In 1759, Ferdinand VI died and Charles III ascended to the Spanish Crown. The new king did not name a Jesuit confessor, and most of his advisors opposed the Jesuits. Soon after taking the throne, Charles III ordered a review of the Treaty of Madrid. Limited progress had been made toward implementing its terms; moreover, the deaths of Foreign Minister Carvajal (1754), Queen María Bárbara (1758), and Ferdinand VI (1759) eliminated the main Spanish proponents of the treaty. In 1760, the Spanish ambassador announced that Portuguese failure to turn over Colonia had forced Charles III to rescind the treaty. Joseph I did not object. A year later, representatives of both Crowns signed the Treaty of El Pardo, which officially repealed the Treaty of Madrid. The Jesuit missionaries ultimately achieved their goal of not having to relinquish Guaraní mission territory, but at a great cost.

A dispute in 1761 over the writings of a French theologian, François Philippe Mesenguy, revealed the Jesuits' waning power in Spain. The Jesuits argued that Mesenguy's writings, which attacked the Jesuits and denied the infallibility of the pope, should be prohibited on account of their heretical content. The pope backed the Jesuits and issued a papal brief to that effect. In sharp contrast to earlier periods, the Jesuits found that the Spanish king did not come to their defense. Unlike Ferdinand VI, Charles III did not acquiesce to Jesuit pressure regarding controversial publications. He reacted vehemently to the papal nuncio. When the inquisitor general published the papal brief condemning Mesenguy's catechism, Charles III did not succumb to Jesuit influence but rather temporarily banished the inquisitor general from court and imposed strict censorship on all papal messages sent to the Spanish clergy.[82]

As in Portugal and France, local events played a pivotal role in the Jesuits' expulsion from Spain. The Hat and Cloak Riots in March 1766 were the breaking point for the Jesuits. Prior to the riots, discontent with the Crown had been on the rise owing to a myriad of reasons, including Charles III's penchant for naming foreigners to high office, the loss of Florida to Britain in 1763, inflation, successive years of bad harvests, and increased taxes. Tensions culminated on March 23, 1766, with the enforcement of a law forbidding men to wear long capes and the common broad-brimmed hats. The ensuing riots in nearly seventy Spanish towns forced Charles III and his family to flee the capital. Reports soon emerged that opponents of Charles III's reforms and enemies of the marqués de Esquilache had planned the riots.

The Council of Castile commissioned an investigation into the riots by one of the two *fiscales* (attorneys general) of the Council of Castile, Pedro Rodríguez, count of Campomanes. During his investigation, Campomanes worked with other Spanish officials to formulate a strategy to incriminate the Jesuits and justify their expulsion from Spain.[83] The resulting work, *Dictamen fiscal de la expulsión de los jesuitas de España (1766–1767)*, was highly critical of the Jesuit order and concluded that the Jesuits had used their influence to incite the protest. The lengthy report contains 746 paragraphs. Only one of its nine chapters focuses primarily on the 1766 riots; the remaining chapters focus on other complaints about the Jesuits. Campomanes dedicated one of these nine chapters to criticizing Jesuit activities related to the Guaraní missions.

Campomanes's criticisms were similar in many ways to those of Pombal and Voltaire.[84] After recognizing that no other missionary endeavor—including those in Asia—surpassed the Guaraní missions in the notoriety of its achievement, Campomanes argued that much of the apparent success was misunderstood. He claimed that both the Spanish Crown and the Guaraní inhabitants of the missions suffered under the Jesuits. In his eyes, the missions' material successes obscured the fact that the Jesuits both disobeyed and defrauded the Crown. According to Campomanes, documents and internal reports concerning the government of the missions revealed that the Jesuits had usurped royal authority.[85] On the basis of taxes and tribute that the missions avoided paying, he believed that the Crown had sacrificed immense sums by allowing the Jesuits to oversee the institution.[86] Moreover, he did not believe that this situation benefited the Guaraní. He argued that the Indians worked excessively hard without receiving adequate compensation, explicitly comparing their condition to slavery: "There is no country in the world in which the subjects are treated with servitude equal to that which the Indians suffer on the part of the Jesuits. . . . The most severe masters are not more rigorous with their slaves."[87]

On December 31, 1766, Campomanes submitted his report to the Council of Madrid. As an important scholar and royal bureaucrat, Campomanes's damning account of the Jesuit order reflected not only his own influential view but royal sentiment as well. On February 27, 1767—less than two months after Campomanes submitted his report—Charles III signed the decree to expel the Jesuits from all Spanish territories and confiscate their property.[88] Over the next months, more than 2,200

Jesuits left Spanish territory.[89] Six years after their expulsion from Spain, the Spanish ambassador, José Moñino, convinced Pope Clement XIV to suppress the Jesuit order.[90]

CONCLUSION

Geopolitics, court intrigues, and European events ultimately led to the Jesuits' expulsion from Portuguese, French, and Spanish territories; but events related to the Guaraní missions played an important role, too. Opponents purposefully criticized Jesuit activities among the Guaraní in order to cultivate anti-Jesuit sentiment and build opposition to the order. In this effort, the Treaty of Madrid was pivotal.

Jesuit missionaries responded to the Treaty of Madrid as they always had to policies that they thought harmed their interests. They lobbied Crown officials and pointed out how the treaty was harmful to Spain. Unlike earlier efforts, however, such actions proved counterproductive. The Crown was not receptive to Jesuit lobbying; Ferdinand VI's move toward absolutism meant that he resolutely demanded compliance with the treaty. The Jesuit hierarchy realized that both their order and the Guaraní had to obey, but the damage had already been done. To many, the missionaries' protest provided convincing evidence that the Jesuits were to blame for the Guaraní War.

The attention drawn to the Guaraní missions during these events provided ample material for propaganda that proved very destructive to the Jesuit order. Pombal, Voltaire, Campomanes, and others argued that the Jesuits had created in Paraguay a state within a state where the Indians lived in slavery and the Crown had no power. Justifications for the expulsion of the Jesuits always referred back to such claims.

The Treaty of Madrid and the Guaraní War radically affected the Guaraní missions. Over a thousand Guaraní lost their lives, and the missions lost thousands of pesos in livestock and property. The missions never completely recovered—the number of mission inhabitants never again reached its 1755 level. Guaraní-Jesuit relations also deteriorated, as the Indians realized that they could no longer count on the Jesuits to protect their interests. Few Guaraní protested the removal of the Jesuits from the missions in 1768, in part because royal officials promised reforms to empower and enrich the Guaraní. The next chapter explains how these reforms bankrupted the missions.

CHAPTER 5

Bankruptcy

Charles III's decree to expel the Jesuits from Spanish territory had a huge impact in the Americas.[1] More than 265,000 Indians living in approximately 222 Jesuit missions spread across frontier regions of Spanish America felt the effects of this decree.[2] In the Río de la Plata region, 78 Jesuits left almost 89,000 Indians residing in the thirty Guaraní missions.[3] The removal of the Jesuits affected the Guaraní and the missions, but their departure did not cause the missions to fail. Rather, the missions became untenable because of reforms that increased the roles of the state and the market economy. While these reforms quickly led to the missions' bankruptcy, many Guaraní chose to continue to reside in and sustain their individual mission for more than thirty years.

This chapter begins with an outline of mission reforms implemented in conjunction with the Jesuit expulsion and an explanation of how these changes fit with absolutism, concepts of liberalism, and new perspectives about Indians and missions. By separating temporal and religious affairs in the missions, reformers sought to increase the role of the state. Reformers also used the market economy to encourage commerce and stimulate trade in an effort to increase revenue and more effectively Europeanize the Guaraní.

Instead of outsourcing all of it to a single religious order as under the Jesuits, the state inserted itself into mission management. Economic and political matters were now the jurisdiction of state-appointed civilian administrators. Only religious matters were left to priests. This separation of secular and temporal affairs prevented a unity of purpose among the new appointees, ended the subsidy provided by a single religious order, and generated insurmountable overhead expenses. The missions' exceedingly high salary expenditures erroneously suggest that rampant corruption caused the missions' financial collapse. Close examination of accounting books, however, reveals that salary expenditures approximated market wages. Instead of corruption, the insertion of the state into mission management caused salary expenditures to soar.

While revenues initially rose in response to greater emphasis on trade, they were not enough to solve the missions' financial problems. For over a decade sales revenues remained relatively high, but expenses continued to exceed revenues. Furthermore, the emphasis on trade siphoned goods away from the Indians. The Guaraní simply did not produce enough trade goods under the missions' communal structure to support the shift toward the market economy. By the late 1780s, the missions no longer sent large quantities of trade goods to their trading center in Buenos Aires, and sales revenue plummeted.

REFORMS AND CHANGING VIEWS ABOUT
INDIANS AND MISSIONS

In carrying out the Jesuit expulsion, Crown officials wanted to ensure that the new missionaries never achieved the same level of autonomy as the Jesuits. As described in the previous chapter, Jesuit influence conflicted with Bourbon absolutism, and in large part, the expulsion resulted from the Crown's desire to centralize power in its own hands and eliminate any challenge to its authority. Over the previous two decades, opponents had widely promulgated anti-Jesuit propaganda that depicted the Jesuits as creating a state within a state in the Guaraní missions; as a result, the missions became a major target for reform.

Charles III assigned the condé de Aranda, president of the Council of Castile, to execute the Jesuit expulsion. Aranda took the opportunity to order extensive reforms for all of the former Jesuit missions in the Americas and the Philippines.[4] Less than a week after Charles III signed the expulsion decree, Aranda issued supplemental instructions about separating temporal and spiritual management and encouraging commerce.[5]

In an effort to prevent any one religious order from gaining a stronghold over the former Jesuit missions, Aranda specified that regardless of whether a secular priest (a priest who was not a member of a particular religious order) or a priest belonging to a different religious order replaced a Jesuit missionary, the priest would always report to a bishop or archbishop and not to the hierarchy of a religious order.[6] He instituted this measure to ensure loyalty to the Crown, because bishops and archbishops owed their allegiance directly to the Crown and not to a particular religious order. And he took even more radical measures to limit the new missionaries' management powers and create a greater role for Crown officials in the missions.

In order to prevent the new missionaries from gaining too much power in their respective missions, Aranda limited the new priests' responsibilities to spiritual matters.[7] Unlike under Jesuit management, when the missionaries oversaw all aspects of mission life, their replacements did not exercise power over temporal affairs. Instead, Aranda inserted the state by awarding this role to government appointees. In the name of the king, an interim gobernador would oversee all the missions in a particular province.

In addition to these high-level managers, Aranda recommended naming Spaniards to develop and promote trade in the each of the missions.[8] In essence, Aranda mandated the separation of church and state in the missions, with civil authorities gaining the upper hand. Going forward, priests would deal only with religious affairs, while government officials would oversee political and economic affairs. By bringing government officials to live in and manage the missions, the Crown thus sought to insert itself in mission operations.[9]

In addition to creating a larger role for Crown officials, Aranda's instructions also reflected changing ideas about Indians and missions. By the mid-eighteenth century, many in the Spanish Empire had become convinced that new and different efforts needed to be made to integrate and acculturate Indians into colonial society. In their opinion, missions had not yielded the desired results. Native peoples had resided in missions for decades and yet the missionaries still claimed that Indians required their tutelage and protection. The missions had always been envisioned as a temporary institution to acculturate Indians and mold them into loyal subjects. Given that the missions had not transformed the Indians into productive, acculturated members of the Spanish empire, reformers deemed the prevailing mission model a failure.

In contrast to the Habsburgs, who advocated separating and protecting Indians from colonial society, Bourbon reformers promoted what David Weber calls a "new method of spiritual government" that advocated the breaking down of barriers between mission Indians and non-Indians.[10] Such reformers believed that given the opportunity and the right incentives—something they believed did not exist in the Jesuit missions—Indians would choose to become productive members of colonial society.

In his *Dictamen fiscal* justifying the expulsion of the Jesuits from Spain, Pedro Rodríguez Campomanes claimed that the Jesuits and their model of managing the missions held back the Guaraní. Rather than trying to help the Indians develop into independent and productive individuals, he argued, the Jesuits cosseted the Indians and prevented their advancement. He pointed to Jesuit discourse as evidence that the missionaries believed the Indians incapable of advancing on their own: "The missionaries frequently cause injury by calling the Indians, with a type of insulting remark, castrated animals (*capones* or *capados*), alluding to the scanty beards that they always have. With these injurious words, the Guaraní know well who is the master and who is the servant."[11] Campomanes believed such racism turned the Indians into virtual slaves and reinforced the Jesuits' desire to oversee all aspects of the missions. In contrast, he praised other missionaries who allowed Indians to freely trade the goods that they produced and did not assume control over everything.[12]

Campomanes's assertions reflected the growing belief that Indians were capable individuals who could become loyal, productive subjects through exposure to trade and the market economy. Such reformers envisioned commerce as a tool of equal or greater importance than conversion for assimilating Indians into colonial society. Proponents of such ideas believed that self-interest motivated all individuals, including Indians. Based on this line of reasoning, Indians should have the ability to own, dispose of, and accumulate property. Under such conditions, Indians would realize the benefits of producing goods, trading, and accumulating property and as a result would become productive members of society.[13]

This new approach fit with other ideas of enlightened reform that circulated in the Spanish Empire. Campomanes and others promoted the modernization of property to stimulate trade and revitalize the economy. They believed that entail privileges and collective property ownership stifled production; in contrast, private ownership stimulated production and thus increased both trade and revenues. Such ideas, along with individual liberty and equality, played a key role in postindependence liberalism.[14] Mariano Moreno, an important independence figure in the Río de la Plata region and the secretary of the first junta that replaced the viceroy, argued that all men had four natural rights—liberty, equality, property, and security.[15]

The desire to develop agriculture and trade throughout Spanish America also influenced the mission reforms. For several decades, intellectuals and statesmen had criticized Spain's failure to develop America's agricultural potential. After spending ten years in South America, Jorge Juan and Antonio de Ulloa argued in a secret report to the king dated 1749 that any other nation would have taken steps to exploit the region's agricultural potential.[16] The two thought that trade would release such potential. In 1765, a junta assigned to review Spain's commerce with its colonies and other nations also claimed that trade "[is] the foundation of a state's well-being in the development of its agriculture and crafts, the real way to abundance, independence, and population growth."[17] To such reformers, the Jesuits' focus on religion did not fully develop the mission economy, especially not for the benefit of the Indians or the Crown.

Aranda reflected this shift to developing trade and agriculture by recommending the placement of Spaniards in the missions. He charged these
individuals with both removing obstacles to trade and finding ways to
facilitate trade. In such efforts, they were to take into account the particular conditions and circumstances of each mission.[18] Aranda issued only
limited instructions; he left it for officials on the ground to interpret and
expand upon his ideas.

Francisco Bucareli y Ursúa, governor of Río de la Plata, expelled the
Jesuits from the Guaraní missions and reinforced and built upon Aranda's
reforms with his own instructions.[19] At the beginning of April 1768—ten
months after having expelled the Jesuits from the major cities—Governor
Bucareli was finally ready to remove the Jesuits from the Guaraní missions.[20] He complained to Aranda that identifying priests to replace the
Jesuits caused much of the delay; he could not find sixty secular priests
who spoke Guaraní and were willing to go to the missions. Hence he
turned to Franciscan, Dominican, and Mercedarian priests. He divided
the missionary posts among these three orders to prevent any one order
from gaining too much power, and he configured the geographic location
of their assignments so as to hinder communications among members of
any particular order.[21]

Bucareli also decided that a single gobernador could not effectively
oversee all thirty missions. Thus, he named a general administrator in
Buenos Aires to oversee the trade of mission-produced goods and two
interim gobernadores to oversee the rest of the missions' affairs.[22] In 1769,
Bucareli modified the structure to a single gobernador in Candelaria assisted by three lieutenant gobernadors, each of whom was in charge of one
of the three other departments—the six missions (San Miguel, San Nicolás, San Juan Bautista, San Lorenzo, San Luis, and San Ángel) of the San
Miguel department, the five missions (Santiago, San Ignacio Guazú, Santa
María de Fe, Santa Rosa, and San Cosme) of the Santiago department,
and the four missions (Yapeyú, La Cruz, Santo Tomé, and San Borja) of
the Yapeyú department. In 1774, Bucareli's successor further revised the
mission structure by adding another lieutenant gobernador to oversee the
seven missions of the Concepción department (Concepción, San Xavier,
Santa María la Mayor, San José, Apóstoles, Santos Mártires, and San Carlos). The department of Candelaria consisted of Candelaria, Santa Ana,
Loreto, San Ignacio Miní, Corpus Christi, Itapúa, Trinidad, and Jesús.[23]

Bucareli issued several sets of detailed directions for further reforming the Guaraní missions. These reforms fell in line with and advanced
Aranda's goals and ideas. In his original instructions of 1768, the ad-
ditions of 1771, and his orders about commerce dated 1771, Bucareli

not only articulated revised priorities for the missions but also provided specific guidelines for how to achieve the new goals.

In accordance with Aranda's instructions, Bucareli's instructions asserted the two principal objectives of the Guaraní missions to be the teaching of the Catholic faith to the Guaraní and "providing these Indians those temporal benefits and conveniences that are acquired through civility, culture, and commerce."[24] The latter objective marked a revision of the missions' priorities. In contrast to the Jesuit period, Bucareli officially elevated temporal concerns onto an equal footing with spiritual matters. Although his instructions discussed temporal concerns after spiritual concerns, neither was subordinate to the other. Rather, the strict separation of religious and temporal affairs indicated that both were equal priorities.[25]

In his initial instructions, Bucareli spent less than one paragraph describing the first objective. He ordered the Indians to treat their priest with veneration commensurate with his character and devotion. He concluded the paragraph with the reminder that "these priests should not involve themselves in other matters than their ministry given that they have no other occupation than that concerning the spiritual good of the [Indians'] souls."[26] Bucareli dedicated the rest of his initial instructions to guiding mission administrators "in all that I judge conducive to the government and direction of said pueblos."[27] Given that the priests no longer oversaw the temporal administration of the missions, he issued detailed instructions for directing the mission economy and the governing structure.

Trade gained even more importance after Bucareli issued a document titled "Orders for Regulating Commerce between Spaniards and the Missions" in January 1770. This document included three sections with a total of twenty-seven chapters, providing explicit instructions regarding the mission economy and trade.[28] In this document, Bucareli specified that a general administrator reside in Buenos Aires to conduct trade on behalf of the thirty missions and oversee their economic affairs.[29] In addition, he confirmed that a Spanish administrator should reside in each mission to oversee all nonreligious matters and emphasized that he should show special dedication to economic affairs.[30]

Bucareli began "Orders for Regulating Commerce between Spaniards and the Missions" with the assertion that trade is necessary and that the missions cannot be completely self-sufficient. Expressing sentiments about the importance of trade that are remarkably similar to the 1765 conclusions of the junta assigned to review Spain's commerce with its colonies and other nations, he stated: "No matter how fertile and abundant, a province can never produce naturally all of the necessary amenities for life if it does not cultivate trade of its fruits with its neighboring provinces."[31] He went on to argue that owing to such trade, the Guaraní will become convinced of the benefits to be gained from engaging in the market economy: "They will not only become civilized and enjoy the benefits of rational society, they will also understand the advantages and utility of giving value to the fruits that nature produces for them."[32]

Bucareli's emphasis on the importance of trade not only fit in with Aranda's reforms, it also mirrored ideas circulating beyond the Spanish Empire. In his instructions about commerce, Bucareli asserted that "of all the means that can steer any republic to a complete happiness, none is more effective than the introduction of commerce, because [it] enriches the people and civilizes the nations."[33] Such phrasing is almost identical to that of the 1758 Portuguese plan for reforming the Pará and Maranhão missions of Brazil: "Among the ways in which any republic can be brought to complete happiness, none is more effective than the introduction of commerce, because it enriches the populace, civilizes nations, and consequently constitutes the power of monarchies."[34]

Likewise, decades later, Manuel Belgrano (the first general of Argentina and an important independence leader) strongly promoted commerce, together with agriculture: "Agriculture only flourishes with great consumption and this, how can this be done in an isolated country without commerce?" Elsewhere he wrote, "Yes, my son, the lack of freedom for the seller discourages him to such an extent from continuing in his labours, that before long he will surrender himself to the most embarrassing laziness."[35]

According to Bucareli, under the old model—where the Jesuits oversaw and managed all mission trade and the distribution of goods—the Indians did not benefit from mission trade. He believed that the Jesuits instead used the missions' fertile resources for their own comfort and grandeur, forcing the miserable Indians to suffer under their tyrannical rule. In his view, the expulsion had ended such exploitation and the Indians would now become the primary beneficiaries of mission trade.[36] Furthermore, he gave Indian leaders a greater role in managing their missions—a topic discussed in more detail in Chapter 7.

Bucareli argued that incorporating the Guaraní into the world outside of the missions would advance the Indians in terms of civilization, culture, and commerce more than isolating them would. One means for achieving this was teaching the Guaraní Spanish: by learning Spanish, the Indians could better communicate with Spaniards, better understand Spanish ways of doing things, and become more civilized.[37] He also promoted interactions between the Guaraní and the world outside the missions. The Indians could directly trade with outsiders by selling the fruits of their labor and buying goods, with the caveat that the Spanish administrator residing in the mission would make sure that the terms of trade were fair.[38]

In order to further facilitate the introduction of the Spanish language and culture and to stimulate trade, Bucareli ordered that meritorious Spaniards—good Christians and model citizens—reside in the missions. This policy was intended to provide the Indians with solid examples of how to work the land and pursue lawful and virtuous means for temporal advancement. He hoped that ultimately this would "extinguish the abhorrent separation that has until now been maintained between the Indians and the whites."[39]

Bucareli believed that as a result of these reforms, the Indians' hard work combined with the land's fertility would make the missions prosperous, even opulent.[40] More trade would increase mission revenues, and since the Guaraní owned all mission property, they would be the ultimate beneficiaries. But the missions never achieved his lofty goals of prosperity and opulence. The new management structure that separated religious from temporal affairs proved too unwieldy and expensive. Intolerable financial shortfalls resulted from at least three factors related to the separation of religious and secular management—the loss of cohesion among managers, the end of an unofficial subsidy from a single religious order, and skyrocketing overhead expenses.

LACK OF UNITY

Before these reforms, management by one single religious order guaranteed unity. A Jesuit took a vow of obedience that meant he had to obey orders even if he did not agree with them. He could protest to higher levels of the order, but ultimately he had to obey directives. This sense of discipline and obedience generally promoted consistent policies throughout the thirty missions, a unified vision, and efforts to work together across missions.

Regular *visitas* (audits) by higher Jesuit officials were meant to check any disobedience, errant behavior, or abuse. Regardless of the cause of such shortcomings, oversight by upper levels of Jesuit management worked to resolve them. According to José Cardiel, the head of the province (the provincial) visited all of the missions twice during his three-year term, and during his visit, he inspected the mission's operations and account records. In addition, the head of the missions (the superior) visited all of the missions every six months, staying at least four days in each mission.[41]

After the Jesuit expulsion, inspection by upper management did not have the same effect; the gobernador and lieutenant gobernadors oversaw groups of missions, but they could not guarantee the same degree of obedience as among the Jesuit order. The lack of discipline and unity among the numerous Spanish priests and officials led to administrative chaos and inefficiency. Instead of the members of one religious order working together to manage the missions, post-Jesuit reforms mandated the naming of a number of individuals with differing loyalties and undefined and overlapping powers. Priests from three different orders oversaw religious affairs, Spanish administrators residing in each mission oversaw political and economic issues, a gobernador and lieutenant gobernador oversaw the political affairs of mission departments, and a general administrator managed economic affairs.[42] Such a governing structure did not function smoothly.

Mission officials lacked the discipline and obedience demanded by a single religious order. Conflict existed between all levels of mission bureaucracy—between the general administrator and the gobernador, between the gobernador and lieutenant gobernadors, and between administrators and priests. The Guaraní were also involved in such conflict. This discord was due to three factors: ill-defined and overlapping responsibilities, personal disagreements, and different opinions about what was best for the missions. The resulting conflicts were often drawn out as each party provided a large amount of supporting evidence in the hope that the problem would be resolved in its favor. Higher levels in the bureaucracy had to gather evidence and evaluate the attacks, counterattacks, and claims of innocence. Sorting all of this material was time-consuming, chaos often ensued, and resolution took a long time.

At the highest level, the gobernador and the general administrator frequently clashed. Formally, the general administrator's duties were limited to economic and trade matters, while the gobernador oversaw all other nonreligious matters. In practice, such a clear division of responsibilities and authority did not work well. Complaints about the general administrator's involvement in matters beyond his realm of responsibility multiplied until they reached the ears of the king. In response, the king issued a royal decree in 1778 that expressly prohibited the general administrator from involving himself in issues relating to the governing of the missions. Instead, the king restated that the general administrator needed only to attend to the goods that he received from the missions.[43] Despite these regulations and the official separation of duties, conflicts between the general administrator and gobernador still arose. After visiting the missions in the 1780s, Félix de Azara, a member of the Spanish delegation charged with determining the border between Spanish and Portuguese territory in

South America who lived in and explored the Río de la Plata region from 1781 to 1801, reported: "The [general administrator] proposes people for the position of administrator to the viceroy, and this [general administrator] has more credit in the missions than anyone else. As a result, this has incited disputes with the gobernador since the beginning."[44]

The differing priorities of the administrators involved in secular affairs and the priests involved in religious affairs also created conflict. Almost a year after the departure of the Jesuits, Francisco Bruno de Zavala, gobernador of the missions, complained: "Those Religious annoy me with frivolous pretexts, and in each mission I have new difficulties. [The priests] want to make convents, monasteries, cloisters, and cells in the principal buildings of the mission where the storage faculties and workshops are."[45] Prior to the Jesuit expulsion, these central buildings had served both secular and religious functions. As this example highlights, dividing secular and religious matters was not straightforward: the Jesuits had incorporated Catholic ritual into almost every aspect of mission life.[46]

This conflict led to a power struggle between administrators and priests that the Guaraní exploited for their own benefit.[47] Zavala highlighted such a power struggle in the letter referred to above: "It is certain they [the priests] do not like the authority of the gobernadors and that they want to lessen or extinguish it. And even though they saw the severe punishment of the Jesuits, they want to be as despotic as [the Jesuits]."[48] Such division created an opening for the Guaraní; when they did not like the instructions of one party, they could appeal to the other. In the assessment of lieutenant gobernador Gonzalo de Doblas: "The Indians, accustomed to obeying only their priests, looked with indifference at first, at whatever the administrators suggested to them, and as such, [they] did nothing without consulting the priest first. From these beginnings, great discord originated between the priests and administrators."[49] In other instances, the Guaraní sided with their administrator against their priest.[50]

Personality clashes and different management styles often aggravated such conflict between individuals. Various disputes involving gobernador Zavala provide a prime example. During his long tenure (1769–1777, 1784–1800), Zavala quarreled with numerous individuals from all levels of mission management—General Administrator Juan Ángel de Lazcano, at least three different lieutenant gobernadors, and various mission priests.[51] Such conflicts hindered smooth operations. During the seven-year interval between 1777 and 1784, Zavala was removed from his appointment as gobernador owing to investigations into his management.[52] Such disputes frequently required intervention from the highest levels of government. Lieutenant gobernador Juan Valiente implored the governor of Río de la Plata, Juan José de Vértiz, for assistance before departing for Spain. Valiente requested that the governor "deign to favor me with retirement because without your shelter, there is no doubt that this gobernador [Zavala] will take vengeance against me."[53] Such quarrels prevented coordination between the missions as well as unified policies.

Differences in opinion about what was in the best interest of the missions further disrupted coordination and unity of purpose. Even higher management disagreed about the best policies for the missions. Governor Bucareli wanted the Guaraní to take a stronger role in managing the missions. He believed that "under their despotic reign, the Jesuits' tyranny had made the Guaraní miserable" and that the Indians had recovered their liberty with the expulsion.[54] With proper instruction and example, Bucareli believed, the Indians were capable of learning and eventually would not need direction. For example, Spaniards residing in the missions as role models would inspire the Indians; their residence would "facilitate better reciprocal trade, and by this means and that of communication, the desired civility of these people [the Guaraní] will be achieved."[55] In contrast, lieutenant gobernador Valiente believed the Guaraní to be incompetent and in need of strict discipline. Less than a decade after Bucareli's instructions, Valiente blamed him for destroying the missions: "Francisco de Bucareli has been the principal instrument for [the missions'] total decadence, having published in all of them that [the Indians] were now free and that everything was theirs, that they could do whatever they wanted with all of the goods that they possessed, that they were absolute owners." Valiente continued: "In order that [the missions] do not fall apart completely, or can partially recuperate, it is necessary for your honor and for the good of this republic and royal service to his Majesty that the old method and government that these missions formerly had be reinstated."[56] Such diametrically opposed opinions about treatment of the Guaraní translated into drastically different management practices.

Whatever the cause, clashes between officials not only led to bureaucratic inefficiency but also translated into economic inefficiency. When conflict arose, officials were less likely to work together or act in a unified manner for the benefit of the missions. In turn, the missions incurred more expenses as each official or group of officials pursued a different agenda. Furthermore, the lack of unified policies hindered efforts to streamline operations or enact reforms to increase economic efficiency. And resolving disputes between officials channeled time and resources away from more productive uses as the officials' superiors investigated and judged the disputes instead of trying to find ways to advance the missions. As Azara concluded, the missions "were reduced to the ultimate

misery and incredible disorder because, in addition [to the conflict between the general administrator, gobernador, and administrators], the
priests were in conflict with the administrators, and everything was divided and in a chaos of confusion."[57]

END OF SUBSIDY

The missions lost a valuable indirect and informal subsidy with the restructuring of the missions. Having a single religious order manage the
missions meant that Jesuits provided a subsidy that increased mission
revenues and decreased mission expenses. The Jesuit order's network facilitated trade, negotiated favorable prices, and successfully lobbied the
Crown for special privileges and concessions. While the impact of this
indirect and informal subsidy cannot be quantified, it was significant.

After the expulsion, revenues declined and expenses increased because the missions no longer had access to the Jesuit order's extensive
trade network. The accounting records for the missions' two trading offices in Buenos Aires and Santa Fe reveal relationships with four other
Jesuit oficios in South America—Córdoba, Salta, Potosí, and Santiago
de Chile. These oficios were commercial offices with full-time personnel
dedicated to business transactions. The missions used this larger network
to purchase and sell goods at better rates. The oficios not only facilitated
trade but also provided valuable information about prices and markets
in their respective regions. They also traded with twelve Jesuit colleges
in modern-day Argentina, Chile, Bolivia, and Paraguay.[58] Trading within
this Jesuit network led to mutually beneficial prices, market information,
and access to markets. The expulsion ended this extended network. Furthermore, centralized mission trade shrank from the two oficios to one
general administration in Buenos Aires.[59]

The missions also experienced financial losses indirectly; the end of
the larger Jesuit network translated into fewer privileges and, as a result,
greater inefficiency and expense. The Jesuit order served as a powerful
and effective lobbyist on behalf of the Guaraní and their missions. The
Jesuit province of Paraguay sent a procurador to Spain and Rome approximately every seven years or as needed. The procurador lobbied on
behalf of the missions and the province—informing the Jesuit hierarchy
and Spanish leaders about conditions and the needs of the province, procuring missionaries, and obtaining supplies. These lobbying trips were
expensive—Procurador Juan Joseph Rico spent tens of thousands of pesos during his European trip in the early 1740s.[60] In Seville and Madrid,
the procurador reported to a *procurador general*, who was responsible

for all of the Jesuit provinces in the Americas and lobbied on their behalf before the general of the Jesuit order. The general, in turn, had privileged access to the Spanish court and papacy.[61] As described in earlier chapters, the Jesuits effectively utilized this network to lobby for special privileges on behalf of the Guaraní missions.

While numerous officials, mission employees, and observers wrote extensive reports throughout the postexpulsion period about mission conditions and offered ideas for improvements, Spanish authorities implemented relatively few of these suggestions. This failure can be explained in part by the lack of an effective lobbying structure like that under the Jesuits. Furthermore, Spanish authorities did not, and could not, dedicate as much time and effort to resolving the missions' problems as Jesuit leaders. Crown officials oversaw an entire province or viceroyalty, with many different institutions and concerns. The Guaraní missions frequently fell low on their list of priorities. From 1784 to 1799, viceroys barely mentioned the Guaraní missions or left them out completely in the final reports about their time in office (*memorias*).[62] Without the extensive Jesuit network, the missions did not have effective lobbyists to catch the attention of important officials and obtain special privileges and concessions.

OVERHEAD EXPENSES

Compliance with Aranda's orders to separate religious and secular affairs inherently generated huge overhead expenses that the missions found insurmountable. Hiring secular employees who needed salaries, in addition to maintaining priests in each of the missions, caused overhead costs to spiral out of control. Between 1767 and 1773, the missions' salary expenses jumped from 13,999 to over 32,600 pesos—an increase of 133 percent (see Table 4). In calculating the financial impact, two main factors need to be considered—the number of employees and their salaries.

Before the expulsion, the Jesuits were responsible for all aspects of the missions. A superior who resided in Mission Candelaria oversaw the spiritual and temporal matters for all of the thirty missions; procuradores in Buenos Aires and Santa Fe managed mission trade; and two Jesuits in each mission (the priest and the priest's companion) directed both spiritual and temporal affairs. In addition, other Jesuits specialized in particular skills or trades such as medicine, painting, architecture, or music.[63] Many of the Jesuits who focused on such temporal matters were lay brothers or coadjutors.[64]

At the time of the expulsion, royal officials removed seventy-eight Jesuits from the Guaraní missions. In addition to the thirty priests and

TABLE 4. *Administrative expenses of the thirty missions, 1767 and 1773*

Position	Jesuit administration 1767			Government-appointed administration 1773		
	Salary	Quantity	Expense	Salary	Quantity	Expense
Priest	467	30	13,999	300	30	9,000
Priest's companion	—	30	—	250	31	7,750
Gobernador	—	1	—	1,200	1	1,200
Lieutenant gobernador	—	1	—	400–700	3	1,600
Assistant	—	1	—	100	4	400
Teacher				150–300	6	1,550
Surgeon/apothecary	—	2	—	350	2	700
Blacksmith				350	1	350
Carpenter				650	1	650
Undefined capacity		13				
Subtotal		78	13,999		79	23,200
Increase, 1767–1773:						66%
Administrators at the thirty individual missions				300–400p.	31	9,400
Total			13,999			32,600
Total increase in administrative costs, 1767–1773:						133%

SOURCE: Cardiel, "Breve relación," 102; list of Jesuits expelled from the Guaraní missions, Brabo, *Colección de documentos relativos a la expulsión de los jesuitas*, 212–22; "Estado general de los pueblos," n.d., AGN, IX 18-7-6.

their thirty companions, officials encountered an additional eighteen Jesuits in the missions. Three of these oversaw the affairs of all of the thirty missions—the provincial, superior, and secretary; two attended to the Indians' health—one surgeon and one apothecary; eight oversaw temporal affairs—one coadjutor and seven laymen; and five others had unspecified roles.[65] These seventy-eight Jesuits did not receive a salary for their services but instead shared the stipend paid by the Crown regardless of the size of the Indian population or any other factor. The Crown paid the Jesuits 466 pesos and 5 reales per mission, which totaled 13,999 pesos.[66]

According to a 1773 report, salary expenses almost tripled from the Jesuit period to at least 32,600 pesos.[67] The true cost of salary expenses was even more: this figure did not include the general administrator's commission and other expenditures. Some employees, such as those working in the transportation of mission goods, only appeared deep in mission account records; for example, Yapeyú paid 315 pesos to Jacinto Gonzalez—the overseer of that mission's boats—in September 1773.[68] Even without these omitted salaries, the 32,600 pesos in salary expenses was a huge outlay and a marked increase of 18,601 pesos compared to the Jesuit period. The shocking increase in salary expenses was generally not due to corruption on the part of mission employees; rather, salary expenditures ballooned because of the need to pay salaries rather than living stipends to mission employees. For the most part, such salaries were largely legitimate and approximated market wages.

Aranda's separation between religious and nonreligious management at the individual mission level led to the hiring of a substantial number of new officials. The missions hired thirty-one administrators (Yapeyú hired an additional manager to oversee its cattle operations) to manage non-religious affairs, and all but one earned 300 pesos per year. These thirty-one administrators cost the missions 9,400 pesos per year as of 1773 and accounted for just over 50 percent of the salary increase between 1767 and 1773.

Other than administrators, no surge in the number of mission employees occurred. Excluding these thirty-one individuals, the number remained virtually the same between 1767 and 1773: at the time of the expulsion royal officials found seventy-eight Jesuits in the missions, while in 1773 the mission complex employed seventy-nine individuals (plus the thirty-one administrators at the individual-mission level). These seventy-nine included the thirty priests and their thirty-one companions— only one more than during the Jesuit period—together with another eighteen people fulfilling similar occupations as during the Jesuit period: eight (the gobernador, three lieutenant gobernadors, and four assistants) oversaw the affairs of all thirty missions; two (surgeons) attended to the Indians' health; two (a blacksmith and a carpenter) attended to the missions' physical infrastructure; and, six (teachers) oversaw the Indians' mental development. Even though the number of employees (excluding the administrators assigned to each mission) was essentially the same, salary costs more than doubled—from 13,999 pesos to 23,200 pesos—because the new employees earned market wages.

A small portion of the increase went to the new priests and their companions. While the Jesuits shared the 466 pesos 5 reales stipend awarded to each mission, their replacements received individual stipends. In 1773, the Franciscan, Dominican, and Mercedarian priests received 300 pesos and their companions 250 pesos. In sum, the stipend expense increased moderately, to an average of 550 pesos per mission, which accounted for 2,751 pesos, or 15 percent, of the 18,601-peso increase in total salary expense. The higher stipend rate was not permanent; a royal decree on October 5, 1778, reduced both the priests' and their companions' stipends to 200 pesos per year—a total which summed to less than in the Jesuit period.[69]

A significantly greater portion of the higher salary expense went to paying the other eighteen people employed by the missions. These eighteen salaries summed to 6,450 pesos—all of which the Jesuits had previously covered with their stipend—and accounted for 35 percent of the total salary increase. Unlike during the Jesuit period, these employees did not live off the religious officials' stipends. Moreover, in contrast to religious officials, civilian employees could not receive only stipends to cover their expenses; they had to receive salaries, and such salaries had to reflect the requirements of the position and the employee's skills and experience. In 1773, salaries paid to mission employees ranged from 100 pesos for an assistant to 1,200 pesos for the gobernador.

Many people complained about the huge amount of money spent on salaries. In 1793, Juan Francisco Aguirre, a member of the commission mandated with defining the Spanish-Portuguese border, asserted that the missions paid too much in salaries and got too little in return: "One could not see the extraordinary consumption [of resources] suffered by the mission communities without feeling pain; between the administrators, school teachers, and their projects [*obras*], their maintenance rises to more than one thousand pesos without their utility reaching so much."[70]

A decade and a half earlier, the general administrator of the thirty missions, Juan Ángel de Lazcano, foresaw such a situation but attributed the employees' incompetence to their low salaries. In 1778, Lazcano complained that an administrator's salary of 300 pesos was so low that potential employees of the necessary quality could not be found.[71] Without paying market wages, or close to market wages, the missions attracted mostly incapable or corrupt job candidates. In 1784, Viceroy Juan José de Vértiz y Salcedo confirmed that such a situation had occurred. In the report about his tenure as viceroy, Vértiz wrote at length about the incompetence of all those employed by the missions—upper management, administrators, and priests alike. Specifically, he said that the administrators "did not have any knowledge and suitability other than being scurrilous. . . . They receive three hundred pesos as administrator, and this can be acquired by anyone in Buenos Aires with very moderate work and without the difficulties of a sad life like in those destinations [the missions]."[72]

Some mission officials indicated what they thought were appropriate salaries for mission employees. In 1786, gobernador Zavala suggested that proficient administrators receive salaries of 400 pesos instead of the normal 300 pesos.[73] According to Zavala, "This increase of one hundred pesos yearly would serve as a reward and bonus for their work and performance."[74] Lieutenant gobernador Gonzalo de Doblas's 1785 plan to reform the missions presented a detailed budget for mission salaries. He recommended that Spanish employees receive commissions rather than fixed salaries, and he argued that mission Guaraní should receive wages for their work. Based on each of the thirty missions generating revenues of 10,000 pesos (300,000 pesos in total), Doblas estimated that commission-based salary expenses for Spanish employees should total 55,500 pesos—30,000 pesos for administrators and their assistants, 9,000 pesos for the priests, 7,500 pesos for the gobernador and lieutenant gobernadors, and 9,000 pesos distributed among other employees (a lettered lieutenant, assistant, treasurer, protector, and clerk). According to Doblas, salaries for Guaraní officials should total another 37,500 pesos—6,000 pesos for mayordomos, 6,000 pesos for corregidors, 4,500 pesos for military officials, and 21,000 pesos shared among the members of the cabildo. Doblas's combined salary expenses for Spanish employees and Guaraní officials totaled more than 93,000 pesos. His estimate for the salary expense of Spanish employees alone—55,500 pesos—was greater than the mission complex's total 1773 salary outlay.[75]

Although most mission employees received salaries that were below the going rate, at least one official received an excessively high salary: in addition to the fixed salaries of 32,600 pesos in 1773, the missions had to pay the general administrator a commission on all mission trade. According to Bucareli's instructions, the missions paid the general administrator 8 percent of gross revenue from the sale of mission goods and 2 percent of monies paid for purchases on behalf of the missions.[76] In 1773, the general administrator's 8 percent commission on mission sales alone reached approximately 6,500 pesos.[77] As will be discussed in Chapter 8, the general administrator subsequently earned a significantly higher salary when Mission Yapeyú began selling large amounts of cattle hides.

While a salary expense of over 32,600 pesos was high, the missions paid even more in salaries in later years. Over time, the missions hired additional employees: more people to work in administration and management as well as skilled employees to fill specialized needs. By 1776, salary costs had increased by another 10,271 pesos, to a total of 42,871 pesos, which resulted from the hiring of another lieutenant gobernador to oversee the seven missions of the Concepción department, an additional surgeon, three more teachers, and—as the Jesuits had done—managers to oversee the missions' estancias.[78]

Over time, most if not all of the missions hired a teacher (*maestro de primeras letras*). Originally, Bucareli's instructions had placed the responsibility for education in the hands of the priests and their companions.[79] In 1769, however, gobernador Zavala decided that the priest and companion assigned to Mission Yapeyú could not educate the large number of Guaraní students, and therefore a teacher needed to be hired.[80] The same occurred in other missions as officials assessed the priest and companion as being unable or unwilling to effectively teach the Guaraní.

By the mid-1780s, at least sixteen missions had secular teachers.[81] These new hires diminished the role of the priests and generated additional salary expense for the missions.

Salary expense also increased owing to raises given to mission employees. Numerous requests for salary increases, from various administrators and upper management, can be found in mission records, and some were granted. For example, in 1788 the administrator of Mission Apóstoles, Pablo Tompson, threatened to resign if he did not receive a raise. Tompson's request was approved, and he subsequently received a salary of 400 pesos per year.[82] Other administrators also had their salaries increased to 400 pesos per year.[83] In 1786, lieutenant gobernador Doblas initiated a dispute about his salary. Based on a promise from Viceroy Vértiz, Doblas asked for a yearly salary of 800 pesos for managing the seven Concepción missions rather than the 600-peso salary of his predecessor.[84] Doblas submitted numerous documents in support of his request, including supporting documentation from Guaraní leaders, but even after two years Crown officials still had not made a decision in his case.[85]

Paying employees cost the missions a great deal of money, but the missions also sold a lot of goods to generate income. Even though mission sales revenues remained relatively high through the mid-1780s, however, they still could not cover mission expenses.

CENTRALIZED TRADE

For approximately two decades after the Jesuit expulsion, mission trade generated tens of thousands of pesos in revenue. During this period, mission trade was centralized and coordinated under the general administrator in Buenos Aires. This focus began soon after the Jesuit expulsion. Bucareli's initial instructions recommended that the administrators send any goods not consumed within a mission to Buenos Aires or Santa Fe, where "without a doubt the trade in such goods would be most useful and profitable."[86] Subsequently, he specified that the general administrator in Buenos Aires conduct all mission trade.[87] Charles III agreed with Bucareli's instructions to centralize mission trade under the general administrator in Buenos Aires; on October 10, 1778, the king issued a royal decree declaring that "it is indispensable, for achieving this end [payments of taxes and salaries] and for supplying [the missions] with necessities that they need, that they remit the goods that they produce to the general administration in Buenos Aires."[88]

The following discussion of mission sales is based primarily on *entrada y venta* accounting books. In general, every two years the general administrator compiled three separate account books—entrada y venta, *cuenta corriente*, and *relación jurada*. He submitted these summary accounts of the mission economy to the Tribunal Mayor de Cuentas, to which treasury departments submitted account records and from which summaries were sent to Spain. The entrada y venta book was separated into sections for each of the thirty missions and contained entry (*entrada*) information—a list of all the items sent to the general administration for sale, their quantity, any shrinkage or damage, expenditures to bring the goods to market (such as transportation costs), and sometimes additional information (such as the quality of the good and the transaction date). The entrada y venta book also contained exit (*venta*) information about each sales transaction—the quantity of a good sold, its price per unit, the name of the purchaser, and sometimes other information (such as the quality of the good and the transaction date). Expenditures to bring the goods to market were deducted from total sales revenue to arrive at net sales revenue, but this figure is highly inaccurate because the calculation did not include expenses incurred to produce the goods. The entrada y venta books also did not include goods produced by the missions and sold through other channels. Individual Guaraní and the missions sometimes traded goods with merchants and/or people in the region, especially the northwestern missions that were closest to Asunción and Corrientes. Such outside sales were small compared to the centralized trade through the general administration. The sales revenue figures also did not include non-sales sources of revenue such as the collection of debt from outside parties. Despite such shortcomings, the entrada y venta books provide very detailed information about the thirty missions' revenues and expenditures over thirty-five of the thirty-seven years between 1770 and 1806.[89]

As with all historical information, weaknesses in the data need to be considered. The record keeper could intentionally or unintentionally omit, change, or distort the numbers. The massive paper trail of receipts, the three interlocking account books, and multiple levels of review limited some of these problems, but the complexity could also hide such distortions. Given these shortcomings, the numbers should be considered ballpark figures. Trends—which imply that something is improving, deteriorating, or staying the same—should be given the most weight.

At first glance, mission revenues seem to have boomed between 1772 and 1784 (see Table 5). Between 1770 and 1788, the general administration generated an average of 105,000 pesos per year in sales revenue on behalf of the thirty missions. In contrast, between 1731 and 1745, the Jesuit-managed oficios in Santa Fe and Buenos Aires generated a yearly average of 69,000 pesos in sales revenue. These figures are deceptive, however: almost half of the missions' sales revenue during the post-Jesuit

TABLE 5. *Yearly sales revenue (in pesos), 1731–1806*

Year	Total sales revenue of thirty missions	Total revenue, Yapeyú	Percentage of total	Total sales revenue of twenty-nine missions
1731	65,704	3,458	5	62,246
1732	65,704	3,458	5	62,246
1733	65,704	3,458	5	62,246
1734	65,704	3,458	5	62,246
1735	65,704	3,458	5	62,246
1736	66,759	3,954	6	62,805
1737	66,759	3,954	6	62,805
1738	91,613	2,969	3	88,644
1739	91,613	2,969	3	88,644
1740	70,709	3,299	5	67,410
1741	70,709	3,299	5	67,410
1742	70,709	3,299	5	67,410
1743	61,351	3,424	6	57,927
1744	61,351	3,424	6	57,927
1745	58,072	1,537	3	56,535
Average yearly revenue (1731–1745)	69,211	3,295	5	65,916
1768				
1769				
1770	62,039	3,522	6	58,517
1771	62,039	3,522	6	58,517
1772	81,659	6,706	8	74,953
1773	81,659	6,706	8	74,953
1774	51,817	7,870	15	43,948
1775	51,817	7,870	15	43,948
1776	109,252	55,806	51	53,446
1777	109,252	55,806	51	53,446
1778	88,463	38,091	43	50,373
1779	88,463	38,091	43	50,373
1780	98,730	30,497	31	68,233
1781	98,730	30,497	31	68,233
1782	222,947	149,294	67	73,653
1783	222,947	149,294	67	73,653
1784	222,947	149,294	67	73,653
1785	43,157	5,585	13	37,572
1786	43,157	5,585	13	37,572
1787	62,985	19,893	32	43,092
1788	62,985	19,893	32	43,092
Average yearly revenue (1770–1788)	105,177	50,891	48	56,907

(*continued*)

TABLE 5. *(continued)*

Year	Total sales revenue of thirty missions	Total revenue, Yapeyú	Percentage of total	Total sales revenue of twenty-nine missions
1789				
1790				
1791	15,948	6,199	39	9,749
1792	15,948	6,199	39	9,749
1793	27,650	3,697	13	23,954
1794	27,650	3,697	13	23,954
1795	7,551	4,043	54	3,508
1796	7,551	4,043	54	3,508
1797	5,597	2,888	52	2,709
1798	5,597	2,888	52	2,709
1799	16,547	2,552	15	13,996
1800	16,547	2,552	15	13,996
1801	29,945	6,782	23	23,163
1802	29,945	6,782	23	23,163
1803	16,230	9,347	58	6,883
1804	16,230	9,347	58	6,883
1805	8,320	5,093	61	3,228
1806	8,320	5,093	61	3,228
Average yearly revenue (1791–1806)	15,973	5,075	32	10,899

SOURCE: See Table 2 and Chapter 5, note 91.

period derived from Yapeyú's sale of cattle hides—an anomaly described in Chapter 8. After removing Yapeyú, average yearly sales revenue for the twenty-nine missions was actually smaller in the post-Jesuit period than during the Jesuit period.

Other than Yapeyú, all of the missions responded similarly to the pressure to send trade goods to the general administration. Of the twenty-nine missions, each contributed almost equally to the sales revenue generated at the general administration. Over the period from 1770 to 1806, all of the trade goods sent by a single mission generally accounted for 1–8 percent of the gross sales revenue. Only four times during the thirty-seven-year period did a single mission (other than Yapeyú) account for more than 25 percent of the gross sales revenue at the general administration.

Higher sales revenues between 1770 and 1788 as compared to later years resulted, in large part, from pressure by Juan Ángel de Lazcano (the third general administrator of the missions). He wanted the missions to conduct all of their trade through the general administration. Lazcano eloquently expressed his views on mission trade in a 1773 letter to Governor Vértiz. The stated purpose of his letter was to stop missions from independently trading with private individuals in order to obtain livestock rather than sending all of their trade goods to Buenos Aires: by "sending their tradable goods and commodities to this Administration, they [the missions] can purchase the same goods at a better price and sell their products at a higher price."[90]

The Guaraní spoke out about this pressure to send trade goods to the general administration and its negative consequences for them. In a 1776 report concerning the deterioration of their mission, the Guaraní cabildo and Spanish administrator of Mission Jesús described the problems that they experienced when much of the fruit of their labor was sent to the general administration in Buenos Aires:

[Our] labor produces little result [for us] because even though [our] toil yields a quantity of fruit each year, the outcome [for us] is minimal because it is necessary to send [trade goods] to the General Administration. The remaining [goods] need to be applied to the daily expenses and consumption of the mission and, as necessary, to help when various emergencies arise. There are no other assets that can be used, since what was acquired has been spent, and many times it is not enough. Not because less work has been done than before, but because, even though [our] labor has produced a considerable amount in a year, as we have said, we cannot conserve [it] on account of the obligation we have to contribute to—so many annual expenses that did not occur in the time of the Jesuits.[91]

In their letter, the cabildo members requested a change; they found the many new expenses incurred under the post-Jesuit administration to be excessive and complained that mission inhabitants received minimal compensation for their labor. Despite such complaints, the missions continued to send large quantities of trade goods to the general administration and sales levels remained high through the mid-1780s.

As discussed in Chapter 9, the missions could not continue to produce such quantities of trade goods. Additionally, the removal of Lazcano as general administrator contributed to a plummet in mission sales through the general administration. On January 7, 1785, the Buenos Aires office of the royal treasury (Junta Superior de Real Hacienda) temporarily removed Lazcano from office in order to resolve accounting issues related to his administration.[92] The investigation dragged on, and he never returned to his position as general administrator; his accounts remained unresolved at the time of his death in 1803.[93] With Lazcano discredited, the missions no longer felt as much pressure to send trade goods to the general administration.

In 1786, gobernador Zavala offered a clear explanation of why many of the missions had lost faith in the general administration. In a letter attached to Mission Concepción's summary accounting records, Zavala discussed the mission's accounts with the general administration.[94] Between

1779 and 1782, Concepción had sent 6,365 arrobas of yerba maté and 50 fanegas of beans to the general administration. Based on the average prices received by the general administration during this period, the yerba maté and beans should have generated approximately 11,143 pesos and 550 pesos, respectively. In addition, in 1784, Concepción provided supplies worth 493 pesos to Paraguayan soldiers and an advance of 600 pesos and a promissory note of 72 pesos to the mission priests. Zavala's estimated revenues for Concepción together with the mission's expenditures on behalf of the soldiers and priests amounted to 12,858 pesos. Zavala complained that the general administration did not compensate Concepción anywhere near that amount. The general administration had only sent six invoices amounting to 1,722 pesos—a small fraction of the total expenditures. Given that the general administrator had not reconciled Concepción's account with the general administration as of November 1786, Zavala asserted that this mission did not recognize its account with the general administration.[95]

Simply put, the general administration had difficulties meeting obligations because mission expenses exceeded revenues. During the period of peak revenues, between 1770 and 1788, the sales revenue of the twenty-nine missions excluding Yapeyú averaged almost 57,000 pesos per year. As discussed earlier, salary expenses as of 1776 amounted to over 47,000 pesos.[96] Additionally, the missions had to pay tribute of 1 peso for each Guaraní male between the ages of eighteen and fifty and 100 pesos in tithes per mission, for a total of 20,611 pesos per year.[97] Between salaries and taxes alone, the missions accrued expenses of at least 68,042 pesos—an amount which far surpassed the missions' average yearly revenue.

As a result of this shortfall, the missions did not meet all of their financial obligations. Complaints by mission employees about unpaid salaries abound in the archives. For example, in 1786 lieutenant gobernador Doblas complained that he had served four years and five months without any salary. Most of this time was during the period of the missions' highest sales revenues—Doblas began work on March 29, 1781. He said that he had received only a few supplements from the general administrator and the missions during this entire period and thus could not meet his daily subsistence needs or pay his debts.[98] Doblas was not the only employee to protest salary arrears; a number of administrators and teachers wrote letters of complaint about not receiving their salaries.[99] Officials and priests frequently were forced to rely on goods provided directly by the mission, since they did not receive cash payments of their salaries or stipends for long periods of time.

Salaries were not the only expense to go unpaid. The missions consistently failed to meet their tax obligations. Throughout the post-Jesuit period, the missions were in debt to the Crown for back taxes.[100] For only three of the fourteen years between 1772 and 1795 did they fully pay the taxes accrued during the year. After 1779, the general administrator did not pay any tax monies directly to the royal treasury. In 1781, 1783, and 1784, the missions made significant payments toward the taxes they had accrued over the years, but none of these payments was made in cash to the royal coffers; instead, the missions received tax credits for provisions supplied to militias, other government officials, and mission employees. In 1796, the viceroy commissioned an official investigation into the missions' accumulated tax arrears. He found that in 1772, the thirty missions owed the Crown 8,063 pesos; by the end of 1796, mission tax arrears had grown to 131,558 pesos. As this growing tax debt confirms, the missions were unable to cover their expenses.

CONCLUSION

While Crown officials believed mission reforms would benefit the Crown, the missions, and the Indians, such reforms actually undermined the very institution they sought to strengthen. By removing the Jesuits and giving the state a greater role in managing the missions, Charles III hoped to strengthen the Crown and expand his rule. Crown officials built on these reforms and expressed their belief that both the missions and the Indians would flourish under the new structure: trade and private property—essentially engagement in the market economy—would create prosperity for all and empower the Indians. The push for centralized trade did lead to high sales revenues, but expenses rose even more. The surge in salary expenditures was not due to corruption; salaries approximated market wages. The root problem was that the missions' communal structure could not support the market-based ideology of salaried officials and the focus on trade.

Under the Jesuits, outsourcing the management of the missions to a single religious order reduced costs and made the missions financially viable. In contrast, sharing management between government and religious officials created excessive costs and inefficiencies. By separating temporal and religious affairs, reformers created a whole new bureaucracy that bankrupted the missions. They replaced management by a single religious order with a combination of Spanish employees and priests from three different religious orders, thereby destroying unity, cohesion, and discipline. The ensuing conflicts were costly and prevented officials from working together to advance the missions. Doing away with management by a single religious order also ended the subsidy that the missions received from being a part of the Jesuit network. As a result, the missions lost both valuable trade connections and a useful lobbying apparatus. The extra level of bureaucracy added to the unmanageable burden of expenditures. While they could pay stipends to the priests and their companions to cover their expenses, the missions now had to pay salaries to all of the other employees as well. As a result, salary costs skyrocketed, and the missions could not generate enough income to cover all their expenses.

Even though revenues failed to cover expenses, the missions continued to survive with a significant number of Guaraní inhabitants for more than thirty years. Only in 1800 did Viceroy Gabriel de Avilés begin to dismantle the missions by distributing mission property and freeing the Indians from communal labor obligations. The following chapters seek to explain how the Guaraní shaped and responded to mission life during the intervening years.

CHAPTER 6

Should We Stay or Should We Go?

Less than five years after the Jesuit expulsion, six caciques from Mission San Juan Bautista informed the governor of Buenos Aires that "the poverty of this mission puts all of us in penury, the first, us caciques, and likewise the rest of the Indians, including children, married women, and widows. Harassed by misery, they flee."[1] In response, Gaspar de la Plaza, the lieutenant gobernador in charge of the six missions that included San Juan Bautista, investigated this and other claims. De la Plaza concluded, "The proposition *that harassed by misery, [Indians] flee and are lost* is for the most part false. Even though I do not doubt that [some Indians] are missing from their mission for some time, they do this because of their natural propensity and to satiate the ambulatory and flighty nature of their spirit and not because they lack clothing and necessities."[2] Several months later, fifteen caciques from San Juan Bautista—the initial six plus nine more—wrote another letter to Governor Vértiz reiterating their complaints. The caciques again emphasized flight as a major problem: "That which most hurts our spirit and heart is, señor Governor, to see that many [Indians] have taken to the countryside for shelter with the unbelieving Minuanes [*infieles minuanes*] only in order to liberate themselves from the severity of hunger."[3] While the caciques and de la Plaza vehemently disagreed about the reasons, both parties concurred that Guaraní inhabitants were leaving San Juan Bautista.

Demographic data confirm that during the decade or so after 1772, many Guaraní opted to leave their mission. Some may have left owing to caprice, but most left in an effort to improve their quality of life. By this time, the financial difficulties associated with the separation of religious affairs from economic and political affairs had reached the mission level. Mounting economic pressures threatened the mission system and burdened the Indian inhabitants. Increasingly indebted, the mission system passed the burgeoning salary and overhead expenses to individual missions. In order to fulfill their financial obligations, the missions clearly needed to generate more revenues. Since the Guaraní inhabitants were both the labor force that produced mission goods and one of the major recipients of mission production, they bore the brunt of this pressure. The effort to produce more trade goods not only meant more work for the Indians, but the diversion of mission goods to pay debts and expenses came at the cost of distributing material goods to the Indians. In addition to worsening conditions inside the missions, improving conditions outside the missions spurred Indians to leave.

Many Indians found life outside of the missions an attractive alternative. Just like the missions, the entire Río de la Plata region underwent drastic changes in the late eighteenth century. While conditions worsened in the missions, the expanding Río de la Plata economy created openings elsewhere for mission Guaraní with more freedom and better remuneration. As a result, large numbers of Indians fled the missions and the mission population fell. Between 1772 and 1783, the Guaraní mission population declined by almost 25,000, from almost 81,000 Indians to just over 56,000 (see Table 6). This loss, though significant, amounted to a decline of just over 30 percent in eleven years, which cannot be considered precipitous. Many Guaraní remained in the missions, and all Native American populations experienced high mortality rates as the result of European diseases. Over the following decade, the decline in the mission population slowed to less than 5,000 Indians, and by the last decade of the eighteenth century, mortality rates in the missions surpassed flight rates. Instead of a rapid collapse, the missions thus experienced a gradual decline.

By reducing the missions' labor supply, Guaraní absences struck at the communal structure that was the foundation of the missions. The Guaraní worked in their mission's fields, pasturelands, orchards, and workshops collectively. The items that they produced were consumed within the mission and sold to generate revenue for purchases and other expenses. As described in Chapter 3, private production for individual consumption existed, but a mission's condition and its future depended on collective projects. The returns funded all operational costs, religious activities, educational programs, festivities, infrastructure investment, and emergency reserves. Legally, the Guaraní as a collective unit had ownership rights over the fruits of communal projects. The Guaraní—not the Crown or the church—owned all the mission's assets, not just the items in the mission storeroom. This communal structure was the mission's distinguishing characteristic; without it, a mission would no longer have been a mission but a town with Indian inhabitants.

While many Guaraní fled the missions, others opted to stay. These Indians found ways of making mission life tolerable. Exploitation of

TABLE 6. Post-Jesuit mission population

Mission	Total population					Average percentage change per year					Total percentage change
	1768	1772	1783	1793	1801	1768–1772	1772–1783	1783–1793	1793–1801	1768–1801	1768–1801
Ana	4,334	5,643	1,834	1,454	1,293	7	–10	–2	–1	–4	–70
Angel	2,362	2,039	1,926	1,448	1,092	–4	–1	–3	–3	–2	–54
Apóstoles	2,127	2,277	1,571	2,052	1,314	2	–3	3	–5	–1	–38
Bautista	3,701	3,087	2,338	2,018	1,292	–4	–2	–1	–5	–3	–65
Borja	2,583	2,131	2,906	2,154	2,413	–5	3	–3	1	–0	–7
Candelaria	3,064	3,077	1,513	1,490	1,343	0	–6	–0	–1	–2	–56
Carlos	2,367	1,968	977	1,023	1,013	–5	–6	0	–0	–3	–57
Concepción	1,475	2,935	1,950	1,349	1,127	NA	NA	0	–2	–1	–24
Corpus	4,587	4,881	2,727	1,946	2,335	2	–5	–3	2	–2	–49
Cosme	2,337	1,709	1,103	1,550	860	–8	–4	3	–7	–3	–63
Cruz	3,243	3,402	3,746	3,871	3,238	1	1	0	–2	–0	–0
Fé	3,954	2,294	723	809	1,233	–13	–10	1	5	–3	–69
Guazú	1,926	1,655	800	1,354	712	–4	–6	5	–8	–3	–63
Itapúa	4,784	4,505	3,037	2,066	2,131	–1	–4	–4	0	–2	–55
Jesús	2,866	2,392	1,306	1,066	1,036	–4	–5	–2	–0	–3	–64
José	2,122	2,180	1,007	1,086	865	1	–7	1	–3	–3	–59
Lorenzo	1,242	1,454	1,273	1,171	1,037	4	–1	–1	–2	–1	–17
Loreto	2,462	2,492	1,472	1,261	1,164	0	–5	–2	–1	–2	–53
Luis	3,353	3,420	3,500	3,312	2,776	0	0	–1	–2	–1	–17
Mártires	1,662	1,724	1,197	892	708	1	–3	–3	–3	–3	–57
Mayor	2,839	1,398	978	690	559	–16	–3	–3	–3	–5	–80
Miguel	3,164	2,118	1,973	2,334	1,664	–10	–1	2	–4	–2	–47
Miní	3,306	3,738	1,021	664	906	3	–11	–4	4	4	–73
Nicolás	3,811	3,741	3,667	2,984	2,406	–0	–0	–2	–3	–1	–37
Rosa	2,243	2,265	1,266	1,910	1,261	0	–5	4	–5	–2	–44
Santiago	2,822	3,585	1,119	1,412	1,262	6	–10	2	–1	–2	–55
Tomé	2,172	2,317	1,837	1,483	1,786	2	–2	–2	2	–1	–18
Trinidad	2,365	1,477	1,101	997	877	–11	–3	–1	–2	–3	–63
Xavier	1,527	1,655	1,477	895	959	2	–1	–5	1	–1	–37
Yapeyú	7,974	3,322	4,747	5,170	4,948	–20	3	1	–1	–1	–38
Total:	88,774	80,881	56,092	51,911	45,610						–49
Average percentage change per year:						–2.3	–3.3	–0.8	–1.6	–2.0	

SOURCE: 1772 from AGN, IX 18-8-5, 18-8-6, and 18-8-7; 1801 from AGN, IX 18-2-6; the remaining years from Maeder and Bolsi, "La población guaraní" mission Indians clearly occurred, but it should not be overstated; the Indians were not powerless against pressure from Spanish officials. They took action to lessen or stop perceived abuses and exploitation both by Spanish officials and by other Guaraní, making use of official channels as well as direct action. Their complaints—often in the form of letters to high-level bureaucrats—limited abuse and restrained Spanish officials and native leaders, at least to some extent, while lack of compliance and evasion of collective labor projects made mission obligations less burdensome without officially challenging mission management. By means of such actions, the Guaraní continued to shape the missions and limit the demands made of them.

DEMOGRAPHICS

After the Jesuit expulsion, the number of Guaraní residing in the thirty missions declined.[4] Administrators counted the entire population of the thirty missions in 1768, 1772, 1783, 1793, and 1801 (see Table 6).[5] Each census recorded a smaller population than the previous one. This continuous decline contrasts starkly with the Jesuit period, when the mission population regularly fell because of epidemics, other hardships, and flight but always began to recover after a couple of years. For example, in the 1730s, when the missions suffered a series of calamities—epidemics, extended military service, drought, and upheaval associated with the Comunero Revolt in Asunción—the mission population plummeted from over 140,000 Indians in 1732 to less than 74,000 in 1740. But it quickly recovered thereafter: fifteen years later—in one generation or less—the population had reached over 104,000.[6] Such a recovery never took place during the post-Jesuit period.

While the mission population as a whole decreased continuously over the post-Jesuit period, however, this decline should not be overstated. A massive exodus from the missions did not occur. The mission population fell by less than 10 percent over the first four years after the Jesuit expulsion, and even after thirty-three years, over 45,000 Guaraní still resided in the thirty missions. Moreover, individual mission populations sometimes increased during this period. Between 1768 and 1772, the sharp population losses of a few missions obscure the fact that more than half of the missions (sixteen) experienced population growth. In subsequent years, some missions—between five and eleven—likewise recorded population growth. Only six missions never experienced population growth during the post-Jesuit period.

The rate of decline also fluctuated during the post-Jesuit period. For the first four years after the Jesuit expulsion (1768–1772), the mission population declined by 2.3 percent per year. During the following decade (1772–1783), the rate of decline peaked at 3.3 percent per year. In the subsequent decade (1783–1793), the rate of decline dropped dramatically to .8 percent per year; but in the last period (1793–1801), the rate of decline increased again to 1.6 percent.

In addition to flight, this decline in population was due to epidemics, which remained a major problem in the post-Jesuit period. As lieutenant gobernador Doblas explained:

Only smallpox and measles cause atrocious decimation. This results, in part, because many years elapse without undergoing these epidemics. When they attack, the contagion is promptly spread because few of those alive have had [the disease]. There are not any people to attend to the sick because all flee to avoid contagion. As a result, it is not surprising that almost all die and it is a wonder that anyone escapes the forces of nature.[7]

Both smallpox and measles continued to plague the missions on a fairly regularly basis. Severe smallpox epidemics struck the missions in 1770–1772, 1772–1777, 1778, 1785, and 1796.[8] The sporadic nature of the census data from the post-Jesuit period prevents a systematic comparison with the Jesuit period. On the basis of limited evidence, Robert Jackson asserts that epidemics did not take as many lives in the post-Jesuit period as in the Jesuit period.[9] Anecdotal descriptions suggest that epidemics still devastated the mission population in the post-Jesuit period but perhaps to a lesser degree, especially after the 1770s.

In 1771, smallpox attacked Yapeyú, and some 80 to 90 Guaraní died each day;[10] according to Mariano Ignacio de Larrazabal's 1772 census, more than 5,000 Indians died in the epidemic. After it had run its course, Yapeyú had a population of only 3,322—less than half the pre-epidemic figure.[11] Jackson erroneously claims this to be the only instance during the post-Jesuit period where mortality levels were comparable to the outbreaks of the 1730s and 1760s.[12] Between May 1777 and August 1778, smallpox struck Mission Santa María de Fe, killing 697 Indians of both sexes and all ages. According to José Barbosa, lieutenant gobernador of the five missions of the Santiago department, "As a consequence [of the epidemic], the mission is left with very few people who can work."[13] In total, the epidemic killed about half the population of Santa María de Fe. In 1779, after the epidemic had run its course, the mission had only 723 inhabitants, including an estimated workforce of 158 adult males.[14]

Anecdotal information suggests lower mortality rates for epidemics in the 1780s and 1790s. A smallpox epidemic struck the six missions of the San Miguel department in 1785. Of the estimated 3,672 Indians who contracted the illness, only a quarter (916) died.[15] Likewise, a small-pox epidemic struck Mission San Borja in 1796, killing from 600 to 800 Indians—between 20 and 25 percent of the population.[16]

Well aware of the high death tolls and other devastation caused by epidemics, post–Jesuit era mission officials made a concerted effort to minimize the impact of viruses and stop their spread. They tried to isolate the sick so as not to infect others, and each mission department employed surgeons and bleeders to treat the sick.[17] In a more radical effort to stop the spread of the disease, some mission Indians received highly contro-versial smallpox inoculations. Rarely practiced in Spain until the 1770s, inoculations were given to Indians from missions in the San Miguel de-partment in 1785 by order of lieutenant gobernador Manuel de Lazarte.[18] Inoculation (also called variolation) was hotly contested in both Europe and the Americas. Proponents argued that inoculation produced milder cases of smallpox and reduced mortality rates, while opponents argued that inoculation actually contributed to the spread of smallpox. Both sides of the debate were correct. Inoculation—derived from the Latin *inoculare*, meaning "to graft"—involved injecting a small amount of liq-uid from a smallpox blister into the subcutaneous tissue of a healthy person.[19] In a successful outcome, the patient acquired a mild case of smallpox and, in the process, immunity to the disease. In an unsuccessful outcome, an inoculated patient contracted a more severe case of small-pox, which could even result in death. Opponents argued that inocula-tion unnecessarily exposed people to smallpox: the inoculated individual might never have contracted smallpox naturally. Furthermore, when the inoculated person contracted smallpox, she exposed other individuals to the illness. If the exposed individuals had not been inoculated against smallpox or had not already had the virus, the resulting outbreak could be especially devastating. Consequently, inoculation sometimes had the paradoxical result of sparking epidemics.[20]

Although reports indicate that inoculation showed some positive re-sults in the missions, its partial implementation meant that epidemics still occurred. Only a small fraction of the population received inoculations against smallpox or measles. For example, in 1785, 362 of the several thousand Indians from the six missions of the San Miguel department were inoculated; 11 died from the procedure.[21] In 1797, a Spanish physi-cian inoculated another 63 Indians at Mission Santa Rosa; the patients acquired a mild case of the virus but then recovered.[22] These patients may have passed the illness to non-inoculated individuals, and thus the inoculation of only a small portion of the mission population may have facilitated the spread of smallpox in this case.

Scholars disagree about whether population loss during the post-Jesuit period derived more from deaths or flight.[23] Regardless of their overall impact, however, evidence shows that the relative importance of both factors varied over the period. During the first couple of years after the Jesuit expulsion, relatively few Guaraní left the missions. Much of the decline between 1768 and 1772 can instead be attributed to epidemics. The deaths in Mission Yapeyú from the 1771 smallpox epidemic accounted for more than half of the total population decline for all of the thirty missions combined during this period.[24]

In the 1770s, the decline in the mission population accelerated and flight became a more important factor. Between 1772 and 1783, the missions lost an additional 1 percent of their population per year as compared to the preceding four years. Most of the decline in the mission population during this latter period was likely due to flight rather than deaths, a conclusion confirmed by two quantitative studies from the period. Between 1772 and 1777, in the eight missions of the Candelaria department, the number of male Guaraní who fled surpassed the number who died by 18.5 percent; deaths totaled 967, while the number that abandoned these missions reached 1,146.[25] Flight was an even greater problem for the five missions of the Santiago department: for each of the eight years between 1773 and 1780, the number of Guaraní males who fled surpassed the number of deaths (see Figure 9). In total, the number of Indians who abandoned these five missions was more than twice the number that died (1,573 versus 736).[26]

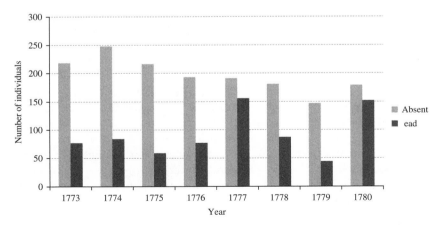

Figure 9. Adult male population loss in Santiago department, 1773–1780
SOURCE: 1781 censuses for the five missions of the Santiago department, AGN, IX 7-9-2.

Subsequently, from 1783 to 1793, the yearly decline in the mission population dropped significantly to an average of .8 percent per year. During this period, more Indians died than fled their mission. Between 1797 and 1799, the number of mission Indians who died was almost double the number who fled (7,221 versus 3,872).[27]

PUSH AND PULL FACTORS

Tracking the size of the mission population in general, and the rate of flight in particular, is one way to gauge Guaraní sentiment toward the missions versus their other alternatives. During good times, when life in the missions compared favorably with other alternatives, the total population increased; in other words, the number of births more than compensated for the number of deaths and flights combined. In contrast, during periods of hardship in the missions and when better opportunities existed elsewhere, the population fell as the result of high mortality rates and/or flight. Flight is a particularly salient index of Guaraní attitudes toward conditions in the missions. Some flight, especially temporary absences from the missions, was to be expected; consistently high levels of flight leading to a decline in the total mission population, however, were a different matter. Abandoning one's mission was a major decision: it entailed lifestyle changes as well as disruptions in social relations with one's community and likely with one's family, at least to some degree. Furthermore, since any unauthorized absence was officially illegal, one risked punishment if caught outside one's mission without permission.

Despite the potential consequences, Guaraní often resorted to flight when faced with difficulties or hardships in the missions.[28] Flight was not unique to the post-Jesuit period; even under Jesuit management Guaraní left the missions.[29] Some Guaraní fled because they did not want to obey mission rules and feared punishment; others left only when mission life came under threat. Accordingly, flight rates increased during periods of hunger, disease, or warfare.[30] In the post-Jesuit era, motivations for leaving the missions intensified—the Guaraní fled for new reasons as well as old ones.

The Guaraní accepted and, according to most accounts, initially welcomed the changes associated with the Jesuit expulsion. Before the expulsion, the governor of the Río de la Plata region, Francisco Bucareli y Ursúa, took great pains to gain the support of Guaraní leaders. Both his actions and words convinced many Guaraní of the benefits to be gained from the expulsion of the Jesuits and reforms to the missions. For a period of more than six months, Governor Bucareli showered fifty-seven

Guaraní leaders with great hospitality in Buenos Aires at the expense of the king. He wanted to teach them about the "benevolent piety with which the King sees them, removing them from the slavery and ignorance in which they have lived."[31] During this time, Bucareli repeatedly made grandiose promises to the Guaraní. He said that he had come to liberate mission inhabitants from the slavery that they had experienced under the Jesuits. He told them that that they, not the Jesuits, were the owners of all mission property, and that after the expulsion they would benefit from this property that heretofore had not been in their possession.[32] Furthermore, he told them that their children could become priests if they so desired.[33]

Bucareli's efforts to convince Guaraní leaders that they had much to gain from the impending changes were largely effective. According to anthropologist Guillermo Wilde, many Guaraní leaders saw the changes both as an opportunity to improve relations with the Crown and as an opening for personal advancement.[34] In early 1768, fifty-four of the fifty-seven Guaraní leaders feted by the governor wrote a letter to Charles III, thanking him profusely for sending Bucareli. In addition to such expressions of gratitude, the Guaraní authors echoed some of Bucareli's grand hopes for their missions' future.[35]

The gratitude of the Guaraní and their hope for their missions' prosperity in the future did not end with this letter. During the process of removing the Jesuits, the Guaraní warmly welcomed officials, with food and festivities. Only in Mission San Ignacio Guazú did Crown officials encounter some (minor) opposition from Guaraní inhabitants; according to these officials, the Jesuit priest incited the Indians to ask to see the papal bull mandating the expulsion of the Jesuits.[36] Aside from this incident, the Guaraní showed very little opposition to the end of Jesuit administration. One of the few written documents showing such opposition is a letter from Mission San Luis. Most likely, however, the authors were not fully informed about the governor's intentions, given that the letter was written before their mission's leaders had returned from the meeting with Bucareli in Buenos Aires.[37]

Although the authors of this and other Guaraní letters often asserted that they were writing on behalf of their entire cabildo and mission, such letters reflected the views of the Guaraní elite and not necessarily those of the entire mission population. Only a select few of the Guaraní elite were literate and so could write such letters. Furthermore, the letter-writing process could distort a letter's content. Most often the Guaraní wrote letters in Guaraní, which then had to be translated into Spanish. This process of translation had the potential to accidentally or purposefully alter the letter's intended content. The possibility of misrepresentation increased when either the Guaraní leaders dictated the letter or someone else composed it and the leaders only signed it; such reliance on others left the Guaraní open to becoming the mouthpiece of the translator or scribe. Taking into account such limitations, however, Guaraní letters still provide insights into the ideas and perceptions of the Guaraní elite and, to a lesser degree, the mission population in general.

A year after the Jesuit expulsion, interim gobernador Carlos Joseph de Añasco ordered that principal caciques from each of the twenty Guaraní missions under his care deliver letters from their cabildo and administrator attesting to their obedience to him.[38] Governor Bucareli had recently appointed Añasco to replace Juan Francisco de la Riva Herrera, who had expressed strong opposition to this change,[39] and Añasco wanted the letters as a sign of the missions' loyalty to him. The cabildo members and administrators complied and sent letters attesting to their obedience.[40] Most of the letters were brief and formulaic in expressing obedience, respect, and gratitude to Añasco, as one would expect from letters written in response to such an order. But some of the Guaraní leaders took this opportunity to highlight their expectations for the reformed missions.[41] Such content that strayed from the standard of respectful compliance with Añasco's request yields insight into the Guaraní elite's understanding of post-Jesuit reforms.

In their letter, which was written in Guaraní and translated into Spanish, twelve cabildo members from San Ignacio Guazú addressed the great changes that they understood to be occurring in their mission. After presenting themselves to Añasco "with all humility," the leaders affirmed their compliance with the post-Jesuit changes at their mission. In contrast to an earlier request for official confirmation of the Jesuit expulsion, they now expressed support for these same changes. They said that they had welcomed and treated both the new priest and the administrator with love. In addition to such standard assertions of compliance with the king's orders, however, the San Ignacio Guazú leaders hinted at their independence and autonomy. Rather than obsequiously offering their submission and deference to the administrator and priest, they declared that the king had sent the administrator to be their partner (*compañero*) and the priest to teach them. The leaders then concluded their letter with "much thanks to God and our Catholic King, who with great love has liberated us from the bondage that we lived in as slaves."[42] These references to slavery under the Jesuits and liberty under the new regime echo Bucareli's proclamations.

In a letter of the same year to Governor Bucareli, Yapeyú's cabildo members similarly expressed appreciation and communicated their hopes for the future. Like San Ignacio Guazú's leaders, Yapeyú's cabildo made reference to their newfound liberty, offering "thanks to the King, Our Señor, for the liberty in which he has placed us." They also thanked Governor Bucareli for naming cacique don Benito Tañuiya as corregidor, cacique don Christanto Tauaré as lieutenant corregidor, and Francisco Sanchez Franco as administrator. With the naming of these individuals, Yapeyú's leaders hoped that "this mission will experience greater progress and that soon its Indians can enjoy the benefits and prerogatives conceded by His Majesty."[43]

After the first couple of years, the initial excitement about the regime change died down, and the outlook of many Guaraní changed. It soon became apparent that the optimism expressed by Governor Bucareli and the Guaraní leaders was not coming to fruition. In the individual missions, the shift from Jesuit administration to separate civil and religious administrations had not proceeded as smoothly as envisioned. Almost all of the first Spaniards assigned to oversee the individual missions were removed owing to incapacity and corruption.[44] Various priests also failed to fulfill their duties, abused the Indians, or were removed for inappropriate behavior.[45] Clearly such upheaval disrupted life in the missions.

The mission system was also a financial wreck. As explained in the previous chapter, the separation of the missions' secular and religious affairs meant that expenses far surpassed revenues. In order to close the gap, the missions sent more trade goods to Buenos Aires, and during the tenure of Juan Ángel de Lazcano as general administrator, from 1772 to 1784, the sale of mission trade goods surged. Mission inhabitants, who formed the labor force that produced these goods, bore the brunt of the pressure to increase production, and in response many fled the missions. This period coincided with the steepest annual decline in the mission population, with the number of Guaraní fleeing the missions surpassing the number who died.

After 1784, pressure to send trade goods to Buenos Aires lessened. As detailed in the next chapter, living conditions in the missions deteriorated, but the Guaraní who remained found ways of making mission life tolerable. The mission population continued to decline, but at a slower rate; flight played less of a role compared to the high mortality rate, at least in the last years of the century.

The Guaraní fled not only because conditions within the missions were deteriorating, but also because conditions outside of the missions were improving. By leaving the missions, the Guaraní sought to better their quality of life. Such betterment did not necessarily mean higher compensation for their labor; it could mean direct compensation in wages or goods in return for labor, greater freedom and independence, or escape from perceived abuse. Rapid regional economic growth created such opportunities. The Río de la Plata region remained a minor offshoot of the Viceroyalty of Peru until the Crown implemented a broad package of reforms in the second half of the eighteenth century. These reforms were driven in large part by Spain's loss to Britain in the Seven Years' War (1756–1763) and the British occupation of Havana.[46]

In an attempt to consolidate power, protect against foreign encroachment, and increase tax revenues in the Río de la Plata region, the Spanish Crown implemented a series of reforms to stimulate political and economic development. The most dramatic and best-known of these reforms were the creation of the Viceroyalty of Río de la Plata in 1776, which made the region Peru's political equal, together with the implementation of *comercio libre* (free trade) in 1778. Comercio libre did not mean free trade such as the name implies; rather, it permitted direct trade between various American ports (including Buenos Aires and Montevideo) and Spanish ports, while also simplifying taxes and bureaucracy. Previously, most legal transatlantic trade goods from Buenos Aires traveled by donkey across the Andes to Peru, by boat to Panama, and by mule train across the isthmus, before finally joining the fleet bound for Cuba and then Spain. Only goods with a high price-to-weight ratio could bear such high transportation costs, and the Río de la Plata region did not produce any goods that commanded such a high price. After comercio libre, both transatlantic trade and the Río de la Plata regional economy grew rapidly; between 1779 and 1784, the number of ships legally entering Buenos Aires each year more than doubled the average between 1760 and 1776.[47]

As a result of such reforms, the Río de la Plata region became one of the most dynamic parts of the Spanish Empire. Economic opportunity, along with new bureaucratic posts and expanding military garrisons, drew people to the region. The number of merchants in Buenos Aires—one measure of the region's economic vibrancy—increased from approximately 75 in 1738 to 653 in 1778.[48] The number of soldiers—a sign of the city's growing political importance—increased from about 500 in 1715 to almost 7,000 by 1776.[49] Likewise, Buenos Aires's total population grew from a little over 10,000 at midcentury to almost 30,000 by the date of comercio libre in 1778 and over 60,000 by the end of the colonial period.[50]

With the increase in population, a commensurate need arose for labor to furnish the growing market for goods and services. Carpenters and masons constructed residences, businesses, and public buildings. Boatmen and muleteers transported merchandise, and an array of domestic laborers met the day-to-day needs of the growing population. Free immigrants filled some of the demand, along with an even larger number of slaves.[51] Still, a labor shortage continued to exist.[52]

There was a growing need for labor in the rural economy as well. Workers produced foodstuffs and supplies for the expanding domestic population. They also supported the booming export trade. In response to trade reforms, transatlantic trade grew rapidly, especially the export of cattle hides. From less than 200,000 per year, cattle hide exports jumped to about a million or more per year by the end of the century.[53] Laborers produced this growing number of hides.

Some employers turned to mission Guaraní to fill these positions. Employers could no longer rely on coercive labor regimes—the encomienda and enslavement—to force the Guaraní to work for them as they had in the seventeenth century. In conjunction with the growing demand for labor, population decline reduced the supply of Indian labor; this increased competition limited the ability of employers to use coercive labor regimes with the Guaraní.

In some cases, lower labor costs made the Guaraní attractive employees. Spanish, mulatto, and mestizo peons in Corrientes and Paraguay received wages according to their ability—six, eight, ten, or in rare cases twelve pesos per month in goods. In contrast, travelers regularly encountered Guaraní laborers receiving only four or five pesos per month in goods. The wages of the Guaraní were often much less in real terms because the markup on the goods that they received in lieu of currency could be as high as 300 percent.[54] Even mission Guaraní employed in the service of the Crown received below-market wages. The commission in charge of settling the boundary between Spanish and Portuguese lands reported that they failed to attract Spanish peons at the going wage of nine pesos per month. Instead, the commission hired mission Guaraní for less than half the price—four pesos per month plus daily rations. The director of the commission, Josef Varela y Ulloa, defended the lower wages paid to the Guaraní by claiming this was "the custom of the land."[55]

The Guaraní did not always receive lower wages. In at least one instance, an *estanciero* offered to pay mission Guaraní the same wages as other employees. Juan Bautista Dargain requested permission from the Crown to hunt cattle in the Banda Oriental with the qualification that he be allowed to employ Indians from Yapeyú. He specified that he would pay them "in the same form as Spanish peons that are hired for the same purpose."[56] For Dargain, the Guaraní were an attractive labor force even without discounted wages.

Contact with other sectors of colonial society exposed the Guaraní to opportunities outside of the missions. Indians in closer contact with outsiders—especially those residing in missions near Portuguese and Spanish settlements—were more likely to flee.[57] The high rate of flight from the five missions of the Santiago department, for example, was likely due in part to their relatively close proximity to Asunción and Corrientes.

Although Guaraní of both genders and all ages fled the missions, more working-age males and females left than Guaraní in other age brackets. According to one observer, 90 percent of the working-age males from Missions Santa Ana and San Ignacio Miní fled between 1772 and 1798.[58] Even without special skills, adults in their prime could easily find employment in the booming regional economy.

While Guaraní of both sexes abandoned the missions, more fugitives were male than female. Censuses from the end of the eighteenth century confirm that more of the 3,875 Indians missing from the missions were male than female. Between 1797 and 1799, 57 percent of the fugitives were male, 35 percent were female, and 8 percent were unclassified.[59] As a result, females made up a greater proportion of mission residents in every age bracket except for the very young.[60] Some of the Guaraní women who fled accompanied their husbands; other Guaraní women left of their own accord. Female fugitives found employment as seamstresses, cooks, bakers, laundresses, and domestic servants.[61]

Indians with marketable skills also left the missions in greater numbers. Skilled Guaraní such as silversmiths, ironworkers, gunsmiths, carpenters, cobblers, masons, weavers, tailors, lathe operators, rosary makers, tanners, tile makers, brick makers, and potters could easily find employment in the expanding economy.[62] In addition to such craftsmen, Guaraní boatmen and muleteers worked in the expanding trade networks and Guaraní cowboys and peons hunted wild cattle and cared for livestock in estancias. All of these skills easily transferred to enterprises outside of the missions. José Barbosa, the lieutenant gobernador in charge of the five Santiago missions, observed that a large percentage of mission fugitives were skilled laborers. After sending troops in search of fugitives in 1773, Barbosa reported that "most of the fugitive Indians gathered in Paraguay are tradesmen (*de oficio*) such as weavers, carpenters, tile makers, etc."[63] Such tradesmen and artisans generally received higher wages because of their skills.[64]

The impact of flight by Guaraní artisans and tradesmen was apparent years later in the missions' decrepitude. In 1798, the intendant governor of Paraguay, Lázaro de Ribera, commented that "those artists have disappeared that gave the pueblos the majesty that they still breathe in all the visible works of architecture, sculpture, carpentry, and blacksmithing."[65]

Guaraní leaders likewise fled the missions in large numbers after 1772 (see Table 7). As of that date, none of the caciques or those immediately in line for this position at Missions Santa Ana and Corpus Christi were

TABLE 7. *Fugitive caciques and their immediate family members, 1772–1801*

	Mission Santa Ana						Mission Corpus Christi				
Cacique	Cacicazgo	1772	1784	1799	1801	Cacique	Cacicazgo	1772	1784	1799	1801
1	Cabiñurá		X	X	X	1	Abaró				
2	Buray		X	X	X	2	Caribé			X	X
3	Apucá		X	X	X	3	Sayobí		X	X	X
4	Guaiquí[a]					4	Arayrá				
5	Aruarí			X		5	Ybapé		X	X	X
6	Tarupí		X	X	X	6	Toribiyú		X	X	
7	Potí					7	Depichó			X	X
8	Añemboé					8	Cuyabí		X	X	X
9	Ysapí					9	Yacaré			X	X
10	Yaseó		X	X	X	10	Pindobí		X	X	X
11	Mbacató		X	X	X	11	Paraguayó		X	X	X
12	Guaibipó		X			12	Guirayá		X	X	X
13	Guandapí		X	X	X	13	Ocarití		X	X	
14	Guaracú		X	X	X	14	Aretú			X	X
15	Yriapí		X	X	X	15	Añengará		X	X	X
16	Arezá			X	X	16	Ayuruyú		X	X	X
17	Caitú		X	X	X	17	Guirapepó			X	X
18	Tamuirá				X	18	Pareyú			X	X
19	Ymbí			X	X	19	Oquedá			X	X
20	Abuyré					20	Mandaguy			X	X
21	Tapayú[b]					21	Mbariré			X	X
22	Caraybobá					22	Papá			X	X
23	Checuá[b]					23	Mbayrobá		X	X	X
24	Cuarasipotí		X	X	X	24	Arazay				
25	Mbarasí				X	25	Pyzé		X	X	X
26	Abaibí		X	X	X	26	Caitú				
27	Arareté		X	X	X	27	Pataguy		X	X	X
28	Peá			X	X	28	Tamapá		X		
29	Checurí		X	X		29	Chavé			X	X
30	Ñacandey		X	X	X	30	Zumey				
31	Yasí		X	X	X	31	Ñatimú[a]				
32	Taburá[a]					32	Piyú			X	X
33	Araró[a]					33	Quarací		X	X	X
34	Cuñambó			X	X	34	Quararay			X	X
35	Guirayaguá					35	Mbaynayú			X	X
36	Ñeatí		X	X	X	36	Chapay				
37	Chabiquí		X	X	X	37	Ará[c]				
38	Arambayú		X	X	X	38	Guarapé			X	
39	Yasucá			X	X	39	Bié				
Total:		0	20	25	25	40	Tayaó				
Percentage:		0%	51%	64%	64%	41	Moacatí				
						42	Ñanguarendí		X	X	X
						43	Coingué				
						44	Pinchará		X	X	X
						45	Camuná			X	X
						Total:		0	16	33	30
						Percentage:		0%	36%	75%	68%

SOURCE: Mission Santa Ana and Mission Corpus Christi censuses, AGN, IX 18-2-2, 18-2-6, 18-7-2, 18-8-6, and 18-8-7.
[a]No cacique listed in 1784, 1799, or 1801.
[b]No cacique listed in 1799.
[c]Cacicazgo disappeared after 1772.

recorded as fugitives.[66] In striking contrast, 51 percent of Santa Ana's cacicazgos (twenty out of thirty-nine) and 36 percent of Corpus Christi's cacicazgos (sixteen out of forty-four) recorded the cacique or a potential successor to the position as a fugitive as of 1784.[67] In subsequent years, most of these individuals did not return to the missions, and more Guaraní leaders fled. By 1799, the percentages of caciques or potential successors to the position who were fugitives increased to 64 percent for Santa Ana and 75 percent for Corpus Christi.[68] The absence of these individuals disrupted mission leadership, reflecting the acceleration of the missions' general decline in the 1770s.

The Guaraní who fled, however, did not always break ties with the missions. Many Guaraní left their own mission but remained in mission territory. Some Indians hid in their mission's agricultural plots and estancias; others sought shelter in territory belonging to another mission.[69] Gobernador Zavala complained, "The Indians go about as vagabonds and fugitives from their respective pueblo. Going to other pueblos or being in the [mission] fields or passing through the estancias, they are harmful. They only perform wrongdoings in the missions and the fields, and destruction in the estancias."[70] Moreover, according to lieutenant gobernador Doblas, these Indians did not contribute to communal labor projects.[71] By fleeing to other missions or unsupervised parts of mission territory, fugitives maintained ties to the missions while evading the demands and laws that regulated mission life.

Fugitive Guaraní could also maintain personal connections by seeking employment near their mission. Married males with children frequently sought positions on nearby farms and estancias, while single and widowed men more frequently left mission territory altogether. This difference likely reflected married men's connections to their families.[72] Still, marriage ties should not be overemphasized: not all married fugitives wanted to maintain ties to the families that they left behind. According to gobernador Zavala, Guaraní couples separated easily because they were compelled to marry at an early age. He also maintained that fugitive couples were generally not man and wife; rather, fugitives sought new unions outside the missions.[73]

Mission fugitives spread throughout the Río de la Plata region, fleeing to both the cities and the countryside.[74] Many went to Buenos Aires, the center of the viceroyalty. In 1790, the general administrator of the thirty missions, Diego Casero, asserted that fugitives from the missions worked in the city, farms, public land, and brick ovens.[75] Mission fugitives also went to other towns and cities throughout the region.[76] In Corrientes, there were a "large number of Indians that work[ed] in farming, estancias, factories, labors, livestock, transportation, and other [enterprises] in service to the Spanish."[77] A decade after the Jesuit expulsion, Juan de la Granja, administrator of Mission Jesús, estimated that there were more than seven thousand Guaraní in Corrientes and the surrounding area.[78] Mission fugitives also helped fill the constant labor shortage in the Banda Oriental. The 1772–1773 census of Montevideo and its jurisdiction shows a high percentage of Guaraní from the missions working as peons in rural enterprises.[79] Some Guaraní combined temporary wage labor with settled agriculture. The military commander Josef de Urquiza reported in 1800 that "this town [Concepción de Uruguay, Entre Ríos] and its jurisdiction is surrounded by Guaraní Indians, fugitives from their missions, maintaining themselves as wage earners and with their labors in sowing [crops]."[80]

Not all of the Guaraní who fled the missions relied on wages or independent farming for sustenance; some resorted to theft. According to gobernador Zavala, the governor of Paraguay, Agustín Fernando de Pinedo, complained in two separate letters about the "many abuses, thefts, and crimes that the fugitive Indians from the missions commit in that province [Paraguay]."[81] At least one of Governor Pinedo's letters was written at the request of the residents of Paraguay. Livestock theft was their main concern; they claimed that fugitive Indians stole livestock from their estancias. Ironically, some estancieros were knowingly or unknowingly complicit. In response to Governor Pinedo, gobernador Zavala said that the residents of Paraguay exacerbated the problem: "I cannot help but wonder at how these residents complain so bitterly about the Indians of these missions when, in order to make use of [the Indians], they admit them into their estancias. They shelter and defend them even when people have gone to look [for fugitives] with Superior Orders of this Government." As an example, Zavala cited the estanciero don Joseph Luis Báez. Báez went so far as "withholding the Indians that he had in his estancia. Not only did he do this but also [he] has entreated Indians that are in the missions to flee so that they may serve as peons."[82]

Spanish managers of the missions agreed that livestock theft by fugitives was a problem. Lieutenant gobernador José Barbosa wrote to Governor Vértiz that the "theft of all sorts of animals in the estancias [by fugitive Indians] are excessive." Barbosa claimed that in the previous month, patrols had discovered two groups of fugitives with stolen livestock. In the first encounter they found about seventy fugitives with dried beef, seventy cows, four oxen, ten horses, and two mules, and in the second encounter they found fifteen fugitives with twenty horses and ample dried beef.[83] The Guaraní sold the livestock as well as used it themselves.[84]

Some fugitives contributed to lawlessness in the region by joining nonmission Indians. In 1778, the corregidor, administrator, and other

Guaraní deputies of Yapeyú complained to the viceroy that the Minuane Indians not only stole cattle and killed mission inhabitants, they also sheltered many Guaraní who deserted the missions.[85] In 1785, lieutenant gobernador Doblas likewise complained that the Minuanes sheltered mission fugitives, engaged in contraband with the Portuguese, and wreaked havoc in the countryside.[86]

By joining nonmission Indians and fleeing to Portuguese territory, mission fugitives weakened Spain's hold on the frontier. Flight to Portuguese territory began before the Jesuit expulsion. Recognizing that populating this frontier region was indispensable to defending their territory, the Portuguese sought to attract Guaraní from the missions. In a secret letter dated 1751, the marquês de Pombal instructed the Portuguese envoy charged with enforcing the Treaty of Madrid in the Río de la Plata region to eliminate all differences between Indians and Portuguese and encourage intermarriage in order to populate the Brazilian frontier.[87] After initially taking up arms in the 1750s to prevent the transfer of the seven eastern missions to the Portuguese, Guaraní sentiment toward the Portuguese increasingly became ambivalent. After defeating the Indians in the Guaraní War, Portuguese troops befriended the Guaraní. When Portuguese troops left mission territory in 1761, a considerable number of mission Indians also migrated to Portuguese territory. In the following years, mission Guaraní continued to flee to Portuguese territory.[88] During the War of the Oranges between Spain and Portugal (1801), Guaraní ambivalence about the Portuguese was readily apparent: the Guaraní assisted both sides, and the Portuguese seized Spanish territory that included the seven eastern Guaraní missions without much opposition from mission inhabitants.[89]

But while Guaraní flight sometimes threatened imperial designs, legal Guaraní absences directly served the Crown's interests. Royal officials repeatedly requested Guaraní assistance in defending the region. One of the principal tasks was militia service against foreign incursions and Portuguese and Spanish marauders. Guaraní called into service to the Crown traveled far from their homes, primarily to the Spanish-Portuguese borderlands, Buenos Aires, and Montevideo. For example, in 1779 six hundred armed Indians defended Montevideo for the duration of Spain's involvement in the American Revolutionary War; afterwards, another three hundred Indians repaired Montevideo's defenses.[90] Guaraní militias also helped defend Montevideo during the British invasions of 1806 and 1807, and on the eve of independence two poorly armed companies of mission Indians remained.[91] In addition, the Crown often ordered Guaraní from the missions to participate in labor projects for the public good. Guaraní men constructed numerous public works and provided firewood to Buenos Aires and Montevideo.[92]

Absences for labor service to the Crown took a great toll on the missions. In 1776, lieutenant gobernador Juan de San Martín complained to Governor Vértiz that defending the frontier was too burdensome for the six missions of the Yapeyú department. These missions alone withstood the loss of more than two hundred Guaraní men for the extended period of a year—one hundred at the Santa Tecla fort, forty at the Santa Teresa fort, twenty-five in Yaguari, and fifty in the Paso de Santiago del Monte-Grande. In addition to supplying Indian labor, the missions also had to provide the Indians with arms, ammunition, and other necessities.[93] Such projects for the Crown not only reduced the number of working-age males in a mission and consumed mission supplies, they also facilitated Guaraní flight. Mission Guaraní came in contact with Spaniards and Portuguese, and many seized the opportunity to flee.[94]

Efforts to force Indians to remain in the missions were largely ineffective. Unauthorized absences were illegal, but mission officials could do little to prevent Indians from leaving. With a population of generally over one thousand in each mission, the handful of Spanish officials had little power to stop an Indian from leaving the mission. Spanish officials relegated policing activities to Guaraní leaders, but cabildo members and caciques were ambivalent in regard to flight. The native leaders' allegiances were often torn between the welfare of the mission, their followers, and themselves. As a result, Guaraní leaders, especially the caciques, often did not prevent their followers from leaving the missions.[95] As noted earlier, caciques also fled their missions in increasing numbers after 1772.

Prohibitions against hiring mission fugitives had little effect in preventing Guaraní flight. Crown officials issued various decrees against hiring mission fugitives and ordered employers to return any Indians under their supervision to the mission of origin. In 1769, Spanish officials ordered employers to pay Guaraní fugitives six pesos per month for their labor and return them to the missions.[96] Over a decade later, Viceroy Vértiz issued another decree forbidding the hiring or use of mission Guaraní as laborers on estancias or in any other capacity. The penalty for disobedience was a two-hundred-peso fine, with a fifty-peso reward to anyone reporting a violation.[97] Again in 1790, Viceroy Arredondo reiterated his predecessor's order to return Guaraní fugitives to their missions.[98] Such repeated attempts to put an end to the hiring of Guaraní fugitives attest to its continued practice.

Fugitives forcibly returned to their mission frequently did not remain there. Of the minority captured and returned to their missions, many escaped again. A letter by lieutenant gobernador Barbosa highlights some of the obstacles to successfully reintegrating fugitives into their mission.

After learning that some fugitive Guaraní from Mission Santiago were in the jurisdiction of Paraguay, Barbosa sent the corregidor and three Guaraní officials with orders "that they lovingly collect [the fugitives]." Of the forty-four fugitives, only seventeen arrived back in Santiago. Along the way, the others hid in the back country and returned to Paraguay. In another instance, thirty-eight mission fugitives were returned from Corrientes; very few of them stayed, even though they received a ration of meat every day in the mission. According to Barbosa, "In this manner, it is shown that the various steps taken to bring them back to their missions are useless because those that are brought back leave again, and the worst is, that they take others."[99]

As the failure of so many efforts to compel Guaraní to remain in the missions demonstrates, the use of force and coercion yielded poor results. Some Spanish officials even perceived a direct relationship between coercion and flight. After spending five years in the missions, Lorenzo de Ugarte came to the conclusion that most fugitives were "disgruntled by the violence that some thoughtless [individuals] do to them."[100] Despite such drawbacks to using force, the threat of punishment persisted in the missions, especially with respect to collective labor projects. According to lieutenant gobernador Doblas, given that remuneration was based on redistribution and not on wages, only the fear of punishment could be employed to motivate men to work. Although an Indian worked harder when overseen by someone with a whip, such a measure could not be employed consistently. There were not enough Spanish officials to oversee all labor projects, and furthermore, in Doblas's opinion, relying on native leaders was ineffective; the corregidor and cabildo members would not force other Guaraní to work. When these native leaders punished their fellow Guaraní for not working on collective projects, the Guaraní responded with complaints about abuse of power; the corregidor and cabildo members would then be reprimanded, and as a result they stopped trying to make their followers work.[101]

As Doblas observed, mission inhabitants found ways to mitigate the use of coercion, force, and exploitation. They not only complained about Guaraní leaders, they also denounced Spanish administrators and priests. Spanish officials took these complaints seriously. They understood that the Guaraní did not have to remain in the missions and that expanding opportunities outside the missions meant that Indians could easily flee if they felt exploited or abused. The Guaraní employed this credible threat in letters of complaint that reached far beyond their own missions, sending letters to various Spanish officials throughout the mission hierarchy and even to the governor and viceroy.

GUARANÍ AGENCY WITHIN THE COLONIAL STRUCTURE

The Mission San Juan Bautista dispute mentioned at the beginning of this chapter is a prime example of mission Indians using official channels to protest what they perceived as abuse and to improve living conditions within the missions. During 1772 and 1773, a power struggle divided the mission, with the Spanish administrator on one side and the priest on the other. Both sides included factions of Guaraní leaders. The various claims and counterclaims make the dispute worthy of tabloid news. Each side accused the other of abuse of power, exploitation, laziness, and drunkenness. Such vivid and detailed descriptions are compelling but make it difficult if not impossible to determine what really happened. In any case, both sides felt wronged and took their complaints to higher authorities. These narratives show how mission Guaraní used official channels to voice their complaints. Furthermore, the paper trail from this dispute demonstrates that mission authorities and royal officials outside the missions took Guaraní complaints seriously.

The paper trail begins on October 13, 1772, with a letter written by administrator Juan Antonio Ysasviribil and signed by the corregidor, other cabildo members, and some caciques from San Juan Bautista. In the letter, the authors accused the priest, Juan Bautista Fretes, of calling cacique don Ignacio Mbaeque away from work. From nine in the morning until two in the afternoon, the two drank excessive amounts of *aguardiente* (brandy). The goal, according to administrator Ysasviribil, was to incite rebellion among other caciques against his own good name and conduct. Subsequently, the priest and the administrator exchanged physical blows; Ysasviribil blamed the priest for the fight and the continued conflict.[102]

Four days later, gobernador Zavala gave instructions for resolving the problems. Zavala sent three separate letters to the mission—one to the corregidor, other cabildo members, and caciques; one to the administrator; and one to the priest. He urged the Indians to obey the administrator and respect the priest. He also ordered cacique Ignacio Mbaeque punished for his drunkenness and his efforts to agitate among the mission population. In addition, in his letter to the native leaders Zavala informed them that he had forwarded a copy of their letter dated October 13 to the governor of the Río de la Plata region.[103]

Almost a month later, administrator Ysasviribil sent another letter of complaint about Father Fretes to gobernador Zavala.[104] In response, Zavala again sent separate letters to the Guaraní leaders and the administrator of the mission. He urged the Indians not to lack respect for the priest and not to be absent from work. As in his earlier letter, Zavala again informed the native elite that he had forwarded a copy of Ysasviribil's letter to the governor of the Río de la Plata region.[105]

In the meantime, the priest and his companion sent letters accusing the administrator of improper relations with an Indian woman named Andrea. In response to all of these accusations, Zavala sent to the mission someone he believed to be impartial—Francisco Colina—to confidentially investigate the ongoing dispute.[106] On November 24, Colina reported that he found that the priest had behaved improperly and had provoked the administrator.[107] Despite Colina's conclusions, however, the dispute was far from over.

On January 30, 1773, less than three months after the initial letter from the administrator and cabildo, six caciques from San Juan Bautista wrote a letter to Governor Vértiz complaining about their corregidor and administrator.[108] One of the caciques was the same Ignacio Mbaeque accused of drinking with the priest and trying to incite rebellion. The caciques' letter was not only detailed and eloquent; it presented their accusations in a skillful and compelling manner as well.

From the very beginning, and before making any accusations, the caciques underscored what they claimed to be the result of the perceived abuses—flight. After introducing themselves and voicing their respect for both God and king, they wrote: "The poverty of this mission puts all of us in great penury, first us caciques and then the rest of the Indians, children, married women, and widows. Harassed by misery, they flee and are assumed to be lost." They then pleaded with the governor to resolve this situation by compelling compliance with what they believed to be the king's orders. As they made their accusations, the caciques highlighted how actions by both the corregidor and administrator were inconsistent with promises made by the king's representatives: "Señor Governador, in 1768 señor don Francisco Bucareli explained to us in all of the missions that we will work for our mission three or four days each week; the rest [of the days] we will care for our [own] plots. It was well understood that if the corregidor, cabildo, and administrator usurped some day they would give us the next week in full. This has not been complied with and as a result we are poor in terms of our personal plots, without having enough to eat."

The caciques' letter was over three pages long and listed various alleged abuses such as overwork, excessive punishment, corruption, drunkenness, and insufficient distributions from communal supplies. In conclusion, the six caciques requested that Governor Vértiz dismiss both the administrator and corregidor, and they specifically requested that Siriaco Guaripa be named as the new corregidor.

Gaspar de la Plaza, the lieutenant gobernador in charge of the six missions of the San Miguel department, visited San Juan Bautista to investigate the matter. On May 17, 1773, de la Plaza issued a report responding to the six caciques' accusations. He paid special attention to the issue of flight while refuting the claims made by the caciques. Acknowledging that Indians left the mission, de la Plaza denied that they left because of abuse and poor conditions. He went so far as to underline the claim that *"those harassed with misery, flee and are lost"* was false. In the report, de la Plaza blamed cacique Ignacio Mbaeque for many of the problems in San Juan Bautista, calling him "seditious, rebellious, and a disturber of the peace."[109]

Less than six months later, the original six caciques plus nine more wrote another letter to Governor Vértiz. They began their letter by mentioning that they had written three separate times to don Bruno Zavala, don Gaspar de la Plaza, and don Joseph Urbano in an attempt to remedy the abuses committed by their administrator and corregidor. Again, the caciques described their mission's poverty. They also underscored that what "most hurts our spirit and heart is, Señor Governor, to see that many [Indians] have taken to the countryside for shelter with the unbelieving Minuanes [*infieles minuanes*] only in order to liberate themselves from the severity of hunger." In conclusion, the fifteen caciques requested that Juan Ignacio Aguirre replace Ysasviribil as administrator and suggested yet another individual for the position of corregidor—Raphael Tovias Guaŷbîca.[110]

The paper trail ends with this October 7, 1773, letter by the fifteen caciques. The final outcome of the dispute is unclear. Ysasviribil continued in his post as administrator of San Juan Bautista for another fourteen years, but the corregidor was likely replaced:[111] according to an official report about each of the thirty missions dated several months after this last letter, the Spanish official noted that a corregidor needed to be named for San Juan Bautista.[112] Whatever the resolution, San Juan Bautista fared no worse than other missions in terms of its population figures. Between 1772 and 1783, the population dropped 24 percent, while the average for all thirty missions was 31 percent. Thus, those involved in the dispute likely reached a resolution that did not alienate the majority of San Juan Bautista's Guaraní population so greatly that they fled in massive numbers.

The drama that unfolded in this correspondence reveals not only that mission Guaraní actively protested what they viewed to be abuses, but that Spanish officials took Guaraní accusations seriously. Gobernador Zavala responded immediately to the letters of complaint. In both cases, he sent instructions less than ten days after the initial letters were written. Zavala not only issued his own instructions, he also informed the highest government official in the Río de la Plata region about what was happening in San Juan Bautista. When these steps failed, Zavala sent someone to the mission to investigate the matter. Governor Vértiz likewise took the mission Indians' complaints seriously. After the letter of January 30, 1773, from the six caciques to Governor Vértiz, the lieutenant gobernador of the department—Gaspar de la Plaza—personally investigated the caciques' claims.

Even though the San Juan Bautista dispute may have begun as a power struggle between the Spanish administrator and Spanish priest, Guaraní leaders quickly became actively involved on both sides. Administrator Ysasviribil admittedly sought native support by asking the corregidor and other cabildo members to certify the truth of his initial letter of October 13, 1772. Father Fretes was said to have called cacique Ignacio Mbaeque from work in order to get him drunk and incite rebellion. Even top mission officials undertook efforts to include Guaraní leaders. When Zavala sent letters to the mission, he made sure to send a separate letter specifically to the native leadership.

The Guaraní leaders were cognizant of their power. As their letter of October 7, 1773, attests, the caciques appealed their cause to the highest levels of the mission hierarchy—the gobernador and lieutenant gobernador. They also wrote at least two letters to the most powerful individual in the entire Río de la Plata region, Governor Vértiz. In their letters, they claimed that their cause was just because of the lack of compliance with orders issued by Bucareli and mandated by the king himself.

Another example of Guaraní leaders forcing Spanish officials to revise their behavior is provided by what occurred in Mission Concepción. On February 15, 1788, the corregidor, lieutenant corregidor, and the rest of the cabildo members wrote to Doblas, the lieutenant gobernador who oversaw the missions in their department. The cabildo requested the removal of their administrator, Pedro Fontela, because of his lack of charity toward Indians in need, his failure to perform his administrative duties, and the general impoverishment of their mission.[113] The following day, Doblas wrote to Intendant Governor Francisco de Paula Sanz, criticizing Fontela for not fulfilling his duties, not following Doblas's instructions, and neglecting Concepción's productive enterprises.[114] Although Paula Sanz decided not to remove Fontela from his post, he berated the administrator, ordering that Fontela "be admonished that if he did not undertake his work with the most complete vigilance and care regarding the interests and treatment of the Indians, and benevolence with which he is obligated to see them, helping them with all of their necessities, it will be necessary not only to separate him from his position but also to impose other penalties."[115]

By 1791, the date of the next accounting record, relations between Fontela and Concepción's native leadership seem to have improved. At the end of the accounting record, various Guaraní leaders—the corregidor, other cabildo members, the mayordomo, and the procurador—described in some detail their satisfaction with both Fontela's management and his account records.[116] Fontela continued as Concepción's administrator for three years after the native leaders' complaint and then became administrator of Mission Santa María la Mayor.[117] Presumably the letters written by Concepción's native leadership and the lieutenant gobernador had an impact such that Fontela's behavior improved.

Like the native leaders of San Juan Bautista and the cabildo members of Concepción, many other Guaraní appealed to the mission hierarchy and beyond when they felt exploited.[118] Their complaints reached the highest levels of government, and Spanish officials took steps to address their concerns. These actions reveal that both Spanish administrators and Guaraní leaders recognized that they could not exploit the mission population without consequence. If they did, they risked the Indians either fleeing or filing complaints that would not be ignored. The Guaraní not only made use of such official channels but also employed less confrontational, more covert methods to reduce exploitation.

OTHER FORMS OF GUARANÍ AGENCY

In order to make mission life more tolerable, the Guaraní shirked or applied themselves less than fully to communal labor projects. Evasion improved living conditions in the missions by reducing the workload. The motivations for evasion were similar to those for flight, but the Guaraní who practiced evasion remained within the boundaries of the mission and did not disengage altogether from the communal structure.

The majority of Jesuits and post-Jesuit administrators held the racist view that the Guaraní evaded labor owing to laziness. They frequently described Guaraní indolence in a manner suggesting it was a commonly accepted fact. For example, in a report to the governor of Río de la Plata, the lieutenant gobernador of the Candelaria missions, Juan Valiente, asserted that slothfulness was a dominant character trait of the Guaraní: "First, [they are] lazy by nature, with little probity; their capacity is very little. . . . They will not communally plant [crops] even for their own food unless they are made to with fear or punishment." He then concluded that "because of this [their disinclination to work], those that know them call them bearded children."[119] But if Valiente, like the Jesuits, believed the Guaraní to be inherently lazy, the actions of many Spaniards, especially those outside the missions, show that they disagreed.

Many Spaniards valued Guaraní labor. While acknowledging that there were no other peons in the area besides the Guaraní, the mayor of Concepción del Uruguay, Vicente Ximénez, recognized their value as laborers: "The quality of these people [the Guaraní] is well known."[120] Many Spaniards actively sought mission Guaraní as laborers. Indeed, they valued the Guaraní so much as to illegally shelter them from forced return to their respective missions. Lieutenant gobernador José Barbosa berated the colonialists who "have not stopped sheltering them [the Guaraní], and even hide them, when they are supposed to be returned [to their respective missions]."[121] Not only mission officials complained about people hiring and refusing to relinquish mission fugitives—even the viceroy acknowledged the problem.[122] Overtly breaking the law and thereby risking a fine would not make sense if the Guaraní were lazy and poor workers.

It was not because they were lazy that the Guaraní exerted less effort for communal projects but because they saw little return for their effort. In contrast to Valiente and others, lieutenant gobernador Doblas argued that the Guaraní did not exert themselves on account of poor incentives, rather than a character flaw: "From reiterated experiences I know that the Guaraní Indians are not as lazy as is supposed; they should not even be perceived as lazy." He described how four Indians from Candelaria "very agreeably worked from sunup to sundown for the day's wages [one real per day] that they knew they were earning." He went on: "In all parts where the Tape Indians [from the missions] are paid daily wages, they are very good peons, as is demonstrated in Buenos Aires and other Spanish cities where they are preferred to other peons." Doblas argued that in the missions the Guaraní "are not as industrious because of the lack of motivation due to not being paid [for their work]."[123]

In Doblas's view, then, mission Indians evaded work on collective labor projects because they did not receive wages or another form of reward commensurate with their labor. Moreover, according to Doblas, not only did the Guaraní not apply themselves, but many Guaraní avoided communal labor altogether. And the number of Guaraní who remained idle was large:

At the least, they are more than one-third [of the mission population], if not one-half. Some are employed in things that are not necessary in the colegio, others feign sickness, others are hidden and freed from communal labor by the corregidor and members of the cabildo. . . . Since [the Guaraní] know that their compliance [with the communal system] results in work and no reward, and that they can always excuse themselves with some pretext that exempts them from punishment, they excuse themselves.[124]

Doblas's estimate that one-third to one-half of mission Indians avoided collective labor projects accounts for a large portion of the population. With so many people absent, it should not be surprising that those who did work on collective labor projects did so without enthusiasm or vigor. Such high rates of absenteeism were readily apparent to all and surely demoralizing to the remaining workforce.

While difficult to quantify, motivations for evasion likely increased during the post-Jesuit period. Fewer distributions from communal supplies and the missions' general decay likely deterred Indians from working on collective labor projects. Although mission Indians never received wages for their labor, they did receive indirect compensation—the distributions from communal supplies; as these distributions declined during the post-Jesuit period, there was less incentive to apply themselves to collective labor projects. The poor state of the missions was also a disincentive. Aside from his racist opinion of their indolent nature, lieutenant gobernador Valiente also believed that the "total decadence" of the missions contributed to the Indians' aversion to work. As a result, he concluded, "the Indians feel so exceedingly lax in their duties and labors."[125]

In addition to the abovementioned factors, the promises and discourse used by Spanish officials likely contributed as well to the Guaraní evading or avoiding collective labor altogether. At the time of the expulsion, Governor Bucareli widely promulgated his belief that mission inhabitants lived like slaves under the Jesuits. He did not hold back in describing what he saw as exploitation of the Guaraní:

The inhabitants of these missions, under the pretense of barbarism or coarseness, did not have the least free will. Their labors and work were, for the most part, converted into the benefit of others. The food and clothing, even though acquired with these same labors, are distributed with the greatest stinginess, such that their nudity is notorious and even scandalous. And finally, until these times, they have been made to suffer effective enslavement [*una efectiva esclavitud*], violating the same natural and divine rights and the almost innumerable Royal decrees, orders, and laws with which our Catholic Monarchs have affirmed this same liberty of the Indians.[126]

In addition to criticizing Jesuit abuses, Bucareli made grandiose promises about how life would be different for the Indians after the expulsion. He declared not only that the Guaraní were free but also that they owned and should manage all mission property. In the addition to his original instructions outlining mission reforms, he emphasized that mission officials should exercise the highest vigilance in making sure that the Indians achieved total liberty.[127] Mission Guaraní heard these pronouncements and thanked Bucareli and the king. In their letter to King Charles III, the caciques and corregidors who went to Buenos Aires at Bucareli's request specifically mentioned their promised freedom. They thanked the king that "Bucareli has repaired our missions, in your name, rescuing us from the miserable state that we were in and ending our life as slaves."[128]

Such pronouncements about freedom and property ownership led some Guaraní to re-evaluate their relationship with the missions' communal structure. A few Guaraní expressly requested freedom from the missions. Diego Guacuyú wrote to Governor Bucareli asking permission to leave Yapeyú; he wanted to "work and be paid for the work I do so that all my earnings do not go just to the community."[129] He wanted complete independence from the communal structure. Likewise, the lieutenant corregidor of San Ignacio Guazú, Miguel Charecú, wanted freedom from the communal structure. But unlike Guacuyú, he did not make a request in writing; instead, he complained about his communal duties and then fled to Paraguay with his wife and three other Indians.[130] Not all of the Guaraní wanted complete freedom from the missions, however. Some interpreted Bucareli's pronouncements only as a release from collective labor projects. Almost a decade after the expulsion, lieutenant gobernador Valiente complained that the Guaraní thought that Bucareli's promises of freedom meant not working: "This is the reason that vices—especially those of laziness, idleness, and vagrancy—have erupted."[131]

Although mission officials tried to assign blame, a variety of factors led the Guaraní to evade collective labor projects. No easy solution could be found, and evasion continued to plague the missions for the duration. Given the numerous demands made upon the communal structure, mission inhabitants would always be pressed to work as much as possible. Evasion was a way for Indians to moderate the demands made upon them and make life more tolerable without breaking ties to their mission.

CONCLUSION

As shown by the demographic trends, the Guaraní responded in a variety of ways to the changing circumstances inside and outside the missions. Some Guaraní opted to leave the missions, while others remained. Even with these contradictory responses, trends can be observed. Initially, flight rates were low, as most Guaraní responded positively to the Jesuit expulsion and the reforms to the missions. As the missions' financial difficulties became apparent and promises of prosperity went unrealized, more Indians decided to leave the missions and flight accelerated. After about a decade of relatively high attrition, flight rates then declined as more Indians opted to remain in the missions.

Changing conditions both inside and outside the missions spurred the Guaraní to flee. Fewer distributions from communal supplies, the deterioration of mission infrastructure, and pressure to produce trade goods pushed them to leave. At the same time, expanding opportunities outside the missions attracted them: the rapidly growing regional economy needed laborers, and so mission fugitives easily found employment or other means of sustaining themselves outside the missions.

Population figures reveal that the collapse of the missions was gradual rather than abrupt. While demographic decline continued from the time of the Jesuit expulsion until the missions' collapse, a mass exodus did not occur. The loss of half of the mission population over thirty years was devastating but not precipitous, and the rates of flight fluctuated. Many Guaraní found ways of making mission life bearable: they used official channels as well as taking direct action to prevent exploitation and limit labor demands. While such responses demonstrate how the Guaraní influenced mission life and contributed to the institution's decline, they provide little insight into standards of living in the missions. Financial pressures, the shrinking labor force, and evasion of collective labor projects meant that distributions from communal supplies had to decline. Under such conditions, how did mission Indians meet their basic needs? Answering this question and showing how their response further contributed to the missions' decline is the focus of the next chapter.

CHAPTER 7

Procuring Necessities in the Missions

Tens of thousands of Guaraní opted to remain in the missions during the more than thirty years of decline. These individuals found ways of making mission life tolerable throughout the prolonged decline. As shown in the previous chapter, the Guaraní used both official channels and direct action to limit perceived abuses and exploitation by Spanish officials as well as other Guaraní. While we now have an understanding of Indian agency, this depiction of mission life so far lacks information about the Indians' material conditions.

Following the expulsion of the Jesuits, Governor Bucareli maintained the missions' communal structure of collective labor, shared ownership, and distribution of mission supplies, but in contrast to the Jesuits, he focused more on commerce and provided a greater role in it to Guaraní leaders. He believed that, given the opportunity and training, Guaraní leaders could manage their mission's communal affairs. In addition to greatly expanding native leaders' participation in mission management, Bucareli also awarded them more social and economic distinctions to reflect their elite status.

Nonetheless, most of the Guaraní did not benefit from mission reforms. The safety net for those in need almost completely disappeared, and the mission population received fewer goods from communal supplies than during the Jesuit period. Given that the mission population had depended on both of these for subsistence, how did mission Guaraní meet their basic needs under these new circumstances? Even though they received less overall from communal supplies, the amounts of some goods that were distributed stayed approximately the same or possibly even increased. Additionally, mission Guaraní found alternate ways of procuring food, clothing, and other necessities. They became more independent and self-reliant than during the Jesuit period. Many engaged directly in commerce with their mission—an activity unheard of previously.[1]

A small number of Guaraní did benefit under the new conditions. With their close ties to the Spanish administration and firsthand involvement in their mission's economic affairs, cabildo members—especially the corregidor—more easily adapted to the changes. Their new role in the missions gave them a better understanding of how market transactions worked and led to stronger connections with Spanish officials and merchants. Guaraní letters and account book entries confirm that at least some cabildo members used their new power to engage in commercial transactions for their personal benefit, and as a result mission society became more unequal.

To a large degree Bucareli achieved his goal of integrating mission Guaraní into the market economy and colonial society, but this process did not occur in the manner he desired. Guaraní leaders played a larger role in mission management, but they could not prevent the missions' decline. Furthermore, the Guaraní did not buy and sell goods independently because they saw how such commerce benefited their mission; rather, they became more self-reliant and independent because the missions' communal structure no longer provided necessities or a safety net.

SOURCES

Estimates of the Indians' living standards in the missions are based primarily on account records for Missions San Juan Bautista (1771–1800), Concepción (1779–1802), and La Cruz (1786–1789, 1798–1805).[2] Each mission kept an assortment of accounting records, including detailed receipts for individual transactions. As for almost all account records, several cabildo members and the administrator signed each receipt. Sometimes one book (or several) listed each transaction chronologically and was signed monthly, while another, separate book listed transactions by party and was signed at the end of each party's credits and debits with the mission. The missions also generally kept a detailed inventory that summarized inflows and outflows by good as well as a summary inventory, each of which was signed at the end. Such signatures by Guaraní cabildo members were a new practice; during the Jesuit period, cabildo members acted as scribes or secretaries, but they did not sign their consent or approval.[3]

All of these books include an immense amount of detail; in order to render the data more manageable, the following analysis primarily makes use of the detailed inventory, which lists the inflows and outflows of each item possessed by the mission over a particular period (most frequently one year). Generally, inflows include preexisting quantities, new production, and purchases, while outflows include consumption, sales, and losses. Sometimes an entry specifies who purchased or sold an item, how the mission procured a good, or for what purpose the mission disposed of an item. Most often the descriptions are vague—for example, consumption by the community (*gasto de la comunidad*). Some descriptions provide more specific details about how goods were procured or who consumed them. With the information in these account books we can trace production and consumption levels over time and gain a basic understanding of how the missions both procured and used goods.

San Juan Bautista, Concepción, and La Cruz exhibit the distinctive characteristics—geographic location, climate, and soil conditions—of all the missions in their respective departments. San Juan Bautista, one of the six missions of the San Miguel department, was one of the easternmost missions; La Cruz, one of the four missions of the Yapeyú department, was one of the southernmost missions; and Concepción, one of the seven missions of the Concepción department, was centrally located along the Uruguay River. Account records after 1784 have not been located for the thirteen Paraguayan missions belonging to the departments of Santiago and Candelaria; other materials discussed throughout the chapter suggest that these missions generally underwent the same types of changes and general decline as San Juan Bautista, Concepción, and La Cruz.

REFORMS: THE COMMUNAL STRUCTURE, COMMERCE, AND GUARANÍ LEADERSHIP

During the Jesuit period, distributions of goods from communal supplies served two main purposes for the Guaraní population. First, they provided a safety net for those who could not provide for themselves. Not only the incapable—the ill, widows, orphans, and the disabled—received foodstuffs from communal supplies; most of the mission population also received distributions of grains and legumes for several months out of the year after having consumed their own production. Second, distributions from communal supplies provided certain basic supplies to the entire mission population—beef rations either daily or several times a week, yerba maté rations twice daily, tobacco at least weekly, cotton cloth twice a year, wool cloth once or twice a year, and occasionally salt. The missions also purchased tools and trinkets with the proceeds from the sale of trade goods produced by mission labor. From these purchases, the Guaraní received valued tools such as axes, knives, and needles at least once a year and scissors, locks, medals, and colored beads sporadically. In addition, the mission populace often received special distributions, including fruit and wheat for bread, on festival days.

For the most part, Governor Bucareli did not try to alter the communal structure of the missions. The Guaraní still had to labor on communal projects. Bucareli did not mention free labor or wages. He specified that, as before, the fruits of communal labor would first sustain and clothe the population; after these needs had been met, then the remaining collectively produced goods were to be sent to Buenos Aires for sale. The proceeds were to purchase goods for the benefit of the community.[4]

While maintaining this communal structure, Bucareli repeatedly emphasized the importance of commerce and free trade.[5] He noted that according to Spanish law, Indians legally had the right to freely trade their goods, and he wanted the missions to comply, albeit with the administrator providing guidance.[6] He believed that the reason for the Guaraní not understanding commerce was their lack of exposure to it during the Jesuit period, and he urged mission officials to "employ the most fervor and effort" in promoting commerce both collectively and individually.[7] Bucareli saw commerce as "one of the most apt means for the missions to achieve the desired results,"[8] that is, prosperity and civilization for both the missions and mission inhabitants. Through this process he believed that the Guaraní would learn to act independently and thus outgrow the need for tutelage by mission officials.

Under Bucareli's plan, the Spanish administrator was not to be authoritarian but rather was to work with the cabildo. As Bucareli explicitly stated, "A Spanish administrator will be named for each mission that will, with his advice and direction, help the cabildo."[9] He expected Guaraní leaders—especially the corregidor and cabildo—to take a greater role in managing the mission, and in his reforms he granted them substantial new powers in order to do so. Instead of functioning solely as an intermediary between Spanish officials and the Guaraní populace as during the Jesuit period, the cabildo's new raison d'être was to oversee mission affairs and govern mission property for the benefit and advancement of the mission population.

In many instances, Bucareli's instructions gave Guaraní leaders powers at least equal to those of the Spanish administrator. Management of mission property provides a case in point. Bucareli ordered that the cabildo must consent to all transactions involving mission property. Thus, an administrator could not sell or trade mission goods or make any purchases on behalf of the mission without the cabildo's prior approval; all receipts required signatures indicating approval by cabildo members. Such receipts needed to include the amount of money paid and the color, quality, and price of each good. Bucareli explicitly instructed the general administrator not to purchase anything on behalf of a mission without the express orders of the corregidor and cabildo.[10]

To further guarantee Guaraní leaders' management powers, Bucareli ordered that access to each mission's storeroom require three keys: the corregidor kept one key, the Guaraní mayordomo another, and the Spanish administrator the third. During the Jesuit period, the mayordomo received such a key, but it served primarily a symbolic rather than practical purpose.[11] In contrast, Bucareli's instructions specified that "without the consent of the three, and after the cabildo's approval, not a single thing can be taken out for trade, or another end, whatever it may be."[12] In sum, cabildo members not only had to sign their consent to any transaction involving mission goods, but Guaraní leaders also held two of the three keys officially required to physically access these goods.

Bucareli's instructions not only granted the cabildo important management powers but also created mechanisms by which native leaders could hold the Spanish administrator accountable for their mission's economic performance. Bucareli ordered the administrator to record all transactions involving the mission's communal goods in two books—one for the administrator and one for the cabildo.[13] The cabildo was to keep a copy so that its members could always know what had been done with the mission's communal supplies.[14] Every year, the administrator had to send the gobernador of the missions a record of all transactions related to communal property. Before doing so, the administrator needed to have the cabildo members sign their approval of the record,[15] which effectively meant that the cabildo was expected to audit the administrator's records. To provide a further means of oversight, Bucareli instructed the corregidor and administrator to meet yearly with the gobernador and lieutenant gobernadors of the missions to examine the account books and the cabildo's resolutions.

While cabildo members had extensive oversight power over their Spanish administrator, ordinary Guaraní did not have similar power over their leaders. Access to the middle level of the political hierarchy—the caciques—was limited by birth, since these were hereditary positions. Mission inhabitants did not elect caciques, and therefore individuals from the lowest level could not move up the hierarchy to this position.

Access to cabildo membership was also, to a degree, restricted to caciques, and Bucareli reinforced the expectation that cabildo members would be caciques. To prevent non-elite Indians from exercising power, as had occurred under the Jesuits, Bucareli ordered that only caciques could be corregidors.[16] While in theory cabildo positions were open to all caciques, access was limited. Outgoing cabildo members chose their replacements and the Spanish governor confirmed the elections; as a result, a candidate could not gain access to a cabildo position without the support of the presiding cabildo members. Further limiting access, official term limits were often ignored.[17] Such restricted access prevented upward mobility and enabled cabildo members to maintain a monopoly over mission management.

Limited upward mobility to the highest levels of power fit with Bucareli's vision for the missions; he wanted a more hierarchical society. Bucareli criticized the lack of hierarchy during the Jesuit period and underscored the importance of building a more stratified society. He believed there to be a direct connection between a hierarchical society and civilization. He maintained that in civilized republics people were divided into various rankings according to their office and that the concomitant signs of honor and respect led their recipients to desire to protect their good names, thereby inspiring upright behavior.[18] In Bucareli's view, as this did not occur under Jesuit management of the missions, much of the Indians' incivility resulted from a lack of distinctions. In order to remedy the situation, he believed, higher-ranking Guaraní needed outward signs of their status. He ordered that the Indians wear clothing and shoes appropriate to their employment and social level and suggested that Guaraní leaders receive greater distributions of certain goods.[19] Furthermore, he strongly recommended that both in private and in public, the administrators honor and treat with distinction the caciques, corregidors, and all other Indians who held high positions or important occupations.[20]

Even before expelling the Jesuits, Governor Bucareli worked to strengthen and intensify the mission hierarchy. When he brought the corregidor and a cacique from each of the thirty missions to Buenos Aires in 1767, Bucareli treated them with great honor and respect as leaders of their missions. According to the fifty-seven Guaraní leaders, he gave them clothing, called them gentlemen (*Señores Caballeros*), and hosted a special mass and dinner for them with the leading men of Buenos Aires. In their letter of gratitude to the king, the Guaraní leaders highlighted his treatment of them:

On November 4, the day of San Carlos, the Bishop [of Buenos Aires] sang a Mass for us in your Majesty's honor; the Governor had us there with great pleasure . . . and after the holy Mass, he took us to the fort, and when it was time to eat, we sat at a table where they fed us; the good Bishop was there along with the priests, and the most important men.[21]

Such treatment was new to Guaraní leaders. Never before had Guaraní authorities had access to privileges or symbols of prestige such as these.[22] Caciques enjoyed some privileges during the Jesuit period—such as the honorific title "Don," exemption from public punishment, and ceremonial clothing to wear during festivals—but nothing like the treatment they received from Governor Bucareli.[23] By awarding more distinctions and power to Guaraní leaders, Bucareli expected them to take a more active role in mission management. Yet even as cabildo members did so, they could not halt the missions' decline.

DISTRIBUTIONS FROM COMMUNAL SUPPLIES

Owing to financial problems and the shortage of labor, mission production could not meet all the demands made upon it. Distributions to mission inhabitants had to decline, but across-the-board cuts did not occur (see Table 8 and Appendix 2). Instead, shifts in allocation patterns mediated the impact of the overall decline in distributions, and thus not all distribution quantities fell during the post-Jesuit period.

Account records for San Juan Bautista, Concepción, and La Cruz suggest that the amount of beef distributed to mission Indians increased substantially compared to the Jesuit period. According to Jesuit sources, most mission Guaraní consumed about .6 head of cattle per year in rations, although the inhabitants of a couple of missions received significantly more beef—the equivalent of 1.6 head of cattle per year.[24] In contrast, between the 1780s and the early 1800s, account records suggest that

TABLE 8. *Per person mission consumption from communal supplies*

	Jesuit period <1768	Post-Jesuit period 1780–1805	Estimates for a well-run mission 1780s
Cotton (ft)	17.4	7.5	9.1
Wool (ft)	5.1	2.2	N/A
Yerba (lb)	6.5	7.3	5.7
Salt (lb)	N/A	1.8	N/A
Beef (number of cows)	0.6	2.7	1.5

SOURCE: Estimates for textile and yerba maté consumption during the Jesuit period from "Relación de las misiones guaraníes" in Hernández, *Misiones del Paraguay*, 1:266. Yerba maté estimates during the Jesuit period also based on Juan de Escandón to Andres Marcos Burriel, 1760 in Cardiel, *Juan de Escandón, S.J.*, 118. Beef consumption during the Jesuit period based on Cardiel, "Breve relación," 83 and 168–169; and Dobrizhoffer, *An Account of the Abipones*, 1:222. Estimates for the post-Jesuit period from Appendix 2. Estimates for a well-run mission in the 1780s from Gonzalo de Doblas, "Memoria histórica, geográfica, política y económica sobre la Provincia de Misiones de Indios Guaraníes," Concepción, Sept. 27, 1785, in *Los escritos de d. Gonzalo de Doblas*, 60–61. Estimate of family size from Maeder and Bolsi, "La población guaraní de las misiones," 14.

Indians in San Juan Bautista, Concepción, and La Cruz consumed much more beef—an average of 2.7 head of cattle per person.[25] The amount of beef consumed in these three missions not only surpassed Jesuit-period levels; it also surpassed lieutenant gobernador Doblas's estimate of the beef rations necessary for a well-run mission—1.5 head of cattle per inhabitant.[26] The amount of beef consumed likewise varied across missions. In 1797, an inspector sent to the thirteen Paraguayan missions reported that the amount of beef distributed per mission inhabitant ranged from 1.0 head to 7.6 head per year. The inspector could not explain the variation; he claimed that the amount of cattle consumed in a mission did not depend on either the size of the population or the abundance of cattle.[27]

While most entries in the San Juan Bautista, Concepción, and La Cruz account records do not specify when and to whom the beef rations were given, the general mission population were clearly recipients. According to Doblas:

Two or three days a week, beef rations are distributed in a mission according to its ability. Ordinarily, one bull is killed for each hundred people and the scraps are distributed to the youth. In addition to the head of cattle distributed during [the aforementioned] days of ration, each day one or two head are killed for the daily consumption of the Spanish priests, administrator, the sick, the corregidor, mayordomos, tradesmen, and generally for those who help in the colegio, all of whom are a great number. Also, several head are consumed for communal projects [*faenas de comunidad*] because [workmen] are regularly given food at midday or after retiring from work, generally when the project is something difficult.[28]

The minimal details in the account records confirm Doblas's description. In addition to rations distributed to the general mission population, entries describe distributions for the colegio, hospital, and Indians sent on work projects outside the mission.

Salt rations also likely increased in the post-Jesuit period. Although no reliable estimate of distribution quantities during the Jesuit period has been found, anecdotal evidence suggests that mission Guaraní did not receive very much salt. Jesuit missionary Juan de Escandón reported that the Guaraní generally ate their food without salt—salt was so expensive that the missions only distributed it to the population occasionally on Sundays and festival days.[29] In contrast, during the post-Jesuit period salt became an important consumption item. In describing the condition of the Guaraní missions in 1798, the intendant governor of Paraguay, Lázaro de Rivera, claimed that lacking a pound of salt, a Guaraní would abandon his home and family.[30] San Juan Bautista, Concepción, and La Cruz prioritized the distribution of salt. Each of the three missions purchased salt during almost every accounting period from the 1780s through the early 1800s. The account books also report relatively high consumption quantities—an average of 1.8 pounds per mission inhabitant per year. In every accounting period, the missions used salt from communal supplies for the daily consumption of the mission (*gasto diario del pueblo*), which included both Spanish employees and Indians as recipients. Salt was also consumed in the colegio and hospital, distributed during community festivals, and given as provisions for Indians working in the estancias, serving in the militia, hunting cattle, and harvesting yerba maté. The missions did not produce salted beef or use salt as a preservative.

While not as dramatic as the increases in beef and salt consumption, the San Juan Bautista, Concepción, and La Cruz account books suggest that the quantity of yerba maté distributed to the Guaraní might have been slightly higher during the post-Jesuit period. Based on the average of two estimates by missionaries during the Jesuit period, the missions distributed about 6.5 pounds per inhabitant per year.[31] The amount distributed by San Juan Bautista, Concepción, and La Cruz—approximately 7.3 pounds per mission inhabitant per year—exceeded both this amount and lieutenant gobernador Doblas's estimate of 5.7 pounds per mission inhabitant for a well-operating mission.[32] Such quantities also compared favorably with the yerba maté rations given to peons in the Banda Oriental.[33]

In contrast to beef, salt, and yerba maté rations, mission Indians received significantly smaller distributions of cloth in the post-Jesuit period. During the Jesuit period, each mission inhabitant received an average of 17.4 feet of cotton cloth and 5.1 feet of wool cloth per year to make clothing.[34] According to the San Juan Bautista, Concepción, and La Cruz account records, the missions distributed an average of 7.5 feet of cotton cloth and 2.2 feet of wool cloth a year to each inhabitant—less than half the amount distributed during the Jesuit period. Furthermore, the Indians did not receive the full 7.5 feet of cotton cloth for clothing during the post-Jesuit period; the missions used some of the cloth for shrouds for the dead, sheets, cushions, pillows, carpets, curtains, tablecloths, and napkins. Although textile distributions fell far short of quantities during the Jesuit period, however, the situation was not necessarily dire. According to Doblas, a well-run mission needed to distribute 9.1 feet of cotton cloth per mission inhabitant—not too much more than the post-Jesuit figure.[35]

Distributions of tobacco fell even more sharply than textiles in the post-Jesuit period. Under Jesuit management, mission inhabitants received weekly tobacco rations. In contrast, consumption levels as recorded in the San Juan Bautista, Concepción, and La Cruz account books were so small as to be almost insignificant.[36] The .3 pounds of tobacco consumed yearly per mission inhabitant was not even enough for one carton of cigarettes in today's terms (see Appendix 2). Moreover, this amount was miniscule compared to the 2.5 pounds of tobacco per month received by peons working in the Banda Oriental region during the same period.[37]

Similarly, distributions of grains and legumes to the general mission population fell sharply in the post-Jesuit period. Under the Jesuits, distributions of grains and beans from communal supplies fed most of the mission population for a significant portion of the year.[38] In the post-Jesuit period, the quantities of corn, beans, wheat, and barley distributed from the communal supplies of San Juan Bautista, Concepción, and La Cruz were so small that they could not have fed mission inhabitants for one-third of the year as they did before. Between the 1780s and early 1800s, these three missions consumed a yearly average of 4.2 pounds of corn, 3 pounds of beans, 9.1 pounds of wheat, and 1.1 pounds of barley per person.

Some sectors of the mission population still received meager distributions of grains and legumes, but consumption was erratic and decreased over time.[39] The account records generally do not specify who received grain and legume disbursements or why they received them; often the records merely state "gasto diario" (daily outlay). Entries with more detailed descriptions show rations of agricultural foodstuffs for Indians engaged in important mission projects: Guaraní laboring in mission workshops (*obrajes*) or working on administrative or religious matters in the colegio. Guaraní laboring outside the mission (*faenas fuera del pueblo*) on projects such as harvesting yerba maté, gathering cattle, transporting trade goods, or providing military service for the Crown also took some grains and legumes with them. Some entries combine distributions to Spanish employees and mission Guaraní into a single entry. According to lieutenant gobernador Doblas, much of the foodstuffs went to Spaniards instead of mission Guaraní; he complained that feeding the administrator, the administrator's family, other Spanish employees, and even passing vagabonds resulted in great expense.[40] Except when they engaged in specialized labor projects on behalf of their mission, the general mission population likely received very little if any grains and legumes from communal production.

The San Juan Bautista, Concepción, and La Cruz account records show some distributions of wheat for bread and sweeteners on special holidays—especially the mission's patron saint's day. The entries do not specify if these goods were distributed to the entire mission population or only to Guaraní leaders, but the small distribution quantities suggest the latter.

Guaraní preferences and the ease of procurement largely explain the changes in the distribution of communal supplies from the Jesuit to the post-Jesuit period—the increase in beef, salt, and yerba maté and the decrease in textiles, tobacco, and grains and legumes. Increases in distribution quantities correspond to goods that the Indians valued and goods that the Indians could not easily procure themselves.

Beef rations meet both criteria. It was widely recognized that the Guaraní enjoyed eating meat, and both the Jesuits and post-Jesuit officials strongly believed that beef rations were the backbone of the missions. Governor Bucareli acknowledged that livestock was the principal means for sustaining the Guaraní.[41] Sixteen years later, lieutenant gobernador Doblas confirmed that livestock continued to be the most important mission resource: "The estancias are the principal force and vigor [*nervio principal*] that assures the subsistence of the pueblos."[42]

Beef rations were also attractive because maintaining collective cattle supplies required less labor than agricultural cultivation, and the operation of mission estancias with large numbers of cattle was more efficient than if each family maintained a few head of cattle. San Juan Bautista, Concepción, and La Cruz domesticated cattle, but they also replenished their herds by hunting and purchasing livestock. Both hunting and purchasing cattle were far less labor intensive than the regular work involved in raising cattle.

Collective cattle supplies also had the added benefit of providing mission Indians with regular beef rations on a daily or almost daily basis. As individual producers, mission Indians would have had to maintain huge herds in order to eat fresh beef on a regular basis, because without refrigeration, meat had to be eaten soon after the animal was slaughtered. The beef could be salted to preserve it, but salt was a precious commodity and mission Indians were unaccustomed to eating salted beef. Thus, collective beef rations were a priority not only because the Guaraní liked beef and communal cattle supplies required less work as compared to settled agriculture, but also because they enabled the Indians to regularly consume fresh beef.

Although its importance was often overlooked, the Guaraní also held salt in high esteem, and they could not produce it themselves. The Jesuits noted that the Guaraní liked salt. According to Escandón: "It is known that they like [salt] a lot, and as such they regularly eat the grains alone or lick it like sheep."[43] Cardiel also mentioned that the Guaraní liked salt very much.[44] Unlike most other necessities, however, the Guaraní could not produce their own salt: they could neither cultivate nor gather it. There were no salt flats in mission territory, and a substitute for salt did not exist. Thus, salt had to be purchased, and San Juan Bautista, Concepción, and La Cruz prioritized such purchases.

Together with salt and beef, the Guaraní also highly valued yerba maté, for which large-scale production was most efficient. In theory, mission Indians could have grown their own yerba maté, but cultivation was a laborious and delicate process. Paraguayans did not grow their own yerba maté trees. Probably because of the high labor costs, the missions largely abandoned their communal yerba maté plantations during the post-Jesuit period and procured much of their yerba maté by sending groups of Indians to distant wild yerbales. Since mission Indians could not easily cultivate yerba maté or gather it nearby, the prioritization of communal distributions made sense.

In contrast to beef, salt, and yerba maté, the Guaraní were ambivalent about clothing. Before joining the missions, the Guaraní did not wear shirts, pants, and tunics. It is unclear the degree to which the Guaraní absorbed Jesuit values about modesty and attire. According to Cardiel, the Indians were content with one simple set of clothes for decency in the summer and a coat in the winter.[45] Repeated descriptions concerning their lack of clothing raise the question whether mission Guaraní even felt such garments necessary.[46] Even during the Jesuit period, when cloth distribution rates were much higher, mission inhabitants were not always adequately dressed by European standards. According to Governor Bucareli, mission Guaraní lacked sufficient clothing, and their nudity was notorious, even scandalous, during the Jesuit period.[47] Clothing, especially European clothing, took on greater value among mission Guaraní after the Jesuit expulsion. When Bucareli invited Guaraní leaders to Buenos Aires, he gave them European clothing to wear as their own. In response, he found that they wore the clothing, honored it, and were thankful for it.[48] Mission Guaraní accepted to some extent European values concerning modesty, status, and proper attire, but their own values, comfort, and the expense made clothing less of a priority for them than other goods.

Just as distributions of beef, yerba maté, salt, and textiles reflected Guaraní preferences, so did the decline in tobacco and grains. Jesuit missionaries did not say that the Guaraní especially liked tobacco, as they did the former items. Tobacco, though addictive like yerba maté, was not as widely consumed by mission inhabitants. Under Jesuit management, the Indians received tobacco rations less frequently than yerba maté—generally once a week rather than twice daily; moreover, unlike everyone else in the region, mission Guaraní only chewed tobacco.[49] Jesuit missionaries did not explicitly discuss Guaraní attitudes about tobacco, but they highlighted Guaraní distaste for wheat and barley.[50] Cardiel explicitly stated that the Guaraní were not fans of wheat and that few cultivated it. Instead of these European grains, the Guaraní prized corn and manioc.[51]

Mission Guaraní may have reduced their consumption of certain items in response to the smaller quantities distributed, but this was only a partial solution. For some items, such as the supplements of grains and legumes that they had relied on for a third of the year during the Jesuit period, they had to find ways of replacing the distributions that they no longer received. How did the Guaraní compensate for this loss?

HOUSEHOLD MANAGEMENT

Reduced distributions from communal supplies forced the Guaraní to become more independent and self-reliant as compared to the Jesuit period. Of course, the Guaraní had been self-sufficient for centuries before European contact, and they had continued precontact hunting, gathering, and fishing practices to a degree even after joining the missions. Still, after over 150 years of residing in the missions, the Guaraní had become accustomed to receiving regular distributions from their mission's communal supplies. When these distributions declined or disappeared in the post-Jesuit period, the Guaraní were forced to adapt. In order to survive, they found ways of meeting a larger portion of their subsistence needs on their own. They generally continued to receive beef, salt, yerba maté, and a small amount of cloth from the mission's communal supplies; but for almost everything else, they had to find other ways of procuring these goods.

Such self-reliance was a marked change from the Jesuit period. Under the Jesuits, mission Guaraní possessed little private property. They did not make wills, and according to Jesuit missionary José Cardiel, an individual Indian only owned whatever he harvested from his seedbed and, if he was especially hardworking, perhaps a few chickens. Cardiel and others further claimed that the Guaraní were not capable of maintaining their own cows, horses, or sheep.[52] Since mission Guaraní had few private possessions during the Jesuit period, they could not trade on their own behalf. Cardiel recorded that during his twenty-eight-year tenure in the missions, he only twice observed a mission Indian selling something that he had produced. In one instance, the corregidor of Candelaria planted his own yerba maté trees and sold about 350 pounds of yerba maté. In another instance, an Indian planted sugarcane and sold between 75 and 100 pounds of sugar on his own account. Cardiel emphasized that these were unique cases: "Among many thousands [of Indians], none like them could be found." Further supporting his view that the mission Guaraní did not engage in commerce, Cardiel stated that he had never heard of any other transaction similar to those he described.[53]

During the Jesuit period, mission Guaraní relied heavily on distributions from communal supplies instead of private property and commerce. Jesuit missionary Juan Joseph Rico claimed that the Guaraní did not know how to take care of themselves. The goods that each individual produced "are so few and his management of them so bad that with total certainty I can affirm that in all of the thirty missions, there are no more than twelve families that have enough to consume and cloth themselves with the goods that they gather from their harvests or acquire by their particular industry. Instead, their priest helps them with goods from communal supplies."[54]

In the post-Jesuit period, by contrast, mission Guaraní independently produced goods for their own consumption, as a way of compensating for some of the distributions that they no longer received from communal supplies. As they had produced corn, legumes, and cotton for their own consumption during the Jesuit period, and a few had also produced some tobacco and sugarcane, the Guaraní intensified such production and met many of their basic needs by engaging in subsistence agriculture.[55]

As they became more self-reliant, the Guaraní also turned to the market economy in order to procure needed or desired goods while continuing to reside in the missions. Engaging in trade was a striking new development: the Guaraní had engaged in subsistence agriculture during the Jesuit period, but they had not bought and sold goods on their own behalf except on vary rare occasions. Although documents detailing transactions between merchants and individual Indians have not been located, post-Jesuit mission account records repeatedly record instances of Guaraní engaging in trade with their mission. In such instances, an Indian exchanged one or several items of his private property for something belonging to the mission's communal supplies. Although currency did not change hands very often, such transactions were equivalent to a Guaraní selling his goods to his mission and using the proceeds to purchase other goods. For example, in 1799 an unspecified number of Indians from San Juan Bautista obtained twenty-six of the fifty-three *sombreros* in their mission's communal supplies through trade—twenty in exchange for yerba maté, one for tobacco, one for onions, two for oxen, and two for silver.[56] Although the entry in the account records describes the various goods that the Indians traded for the sombreros, most entries do not include that much information. Over half the entries provide no information about who purchased or sold the goods during the given year; of the entries that include some description about purchases and sales, most do not mention the other party by name, how many separate transactions occurred, or the other goods that were traded in the transaction.

Despite the paucity of detail, the frequency of purchases and sales by mission Indians noted in the account records indicates that these were not isolated transactions. Whenever an entry includes a description about a mission purchase, it almost always mentions purchases from Indians. Not only did individual Indians regularly trade goods with the missions, the exchanges included a wide variety of items. The Indians sold almost everything produced in the missions—yerba maté, livestock, tobacco, cotton, wheat, corn, beans, and sweeteners.

Mission Indians often sold significant quantities of trade goods. For example, in 1799, San Juan Bautista purchased 19,575 pounds of yerba maté from mission Guaraní. These purchases from Indians accounted for almost three-quarters of the total yerba maté purchased by the mission during that year. In another transaction, Indians sold 286 of the 425 horses purchased by La Cruz in 1799.

Not only do these sales reveal Guaraní activity in the market economy; they also point to the increasing acceptance of private property by mission Indians. In order to sell goods to the missions, Indians first had to possess them. In striking contrast to Cardiel's description, account records reveal that mission Guaraní possessed livestock in the post-Jesuit period. They frequently sold horses and cattle to their missions. In every instance where the account books of San Juan Bautista, Concepción, and La Cruz specify from whom the mission purchased oxen, at least some were purchased from Indians. The Indians did not necessarily raise all of these animals; some were likely either hunted or stolen. The Guaraní, especially mission fugitives, were known to rustle cattle.[57] Nevertheless, even if they did not raise the livestock themselves, their selling stolen or hunted livestock still demonstrates that the market economy had infiltrated the missions.

Mission Guaraní not only sold what they produced; they also engaged in more complex transactions. Mission Indians sometimes sold things that they received as distributions from communal supplies. Almost a decade after the Jesuit expulsion, lieutenant gobernador Juan Valiente reported that mission Guaraní traded the clothing given to them by the community for horses.[58] Similarly, in at least one instance, Indians sold salt to Concepción. This transaction is especially interesting because the Indians did not simply produce the salt and trade it for something else. Instead, they first had to obtain the salt in some other manner—as a distribution from their mission, as a wage, or by theft or trade; only then could they trade the salt with the mission. Such transactions suggest that the Guaraní were deeply engaged in the market economy even while continuing to reside in the missions.

While trade was beneficial to the Guaraní, however, such exchanges do not mean that the Indians' standard of living improved in the post-Jesuit period. Trade expanded the Indians' access to goods beyond what they produced themselves or received from communal distributions. Additionally, they obtained some of the goods that they no longer received from communal supplies through trade. Yet, although commerce opened up new opportunities, its benefits should not be overstated. Mission Indians were forced into trade as a way of getting necessities that they no longer received from communal supplies and could not obtain elsewhere. In other words, they had little choice but to trade. With a few exceptions, mission Guaraní engaged in trade in order to meet their basic needs, not to accumulate wealth.

Guaraní who traded on their own behalf were often taken advantage of by unethical merchants. Given their lack of exposure to currency and commerce during the Jesuit period, the Guaraní often did not understand the terms of trade and how to make a fair exchange. As a result, many merchants and others saw mission Guaraní as easy prey. Governor Bucareli warned about such potential abuses; without the intervention of Spanish officials, he believed, outsiders would manipulate the terms of trade to personally benefit from the Indians' work and sweat.[59] Almost two decades later, lieutenant gobernador Doblas warned that by making unfair exchanges with the Indians without the knowledge of mission officials, Spaniards took advantage of mission Guaraní who did not know the market value of items.[60] Clearly, engagement with the market economy was not a panacea for the Guaraní.

WINNERS AND LOSERS

The biggest losers during the post-Jesuit period were the Guaraní who had previously relied for survival upon the safety net provided by their mission's communal structure. During the Jesuit period, each mission set aside communal fields specifically for widows and orphans, and the Jesuits fed the elderly, widows, orphans, and others who could not provide for themselves from the mission's communal supplies. Those who were ill also received special distributions from communal supplies.[61] (The cotiguazu, or women's dormitory, should not be considered part of such a safety net; rather, the safety net was the material goods—primarily food and clothing—provided to those in need.)

Special assistance to the elderly, widows, and orphans virtually disappeared in the post-Jesuit period. The San Juan Bautista, Concepción, and La Cruz account books never mention fields set aside for widows or orphans, which would have been listed in the inventories if they existed. Yerba maté, cotton, tobacco, and sugarcane fields are listed in the inventories, along with the number of trees or plants in many instances. Even the number of fruit trees is often noted in the accounting records. Both the administrator and native leadership clearly had the incentive to mention as many communal assets as possible in order to highlight their effective management and development of mission resources. Not only do the San Juan Bautista, Concepción, and La Cruz account books fail to mention specific fields as a safety net, they also never specify any distributions of corn, beans, wheat, or barley to their mission's elderly, widows, or orphans. In 1798, governor of Paraguay Lázaro de Rivera complained that the missions' communal system had abandoned the elderly, widows, and orphans. To address this shortcoming, he recommended the reestablishment of communal fields of corn, manioc, and other necessities specifically to serve the above-mentioned mission population.[62]

The main exception to the disappearance of the missions' safety net was assistance to the sick. As part of the effort to stop the spread of and lessen the devastation caused by epidemics, Indians interned in the hospital received extra assistance from communal supplies. San Juan Bautista, Concepción, and La Cruz used some of their communal grain and legume supplies to feed Indians in the hospital (and in at least one case, the prison). The infirm also received distributions of sweeteners—sugar and molasses/honey—to assist in their recovery.

But aside from the hospitals, little assistance was given to mission Indians in need. The only explicit reference to helping destitute Indians is distributions of cloth to those with the least clothing or those most in need (*vestuario a los mas desnudos* or *los mas necesitados*). During 1789 and 1790, the corregidor, cabildo, mayordomo, and procurador of Concepción confirmed that those most in need of clothing received priority. In a note attached to one of their mission account records for 1789 and 1790, they explained: "Because there has not been sufficient [cloth], it has not been distributed equally, but rather to those most in need, giving to them equally, and we have been satisfied and agreeable to this."[63] In contrast to entries pertaining to distributions of cloth, there is no mention of giving grains or legumes to Indians who were hungry or lacked food.

In addition to the sick, some mission Guaraní received more distributions from communal supplies than others. The pattern of San Juan Bautista's 1794 cloth distributions shows that even though cloth was part of the general distribution of communal goods, mission Indians did not receive equal amounts.[64] During that year, San Juan Bautista made 1,395 separate distributions of 6,508 varas to male mission Guaraní. The distributions were not equal in size but rather varied between two and eight varas. The size of the allotments was probably not based on family size; the high frequency of one quantity—five varas—would imply a very unlikely consistency in family size. Rather, the amount likely varied depending on an Indian's contribution to collective labor projects and/or position in society. Weavers received additional cloth as a reward (*gratificación*). Both Concepción and La Cruz also specified distributions of cloth to cabildo members, and Concepción recorded cloth given to students as a prize.[65] Such distributions suggest that even though the missions did not formally pay the Guaraní wages for communal labor, distributions from communal supplies served in part as compensation, based on the amount of time spent on collective labor projects and the level of responsibility and/or skill required.[66]

The San Juan Bautista, Concepción, and La Cruz account books also show native elite receiving special allotments of honey, wheat, cloth, ponchos, and hats. Clothing and related accessories were the most common type of item awarded to native elite. Special clothing for native elite was not new to the missions, but during the Jesuit period these signs of distinction were generally limited only to festival days and were put away when the festivities were over. According to Jesuit missionary Juan de Escandón:

All of the cabildo [members], or at least the principal members, on certain grand days [festival days] go about elegantly dressed "a la española," and that is equivalent to putting on *seda de golilla* [an ornamental silk collar], but after that day or days have passed, all of these clothes belonging to the cabildo members are returned to the communal storage room for another occasion.[67]

After the Jesuit expulsion, in contrast, native elite no longer limited their distinctive attire to ceremonial purposes. Bucareli regarded ceremonial clothing as ridiculous and a waste of money and prohibited its purchase.[68]

In the post-Jesuit era, cabildo members and other privileged Guaraní received Spanish-style clothing for their own personal use instead of extravagant clothing for festivals. This clothing was a change from the uniform dress of the Jesuit period and represented native leaders' new authority, power, and prestige.[69] The San Juan Bautista, Concepción, and La Cruz account books record distributions of ponchos and hats to cabildo members and other native elites. All of the missions frequently purchased such Spanish-style clothing and accessories through the general administration in Buenos Aires.

Detailed analysis of the goods purchased by Yapeyú in 1780 and 1781 shows that a significant percentage of the mission's expenditures went to Spanish-style clothing. During these two years, Yapeyú received 1,106 pesos worth of Spanish-style clothing items from the general administration, which accounted for 18 percent of the money that Yapeyú spent on purchases through the general administration. The quantities—201 ponchos, 192 caps, 42 hats, 79 pants, 54 vests, and 144 buttons—would have been enough for the Yapeyú elite but not enough for the approximately four thousand Guaraní who resided in the mission. In addition, Yapeyú purchased and distributed 1,058 pesos in clothing and knives to seventy-nine Guaraní who worked on the boats that transported goods between Yapeyú and Buenos Aires or Montevideo or who accompanied prisoners from Yapeyú to Buenos Aires.[70] While a Spanish administrator might pilfer some such items for his personal use, the detailed record-keeping process and cabildo oversight described previously provided a deterrent to such theft.

In the San Juan Bautista, Concepción, and La Cruz account books, cabildo members are the most frequent elite recipients of distributions from communal supplies. Ten entries specify distributions to cabildo members, but only one such entry (in this case, honey) to caciques. Another entry vaguely describes recipients as "the most distinguished Indians of the mission."

Lieutenant gobernador Doblas confirmed that cabildo members and other elite received special distributions from communal supplies but did not specify caciques in particular. According to Doblas, the general mission population received only beef, cloth, and yerba maté rations, and the corregidor, cabildo members, and the sick also consumed a little wheat, tobacco, molasses/honey, and sugar. Furthermore, the corregidor, mayordomos, artisans, those who worked in the colegio, and the sick received daily allotments of beef, while the general population received such rations only two or three times a week.[71]

In his 1798 report about how to reform the missions, governor of Paraguay Lázaro de Rivera likewise advocated the distribution of additional goods to cabildo members and others but did not mention caciques as recipients. Rivera recommended distributions of cloth, salt, goods purchased by the general administration, and extra beef to each mission family and to the widows and elderly on holidays. He also recommended the daily distribution of beef rations from the slaughter of one head of cattle and a half pound of yerba maté and tobacco for each of the fifty Indians working on communal projects. In addition to distributions to those working on communal projects, Rivera specified that cabildo members receive extra disbursements; he recommended that each month the regidors, alguacil mayor, and secretary receive one and a half pounds of tobacco, two pounds of soap, and fifteen candles and share four pounds of yerba maté. He recommended greater quantities for the corregidor, principal mayordomo, and two alcaldes—a half pound of sugar, thirty candles, and two pounds of yerba maté, tobacco, and soap per month.[72]

Many caciques reacted to the changes by leaving their mission. As described in Chapter 6, as of 1772—four years after the Jesuit expulsion—all of the caciques and potential successors to the position still resided in Missions Santa Ana and Corpus Christi (see Table 7).[73] By 1784, the cacique or a potential successor to the position had fled from over half of Santa Ana's cacicazgos (twenty out of thirty-nine) and over a third of Corpus Christi's cacicazgos (sixteen out of forty-four).[74] By 1799, the percentages of caciques or potential successors to the position who were fugitives increased to 64 percent for Santa Ana and 75 percent for Corpus Christi.[75] In almost every case, fugitive caciques did not return to the mission between 1784 and 1799—like other mission fugitives, many caciques found conditions outside preferable to life inside the missions.

Cabildo members had the most to gain by staying in the mission and adapting to the changes. Because of their close connection with the administrator and active involvement in mission trade, corregidors were in the best position to benefit from the new emphasis on the market economy. The San Juan Bautista and Concepción account books show corregidors trading with the mission on their own behalf. Not all of these transactions were small: in 1794, the corregidor of San Miguel sold 208 cattle to San Bautista. Although Guaraní corregidors did not attain the same level of wealth as the richest native elite in Mexico City or Lima, at least a few took advantage of the post-Jesuit reforms for personal advancement.

Some cabildo members also took advantage of their position to divert communal goods for their personal benefit. Groups of caciques on various occasions wrote letters of complaint about abuses on the part of their corregidor and other cabildo members.[76] They often complained that, together with the administrator, these individuals had misappropriated communal property; they also complained of excessive punishment, drunkenness, disobedience, and shirking of duties. The corregidor was generally the main subject of such complaints, and frequently the caciques requested his replacement by someone more to their liking. It is difficult to determine how widespread such abuses were. The existing documentation is filled with accusations, counteraccusations, and claims of innocence; determining what actually happened is impossible. While abuses definitely occurred, sometimes factions of disenfranchised caciques lodged such complaints as a way of gaining access to power. Since cabildo members chose their replacements, they held a virtual monopoly over this body. Thus, complaints about abuse were often part of a power struggle between opposing groups of caciques vying for cabildo positions.

An example of such a complaint is a long letter written by cacique Juan Guirayú from Loreto in the name of his fellow caciques to the governor of the Río de la Plata region in 1770. Guirayú asserted that his mission's leadership had not met their obligation to work for the good of all the community, especially those most in need: "We are ordered to provide succor to the poor from mission supplies. This is not done even though the pueblo has supplies, which have been acquired with the work of these same poor. Because of this, us, the caciques, your humble subjects, are disgusted."[77] Guirayú supported such broad claims with specific examples of abuse:

Señor: We assert that the goods that God gives us, and that are acquired through the work of the Poor [mission inhabitants], others benefit and gratify themselves. . . . Based on orders from the corregidor and administrator and the labor of these Poor [mission Indians], only the corregidor is paid. Not only this benefit, [he] has many others. The cabildo [members] also benefit. They are given clothing to wear, and to conceal this, they give the caciques three-quarters of rough cloth, but the Poor do not even get a needle.[78]

Even though a cacique himself, Guirayú felt the unequal distributions unfair and believed that the corregidor abused his power and bought off the other cabildo members and caciques. Furthermore, he argued, the corregidor prohibited any challenge to his authority and acted in a dictatorial and threatening manner. According to Guirayú, when questioned the corregidor responded, "There is no other superior that has the ability to override my orders, not the cabildo and no cacique. I also am a cacique and have had schooling, and thus, nobody can suppress my orders." This dispute clearly documents a power struggle between Guirayú and the corregidor. Whether other caciques felt the same as Guirayú is uncertain; none signed his name to the letter.

Similarly, in the dispute at San Juan Bautista discussed in the previous chapter, a group of caciques complained about what they saw as abuse by their corregidor and administrator. In their letter to Governor Vértiz, the caciques claimed: "Señor, the rations that are given every week are not given equally to the poor Indians. The sick do not get rations. Those who return from their fields do not receive rations either. In this manner, we experience the most misery."[79] Such letters portray both the growing inequality among the Guaraní within the missions and disputes over power among the Guaraní elite.

Some complaints were much more specific and reveal an understanding of market transactions on the part of caciques. In a letter of complaint about their administrator, corregidor, and two cabildo members, six caciques from Jesús provide an example of a transaction with mission goods that they characterized as "without the least utility to our mission." Their description was very detailed: they specified the amounts of items sold (150 varas of cloth, 2 fanegas of wheat flour, and Castilian clothing) and purchased (42 horses, 9 mules, and 24 bulls). They named who was involved—the administrator, the individuals who transported the goods (Carlos Taguacu and a Paraguayan named Lázaro), the corregidor, lieutenant corregidor, and two other members of the cabildo. Last, they included where the transaction occurred (the town of Yuty). Such details show that at least some caciques informed themselves about their mission's finances and wanted to shape the use of mission property. Furthermore, they did not hesitate to highlight what would happen— flight and evasion of collective labor—if conditions did not change. They threatened that if "our children see themselves persecuted, they abandon the Mission. In these terms we will find ourselves without any mind to work for the advancement of our Mission."[80]

As these complaints show, the expansion of the cabildo's power and autonomy sidelined caciques who were not cabildo members. Since caciques were native elite, Bucareli's desire to make the missions more hierarchical and award distinctions based on one's position in Guaraní society erroneously implied that all caciques would benefit: in practice, new power and status went primarily to cabildo members. Still, caciques found ways—including letter writing—to exert influence in their mission.

CONCLUSION

Ironically, Bucareli's goal for the Guaraní to engage in commerce was largely achieved. Both inside and outside the missions, the Guaraní participated in the market economy, but the process by which they became more independent and engaged in that economy did not occur in the manner that Bucareli had hoped. The missions did not flourish; it was declining distributions from communal supplies that forced the Guaraní to become more self-reliant and turn to commerce.

Although the missions declined and the Guaraní received fewer benefits from the communal structure after the Jesuit expulsion, a sudden collapse did not occur. Communal distributions shrank, but across-the-board cuts did not occur. While the social safety net disappeared almost entirely and distributions of most items grew smaller, quantities of a few items remained the same or even increased. The Guaraní played an important role in prioritizing these distributions and shaping the distributions as they declined. Cabildo members used their extensive management power over mission property, and even non–cabildo members made their voices heard. Concurrent with the decline in communal distributions, mission Indians became more self-reliant, disengaged from the communal structure, and engaged in the market economy by buying and selling goods. While most mission Guaraní did not benefit, cabildo members stood to gained the most and at least some personally benefited.

This process was common across the thirty missions, but the unique circumstances of two missions suggest another potential outcome. Yapeyú and San Miguel held rights to innumerable herds of cattle—a very valuable asset in the late eighteenth century. The two missions used these herds to produce cattle hides for the booming transatlantic export market and earned hundreds of thousands of pesos in revenues. Ostensibly, some of this money could have been channeled back to the missions and their Guaraní inhabitants and thus helped to offset the missions' decline. The next chapter explores what happened to these revenues, and why this endeavor failed to staunch the missions' decline.

CHAPTER 8

Failed Promise of Prosperity

At the same time as the thirty Guaraní missions were undergoing general decline, two missions generated hundreds of thousands of pesos in revenue. Between 1776 and 1786, Missions Yapeyú and San Miguel took advantage of their rights to innumerable cattle and became major producers of the Río de la Plata region's primary transatlantic export item—cattle hides (*cueros*). During these eleven years, mission hides accounted for approximately 16 percent of all the hides exported from the entire Río de la Plata region.[1] The high levels of revenue from such sales suggest that these missions were in a unique position to avoid the decline described in previous chapters. Yapeyú and San Miguel seemingly could have channeled their revenues from hide production into supporting their respective missions and their inhabitants and thereby avoided the financial problems and worsening living conditions that were undermining all the missions. While these two missions and their inhabitants benefited to a degree from such sales, however, their orientation to the world economy failed to be a panacea. Hide production generated huge revenues, but it also generated great expense. Moreover, the missions' inability to protect their property rights over cattle made large-scale hide operations unsustainable. By the early 1790s, according to an anonymous source whose writings show him to be knowledgeable about the region, Yapeyú was "one of the most indigent and miserable of the missions."[2] This chapter traces how Yapeyú and San Miguel came to be major hide producers, explores what happened to the revenues, and explains why ownership rights to the most valuable regional export failed to save these missions from decline.

RÍO DE LA PLATA HIDE EXPORTS

Hide exports were foundational for Río de la Plata's economic history and a precursor to Argentina's becoming one of the wealthiest countries in the world in the nineteenth and early twentieth centuries.[3] Río de la Plata's boom in cattle hide exports resulted from Spain's lowering of trade barriers in the eighteenth century, as described in Chapter 6, and hides remained the region's main export through the early 1860s.[4]

Leather making was one of the largest pre-industrial manufacturing industries, owing to the versatility of leather.[5] Especially before the advent of plastic and rubber, leather was used for a wide variety of purposes: people wore leather boots, shoes, breeches, gloves, and other apparel; they furnished their homes with leather furniture, screens, and bedcovers; they stored and transported their things in leather purses, bags, drums, and trunks; and they bound their books in leather. Leather was also used in farming, transportation, and manufacturing as well as for military purposes; buckets, saddles, harnesses, carriages, ship rigging, hoses, couplings, and cords were all made with leather. Most leather, however, was used for boots and shoes: about 80 percent of all leather produced in the early nineteenth century was made into footwear.[6] In South America, the abundance of cattle led to even more diverse uses for hides. River boats (*pelotas*) were made of hides, and even houses were sometimes covered with leather rather than wood or tiles. It was not uncommon for people, especially slaves and those with fewer resources, to sleep on hides stretched on the ground. Hide sacks were used to protect and transport agricultural products such as yerba maté, tobacco, sugar, cotton, and foodstuffs.[7]

Demand for leather grew in the eighteenth century as a result of numerous European wars and the beginnings of the Industrial Revolution; Britain, for example, was at war for 75 of the 114 years between 1689 and 1802. In addition to the great number of wars, armies increased significantly in size during the period. These soldiers were provisioned with a variety of leather goods such as boots, bags, and clothing. In addition to the military's increased demand, changes in agriculture and industry also required more leather; among other things, leather harnesses captured animal power for agriculture and industry, and factories required leather transmissions belts in order to power machines.

As leather consumption increased, domestic cattle herds were no longer sufficient to meet the demand for hides.[8] In Britain, changes in the pastoral landscape resulted in fewer cattle herds at the same time as demand for hides was growing.[9] As a result, Britain, previously an exporter of hides, imported approximately 1.8 million pounds of hides between 1772 and 1774, 4.3 million pounds between 1796 and 1798, and about 20 million pounds between 1810 and 1815 for home consumption.[10]

Spain had also imported hides since the sixteenth century, when the tanning and leather trade shifted from the Moorish preference for more workable goat and sheep skins to cattle hides, which were more durable. Around 1500, Spain imported hides from North Africa, England, and

Ireland but also exported hides to Italy, France, and the Low Countries.[11] Beginning in the 1760s, Spain's trade liberalization enabled the Río de la Plata region to tap into the growing demand for hides. Many of the hides did not remain in Spain; by the late eighteenth century, most of Río de la Plata's hides ultimately ended up elsewhere in Europe.[12]

Although not native, the few cattle brought by Spaniards to the Río de la Plata region in the sixteenth century quickly multiplied into extensive wild herds.[13] During the colonial period, most of the region's hide exports came from an area that ranged north from Santa Fe (approximately four hundred kilometers north of Buenos Aires along the Paraná River), south from the Salado River (approximately two hundred kilometers south of Buenos Aires), west from Córdoba, and to the east included all of present-day Uruguay. The humid and temperate climate, regular rainfall, and extremely fertile soil made the region especially suitable for livestock and agriculture. Tall prairie grass and low, scrubby trees provided abundant food for animals. Natural water sources and year-round rainfall yielded plentiful drinking water. When pastureland and water disappeared owing to drought, the great expanse of largely uninhabited land meant that cattle could generally migrate to suitable conditions elsewhere. Other than wild dogs and jaguars, few natural predators threatened the cattle herds. If disease or drought caused the wild cattle population to decline, favorable natural conditions enabled the herds to quickly reproduce and recover their population.[14]

Until the middle of the eighteenth century, hide production occurred in close proximity to Buenos Aires and Montevideo because of low transportation costs. As overhunting destroyed the wild herds in these areas, hide production moved to the interior. In the 1760s, Spanish, Portuguese, and Indian hide producers shifted their attention to the Negro and Yí River region of the Banda Oriental. This region was especially attractive for clandestine hide production. Although it was illegal, few obstacles prevented interested parties from hunting wild cattle without official permission. The territory was expansive and largely unpopulated; most of the land belonged to the Crown, and royal officials were far away in more settled areas. In the late 1730s, the Jesuits had unsuccessfully lobbied the Crown on behalf of the missions for rights to all of the land between the Negro and Uruguay Rivers.[15] The missions owned only the land to the north of this region and could do little to enforce the rule of law, since few of the Guaraní lived outside the distant mission pueblos. Independent Indian tribes to the west and Portuguese to the east had little reason to enforce the rule of law; they illegally slaughtered cattle for hides. Nobody had both the ability and desire to enforce property rights over cattle and land.

Indians, Spaniards, and Portuguese participated in contraband and illegal hide production. Nonmission and mission Indians frequently hunted cattle illegally, either independently or on behalf of Spanish or Portuguese employers. Outlaws and many prominent estancieros also slaughtered wild cattle illegally for hides; estancieros rounded up wild cattle on royal lands and then herded them to their estancia clandestinely before slaughtering them. Alternatively, they purchased illegally produced hides and then falsely represented that the hides were from cattle belonging to their own estancia. The Portuguese were also integrally involved in the illegal hide trade: they not only purchased large quantities of illegally produced hides from Spanish outlaws and estancieros but also crossed into Spanish territory to hunt cattle and produce hides themselves.

The illegal sale of hides played a big part in the contraband trade that proliferated in the region. Generally, hides or silver were traded for European manufactured goods or tobacco. Such contraband was attractive because it avoided any questions about the ownership of the cattle and evaded Spanish taxes. The Portuguese were deeply involved in this trade; an anonymous source in the 1790s estimated that Portuguese merchants could pay 25 percent more for hides because they did not have to pay the high Spanish taxes.[16] The Negro and Yí River region's proximity to the Portuguese border facilitated such contraband as well as other illegal activities.

Contraband, Portuguese activity, and lawlessness in the region were matters of serious concern for the Crown and Spanish officials. Disrespect for laws, rampant theft, and the cover offered to outlaws were an affront to authority. Equally alarming, rampant Portuguese activity threatened Spanish sovereignty and opened the door to Portuguese territorial expansion. Such a threat was real: the Portuguese had already demonstrated that their interest in the region reached beyond trade to territorial possession. In 1774, the Portuguese colonial secretary admitted: "His Majesty prizes much more the loss of a single league of territory in the southern part of Portuguese America than fifty leagues of exposed sertão in its interior."[17] As of the middle of the eighteenth century, the Portuguese claimed over half of the South American continent (see Map 5).[18] At least as pressing a concern to the overextended and indebted Spanish Crown was the valuable tax revenue lost to contraband trade. Given that the Crown lacked the resources and funds to pacify and bring the rule of law to the region, Spanish authorities had to look for creative solutions. Mission hide production offered the potential for a mutually beneficial solution to problems such as these.[19]

FROM CATTLE SUPPLIER TO HIDE PRODUCER

In the post-Jesuit era, mission officials expected that Missions Yapeyú and San Miguel would continue to play an important role in providing cattle to the other missions. Beef rations were of vital importance to the missions; the Guaraní consumed great quantities of beef. As Governor Bucareli stated at the time of the Jesuit expulsion, livestock from mission estancias was the main source of sustenance for mission Indians.[20] For most of the missions, the Guaraní consumed so much meat that the livestock on their estancias was not self-sustaining, and unforeseen hardships, such as a drought or epidemics, further depleted the herds. Mission officials acknowledged the reality that most missions had to regularly replenish their estancias with cattle from elsewhere. With the hopes of keeping all profits within the mission system, mission officials ordered that whenever a mission needed cattle, the animals should be purchased from another mission.[21] Given that their extensive territory was well suited to livestock, Yapeyú and San Miguel seemed best situated to continue being the main suppliers of cattle to the other missions.

Mission officials also saw opportunity in producing hides. They were well aware that significant amounts of money could be earned from the sale of hides. The Jesuits initiated such sales in 1745, but Yapeyú never sold more than a few thousand hides per year before the Jesuits were expelled. Governor Bucareli recognized the potential in this line of trade: in addition to noting that livestock from estancias provided the principal sustenance of the Indians, he pointed out that with the hides the missions could produce a sizeable amount of a commodity for trade.[22]

Two years after the Jesuit expulsion, the general administrator of the thirty missions, Julian Gregorio de Espinosa, laid the groundwork for large-scale hide operations by ordering infrastructure development for Paysandú (an outpost of Yapeyú along the Uruguay River and south of the Queguay River). Espinosa clearly had hide production in mind when planning the development of Paysandú: he ordered that facilities be constructed for inspecting and storing hides and *sebo* (tallow) before sending the goods to the general administration. In order to begin operations, twenty-four knives for killing the cattle; a thick cord to hang the dead animal; twelve powerful axes to cut the animal in two and skin it; six iron tables for cutting, cleaning, and shaping the hide; and a scale for weighing it were sent to Paysandú. In addition, fifty pounds of hardtack, four reales for meat and salt, and two pounds of yerba maté arrived in Paysandú to feed the workers. In addition to ordering supplies, Espinosa set basic operational guidelines: he explicitly emphasized that the administrator of Paysandú should always follow the orders of the corregidor, cabildo, and administrator of Yapeyú, because the Indians were the owners of the cattle.[23]

The Guaraní leadership of Yapeyú acknowledged the value of cattle hide production. In October 1772, Yapeyú's cabildo elected Gregorio de Soto (administrator of Yapeyú at the time) as the administrator of Paysandú. The fact that the cabildo chose to shift the administrator of Yapeyú to Paysandú indicates the importance of this outpost and its hide operations. In further recognition of the significance of hide production for Yapeyú, the administrators of both Paysandú and Yapeyú received the same salary of three hundred pesos per year.[24]

Although operations in Paysandú commenced in 1770, the quantity of hides sent to Buenos Aires remained relatively small for the first couple of years. After two years as general administrator, Espinosa stepped down. Then, soon after taking office, his successor, Juan Ángel de Lazcano, encountered an opportunity to massively expand hide production while at the same time claiming to be rebuilding the mission's cattle herds. In the early 1770s, Yapeyú's herds migrated south, and the mission did not have the manpower to round up the animals to bring them back.

Both general administrator Lazcano and a cacique from Yapeyú named Francisco Tarara sought the help of the governor of Buenos Aires in rebuilding the mission's cattle herds. Cacique Tarara alerted the governor in a letter that his mission had suffered a double catastrophe. Tarara complained that one-quarter of Yapeyú's cattle had strayed out of mission territory owing to drought and for other, unspecified reasons.[25] The cattle had migrated south into the Negro and Yí River countryside in search of food and water. This southern migration was not surprising: the Jesuits had maintained an outpost in Santa Tecla at the headwaters of the Negro River to prevent cattle from leaving mission territory for the Negro and Yí River countryside.[26] But this time, Yapeyú's inhabitants could neither stem the exodus of cattle nor bring them back. Concurrent with the drought, an epidemic ravaged Yapeyú. Smallpox (*viruela*) killed over half of Yapeyú's population. Fifty to 90 Indians died each day, and at least once the number jumped to 350 in a single day.[27] As of 1772, more than 5,000 inhabitants of Yapeyú had died from the epidemic.[28]

In order to rebuild Yapeyú's cattle herds, Tarara asked Governor Vértiz for official permission to gather stray cattle and produce hides in the Negro and Yí River region. By slaughtering bulls, hide production made the forced cattle migration easier. When cornered or confined, bulls fight and try to kill each other in an attempt to exert dominance over the herd; slaughtering the bulls thus eliminated this obstacle to gathering together the dispersed herds. Furthermore, since only the fertile cows and a few bulls were necessary for reproduction, excess male cattle and barren cows could be slaughtered without endangering future cattle supplies.[29]

Lazcano seconded Tarara's concern about rebuilding Yapeyú's cattle supplies; he had no doubt that Yapeyú had the potential to sell more than thirty thousand head per year to the other missions.[30] A year after taking office, Lazcano claimed that three missions—Yapeyú, San Miguel, and San Borja—had an endless number of cattle in their vast territory together with the royal lands where some of their herds had migrated. He reaffirmed that the cattle belonging to these missions were sufficient to maintain and provide succor to all of the thirty missions combined. There was a problem, however: the missions lacked the horses and manpower to round up the cattle. Moreover, the missions needed to hunt for and return the livestock that had strayed outside of mission territory and into royal lands.[31] Contracting hide producers on behalf of the missions was potentially a solution to the problem.

Lazcano also addressed the financial merits of hide production. He argued that producing and selling hides was the only way for Yapeyú to benefit from its bulls and repair some of the damage caused by the strayed cattle.[32] Lazcano personally stood to gain from this project: as general administrator in charge of the economic affairs of the thirty missions, he received a commission of 8 percent of gross revenues from the sale of all mission-produced goods, including hides. Moreover, he received a 2 percent commission on all goods purchased by the missions, including supplies and items purchased with hide revenues. Given Yapeyú's innumerable cattle, Lazcano's commission promised to be very lucrative. Thus, he likely encouraged the cacique to write to the viceroy; he may even have been the driving force behind the letter.

Although Guaraní leaders, Lazcano, and Governor Vértiz may initially have presented Yapeyú's hide operations purely as a straightforward way for the mission to rebuild its herds, the situation quickly became more complicated. Yapeyú immediately encountered difficulties in executing its plan to produce hides and herd cattle from the Negro and Yí River countryside. The mission simply could not find enough individuals to implement the project; as a result of the epidemic mentioned above, Yapeyú did not have enough manpower. Mission officials tried to attract nonmission labor but to little avail. The lawlessness and disorder in the region discouraged interest in the project. According to Lazcano, no *vaquero faenero* (cowboy hide producer) could be found who would go into the Yí River countryside without the accompaniment of armed troops. Such armed assistance was necessary "owing to the great number of *gauderios* [rural criminals] who roved those countrysides in association with Portuguese troops to produce said *faenas* [of hides]."[33] It is likely that financial motives played an even bigger role; nobody was interested in producing hides for the missions without financial gain.

In an effort to both stop the lawlessness and assist the Guaraní missions, Governor Vértiz approved a proposal by Cristobal Castro de Callorda to patrol the countryside around the Negro and Yí Rivers against illegal activity. Signed on January 9, 1773, the agreement gave Castro Callorda the right to sell hides in order to cover his expenses. He and his twenty-four armed men could seize contraband hides as well as slaughter cattle for hides. In recognition of Yapeyú's rights to the cattle in this region, Castro Callorda promised to give the mission one of every three hides.[34] General administrator Lazcano deemed this agreement beneficial to Yapeyú and urged Governor Vértiz to approve it. In practice, higher-than-expected costs resulted in Yapeyú receiving a smaller percentage of the hides—one out of four—than specified in the original agreement.[35] In total, between 1773 and 1775 Castro Callorda and his troops sent 90,266 hides to Montevideo on behalf of the missions.[36] Despite this large number of hides, Castro Callorda's commission was short-lived. In response to his patrols, the Portuguese raised larger posses, against which Castro Callorda and his troops were ineffective. Thus, after two years Castro Callorda resigned, complaining that the commission was no longer useful or profitable to him.[37]

Upon becoming viceroy in 1778, Vértiz again included the missions in his efforts to stop the lawlessness and contraband in the Negro and Yí River region of the Banda Oriental. He ordered the Guaraní missions and the Montevideo estancieros to establish patrols to protect their cattle and put a stop to illegal activity.[38] In response, the missions contracted and paid the salaries of twelve cavalry under Lorenzo Figueredo. In support of Figueredo's efforts, Vértiz initially supplied him with an additional twelve foot soldiers, but this support did not last long. After Spain joined the American War of Independence in 1779, Vértiz recalled the foot soldiers to defend the province. To compensate for this loss, Figueredo added an additional four cavalry funded by the missions.[39] In the report to his successor, Vértiz emphasized the importance of the patrols and law-enforcement measures. "No other method can contain such a multitude [the Portuguese, mission Indians, Minuanes, Charruas, deserters, and gauderios in the Banda Oriental], and I deem that you will have to dedicate yourself to exterminate it, so that all of the cattle of the Indians do not come to an end."[40]

The patrols under Figueredo lasted much longer than those under Castro Callorda and marked the beginning of a greatly expanded role for the missions in the Negro and Yí River region. Part of the reason for Figueredo's comparative success was a compensation structure better suited to the environment. In contrast to Castro Callorda's salary structure of a fixed portion of the hides, Figueredo and his troops were guaranteed salaries in advance. While Castro Callorda received a profit only after the missions received their cut and all expenses were paid, Figueredo and his troops received a fixed portion of gross revenues—one-third of the sales revenue from the auction of the seized hides—regardless of expenses. Under Figueredo's agreement, the missions received what remained after deducting Figueredo's cut, transportation, storage, auction, and other expenses.[41] If the revenue from the sale of seized hides did not cover Figueredo and his men's salaries, Yapeyú had to pay the difference.[42] Clearly, the agreement with Castro Callorda best suited the missions, while the agreement with Figueredo best suited the hide producer.

Another lucrative concession from Viceroy Vértiz ensured that Yapeyú had the ability to cover any shortfall in Figueredo's compensation. In 1778, Vértiz granted the missions the exclusive right to produce hides in the Negro and Yí River countryside. Furthermore, the viceroy recognized mission ownership of all reddish-colored (*osco*) cattle.[43] As a result, Yapeyú's hide operations produced more than enough revenue to guarantee payment of Figueredo's expenses.

In Vértiz's eyes, awarding Yapeyú this concession might potentially serve as a mechanism for resolving the problem of disorder in the Negro and Yí River region. By formally granting the missions exclusive rights over osco cattle and all hides produced in the region, the enforcement of property rights was outsourced to the missions. These clearly defined, exclusive rights gave the missions both the incentive and justification to protect cattle from theft and illegal slaughter. If the missions were effective, other parties would be unable to access the cattle and presumably most of the illegal activity would cease, given that contraband and the general lawlessness in the region revolved around cattle theft and illicit hide production. By granting Yapeyú exclusive privileges to cattle and hide production, Vértiz effectively turned the problem of stopping illegal activity in the Negro and Yí River region over to the missions.

The missions' exclusive right to slaughter cattle in royal lands mirrored the customary tradition of vaquerías. Since the seventeenth century, government officials had granted individuals licenses to *vaquear*, or hunt wild cattle, on royal lands. Prominent individuals or institutions solicited such licenses from the Buenos Aires cabildo or governor in order to produce hides for export or to provision the local population. Upon receiving the license, the holder organized a group of cowboys to hunt wild cattle. Over time, vaquerías depleted wild herds and private land ownership grew in the areas surrounding Buenos Aires. By the mid-eighteenth century, wild cattle had disappeared from much of the Río de la Plata countryside, and the concession of vaquería licenses had generally ended. But this was not the case in the Negro and Yí River region, where abundant cattle still roamed. Granting the missions permission to slaughter cattle in this region was thus an extension of the vaquería tradition—a productive use of cattle herds on royal lands.

Juan Ángel de Lazcano probably played a more important role in Vértiz's decision to grant this concession to the missions than any other individual or entity. Lazcano was very active in the Buenos Aires economy as the general administrator in charge of the economic affairs of the thirty missions. By arranging all sales of mission goods and purchasing all goods requested by the missions, he worked closely with the merchant community. This role necessitated that he live in Buenos Aires, unlike the gobernador and other mission officials. As a result, Lazcano was likely the most recognized face of the Guaraní missions among Crown officials. Furthermore, his high salary made him wealthy and facilitated both social and professional contact with powerful individuals including Vértiz and other royal officials.

Viceroy Vértiz granted Yapeyú the special privileges and responsibilities related to hide production after Lazcano wrote to the viceroy:

Mission Yapeyú has an urgent need to establish hide production in the countryside of the Yí and Negro Rivers, where its cattle have strayed. Not only because this is the most useful and opportune means to impede the very grave damages caused on one hand by the gauderios and on the other hand by the men of don Manuel Barquin, who against your express orders continue to benefit from hides, but also in order to restore to their old pastures those cattle [that have strayed from Mission Yapeyú].[44]

In making this request, Lazcano garnered support from estancieros and other regional leaders. A representative of the Montevideo cabildo agreed that hide production was the most opportune means for both remedying what had already occurred and preventing future damage to the missions' cattle herds,[45] and a representative of the Santo Domingo Soriano cabildo confirmed that "all the landholders of that area, except for don Francisco de Haedo, are firmly persuaded that all the cattle that are in the northern part of the Negro River belong to Mission Yapeyú, from whose estancias they have strayed."[46]

The Guaraní corregidor, other Guaraní leaders, and the Spanish administrator of Mission Yapeyú contracted Domingo Ygarzabal to oversee hide production in the region less than a month after receiving the concession. The agreement signed by Ygarzabal, Lazcano, the Guaraní representatives, and the Spanish administrator of Yapeyú formalized the terms of compensation and how Ygarzabal should proceed with hide production and record keeping. In return for undertaking this endeavor, Ygarzabal received 10 percent of gross hide sales revenue as compensation. The cattle hands and peons provided their own horses and firearms, but the cost of tools for hide production, weekly rations (or the equivalent value), and salaries were paid from hide revenues. The contract reminded Ygarzabal that neither cows nor calves were to be slaughtered; instead, bulls should be slaughtered strategically in a manner that facilitated the gathering of cows and calves, prevented the cattle from straying over the sierras, and encouraged the herds to return to the western side of the Arroyo Grande. Furthermore, he should take care when slaughtering cattle in the southern part of the region, because by this date Yapeyú's cattle had mixed and procreated with cattle belonging to Montevideo estancias. Thus, Ygarzabal had the additional responsibility of consulting with Montevideo estancieros about the best way for both parties to benefit from the contested cattle.[47] Based on this agreement, Ygarzabal sent a considerable amount of hides to the general administration on behalf of Yapeyú—almost 160,000 hides between 1778 and 1784, in addition to a little over 50,000 hides before the official contract was signed.[48]

The formal relationship between Yapeyú's hide production under Ygarzabal and the troops under Figueredo underscores that Yapeyú's hide operations not only benefited the mission but also addressed royal officials' concerns with disorder in the region. Ygarzabal and Figueredo worked hand-in-hand and supported each other. As noted above, revenues from Yapeyú's hide operations under Ygarzabal guaranteed payment of Figueredo's expenses. By capturing lawbreakers and sending them to Montevideo for prosecution, Figueredo and his troops protected Ygarzabal and his men. In this relationship, Figueredo's patrols took precedence: if for some reason Figueredo could not oversee the patrols, Ygarzabal took Figueredo's place. In at least several instances, Ygarzabal patrolled the countryside with Figueredo's troops when the latter was ill or otherwise absent. During these patrols, Ygarzabal confiscated illegally produced hides and, when possible, captured the gauderios and sent them to Montevideo for prosecution.[49]

Ygarzabal and Figueredo formed only one part of Yapeyú's combined hide production and patrols. In addition, Gregorio de Soto produced hides and patrolled the countryside for Yapeyú.[50] Ygarzabal and Figueredo operated out of Puerto Durazno in the contested Negro and Yí River region, while Soto operated out of Paysandú. Mission territory clearly did not encompass Puerto Durazno (located between the Negro and Yí Rivers); there was debate as to whether or not mission territory included Paysandú (located along the Uruguay River and south of the Queguay River). A Jesuit map from 1750 clearly shows Yapeyú's territory reaching only the northern banks of the Queguay River;[51] later sources claimed that Yapeyú's territory extended closer to the Negro River and encompassed Paysandú.[52] Whether or not mission territory actually included Paysandú, much of the outpost's hide production came from cattle in the disputed region: between 1769 and 1786, Soto sent more than 320,000 hides from Paysandú to the general administration.[53]

As Yapeyú's hide operations grew, its role as provisioner of livestock to the other missions declined. By 1785—a decade after cacique Tarara voiced concern about the state of Yapeyú's livestock holdings—the mission's native leadership recognized that the sale of live cattle played a minor role in the mission's operations. In a letter to the intendant governor of Buenos Aires, Yapeyú's cabildo and administrator claimed, "Our assets consist of the livestock gathered in our ranches, the hides that are dispersed in our countryside, and freight charged for goods transported from the other missions to the general administration. . . . The trade of the first asset only provisions our community with consumption goods and has no other benefit or income than basic support."[54] Yapeyú's leadership highlighted that, in contrast to freight charges and the sale of hides, the mission received only minor benefits from trading livestock. Clearly, Yapeyú's role as provisioner of livestock to the other missions had declined drastically in importance.

Other missions found that they could purchase live cattle elsewhere at a cheaper price than from Yapeyú. In 1773, the corregidor, cabildo, and administrator of Yapeyú offered Missions Santiago and San Ignacio Guazú a contract to supply them with two thousand cattle at 10 reales per head. Rather than paying in cash, the two missions would trade five varas of rough cloth (*lienzo grueso*) produced by the Indians for each head of cattle.[55] Both missions declined Yapeyú's offer despite the general administrator's order that preference be given to inter-mission trade. José Barbosa (the lieutenant gobernador who oversaw the department that included both Santiago and San Ignacio Guazú) justified this decision to Francisco Bruno de Zavala (the gobernador who oversaw all thirty of the missions) by claiming that such an agreement was not in the best interest of these two missions under his charge: Yapeyú's price was too high.

Making matters worse, according to Barbosa, the true price offered by Yapeyú was significantly greater than 10 reales, because it did not include transportation costs; thus Santiago and San Ignacio Guazú would have to pay for carts and oxen to transport the cloth and for horses to herd the cattle from Mission San Carlos (the midpoint where Yapeyú wanted the exchange to take place). Moreover, Barbosa claimed, about a quarter of the cattle would be lost during the extended journey and the crossing of the Paraná River. Santiago and San Ignacio Guazú offered Yapeyú a counterproposal—they would pay the same price, but Yapeyú would have to transport the cattle to Mission Itapúa, north of the Paraná River. Under this proposal, Yapeyú would cover more of the transportation costs and the loss of animals, which effectively meant that Yapeyú would receive less than 7.5 reales per head. Yapeyú declined the counterproposal.[56] Yapeyú received a significantly higher price per head by selling hides than by selling live cattle to other missions: between 1769 and 1786, the missions received on average 11 reales per hide. Although selling hides in Buenos Aires or Montevideo entailed production, storage, and transportation costs, it avoided the high costs and losses incurred by herding live animals long distances and crossing both the Uruguay and Paraná Rivers.

In 1783, Mission San Miguel also began massive hide operations. In that year, Lazcano complained that theft and illegal slaughter threatened San Miguel's cattle herds. His description echoed his account of Yapeyú's herds in 1778: "The miserable Indians suffer daily the theft of cattle, hides, and death at the hands of the Portuguese and Spanish gauderios." Furthermore, he recommended that Viceroy Vértiz approve a twofold approach similar to that implemented under Ygarzabal and Figueredo. On one hand, San Miguel's cattle outside of mission territory should "be gathered according to the plan formed in 1774 according to your [Vértiz's] orders . . . and on the other hand, the object of this patrol should be directed to the remote countryside where the Portuguese produce hides and herd cattle to their dominions. With your goodwill and approval, hide production should be established for those cattle that belong to Mission San Miguel in the distant countryside where Portuguese benefit from them."[57] In the same year, Viceroy Vértiz approved Lazcano's plan. Soon thereafter, Antonio Pereyra, assisted by José Fernandez Castro, initiated hide production on behalf of San Miguel in the frontier between San Miguel's territory and Portuguese dominions.

Vértiz hoped that San Miguel's hide operations would financially benefit the missions while counteracting disorder in the Banda Oriental. Like Yapeyú's hide operations under Ygarzabal, San Miguel's hide operations under Pereyra were designed to put an end to Portuguese activity and the general lawlessness in the region. Pereyra's contract with San Miguel explicitly included his obligation to "exterminat[e] the many gauderios that have for years engaged in clandestine hide production and the taking of livestock to the dominions of Portugal and this Plaza [of Montevideo]."[58] Pereyra, like Ygarzabal, produced significant quantities of hides: between 1784 and 1785, the general administration documented the receipt of almost 53,000 hides from Pereyra. Most likely Pereyra slaughtered more cattle; when he was removed from his position as *comandante de milicias*, he claimed that he left 50,000 hides in the countryside.[59]

As a result of these cattle hide concessions, Yapeyú and San Miguel became major players in the Río de la Plata hide trade and earned huge amounts of revenue. Between 1776 and 1786, the general administration received almost 640,000 hides from the missions, which accounted for over 16 percent of all hides exported from the Río de la Plata region and generated over 820,000 pesos in sales revenue for the missions.[60] Such revenues dwarfed those of the other missions. From 1778 to 1788, Yapeyú accounted for almost half of the total revenue for all thirty missions (see Table 5). These massive operations and enormous revenues stand in sharp contrast to Yapeyú's decline. One might conclude that greedy and corrupt individuals took advantage of the missions' hide operations and siphoned off the benefits. But while greed and corruption definitely were contributing factors, mismanagement does not fully explain the outcome.

HIDE REVENUE AND EXPENSES

Producing such a large number of cattle hides required large-scale, complex operations. Between 1769 and 1786, the missions employed four main contractors to produce hides, three of whom worked for Yapeyú. From 1773 to 1778, Cristobal Castro de Callorda and others operated armed patrols of the Negro and Yí River countryside and produced hides to cover their expenses; from 1769 to 1786, Gregorio de Soto produced hides and oversaw Yapeyú's estancias out of Paysandú; from 1777 to 1785, Domingo Ygarzabal produced hides out of Puerto Durazno for Yapeyú; and from 1784 to 1785, San Miguel contracted Antonio Pereyra to produce hides.[61] The profitability of these operations fluctuated greatly, and not all were profitable. Much of the losses can be attributed to unsold hides and extraordinary and unrelated expenses.

For all of the missions' operations, both hide prices and production costs generally fell within normal ranges for regional hide operations. Hide prices in the Río de la Plata region were not constant but variable, depending on the quality of the hide and market conditions. On a particular date, there was not one single price but rather a range of prices, based on a hide's weight and physical condition.[62] Furthermore, the range of prices was not constant: prices fluctuated, depending on demand, which in turn was highly dependent on how easy it was to ship merchandise across the Atlantic Ocean.[63] Prices paid for mission hides were consistent with such variations and fit with the prevailing market prices.[64] Similarly, the costs incurred in producing and transporting hides fit within the normal range. According to a widely consulted report about the Banda Oriental from the 1790s, the cost of bringing hides to market totaled one peso—four reales for production and four reales for transportation from the countryside to Montevideo.[65] Accounting records indicate that mission hide operations were consistent with such an estimate.[66]

The compensation structure for mission hide operations encouraged efforts to make sure the hides garnered the highest possible prices but did little to restrain expenses. Ygarzabal, Pereyra, and the general administrator received commissions based on gross revenues, which motivated them to maximize both the quantity of hides sold and the price but not to limit expenditures.[67] Ygarzabal and Pereyra would receive no additional compensation if they made their operations more efficient; the general administrator, because he received an additional commission on all mission purchases, actually had an incentive to increase expenditures. Likewise, the flat-rate compensation received by Soto did little to make hide production more efficient. Soto received a fixed annual salary of 300 pesos—only a small fraction of the average of over 3,500 pesos earned by Ygarzabal each year.[68] So large a discrepancy could have encouraged Soto to employ excess labor, make unnecessary expenditures, or pad the books, or he could have diverted such spending for his personal benefit or used it to increase his prestige, power, and ability to ask for favors from dependents.

The compensation structure not only did little to promote efficient operations, it also channeled much of the financial benefit to the general administrator and hide contractors. Compensation based on commissions resulted in very generous compensation packages for both the general administrator and Ygarzabal. The general administrator's commission of 8 percent of all of the missions' hide sales revenue—including that pertaining to Ygarzabal's operations—earned him more than 57,979 pesos, while Ygarzabal's commission of 10 percent earned him 29,428 pesos. If Pereyra had received his commission, he likewise would have received a large amount of money. Such earnings greatly exceeded the salaries of top mission officials: the gobernador of the thirty missions received 1,200 pesos per year, and lieutenant gobernadors received between 400 and 700 pesos per year depending on the number of missions under their supervision.[69] Both Ygarzabal's and the general administrator's compensation were also high compared to that of prominent Crown officials: a commander received 2,000 pesos per year, the superintendent (the financial chief of the entire viceroyalty, who reported directly to Madrid) 10,000 pesos per year.[70]

Critics of the missions' hide operations repeatedly claimed that the missions failed to benefit from hide production owing to corruption on the part of the general administrator and the hide contractors.[71] After Ygarzabal's first sale of 50,142 hides, Pedro Joséf Ballesteros, the accountant for the agency in charge of public property and taxes (Contaduría General de Propios y Arbitrios) wrote to the treasury complaining that Ygarzabal's 5,848 pesos in commission was unjust and excessive.[72] But, while the huge amounts of money that both the general administrator and Ygarzabal received from the missions' hide operations can be considered unjust and excessive, such earnings should not be considered as manifestations of outright corruption. Top Crown officials documented and approved the salary structure. In his instructions for the missions, Governor Bucareli deemed appropriate the general administrator's salary of an 8 percent commission on the sale of mission goods and a 2 percent commission on mission purchases.[73] Likewise, both top Crown officials and mission management knew about and approved Ygarzabal's commission; his contract specified the amount and the cabildo and administrator of Yapeyú and the general administrator signed their approval of this document.[74] Moreover, the viceroy himself also gave his consent.

Both the general administrator and Ygarzabal certainly received excessive amounts of money when compared to the benefits received by the Guaraní, but their earnings were not out of line when compared with large-scale estancieros or *contrabandistas*. According to the anonymous author of the 1790s report about the Banda Oriental, no other trade good yielded as high a profit as hides produced from wild cattle in the Negro and Yí River countryside and sold in Montevideo. The author optimistically claimed that returns on hide production averaged 100 percent but could be even higher.[75] Profits of that magnitude dwarfed the general administrator's and Ygarzabal's commissions of 8 and 10 percent, respectively.

While expenses may have been padded and managers probably had connections with estancieros or people involved in contraband, the keeping of detailed accounting records and extensive oversight hindered, at least to some degree, rampant corruption. Hide contractors and managers had to account for all expenditures. These receipts and records were signed by the general administrator and often by native leaders as well. Furthermore, the Contaduría General de Propios y Arbitrios inspected and approved mission account records. Nevertheless, although the contractors had to provide the general administrator with lists of all of their expenditures in order to receive payment, both Soto's and Pereyra's descriptions of the monies that they spent lacked important details. In many instances, the receipts stated merely that the money or goods were used for producing hides or paying salaries and did not provide any information about how the goods were distributed, the compensation rate, or the number of recipients. Presumably, however, despite such lack of detail, the signatures on the receipts, frequently by five distinct parties—Yapeyú's

Guaraní cabildo and mayordomo, the Spanish administrator, the captain of the boat that transported the goods, the general administrator, and Soto or Pereyra—provided oversight.

But mission hide production, even with extensive oversight, could not remain immune from the thriving contraband trade that pervaded the region. The porous border with Brazil, limited law enforcement, and vigorous market in contraband hides made the illegal production and sale of hides attractive. Not all mission officials and concessionaires remained honest when faced with such opportunities for financial gain.[76] At least some of the missions' hide production was diverted to contraband trade.

Several Spanish managers were accused of corruption and investigated, but the most notorious—Antonio Pereyra—was ultimately exonerated. Because of concerns that he was working with clandestine hide producers and involved in contraband trade, the newly appointed viceroy, the marqués de Loreto, relieved Pereyra in 1784 from his contractor position. His replacement, Félix de la Rosa, was instructed to investigate Pereyra's conduct. In order to plead his case, Pereyra left for Spain before reconciling his accounts and paying the outstanding bills related to hide production. While in Spain, he wrote a report about how to put an end to lawlessness in the Banda Oriental that was highly critical of large landowners. The outcome of Pereyra's case is unknown, but it was likely resolved in his favor given that he subsequently returned to the Banda Oriental and, ironically, became a large landowner, an *alcalde de barrio*, and in 1802 a representative in the political organization for estancieros (*junta de hacendados*).[77]

Whether or not Pereyra was himself corrupt, such accusations serve as a reminder that accounting books should not be taken at face value. Records could be falsified; details or numbers might have been omitted or included unnecessarily. One must always question the accuracy and honesty of the account books. Nevertheless, when used with caution, these records provide valuable information about the mission's economic activities and performance.

While Spanish administrators benefited most from hide operations, mission Guaraní were not entirely left out. In fact, the amount of money spent by Yapeyú on its Guaraní population was not insignificant (see Table 9). Between 1776 and 1784, after paying hide-related expenses (which accounted on average for almost three-quarters of all the monies spent by the mission) and spending another 14 percent on other expenses, such as hide-related salaries and transportation, Yapeyú spent the remaining 13 percent on its Guaraní inhabitants. This money went toward the purchase of livestock, consumption goods, and other remitted goods that, at least in part, benefited the Guaraní. The monies spent on mission

TABLE 9. *Mission Yapeyú expenses during peak cuero production years*

Year	Total expenses	Production costs	Livestock purchases	Goods	Other
1776	42,978	61%	13%	16%	10%
1777	42,978	61%	13%	16%	10%
1778	54,617	55%	24%	14%	7%
1779	54,617	55%	24%	14%	7%
1780	73,642	85%	4%	5%	6%
1781	73,642	85%	4%	5%	6%
1782	117,085	77%	0%	3%	20%
1783	117,085	77%	0%	3%	20%
1784	117,085	77%	0%	3%	20%
Total	693,729	73%	6%	7%	14%

SOURCE: See Appendix 3.
NOTE: Other expenses are primarily salaries and the maintenance of boats.

inhabitants are especially noteworthy in view of the fact that Yapeyú's revenues did not cover all of the mission's expenses (see Appendix 3). The mission prioritized these goods for the Indians over its other expenses: it did not even pay any taxes owed to the Crown during the entire period.

Paradoxically, given its history as a cattle supplier to the other missions, Yapeyú directed 6 percent of its expenditures between 1776 and 1784 to the purchase of livestock.[78] The 44,346 pesos went to purchasing and transporting horses and cattle. Yapeyú needed a large number of horses to herd cattle and operate its estancias. According to the Jesuit José Cardiel, each person on a vaquería needed five horses; Félix de Azara wrote that each worker on an estancia needed ten horses and five mules.[79] In 1778, the corregidor, cabildo, and administrator of Yapeyú together with Gregorio de Soto complained to the viceroy that Minuanes Indians, along with the mission deserters that they harbored, stole large numbers of Yapeyú's horses, making it difficult for Yapeyú to care for its cattle herds.[80] As a result, over 7,695 pesos was spent on horses and some mules.

Yapeyú spent more money (over 30,054 pesos) on the purchase and transport of cattle. According to a report by Yapeyú's Guaraní leaders and administrator, herding cattle from the River Yí countryside was difficult on account of the large distances and numerous rivers, and so the mission resorted to purchasing cattle.[81] In October 1778, Yapeyú paid Pedro Garcia de Zuñiga 14,700 pesos for 14,000 cattle to stock a new estancia near the Mocoretá River and 9,749 pesos for 9,478 cattle to stock another new estancia at Mandisoví. These cattle were purchased from the general administrator's brother-in-law, with whom Lazcano also co-owned a major estancia.[82] Even though the close relationship between

Lazcano and Garcia de Zuñiga might imply corruption, the low sale price suggests otherwise. Both purchases averaged just over eight reales per head, which was significantly lower than the ten reales sale price that Yapeyú wanted less than five years earlier from Missions Santiago and San Ignacio Guazú. Lazcano further defended these purchases by documenting that the Jesuits had purchased even greater quantities of cattle—112,218 head—for Yapeyú in the 1730s.[83] In addition to purchasing cattle, Yapeyú's cabildo and administrator and Paysandú's administrator contracted Ygarzabal to herd 50,000 of its cattle from the Negro and Yí River countryside to Salto for a fee of four reales per head. According to the general administration's accounting records, Yapeyú only received (and paid for) 10,469 of the allotted cattle.[84]

Yapeyú's hide operations facilitated the temporary renovation of its estancias. As cacique Tarara argued, in the early 1770s Yapeyú's estancias were in dire condition. Drought and emigration caused the cattle population to fall from 62,679 at the time of the Jesuit expulsion to 15,726 in 1772–1773 (see Table 10). Yapeyú's hide operations made the temporary recovery of the mission's estancias possible by funding livestock expenditures and facilitating the herding of cattle back to Yapeyú's territory. By 1783, the number of cattle in Yapeyú's estancias had risen to 72,800—surpassing the number at the Jesuit expulsion. But the increase was short-lived. In the subsequent year, the number of cattle fell to 61,300, and by 1798 Yapeyú's cattle supplies had plummeted to 13,068.

Yapeyú derived minimal benefit from its valuable cattle herds and lucrative concessions to produce hides in part because the possibilities for the Guaraní to take advantage of such an opportunity were limited. It is likely that Yapeyú's Guaraní leaders compromised with Spanish administrators and did not demand more from their mission's hide operations because it seemed like the best option under the circumstances. Guaraní

TABLE 10. *Cattle in Mission Yapeyú's estancias, 1768–1806*

Year	Total	Year	Total
1768	62,679	1800	14,021
1772–1773	15,726	1801	7,873
1778	34,508	1802	9,262
1780	48,290	1803	4,273
1783	72,800	1804	640
1784	61,300	1805	5,014
1798	13,068	1806	9,056
1799	17,187		

SOURCE: Mission inventories, AGN, IX 7-7-7, 17-6-3, 18-7-6, 22-6-3, 22-7-6, and 22-9-4.

leaders were unable and unprepared to properly oversee such a massive operation. Supervising hide production, properly reviewing the accounting records, and understanding where all of the money was spent was an enormously complicated task. Mission Guaraní did not have the experience or skills necessary for managing an enterprise employing hundreds of people and generating hundreds of thousands of pesos in revenue. Moreover, even if they had had the ability and desire to actively manage the mission's hide operations, other matters demanded their attention.

When Yapeyú initiated its large-scale hide operations, the mission was recovering from a massive smallpox epidemic. Yapeyú's population had drastically declined, its buildings were in disrepair, and its reserves and estancias were exhausted.[85] Guaraní leaders could not attend to matters in the mission at the same time as overseeing hide production in an extensive territory distant from the mission town; they had neither the time nor the manpower to properly oversee both. Making matters worse, the epidemic had impaired the native power structure. Various caciques and cabildo members had died, including the corregidor; as a result, in 1772, 38 percent (eighteen out of forty-eight) of the caciques were either female or under the age of fifteen.[86] Many of the new leaders, especially the very young, lacked experience and probably did not have the respect or loyalty of the rest of the Guaraní.

Management and oversight efforts were further impeded by the fact that Guaraní laborers did not participate in hide production. Oversight was practically impossible, since the Guaraní population lacked day-to-day contact with the production process. In 1772, only twelve Guaraní families from Yapeyú resided in Paysandú. By 1786, the number had increased to twenty-two families, but the number was still insignificant compared to the hundreds of Spanish peons employed in the mission's hide production.[87] Ygarzabal's contract also specified that he was to hire cowboys and peons.[88] According to Gregorio de Soto, it was immediately necessary to exclude Yapeyú's Guaraní population from hide production because of their uselessness and instead hire Spanish laborers in their place.[89] Such a claim rings hollow, though, given that mission Guaraní had participated in vaquerías and produced cattle hides during the Jesuit period. Furthermore, the Guaraní were valued employees and sought after for producing hides, as shown in Chapter 6.

Nonetheless, Yapeyú's population could not meet the labor needs of the mission's hide operations. When Soto began hide production in Paysandú in 1773, over half of Yapeyú's population had died during the epidemic. The number of tributaries (equivalent to non-cacique working-age males) dropped from 936 before the expulsion to 735 in 1772.[90] Moreover, a large number of fugitives fled the mission to avoid contagion.

As cacique Tarara stated in his request for assistance, Yapeyú did not have the labor force necessary to gather its cattle herds and restore its estancias. Even after the number of Yapeyú's tributaries grew to 1,047 in 1781, the labor force necessary for Soto's and Ygarzabal's hide operations was significantly greater than Yapeyú's capacities. Yapeyú's hide operations lasted for more than a decade, and the mission could not afford to have most of its workforce absent for such an extended period of time, neglecting the rest of their responsibilities to the mission.

Most likely, mission Guaraní also chose not to produce hides because of the minimal compensation that they received for their labor. Within the mission structure, the concept of paying mission Indians wages clashed with the ideas of communal ownership of resources and collective labor. As a result, a dual remuneration system developed: mission Indians received only rations, while Spanish peons received wages. Yapeyú's transportation network used this remuneration system: mission Guaraní who worked on Yapeyú's three boats received only food rations and clothing, while Spanish laborers received wages.[91] Similarly, in 1785 Casero requested eight mission Guaraní to work in Yapeyú's hide storage facilities (*barracas*) in Buenos Aires, explicitly in order to avoid paying the eight-pesos-per-month wages that the mission had to pay to Spanish peons.[92]

Laboring in mission hide production meant both below-market wages for the Guaraní and extended absences from their pueblo. The production, storage, and sale of hides occurred at a distance far from their homes in Yapeyú. Given these conditions, the Guaraní had little incentive to actively participate in the mission's hide operations. And, if they did not want to work in hide production, mission Guaraní could not be forced to do so. They resisted pressure to work not only from the Spanish administrators but also from Guaraní leaders. In 1779, Yapeyú's cabildo and some caciques complained to lieutenant gobernador Juan de San Martín that their corregidor, Abran Guirabó, failed to compel the Indians to work on behalf of the mission, thus endangering the mission and its estancias.[93]

In order to conduct its hide operations, Yapeyú resorted to employing hundreds of outside laborers. Hide production required crews consisting of cowboys who killed the animals, butchers who made the hides, and peons who organized the hides and cared for the horses.[94] After producing hundreds or perhaps several thousands of hides, the crew brought the hides to centralized facilities near a port for storage and classification by size and quality. Here, an overseer and workers were employed to stack and sort the hides. Periodically, boatmen transported the hides to Buenos Aires or Montevideo for sale. Together, these activities required more laborers than Yapeyú could spare. During the course of a year, Paysandú employed over 482 individuals in the production and storage of hides.[95]

Between 1778 and 1784, Domingo Ygarzabal likewise employed hundreds of individuals. He purchased hides from at least forty-one separate crews comprising an unknown number of workers, employed one hundred different individuals at his storage facilities, and paid fourteen individuals to transport hides to Montevideo.[96] Very few of these individuals had Guaraní surnames, and none were identified as mission Indians.

Since Yapeyú had to depend on outside labor and the native leaders were unable to properly oversee hide operations, the arrangement between the mission managers, contractors, and native leadership was a beneficial compromise for the Guaraní. They had no other option for making use of their strayed cattle herds. The financial benefit from hide production and the inability to enforce property rights meant that wild cattle in the Negro and Yí River region were going to be slaughtered whether or not the Indians were involved. Under these circumstances, mission Guaraní gained some material benefit from hide production as opposed to none.

PROPERTY RIGHTS

Vértiz's replacement as viceroy of the Río de la Plata in 1784 marked a sudden end to the missions' hide operations. The new viceroy—the marqués de Loreto—took a radically different stance toward mission hide production than his predecessor. After spending a few weeks in Montevideo before assuming his new position, Loreto was convinced that lawlessness in the Banda Oriental was one of the viceroyalty's most pressing problems. Furthermore, Montevideo estancieros convinced him that the missions' hide operations contributed greatly to the lawlessness.

Within days of Loreto's becoming viceroy, the superintendent of the viceroyalty, Francisco de Paula Sanz, ordered don Francisco Ortega y Monroy to report on the causes of and solutions to the disorder in the Banda Oriental.[97] As *comandante de resguardos* (commander in charge of suppressing contraband), Ortega y Monroy was very knowledgeable about lawlessness and disorder in the region. He concluded that by this date, although cattle belonging to the missions had strayed onto royal lands, the missions could no longer claim ownership. Over the years, he claimed, the missions had taken so many cattle from the region that they had been more than compensated for the animals that had originally strayed out of mission territory. Therefore, in his opinion, those cattle that remained belonged to the king. He recommended revoking the missions' right to any cattle located outside of clearly documented mission territory.[98]

Even before Ortega y Monroy completed his report, Viceroy Loreto began revoking mission privileges. He ordered a stop to all mission hide production outside of legally recognized mission lands. By the middle of September 1784, Yapeyú and San Miguel had discontinued all hide operations in the Negro and Yí River region.[99] Paysandú continued to incur hide-related expenses and send a large quantity of hides to the general administration through July 1786, but quantities plummeted thereafter.[100]

With these restrictions in place, Yapeyú and the general administration looked for alternate ways to generate income using wild cattle in Yapeyú's territory, but with very limited success. On November 23, 1786, Yapeyú's Guaraní representatives and administrator signed a contract to sell Francisco Medina 30,000 cattle gathered from Yapeyú territory for 6.25 reales per head.[101] Superintendent Paula Sanz wrote to the corregidor, cabildo, and administrator of Yapeyú that this agreement was most advantageous for Yapeyú because the mission could not get as high a price for hides after deducting production and storage costs.[102] Medina, who opened the first factory for producing salted beef in the Río de la Plata region, used the cattle for this purpose.[103] In 1787 and 1788, Yapeyú sold Medina 11,630 and 1,265 cattle, respectively, but the mission never fulfilled the rest of the contract.[104]

Thereafter Yapeyú's condition deteriorated even further. In 1791, Yapeyú's native leadership and the administrator claimed that the mission lacked the necessary industries for its subsistence—cotton, yerba maté, tobacco, and carts. In order to remedy the situation, they requested permission for Yapeyú to slaughter cattle and sell hides to pay for the purchase of these goods.[105] In the same year, Yapeyú's corregidor, cabildo, and caciques wrote to the viceroy, saying that Yapeyú's territory was threatened with immediate ruin because gauderios infested the region and were destroying the mission's cattle herds. According to the leadership, the situation was all the more serious because livestock was the mission's only means of subsistence. The letter was written to express the gratitude of Yapeyú's leaders to the viceroy for sending a troop of *blandengues* (cavalry), who they hoped would stop the gauderios from destroying their cattle herds.[106] Yapeyú's condition did not improve. In 1793, Juan Francisco Aguirre, a member of the commission to define the Spanish-Portuguese border, described Yapeyú as the poorest of the missions, saying that Yapeyú owned only about ten thousand cattle, which was barely enough to feed the Guaraní inhabitants.[107] Yapeyú had become the barest skeleton of what it once had been (see Table 10).

While Yapeyú rapidly collapsed after the end of its large-scale hide production, Viceroy Loreto's revocation of Yapeyú's cattle rights merely sped up an inevitable process. As they had elsewhere in the Río de la

Plata region, the missions' undomesticated herds were bound to disappear as a result of overslaughter. A scenario like the so-called tragedy of the commons unfolded, with the added complication of the border with the Portuguese. Such a scenario occurs when multiple parties independently pursue their own self-interest, leading them to overuse, and ultimately destroy, a shared limited resource. The typical tragedy of the commons story is a pasture that is commonly shared by all: each herder captures all of the benefits when he lets an additional animal graze, but the damage caused by the additional grazing animal is shared equally among all the herders. The key point is that the costs and benefits of grazing are unequally shared. Each herdsman seeks to maximize his gain by adding as many livestock as he can to the pasture; the compounded result is overgrazing, degradation, and ruin of the pasture.[108] A similar scenario unfolded with cattle in the Banda Oriental. There was no incentive for anyone—including the missions—to protect the wild herds by limiting the quantity of cattle slaughtered; if one producer practiced restraint, someone else would slaughter the cattle instead. Thus, Yapeyú, like the estancieros, gauderios, Portuguese, and mission and nonmission Indians, participated in the overslaughter. Despite his good intentions, Viceroy Loreto's efforts failed to stem illegal hide production; contraband hides continued to be exported from the region through at least the early 1790s.[109]

CONCLUSION

Given the conditions in the Banda Oriental, Mission Yapeyú could not defend its rights to huge numbers of wild cattle. The high economic incentive and relatively low risk of being caught made clandestine hide production very attractive. Yapeyú hired troops to patrol its territory but was unable to stop the theft and slaughter. Gauderios found by the troops easily fled to Portuguese territory or the other side of the Negro River into the jurisdiction of Santo Domingo Soriano.[110] In 1786, Diego Casero, who replaced Lazcano as general administrator, asserted that Yapeyú could not effectively defend its cattle herds even on its own territory. He acknowledged that Yapeyú's estancias alone were not sufficient for maintaining the large number of cattle needed to sustain the Indians; rather, the estancias functioned as repositories for a yearly supply of cattle. Wild cattle dispersed throughout the countryside were needed to restock the estancias. Casero blamed both gauderios and nonmission Indians for raiding and killing Yapeyú's cattle; moreover, their activities frightened the cattle and caused them to flee to land outside of mission territory. Even in the face of such dismal conditions, Casero still hoped that Yapeyú could protect its cattle by fortifying Paysandú and rebuilding the posts of San Xavier and San Estevan along the Negro River.[111] But despite such hopes, containing Yapeyú's undomesticated and undefended cattle was an impossible task; the mission's property rights were virtually unenforceable and meaningless.

Yapeyú lacked the capability to domesticate and protect its cattle. Given the intense competition for cattle and lack of effective law enforcement, direct oversight of the herds was the only way to prevent theft, but the population of Yapeyú was not large enough to domesticate or defend the wild herds upon which the mission subsisted.[112] Likewise, Guaraní leaders had neither the manpower nor the skills to effectively oversee the mission's special concession to conduct large-scale hide production in the Negro and Yí River region of the Banda Oriental. Still, despite high overhead costs and corruption, Yapeyú derived some temporary benefit from the hundreds of thousands of pesos generated from such operations.

Recognizing the opportunity presented by Yapeyú's inability to defend its property rights, everyone—including contractors working on behalf of the missions, estancieros, and Indians—produced as many hides as they could before the herds disappeared. As a result of such overslaughter, Yapeyú could not maintain the necessary number of cattle for the health of the mission and the well-being of its inhabitants.

Like the other missions, Yapeyú and San Miguel suffered decline. All of the missions faced great financial pressures, in response to which their Guaraní inhabitants both disengaged from the communal structure and fled altogether. The question thus arises, how were the missions able to continue functioning over a prolonged thirty-year decline? The next chapter details this long decline and the final end of the Guaraní missions.

CHAPTER 9

Prolonging the Collapse

From the expulsion of the Jesuits in 1767–1768 until Viceroy Gabriel de Avilés began dismantling the missions' communal structure in 1800, a variety of factors pointed to the impending collapse of the Guaraní missions: mounting financial problems due to the separation of religious and secular affairs bankrupted the mission system; Guaraní evasion of work and outright flight struck at the heart of the collective labor projects that funded the mission; and the increasing self-sufficiency of the Guaraní weakened the role of the mission's communal structure. Yet despite all these pressures, the mission's communal structure of collective labor, shared ownership of mission assets, and redistribution of goods from communal supplies continued for over thirty years after the expulsion. What enabled the missions, and the communal structure that defined them, to endure for so long?

The longevity of the missions and their communal structure were made possible by adaptations and compromises among Spanish administrators, native leaders, and the rest of the Guaraní population. The Guaraní made mission life tolerable adeptly protesting against abuse and credibly threatening flight in order to limit Spanish and native officials' ability to use coercion or practice exploitation. Pressured by growing budget deficits, on one hand, and finding their ability to extract greater amounts of labor limited, on the other hand, mission officials needed to come up with new strategies to keep the communal structure afloat. In essence, they prioritized—they avoided paying some expenses in order to meet the mission's most pressing obligations. This strategy resulted in individual missions severing many of their ties to the coordinated mission system, restructuring their spending, and resorting to labor-saving practices. While buying time in the short run, this process undermined a mission's viability in the long run.

The adaptations and compromises that enabled the communal structure to survive until 1800 came at the cost of disinvestment—the running down of capital by either selling or not replacing capacity as assets reach the end of their useful lives.[1] Mission supplies declined as Spanish and native officials either distributed inventories to the Indians or sold them off; skilled Guaraní artisans and other laborers left and were not replaced; buildings deteriorated; and infrastructure was depleted. As a mission's population declined and labor demands pressed upon the remaining Guaraní, a mission lacked the labor supply necessary to properly maintain and invest in its productive resources. As valuable resources such as yerba maté plantations, cotton fields, tobacco fields, and cattle herds disappeared, a mission had to look elsewhere for trade goods and necessities. Such reliance on external sources, however, was unsustainable owing to excessive cost and competition. Thus, while collapse was not immediate, the missions were gradually destroyed by both internal and external pressures.

ADAPTATIONS AND COMPROMISES

Under the Jesuits, the mission economy was based on a communal structure of collective labor, shared ownership, and distribution of mission supplies, with an emphasis on self-sufficiency at the individual mission level and mutual support among the missions. The Jesuits limited external trade to paying taxes and purchasing items that the missions could not produce themselves. Bucareli's reforms maintained this communal structure: mission Indians still had to work on the collective labor projects that funded the economy, and they continued to receive distributions of goods from mission supplies, albeit in smaller quantities and of less diversity. The biggest change was the emphasis on the market economy and the insertion of state-appointed officials into mission management. Bucareli also adamantly opposed the idea of a mission's being self-sufficient; instead, he advocated trade as a means of wealth accumulation for both the missions and the Indians. The imposition of a market-based ideology, while maintaining the missions' communal structure at the same time, became excessively burdensome.

After the regime change, the communal structure not only was subject to the same pressures as during the Jesuit period but faced new demands associated with the turn to the market economy as well. As before, collective labor was needed to produce goods for redistribution, repair buildings and infrastructure, invest in future production, and generate trade goods, but now the communal structure also needed to substantially increase revenues through the sale of more trade goods. Moreover, Spanish administrators, other mission employees, and various non-Guaraní skilled laborers required market wages. Overhead for operating the mission system—commissions and salaries for upper-level management, transportation fees, and other miscellaneous expenditures—generated new expense. In addition, outstanding debts from before the Jesuit expulsion and accumulated deficits needed to be repaid. The communal structure could not meet all of these demands. Simultaneously, the Indians resisted when pressed to work more than they wanted. In response to these many pressures, both Spanish administrators and mission Indians adapted to the changing circumstances and compromised. Out of necessity, they prioritized the most pressing collective labor projects and abandoned the least pressing.

Making sure that communal supplies covered his salary—either in currency or goods—was of primary importance to a Spanish administrator. The desire to provide for himself and his family sometimes led to corruption and abuse of mission assets. The large quantities of land, labor, and other resources belonging to the mission were attractive targets for dishonest individuals. Possibilities for diverting benefit abounded: an administrator could overtly steal mission assets, indirectly usurp mission lands, take a cut of trade, or hire his underlings to work for the mission.

Although corruption was definitely a problem, however, oversight from the Guaraní themselves, priests residing in the same mission, and Spanish superiors in the mission system bureaucracy limited some such abuses. Bucareli's reforms mandated that the administrator work closely with Guaraní leaders and that any action taken regarding mission supplies have their consent. The thousands of pages of receipts and account records with cabildo members' signatures show that Guaraní leaders played a role in their mission's affairs and had some knowledge of their administrator's actions. Even if they did not fully understand what they signed, their signatures indicate some level of compliance. Moreover, when they felt that abuses occurred, Guaraní leaders, priests, and others lodged complaints with higher-level officials, as evidenced by the cases at San Juan Bautista and Concepción described in Chapter 6.

An administrator could not autocratically cut distributions to mission inhabitants in order to reduce expenses or ensure payment of his salary. If he did, he risked the Guaraní fleeing, writing letters of complaint, or rebelling in other ways that would reflect poorly on him and lead to reprimand. In order to maintain his position, an administrator had to ensure that relative peace existed in the mission. He had to distribute enough goods to placate the Guaraní—especially the native elite—lest they complain that he lacked compassion and shirked his duties. As detailed in

Chapter 8, distributions to the Guaraní generally declined, but the Indians continued to receive items that they valued.

In addition to paying his own salary and making distributions to the Indians, for the first decade or so after the expulsion an administrator also felt strong pressure to send trade goods to the missions' trading center in Buenos Aires. Mission sales revenue remained high owing to the large volume of the most important trade goods—cattle hides, yerba maté, and textiles. The quantity of cattle hides sold by the general administration on behalf of the missions from 1776 to 1784 greatly exceeded Jesuit levels; the same held true for yerba maté from 1770 to 1788 and textiles from 1770 to 1773.

In the years following the Jesuit expulsion, however, while the missions' sales volume of yerba maté and textiles greatly expanded, revenues did not (see Table 11). Under Jesuit management, the missions sold an average of almost 310,000 pounds of yerba maté per year between 1731 and 1745; this rose to almost 594,000 pounds of yerba maté per year between 1770 and 1788. Between 1770 and 1773, the volume of textiles sold also surpassed the highest Jesuit levels. Yet despite high volumes, these figures do not reflect economic growth: average yearly sales revenues between 1770 and 1788 fell below the average for the Jesuit period.

The initial increases in volume are all the more striking given that the total number of mission inhabitants—in other words, the labor

TABLE 11. *Yerba maté and textile sales, twenty-nine missions (excluding Yapeyú), 1731–1806*

Year	Yerba quantity (lb)	Yerba revenue (pesos)	Yerba average price	Textile quantity (ft)	Textile revenue (pesos)	Textile average price
1731	259,150	44,924	0.17	73,099	14,054	0.19
1732	259,150	44,924	0.17	73,099	14,054	0.19
1733	259,150	44,924	0.17	73,099	14,054	0.19
1734	259,150	44,924	0.17	73,099	14,054	0.19
1735	259,150	44,924	0.17	73,099	14,054	0.19
1736	214,169	42,340	0.20	48,907	14,055	0.29
1737	214,169	42,340	0.20	48,907	14,055	0.29
1738	381,406	68,110	0.18	80,653	16,860	0.21
1739	381,406	68,110	0.18	80,653	16,860	0.21
1740	331,835	49,693	0.15	122,325	15,870	0.13
1741	331,835	49,693	0.15	122,325	15,870	0.13
1742	331,835	49,693	0.15	122,325	15,870	0.13
1743	317,973	44,461	0.14	55,673	10,077	0.18
1744	317,973	44,461	0.14	55,673	10,077	0.18
1745	352,157	46,397	0.13	45,038	8,116	0.18
Average (1731–1745)	309,448	49,321	0.16	70,949	13,172	0.19

(*continued*)

TABLE II. *(continued)*

Year	Yerba quantity (lb)	Yerba revenue (pesos)	Yerba average price	Textile quantity (ft)	Textile revenue (pesos)	Textile average price
1768						
1769						
1770	529,271	33,503	0.06	120,174	16,286	0.14
1771	529,271	33,503	0.06	120,174	16,286	0.14
1772	862,419	51,189	0.06	83,767	11,656	0.14
1773	862,419	51,189	0.06	83,767	11,656	0.14
1774	N/A	N/A	N/A	N/A	N/A	N/A
1775	N/A	N/A	N/A	N/A	N/A	N/A
1776	533,055	30,011	0.06	50,650	6,938	0.14
1777	533,055	30,011	0.06	50,650	6,938	0.14
1778	522,404	32,440	0.06	24,368	3,365	0.14
1779	522,404	32,440	0.06	24,368	3,365	0.14
1780	779,815	59,939	0.08	23,201	3,194	0.14
1781	779,815	59,939	0.08	23,201	3,194	0.14
1782	580,816	48,228	0.08	27,950	3,875	0.14
1783	580,816	48,228	0.08	27,950	3,875	0.14
1784	580,816	48,228	0.08	27,950	3,875	0.14
1785	455,613	35,898	0.08	8,791	1,159	0.13
1786	455,613	35,898	0.08	8,791	1,159	0.13
1787	494,211	41,196	0.08	17,488	2,230	0.13
1788	494,211	41,196	0.08	17,488	2,230	0.13
Average (1770–1788)	593,884	41,943	0.07	43,572	5,958	0.14
1789						
1790						
1791	106,073	6,967	0.07	10,587	1,220	0.12
1792	106,073	6,967	0.07	10,587	1,220	0.12
1793	157,294	7,522	0.05	—	—	
1794	157,294	7,522	0.05	—	—	
1795	38,953	2,472	0.06	—	—	
1796	38,953	2,472	0.06	—	—	
1797	27,684	2,251	0.08	1,500	188	0.13
1798	27,684	2,251	0.08	1,500	188	0.13
1799	156,869	12,808	0.08	1,716	259	0.15
1800	156,869	12,808	0.08	1,716	259	0.15
1801	225,222	15,242	0.07	13,329	3,031	0.23
1802	225,222	15,242	0.07	13,329	3,031	0.23
1803	55,980	4,333	0.08	8,082	1,648	0.20
1804	55,980	4,333	0.08	8,082	1,648	0.20
1805	6,500	544	0.08	—	—	
1806	6,500	544	0.08	—	—	
Average (1791–1806)	96,822	6,517	0.07	4,402	793	0.16

SOURCE: See Table 5.
NOTE: The missions could legally sell 12,000 arrobas (300,000 pounds) per year. The Jesuit accounting periods are not divided into 12-month periods. The average over the entire period is within 3 percent of 300,000 pounds.

TABLE 12. *Productivity per worker, twenty-nine missions*

Year	Revenue per mission inhabitant (pesos)	Quantity of yerba sold per mission inhabitant (lb)	Quantity of textiles sold per mission inhabitant (ft)
	Jesuit period		
1731	0.5	1.9	0.5
1733	0.5	2.1	0.6
1736	0.6	2.2	0.5
1738	1.0	4.5	1.0
1739	1.3	5.6	1.2
1740	1.0	4.9	1.8
1741	0.9	4.7	1.7
1744	0.7	4.1	0.7
1745	0.7	4.3	0.6
	Post-Jesuit period		
1772	1.0	11.1	1.1
1783	1.4	11.3	0.5
1793	0.5	3.4	0.0
1801	0.6	5.5	0.3

SOURCE: See Table 5 and Appendix 1.

force—had declined. The smaller size of the labor force would suggest that each worker had to be more productive (in other words, work harder) during the peak period of mission sales in the 1770s and 1780s. Productivity estimates are less conclusive (see Table 12).[2] While the missions sold more than double the quantity of yerba maté per mission inhabitant in 1772 and 1783 as compared to the highest levels during the Jesuit period, sales revenue per mission inhabitant approximated Jesuit-period levels. The quantity of textiles sold per mission inhabitant during peak years likewise approximated Jesuit-period levels.

The main reason why the missions sold much greater quantities of yerba maté without realizing a commensurate increase in total sales revenue is that, in contrast to the Jesuit period, they almost exclusively sold an inferior grade of yerba maté—yerba de palos. During the Jesuit period, the missions sold mostly yerba caaminí (63%), some yerba de palos (11%), and a significant portion of unspecified yerba (26%). In the post-Jesuit period, the missions resoundingly sold yerba de palos (95%), a minute amount of yerba caaminí (2%), and a small amount of unspecified yerba (3%). Yerba caaminí was a superior grade of yerba maté that required more labor to produce and consistently garnered a lower price. Between 1731 and 1745, the price that the missions received for yerba caaminí was double the price they received for yerba de palos. Hence, the shift to almost exclusively selling yerba de palos in the post-Jesuit period meant lower prices; between 1731 and 1745 the missions received on average .16 pesos per pound of yerba maté and .07 pesos per pound between 1770 and 1788. As a consequence, while the average amount of yerba maté sold by the missions increased from almost 310,000 pounds per year to over 590,000 pounds per year, average revenues from these sales fell.

Declining demand in markets that preferred yerba caaminí to yerba de palos partly explains why the missions shifted from selling yerba caaminí to selling yerba de palos. In the late eighteenth century, chocolate, coffee, and tea began to replace yerba maté in Chile and the Andes.[3] Even before the expulsion, José Cardiel noted the effects of declining demand, complaining that "in the past ten years [prior to 1766], yerba maté's price has fallen greatly and there is little consumption of it because chocolate has been introduced in its place in the realm of Chile and Peru."[4]

Even more important, the missions shifted away from producing yerba caaminí because its price likely did not compensate for all of its labor costs. By definition, yerba de palos included the sticks or small branches from the yerba maté tree, while yerba caaminí contained only the leaves. Separating the leaves from the sticks and small branches required more labor and yielded less finished product than did yerba de palos. Only the missions, under the Jesuits, opted for this labor-intensive type of yerba maté production; other producers preferred yerba de palos, in all likelihood because the costs of producing yerba caaminí exceeded its higher price. Shifting from yerba de caaminí to yerba de palos was a way for the missions to reduce labor demands made upon the Guaraní.

As with yerba maté, the missions focused on low-quality, less labor-intensive textiles after the Jesuit expulsion. During the Jesuit period, the missions sold a variety of textiles in a range of qualities.[5] In the post-Jesuit period, the missions shifted almost exclusively to the rough cloth of the poorest quality (*lienzo grueso*),[6] which took less labor to produce than higher-quality cloth. In both cases—yerba maté and textiles—the missions found ways of increasing volume without a commensurate increase in labor.

Producing lower-quality yerba maté and textiles affected sales revenue. While the volume of yerba maté sold almost doubled between 1770 and 1788 in comparison to the Jesuit period, revenues fell by 15 percent (see Table 11). Likewise, the missions almost consistently received a lower average price for their textiles than during the Jesuit period, and their average sales revenue was correspondingly lower as well.

Limiting maintenance, upkeep, and investment in productive resources was another way of reducing the demands made on mission labor with minimal short-term sacrifice. Over time, all physical structures and objects age and depreciate; they deteriorate and break down owing to wear and tear, the passage of time, weather, and myriad other factors. Keeping buildings, machinery, tools, and furniture in good working order requires regular maintenance and upkeep. Such effort generally prolongs the life of physical structures and objects; in essence, maintenance and upkeep are done primarily with a view to the long term rather than the present. Yet, even with regular attention and care, physical structures and objects eventually wear out beyond repair and need to be replaced. Thus, for their long-term well-being, the missions not only needed to repair and maintain their productive assets, they also needed to invest in new buildings, machinery, tools, and furniture. Since maintenance and investment are done primarily with an eye to the future, however, missions could avoid doing either or both with minimal effect on current conditions. With the numerous demands made upon collective labor, it made sense to sacrifice maintenance and investment. Tools, machinery, furniture, and mission buildings such as the church, workshops, and lodgings could still be used without expending such effort.

Lieutenant gobernador Doblas described this process and its results in his 1785 report on conditions in the missions:

> In the beginning nothing was cared for, and later it was necessary to attend only to populating the estancias with livestock. As a result, the other objectives of [Bucareli's] instructions, which merit the attention of all good government, were neglected. The repair and construction of the buildings, equally the principal buildings called colegios as those of individual Indians, have been neglected. As a result, the mission towns are ruined and some churches are threatened with ruin.[7]

Similarly, the missions stopped maintaining or investing in many of their productive resources. Farmlands (*chacras*), together with fields of cotton (*algodonales*), yerba maté (*yerbales*), tobacco (*tabacales*), and sugarcane (*cañaverales*), require proper maintenance and replanting in order to ensure future production. As they age over time, cotton and tobacco plants, sugarcane, yerba maté trees, and the like produce less and less. External factors, such as drought, insects, and disease, likewise threaten productive resources. As a result, plants and trees need care and replanting in order to maintain production levels.

In his 1785 report, Doblas also described the missions' failure to properly care for and invest in these productive resources:

> Because maintenance and replanting required labor in the present with the returns realized only at a later date, the missions often opted to channel Guaraní labor to more pressing immediate needs. The yerbales that are cultivated next to the mission towns have been left almost to be lost. Nothing is done except taking from them whatever utility is possible, without caring to put in new plants to replace those that are being lost or dying from old age.[8]

Inventories, which document increases and decreases in communally owned property, confirm that missions invested in new productive resources infrequently at best. During the last two decades of the eighteenth century, San Juan Bautista, Concepción, and La Cruz occasionally planted cotton, but only San Juan Bautista produced enough cotton to meet most of its needs. Inventories further reveal that San Juan Bautista also planted some yerba maté trees, tobacco plants, and sugarcane during the first years, but none after 1790.

This focus on meeting short-term needs came at the cost of a mission's long-term welfare. An administrator was held accountable for his mission's overall condition; his duties included both the short- and long-term viability of the mission in his charge. While the lieutenant gobernadors, gobernador, and others visited and inspected the missions, they could not ensure the short- and long-term viability of the missions. Not only were the demands too great, emergencies frequently focused attention on the current condition of a mission. An epidemic, drought, shortages of one good or another, or management problems that struck a mission required immediate attention—issues such as these could not be ignored. Furthermore, emergencies contributed to low standards of evaluation on the part of mission administrators. Upper management tended to be distracted by an emergency in one or more of the missions under their care; since emergencies required immediate attention, they focused on such crises rather than the long-term well-being of the other missions also under their care. As a result, upper management's evaluations of the individual missions generally concentrated on short-term conditions rather than long-term prospects.

The process by which missions sacrificed their long-term welfare was disinvestment: the missions used up their assets. They consumed or sold inventories, did not maintain productive assets and infrastructure, and failed to invest in future productive capacity. Disinvestment was an extended process: the missions went through several steps to prolong the decline and forestall the end of the communal structure.

DISINVESTMENT

The failure to maintain and invest in productive assets and infrastructure began to cause problems in the 1780s. By this time, most of the productive resources developed by the Jesuits almost consistently could not meet an individual mission's needs, and yields on productive resources continued to worsen over time. Mission account records rarely mentioned chacras, tabacales, and cañaverales, and production was minimal. While account records regularly included yerbales, algodonales, and estancias, these productive assets generally did not produce enough to meet a mission's needs. Yerba maté trees and cotton plants can produce for twenty, thirty, or more years when cared for properly.[9] Just shy of twenty years after the Jesuit expulsion, by the mid-1780s the algodonales and yerbales planted near the mission towns during the Jesuit period had begun to reach the end of their life cycle, and the estancias were suffering from growing competition for cattle that impeded the missions' ability to restock their herds.

But even though the missions were depleting domesticated yerbales, algodonales, and estancias, they continued to need these resources. Other items, such as sugar, tobacco, and foodstuffs, the Indians could procure for themselves; but yerba maté, textiles, and cattle were vital to maintaining the missions' communal structure. Yerba maté and cotton for textiles served as rations for mission inhabitants and trade goods for procuring other necessities; cattle provisioned the Indians. The depletion of resources that produced these necessities—the algodonales, yerbales, and estancias—forced the missions to look for alternate sources. As a result, the missions resorted to harvesting wild yerba maté, purchasing cotton and cattle, and hunting wild cattle.

The missions' abandonment of their domesticated yerba maté plantations marked a striking change from the Jesuit period but one that made sense given the existence of wild yerbales. The Jesuits commended themselves for figuring out how to domesticate yerba maté, but they also admitted that it required a great deal of labor and attention: domesticated yerbales were difficult both to establish and to maintain. The yerba maté tree is delicate, even more so when young; a yerba maté seedling requires watering and special care for two to three years before being transplanted. Only after eight to ten years could a yerba maté tree yield a harvest.[10] Even though knowledge about domesticating yerba maté existed, Spanish Americans generally avoided yerba maté cultivation. Instead, as long as wild yerba maté trees remained relatively abundant, yerba maté producers preferred wild yerbales to domesticated yerbales; only after the 1870s did large plantations cultivate more yerba maté than the amount extracted from wild yerbales.[11] It is likely that Spanish Americans avoided yerba maté cultivation because domestication was so labor intensive and time-consuming and thus expensive. By not maintaining or replanting the domesticated yerbales, the Guaraní also made a choice to forgo this labor-intensive process in favor of the wild yerbales, like other yerba maté producers.

As with yerba maté, the missions found alternate sources for cotton, in this case resorting to purchasing cotton. In many instances, missions obtained the cotton in a hotly contested transaction. A mission contracted with a private party for a specified amount of cotton; in return for the cotton, the mission promised to pay the other party a percentage of the thread or cloth produced by mission Indians.[12] Such purchases of cotton were costly. According to one source, a mission had to give half of the resulting thread or cloth in return for the raw cotton.[13] According to Lázaro de Rivera, the intendant of Paraguay, such transactions were detrimental to the missions and should be prohibited. Not only did he believe such purchases to be excessively expensive, he also believed that they led the missions to neglect cotton cultivation.[14] Rivera claimed that the missions of the Santiago department intentionally abandoned their cotton fields so that the administrators could financially benefit from such exchanges.[15] Guaraní preferences probably played an even greater role in the decline of cotton cultivation. The Guaraní did not like to grow cotton. When discussing the effort expended by the missionaries to get the Guaraní to grow crops, Jesuit José Cardiel said that "getting them to cultivate cotton for their clothing takes the most work."[16] In any case, regardless of the reasons behind the decreasing cotton yields from mission algodonales, missions had to obtain cotton elsewhere in order to meet their needs. Since wild algodonales were not an option, purchases and exchanges of thread and finished textiles were a viable alternative.

Likewise, as with cotton and yerba maté, insufficient livestock supplies forced most missions to either purchase or hunt cattle. There were a variety of reasons for the shortages. Wild animals or hostile Indian attacks plagued some estancias; for example, San Juan Bautista's leadership wrote in their 1794 account record that the mission's "estancias did not yield any procreation because of the poor pastureland and infestation of jaguars and pumas." Others lacked suitable pastureland or water for sustaining their herds. Even estancias without these problems went through periods of crisis that precipitously reduced the herds: pests and disease regularly struck cattle herds, and droughts inevitably resulted in the death or migration of many cattle.

Both Indians and Spanish administrators widely engaged in practices that hindered self-sufficiency in cattle. According to a Portuguese military engineer in 1789, "The Indians cause much damage to the cattle herds when they hunt cattle. . . . They kill [the cattle] to eat, leaving the majority abandoned in the countryside. It gets to the point that they kill a cow only to take out the tongue and some ribs, and if this meat is not to their liking, they kill another."[17] Many Spanish administrators did not try to make mission estancias self-sustaining: according to lieutenant gobernador Doblas, "In a few years, [the Spanish administrators] misspent and consumed [the cattle] that had been in the missions and estancias, without thinking of work or restoring that which they consumed."[18] While in hindsight such actions appear destructive, the seemingly endless supply of wild cattle made conservation efforts seemed irrational to both the Guaraní and many Spanish administrators.

The Río de la Plata region was well suited to livestock, and wild cattle multiplied. Such herds continued to be hunted by the missions and others in the Banda Oriental through the 1780s. As a result of this natural surplus, mission estancias never relied solely on natural reproduction. Even during the Jesuit period, the missions replenished their estancias by hunting cattle on royal lands or purchasing cattle from another mission. Missions with abundant supplies, such as Yapeyú and San Miguel, did not domesticate all of their cattle; instead, they set aside extensive territory for cattle to proliferate and sent Indians to hunt the cattle as needed. In 1774, general administrator Lazcano asserted that Yapeyú, San Miguel, and San Borja had innumerable cattle, which he thought could supply the other missions.[19]

But the missions could not depend on replenishing their herds with undomesticated cattle from Yapeyú and San Miguel. Yapeyú never fulfilled expectations as a large-scale cattle supplier in the post-Jesuit period. Instead, the mission focused its efforts on slaughtering cattle and selling the hides to the growing export market. While San Miguel did a better job of supplying other missions with cattle, such assistance did not continue. As explained in the preceding chapter, neither mission could defend its cattle herds in the face of growing competition.

Many missions resorted to purchasing cattle from private individuals outside the mission system. Such efforts to procure cattle and other necessities from outside served as a stopgap measure that provided necessary aid in the short run but not a permanent long-run solution. By the 1790s, cost, overuse, and competition made external supplies increasingly unreliable and unattainable. Over the short term, the missions could divert money toward purchasing cotton and cattle, but over time such expenses were untenable. The amount of money available for such purchases fell as mission sales revenues declined. Furthermore, the fall in the price of rough cloth—the main item traded for both cotton and cattle—made such purchases even more onerous.[20] Despite the higher price of cattle as compared with lienzo grueso, the missions continued to purchase large amounts of cattle for as long as they could. Corrientes estancieros, the primary cattle suppliers, sold over 183,000 cattle to the missions between 1780 and 1797; thereafter, mission purchases declined and never recovered.[21]

In the long run, dependence on wild yerbales was also unsustainable. Like wild cattle, wild yerbales initially seemed to be an unlimited natural resource. They attracted not only the missions but also Spanish Americans who sought to make a profit; such competition led to overuse. As a result, the wild yerbales in the north, close to the Paraguay River, were largely exhausted by the 1790s.[22] This depletion explains much of the missions' declining harvests.

Labor shortages further constrained the missions' ability to exploit wild yerbales. Few missions could spare Indian labor to harvest wild yerba maté for an extended period. At least one mission dealt with the labor shortage by hiring nonmission peons to harvest yerba maté. From 1785 to 1787, Jesús hired at least twenty-three peons to work as *yerberos*.[23] But hiring peons to harvest yerba maté from yerbales silvestres was expensive and unsustainable, and over time the missions could not afford the expense.

An anecdote from the department of Concepción reveals how mission administrators sought external sources and how reliance on wild yerbales proved not to be a solution to the missions' problems. On March 19, 1798, the lieutenant gobernador of the department of Concepción, Feliciano Cortez, wrote to Viceroy Antonio Olaguer Feliú about his failed attempt to advance the seven missions under his care. The previous year, Cortez had ordered a general expedition from all seven of the missions to go to Ñùcora-guasù—the location of a distant wild yerbal—in order to harvest yerba maté. Visiting Ñùcora-guasù had convinced Cortez of the benefit to be gained from such an expedition: he envisioned that the sale of yerba maté from the expedition would yield enough revenue that, in addition to meeting current obligations, some of the proceeds could be used to repay debts and expenses accrued at the general administration. Convinced of such profitable returns to be gained from harvesting these distant, wild yerbales, Cortez contracted a boatbuilder to construct a *piragua* (canoe) in order to transport great quantities of yerba maté.

But Cortez's project encountered obstacles from the beginning. Administrators from five of the seven missions informed him that no Indians could be spared for the expedition because "they needed to attend to the repair of the buildings that are all threatened with ruin, especially the churches."[24] Only Guaraní from Concepción and Apóstoles went on the expedition.

Even these two missions were unable to take full advantage of the Ñùcora-guasù yerbales to the degree expected by Cortez. Shortly after undertaking the project, Cortez had to cancel it. Hostile Tupí Indians and the beginnings of war with Portugal threatened the region, and so Cortez ordered the expedition to return with the small amount of yerba maté already gathered. Because of its premature conclusion, Cortez complained, the project produced little more yerba maté than what was needed to cover its costs. Only one of the two missions—Apóstoles—set aside some yerba maté for repayment of its debts with the general administration.[25]

Cortez's experience highlights how procuring necessities outside of the missions made sense but was unsustainable in the long run. Harvesting yerba maté from wild yerbales was clearly profitable: even given its short duration, the expedition brought in a significant amount of yerba maté, as demonstrated by Apóstoles' ability to repay some of its debt. Despite this profitability, however, only two of the seven missions had the capacity even to embark on such an expedition; the other five did not have enough Guaraní laborers to spare and were plagued by more pressing concerns. Although conditions outside the missions' control cut short this particular project, reliance on wild yerbales was at best only a short-term solution: depletion, the result of overuse, soon destroyed the yerbales silvestres.

Account records for San Juan Bautista, La Cruz, and Concepción from the late 1780s through the early 1800s further confirm that disinvestment and the procurement of necessities from outside the missions were not sustainable in the long run. By the early 1800s, supplies of livestock and mission production had plummeted (see Appendix 2). San Juan Bautista was in the worst condition. Its population continuously declined over the post-Jesuit period and between 1768 and 1801 had fallen by 65 percent. As of 1794, its cattle herds also went into rapid decline. Because of the poor quality of its pastureland, San Juan Bautista had to regularly replenish its supplies from elsewhere. The mission relied heavily on annual cattle purchases from San Miguel, but such expenditures were costly. The administrator of San Juan Bautista reported that the mission was deeply in debt, primarily because of these purchases from San Miguel. San Juan Bautista could not continue purchasing cattle owing to the expense as well as the depletion of San Miguel's herds; soon thereafter, the mission's production of cotton and cotton cloth also fell. In contrast, yerba maté production remained relatively consistent through 1800, primarily because of harvests from wild yerbales.[26]

In striking contrast to San Juan Bautista, La Cruz performed comparatively well until the end of the period, although it still experienced decline. While La Cruz recorded only five fewer inhabitants in 1801 than in 1768, such numbers disguise worsening conditions at the end of the period. Between 1768 and 1793 (a quarter of a century), La Cruz's population grew by more than 600, from 3,243 to 3,871 inhabitants. Subsequently, between 1793 and 1801 (less than a decade), La Cruz's population fell by almost the same amount. Like its population figures, La Cruz's production numbers remained fairly strong until these later years. In 1789, La Cruz had over 61,000 head of cattle in its inventory and replenished its supplies by hunting cattle on royal lands. As these herds diminished, La Cruz's cattle supplies consistently fell. By 1801, La Cruz was distributing fewer beef rations, and its herds numbered less than 20,000. Likewise, the rest of La Cruz's communal supplies fell: by 1803, cotton, cotton cloth, and yerba maté production had plummeted.

Concepción underwent a temporary period of recovery during the post-Jesuit period, but like the other missions it went into irreversible decline at the end of the eighteenth century. Five years after the Jesuit expulsion, Concepción was in very bad shape. According to general administrator Lazcano, Concepción "lacked everything for its sustenance" and needed the relief of eight thousand cattle and two thousand mares as of 1773.[27] Within a decade, Concepción was no longer in such dire straits. By 1783, its population had increased by almost five hundred people since the expulsion.[28] Moreover, its livestock estancias recovered: from 1785 through 1802, Concepción maintained cattle herds of approximately thirty thousand (largely through procreation). But sustainable cattle supplies could not stem the mission's decline. In 1793 and again in 1801, the number of Guaraní inhabitants declined. Between 1792 and 1798, cotton production fell, and cotton cloth gradually declined to less than one-third its peak level of 1795. And by 1800, yerba maté had also plummeted.

END OF THE COMMUNAL STRUCTURE

Thirty years after the Jesuit expulsion, the Crown had had enough of the repeated reports about the missions' impoverishment and decay. In 1798, the Crown issued a royal decree for the viceroy of Río de la Plata to contain the disorders and abuses occurring in the government and administration of the missions.[29] A year later, Gabriel de Avilés y del Fierro became viceroy, and he quickly took steps to address the missions' decline and the state of the Guaraní inhabitants.

Many, including Viceroy Avilés, believed the communal structure to be fundamentally flawed and an obstacle to the Indians' freedom. In their view, Bucareli's promise to free mission Indians from virtual slavery under the Jesuits had not been achieved because the communal structure that underlay the missions obligated the Guaraní to work on collective labor projects while giving them little in return. Thus, Viceroy Avilés decided, "the means for obtaining [relief for these wretched Indians] was to put them in their natural liberty."[30] Avilés, other Spanish administrators, and the Guaraní described exemption from the missions' communal obligation as freedom or liberty (*libertad*).[31] Although Avilés's reforms dismantled the communal structure, his underlying goal was consistent with that of Bucareli. In describing his reforms to his successor, Avilés explained that Bucareli wanted mission Indians to be given their freedom once they were capable of governing themselves.[32]

While Avilés explained his actions primarily as a response to the deplorable condition of the missions, the reforms also fit well with the liberal economic concepts growing in popularity at the time. Manuel Belgrano, the first general of Argentina and an important independence leader, advocated individual liberty and property rights, proclaiming, "Working each one for himself, the general good will be reached."[33] In contrast, the inability to sell one's goods is so discouraging to a farmer that it causes laziness.[34] Mariano Moreno, another important independence leader and secretary of the first junta that replaced the viceroy, also embraced notions of liberty and applied such ideas to Indians. He condemned coercive Indian labor practices in the Andes and argued against the belief that Indians were lazy and had to be forced to work.[35] It was Moreno's belief that freedom "is a natural faculty of man to make of himself what he wishes without any coercion."[36] He later wrote that all men had four natural rights—liberty, equality, property, and security.[37]

Some fifteen years prior to Avilés's reforms, Gonzalo de Doblas employed similar rhetoric to lobby for the payment of wages to mission Guaraní. Lieutenant gobernador Doblas argued that doing so would leave the Guaraní "in full liberty so that each one works for his own utility, trades with the fruits and articles of his work and industry. In sum, they would live and be treated as the rest of the King's vassals."[38] By freeing the Guaraní from collective labor obligations and distributing communal property, Avilés's reforms coincided with these ideas of liberty, private property, and equality.

Viceroy Avilés added an important qualification to the decree freeing the Guaraní from their mission's communal regime. He feared that immediate freedom for all mission inhabitants would lead to problems, that in the massive upheaval, mission debts would go unpaid and immoral individuals would take advantage of the situation for their own benefit rather than for that of the Guaraní. To address such concerns, Avilés decided to give mission Indians their freedom gradually, based on their capability to care for themselves and their family. Specifically, he asked the gobernador of the thirty missions, Francisco Bruno de Zavala, for a list of the Indians who were

[the] most industrious in agriculture, industry or wage labor; and whose diligence and good habits are verified in some manner by the way their family lives or by the individuals' behavior if they are single. Concurrently, [they should] also know

our Spanish language at a level sufficient to make themselves understood; and moreover, they should not be known as crafty or that they prefer to live in deception from the good faith, which will be shown by [their] having withdrawn from their original or barbarous habits.[39]

On the basis of Zavala's response, Avilés granted 323 Guaraní individuals along with their families exemption from communal obligations on February 18, 1800. In addition to exempting them from communal labor demands, Avilés ordered that mission officials give each of these Indians a portion of land—containing both an agricultural plot and pasture for livestock—sufficient for maintaining their families. While exempted from communal obligations, the newly freed Indians still had to pay one peso per year in tribute and their share of their mission's tithes.[40]

The number of Indians freed from communal obligations varied greatly among the missions. For example, almost 60 percent of San Juan Bautista's population—744 out of 1,292 Indians—had received their freedom as of the 1801 census; in contrast, less than 3 percent of Santa Ana's population—32 out of 1,293 Indians—had received their freedom by the same date.[41] This variation was due in part to a lack of specificity concerning the requirements for being granted freedom. The description given by Avilés to gobernador Zavala was vague and open to interpretation, and some mission officials employed a more liberal interpretation of Avilés's instructions than others when submitting names for Zavala's list. The Guaraní also took steps to be included among those who gained their freedom. Avilés granted freedom not only to the individuals on Zavala's list but also to family members who lived under their care. With some success, more distant relatives maneuvered to be included as a family member of an individual on the list.[42] Even with such machinations, however, only a minority of the total mission population had received their freedom by the end of Avilés's term. By 1801, Avilés had freed 6,212 Guaraní—about 15 percent of the 42,885 inhabitants of the thirty missions.[43]

The idea of freeing mission Indians from the communal regime received widespread support. Mission officials and other Crown officials agreed with Avilés's plan. Only a small minority opposed the idea, still believing that the Indians were childlike and incapable of governing themselves. Generally the Guaraní were pleased as well with the prospect of freedom, and various individuals wrote letters of gratitude for the decree.[44] However, while the corregidor and cabildo of Mission San José were happy about the declaration of freedom, they also complained that their mission was left without men to care for its estancias, yerbal, and cotton plants.[45]

The Crown agreed with Avilés that the missions' communal structure needed to be dismantled. On May 17, 1803, Charles IV extended Avilés's decree to all mission Indians. Furthermore, he ordered that all land and livestock be distributed and measures implemented to help the Guaraní adjust to the transition.[46] Avilés's decree and the Crown's order to extend the decree to all mission Indians definitively signaled the missions' demise.

Most mission Guaraní did not officially gain their freedom until years after Avilés's initial decree. Despite reformers' efforts and royal officials' intentions to free mission Guaraní from the communal regime, progress moved slowly. Charles IV placed lieutenant colonel Bernardo de Velasco in charge of the thirty missions and the implementation of the reforms. Assuming management duties over the missions in 1804, Velasco encountered various difficulties and was soon distracted by priorities more pressing than the liberation of mission Indians. Three years prior, in 1801, Spain had lost territory—including the seven missions east of the Uruguay River—to the Portuguese during the War of the Oranges.[47] Consequently, Velasco focused his attention on building Spanish defenses against the Portuguese. Then, two years after becoming gobernador of the Guaraní missions, he was also named governor of Paraguay, without relinquishing his initial post presiding over the missions. Soon thereafter, the British invasion of Buenos Aires (1806–1807) diverted Velasco's attention to the center of the viceroyalty and further distracted him from affairs related to the missions. In 1808, Napoleon forced Charles IV to abdicate the Spanish Crown, and in 1810, the May revolution deposed the viceroy and named a junta to govern the viceroyalty of Río de la Plata. As a result of these many events, royal officials did not free all mission Guaraní from the communal regime prior to independence.

The Guaraní missions continued to exist for a number of years even after independence, but only as a shadow of their former selves. The thirteen missions bordering the Paraná River went to the nation of Paraguay, the ten missions between the Paraná and Uruguay Rivers went to the United Provinces of the Río de la Plata, and the seven missions east of the Uruguay River went to Brazil. Of the thirty missions, only the eight that were north of the Paraná River—Santa María de Fe, San Ignacio Guazú, Santa Rosa, San Cosme, Santiago, Jesús, Trinidad, and Itapúa—survived the wars of independence.

Fifteen of the missions were destroyed in 1817 as a result of the quest of the Banda Oriental and the interior provinces under José Gervasio Artigas for greater autonomy from Buenos Aires. In 1811, Artigas appointed a mission Guaraní, Andrés "Andresito" Guacaraví, as general commander of the province of Misiones. In 1815, Artigas ordered

Andresito to take charge of the five missions bordering the southern shores of the Paraná River. Both the Federal League (under Artigas) and Paraguay (under José Gaspar Rodríguez de Francia) claimed these missions. In the face of this conflict, Francia ordered their evacuation, and in 1817 Paraguayan troops destroyed the five missions. In the meantime, Artigas also ordered Andresito to recover the seven eastern missions from Brazil. In response, Portuguese forces destroyed the ten missions belonging to the United Provinces of the Río de la Plata.[48] At the end of this turbulence, only the seven missions in Brazilian territory and the eight Paraguayan missions north of the Paraná River remained.

The seven Brazilian missions east of the Uruguay River—San Miguel, San Luis, San Juan Bautista, San Nicolás, San Lorenzo, San Ángel, and San Borja—lingered on for another decade. In 1828, Fructuoso Rivera invaded Brazilian territory during the extended struggle between Argentina and Brazil that ultimately led to the creation of the nation of Uruguay. Rivera depopulated the region and forced the remaining mission inhabitants to emigrate to Uruguay.[49]

Little is known about the subsequent history of the eight remaining Paraguayan missions—San Ignacio Guazú, Santa María de Fe, Santa Rosa, Santiago, San Cosme, Itapúa, Trinidad, and Jesús. These missions formally ended in the 1840s. In 1842, Francia's successor, Carlos Antonio López, ordered the distribution of communal lands and cattle to capable Indians; six years later, he declared all Indians to be citizens of the Republic of Paraguay. Thus, all mission Guaraní were finally freed from the communal regime almost a half century after King Charles IV's initial decree.

FINAL THOUGHTS

Reforms associated with the Jesuit expulsion exposed weaknesses inherent in the missions. During the Jesuit period the missions seemed to thrive economically and in terms of the number of Guaraní inhabitants, but this success disguised hidden costs. The communal structure that supported the missions depended upon large subsidies: the Jesuits subsidized the missions by receiving stipends rather than market wages. After the Jesuit expulsion, when the Crown limited the missionaries' involvement to religious matters, that subsidy disappeared; mission employees had to be paid market wages. Operational costs increased substantially and bankrupted the missions. Additionally, the communal structure depended as well upon the inefficient use of productive resources. As the regional economy expanded, the missions found that they could not defend their rights to Indian labor, land, and cattle in the face of growing competition.[50]

Reformers believed that exposing the missions and the Guaraní to the market economy would bring prosperity and benefit to all. Such exposure to and engagement with the market economy intensified Guaraní acculturation and assimilation into colonial society, but it also destroyed the missions and only benefited a privileged few. The changes most hurt Guaraní who had difficulty providing for themselves—the orphans, widows, elderly, and disabled; the missions were no longer able to assist such individuals on a regular basis. The standard of living of most mission inhabitants declined: while they continued to work on communal labor projects, they received less in return for their labor. Skilled and well-connected Guaraní gained the most: skilled Guaraní easily found employment in the expanding regional economy, and at least some well-connected Guaraní made use of mission property and commercial exchanges for their own benefit.

In many ways, the trajectory described above resembles what happened in Latin America at the end of the twentieth century. With the exposure of the inefficiencies and costs associated with intervention and protectionism, governments turned to neoliberal free market reforms and privatization. As with the Guaraní, many late twentieth-century Latin Americans suffered as a result of market reforms that included little or no assistance for the poor and vulnerable. Already high, inequality increased in the 1980s and early 1990s. Such hardship led to a backlash against neoliberalism. Recognizing that free markets alone are not the solution, Latin Americans have been looking for alternatives or at least ways of tempering the shortcomings of free markets. Voters elected left-leaning and populist leaders more interested in social equity, and governments increased transfers and other reforms targeted at the poor. As a result, inequality declined in Latin America between 2000 and 2007.[51] In contrast, when the limitations of market reforms became undeniable in the case of the missions, Crown officials responded by accelerating these same reforms. Avilés's decree in 1800 began freeing the Guaraní from communal obligations and privileges, but no measures were instituted to assist the most vulnerable of the Guaraní. Other events in the Spanish Empire disrupted the process begun by Avilés, and although the missions lingered on, the end was imminent. Given the shift to a market-based ideology, the communal structure that underlay the missions could no longer sustain either the institution or its Guaraní inhabitants.

Reference Matter

Total Mission Population, 1700–1801

Year	Population	Year	Population	Year	Population	Year	Population
1700	86,173	1726		1752	99,339	1778	
1701		1727		1753	99,545	1779	
1702	89,501	1728	125,365	1754	101,752	1780	
1703		1729	132,685	1755	104,483	1781	
1704		1730	135,117	1756	89,536	1782	
1705		1731	138,934	1757	102,055	1783	56,092
1706		1732	141,182	1758	101,371	1784	
1707	98,188	1733	126,389	1759	104,184	1785	
1708	101,475	1734	116,250	1760	95,384	1786	
1709		1735	108,228	1761	102,694	1787	
1710		1736	102,721	1762	102,988	1788	
1711		1737	104,473	1763	98,879	1789	
1712		1738	90,287	1764	90,545	1790	
1713		1739	74,336	1765	85,266	1791	
1714	110,151	1740	73,910	1766	87,026	1792	
1715	115,488	1741	76,960	1767	88,796	1793	51,911
1716	121,307	1742	78,929	1768	88,774	1794	
1717	121,168	1743	81,355	1769		1795	
1718		1744	84,046	1770		1796	
1719	103,158	1745	87,240	1771		1797	
1720	105,104	1746	90,679	1772	80,881	1798	
1721		1747	91,681	1773		1799	
1722		1748	94,166	1774		1800	
1723		1749	92,835	1775		1801	45,610
1724	117,164	1750	95,089	1776			
1725		1751	96,749	1777			

SOURCE: 1700–1767 Maeder and Bolsi, "La población guaraní de las misiones jesuíticas"; 1772 from AGN, IX 18-8-5, 18-8-6, and 18-8-7; 1801 from AGN, IX 18-2-6; the remaining years from Maeder and Bolsi, "La población guaraní de la provincia de misiones," 89–92.

Consumption per Mission Inhabitant

Beginning date	End date		Population	Corn Quantity (lb)	Per person	Beans Quantity (lb)	Per person	Wheat Quantity (lb)	Per person	Barley Quantity (lb)	Per person
1786/02/21	1789/12/31	Cruz	3,746	4,672	1.2	801	0.2	31,094	8.3	2,083	0.6
1787/04/01	1790/12/31	Bautista	2,388	15,525	6.5	24,470	10.2	43,765	18.3	—	—
1789/01/01	1790/12/31	Concepción	1,349	13,069	9.7	—	—	—	—	—	—
1791/01/01	1791/12/31	Bautista	2,018	27,394	13.6	18,469	9.2	25,744	12.8	—	—
	1795/09/09	Concepción	1,349	4,931	3.7	—	—	16,031	11.9	—	—
1791/10/29		Concepción	1,349	6,434	4.8	3,273	2.4	13,699	10.2	1,942	1.4
1792/01/01	1792/12/31	Bautista	2,018	17,700	8.8	14,344	7.1	33,825	16.8	—	—
1794/01/01	1794/12/31	Bautista	2,018	23,306	11.5	18,038	8.9	36,544	18.1	27,938	13.8
1795/01/01	1795/12/31	Bautista	2,018	5,231	2.6	15,994	7.9	39,975	19.8	900	0.4
1796/01/01	1796/12/31	Bautista	1,476	39,975	27.1	16,819	11.4	38,325	26.0	10,181	6.9
1796/01/14	1798/05/31	Concepción	1,138	11,058	9.7	1,361	1.2	23,692	20.8	425	0.4
1797/01/01	1797/12/31	Bautista	1,476	11,475	7.8	4,350	2.9	9,319	6.3	—	—
1798/01/01	1798/12/31	Cruz	3,331	1,031	0.3	—	—	25,800	7.7	—	—
1798/06/01	1798/12/31	Concepción	1,138	—	—	1,286	1.1	15,332	13.5	—	—
1798/12/16	1799/12/31	Bautista	1,476	—	—	3,366	2.3	5,166	3.5	684	0.5
1799/01/01	1799/12/31	Concepción	1,127	—	—	2,813	2.5	3,919	3.5	—	—
		Cruz	3,331	—	—	—	—	3,562	1.1	—	—
1800/01/01	1800/12/31	Bautista	1,292	5,775	4.5	1,163	0.9	7,256	5.6	—	—
		Concepción	1,127	—	—	3,338	3.0	4,875	4.3	19	0.0
		Cruz	3,238	2,381	0.7	713	0.2	4,875	1.5	75	0.0
1801/01/01	1801/12/31	Concepción	1,127	—	—	2,025	1.8	8,531	7.6	—	—
		Cruz	3,238	—	—	469	0.1	7,902	2.4	7,500	2.3
1802/01/01	1802/12/31	Concepción	975	—	—	6,131	6.3	10,500	10.8	—	—
1803/01/01	1803/12/31	Cruz	3,458	3,225	0.9	—	—	13,706	4.0	2,325	0.7
1804/01/01	1804/12/31	Cruz	3,458	2,925	0.8	—	—	10,238	3.0	6,225	1.8
1805/01/01	1805/12/31	Cruz	3,458	—	—	844	0.2	16,519	4.8	1,425	0.4
		Cruz	3,458	—	—	—	—	14,475	4.2	281	0.1
Average:											
Bautista					9.1		6.8		14.1		2.4
Concepción					3.1		2.0		9.2		0.2
Cruz					0.5		0.1		4.1		0.7
Overall					4.2		3.0		9.1		1.1

Beginning date	End date		Cattle inventory at end of period	Cattle		Yerba		Wool textiles		Cotton textiles	
				Head	Per person	Quantity (lb)	Per person	Quantity	Per person	Quantity (ft)	Per person
1786/02/21	1789/12/31	Cruz	61,049	8,882	2.4	27,280	7.3	7,018	1.9	16,480	4.4
1787/04/01	1790/12/31	Bautista	27,546	4,966	2.1	17,091	7.2	1,042	0.4	23,231	9.7
1789/01/01	1790/12/31	Concepción	27,551	3,429	2.5	8,445	6.3	3,518	2.6	5,511	4.1
1791/01/01	1791/12/31	Bautista	23,626	7,309	3.6	16,030	7.9	1,445	0.7	26,581	13.2
	1791/10/29	Concepción	31,338	2,610	1.9	9,180	6.8	3,089	2.3	68,831	51.0
1791/10/29	1795/09/09	Concepción	35,363	4,870	3.6	10,416	7.7	17	0.0	5,662	4.2
1792/01/01	1792/12/31	Bautista	21,454	6,903	3.4	14,212	7.0	663	0.3	23,000	11.4
1794/01/01	1794/12/31	Bautista	17,016	7,396	3.7	20,038	9.9	—	—	30,850	15.3
1795/01/01	1795/12/31	Bautista	11,058	7,018	3.5	15,525	7.7	4,262	2.1	20,831	10.3
1796/01/01	1796/12/31	Bautista	4,853	5,956	4.0	29,633	20.1	3,897	2.6	24,737	16.8
1796/01/14	1798/05/31	Concepción	33,697	5,048	4.4	11,929	10.5	—	—	6,753	5.9
1797/01/01	1797/12/31	Bautista	4,711	1,991	1.3	9,863	6.7	624	0.4	5,011	3.4
1798/01/01	1798/12/31	Cruz	23,378	8,069	2.4	24,600	7.4	11,189	3.4	11,964	3.6
1798/06/01	1798/12/31	Concepción	32,056	4,683	4.1	7,368	6.5	2,325	2.0	7,732	6.8
1798/12/16	1799/12/31	Bautista	1,937	3,499	2.4	6,270	4.2	5,394	3.7	2,024	1.4
1799/01/01	1799/12/31	Concepción	33,561	4,589	4.1	9,821	8.7	3,597	3.2	13,993	12.4
	1799/12/31	Cruz	18,674	5,785	1.7	25,895	7.8	26,901	8.1	10,156	3.0
1800/01/01	1800/12/31	Bautista	656	2,882	2.2	7,550	5.8	5,841	4.5	3,657	2.8
		Concepción	33,867	4,296	3.8	8,076	7.2	2,522	2.2	2,342	2.1
		Cruz	18,077	5,640	1.7	21,575	6.7	23,754	7.3	9,414	2.9
1801/01/01	1801/12/31	Concepción	31,711	3,759	3.3	8,111	7.2	389	0.3	1,157	1.0
		Cruz	14,926	5,114	1.6	29,595	9.1	9,324	2.9	11,805	3.6
1802/01/01	1802/12/31	Concepción	29,084	3,603	3.7	5,459	5.6	404	0.4	2,850	2.9
		Cruz	9,520	4,506	1.3	12,758	3.7	10,253	3.0	15,914	4.6
1803/01/01	1803/12/31	Cruz	9,148	4,347	1.3	21,422	6.2	6,423	1.9	14,580	4.2
1804/01/01	1804/12/31	Cruz	8,986	4,479	1.3	10,814	3.1	7,494	2.2	4,179	1.2
1805/01/01	1805/12/31	Cruz	6,299	4,077	1.2	7,522	2.2	4,962	1.4	3,594	1.0
Average:											
Bautista				5,324	2.9		8.5		1.6		9.4
Concepción				4,099	3.5		7.4		1.5		10.1
Cruz				5,655	1.7		5.9		3.5		3.2
Overall				5,026	2.7		7.3		2.2		7.5

Beginning date	End date		Salt Quantity (lb)	Salt Per person	Sugar Quantity (lb)	Sugar Per person	Honey Quantity (lb)	Honey Per person	Tobacco Quantity (lb)	Tobacco Per person
1786/02/21	1789/12/31	Cruz	3,870	1.0	1,292	0.3	3,373	0.9	1,211	0.3
1787/04/01	1790/12/31	Bautista	5,469	2.3	621	0.3	—	—	1,248	0.5
1789/01/01	1790/12/31	Concepción	2,081	1.5	596	0.4	1,666	1.2	857	0.6
1791/01/01	1791/12/31	Bautista	3,343	1.7	693	0.3	—	—	718	0.4
		Concepción	—	—	—	—	1,860	1.4	612	0.5
1791/10/29	1795/09/09	Concepción	2,610	1.9	598	0.4	1,907	1.4	570	0.4
1792/01/01	1792/12/31	Bautista	2,767	1.4	—	—	—	—	660	0.3
1794/01/01	1794/12/31	Bautista	2,891	1.4	150	0.1	250	0.1	1,894	0.9
1795/01/01	1795/12/31	Bautista	4,276	2.1	—	—	—	—	113	0.1
1796/01/01	1796/12/31	Bautista	6,350	4.3	—	—	—	—	1,125	0.8
1796/01/14	1798/05/31	Concepción	3,924	3.4	348	0.3	896	0.8	905	0.8
1797/01/01	1797/12/31	Bautista	1,162	0.8	—	—	—	—	—	—
1798/01/01	1798/12/31	Cruz	8,757	2.6	525	0.2	1,113	0.3	25	0.0
1798/06/01	1798/12/31	Concepción	4,786	4.2	—	—	494	0.4	—	—
1798/12/16	1799/12/31	Bautista	3,384	2.3	198	0.1	771	0.5	159	0.1
1799/01/01	1799/12/31	Concepción	2,031	1.8	421	0.4	850	0.8	594	0.5
		Cruz	5,752	1.7	613	0.2	—	—	—	—
1800/01/01	1800/12/31	Bautista	3,044	2.4	200	0.2	1,023	0.8	—	—
		Concepción	1,977	1.8	561	0.5	1,750	1.6	182	0.2
		Cruz	6,434	2.0	175	0.1	—	—	765	0.2
1801/01/01	1801/12/31	Concepción	956	0.8	125	0.1	799	0.7	287	0.3
		Cruz	3,049	0.9	—	—	1,250	0.4	1,299	0.4
1802/01/01	1802/12/31	Concepción	2,937	3.0	—	—	158	0.2	—	—
		Cruz	3,670	1.1	275	0.1	775	0.2	790	0.2
1803/01/01	1803/12/31	Cruz	4,519	1.3	250	0.1	—	—	425	0.1
1804/01/01	1804/12/31	Cruz	2,255	0.7	250	0.1	—	—	—	—
1805/01/01	1805/12/31	Cruz	2,500	0.7	200	0.1	—	—	—	—
Average:										
		Bautista		2.1		0.1		0.2		0.3
		Concepción		2.1		0.2		0.9		0.4
		Cruz		1.3		0.1		0.2		0.1
		Overall		1.8		0.2		0.4		0.3

SOURCE: San Juan Bautista, AGN, IX 17-3-6, 17-9-1, 17-9-2, and 33-6-2. Concepción, AGN, IX 17-9-5, 18-1-1, and 18-4-4. La Cruz, AGN, IX 22-9-2.

Mission Yapeyú Revenue and Expenses

Beginning date	End date	Cuero revenue	Cuero revenue as percentage of total revenue	Total revenue	Total expense	Revenue less expense
1768/10/01	1769/12/31	4,163	42	9,986	(10,003)	(16.11)
1770/01/01	1771/12/31	3,803	54	7,043	(13,686)	(6,642.99)
1772/01/01	1773/12/31	6,636	49	13,411	(16,226)	(2,815.46)
1774/01/01	1775/12/31	—	0	15,739	(34,240)	(18,501.33)
1776/01/01	1777/12/31	93,119	83	111,612	(85,956)	25,655.42
1778/01/01	1779/12/31	64,693	85	76,181	(109,234)	(33,052.85)
1780/01/01	1781/12/31	38,643	63	60,993	(147,284)	(86,291.78)
1782/01/01	1784/12/31	400,015	89	447,883	(351,254)	96,629.51
1785/01/25	1787/01/24	—	0	11,170	(34,498)	(23,328.19)
1787/01/25	1789/01/24	15,891	40	39,786	(39,624)	162.21
1789/01/25	1791/01/24					—
1791/01/25	1793/01/24	9,845	79	12,397	(11,789)	608.70
1793/01/25	1794/10/18		0	7,394	(7,396)	(2.24)
1794/10/19	1796/07/19	359	4	8,086	(8,344)	(258.06)
1796/07/20	1798/07/20	347	6	5,775	(8,125)	(2,350.21)
1798/07/21	1800/07/20	104	2	5,103	(8,359)	(3,256.23)
1800/07/21	1802/07/20	1,440	11	13,564	(17,996)	(4,431.71)
1802/07/21	1804/07/20	5,873	31	18,693	(10,208)	8,484.59
1804/07/21	1806/07/20	1,574	15	10,185	(7,293)	2,892.00
Total		646,504		875,001	(921,516)	(46,514.76)

SOURCE: Entrada y venta and cuenta corriente accounting books and data and cargo receipts found in AGN, IX 7-7-7, 17-4-2, 17-5-1, 17-5-2, 17-5-3, 17-5-4, 17-6-1, 17-6-4, 17-7-1, 17-7-3, 17-7-4, 17-8-2, 18-3, 18-1-6, 18-3-5, 18-5-6, 18-5-7, 18-6-1, 18-6-6, 18-7-5, 25-7-6, and 27-2-7 and AGN, XIII 47-2-56, 47-2-58, 47-3-19, 47-3-21, and 47-3-30.

NOTE: 1. The years when Yapeyú recognized revenues from the massive cuero operations, 1776–1784, are highlighted in gray.

2. Total expense numbers do not include tribute or mayor serivicio owed to the Crown after 1775 because Yapeyú did not pay tribute or tithes after this date and did not list the amount owed in total expense.

3. My revenue calculation for 1782–1784 is higher than that in the account books because I included approximately 20,000 pesos worth of cuero revenue that was collected in the subsequent period by general administration and not handed over to Yapeyú.

Notes

INTRODUCTION

1. Merino and Newson, "Jesuit Missions in Spanish America," 135–136.
2. Morales, "Reducciones," 112. In 1984 the United Nations Educational, Scientific and Cultural Organization (UNESCO) declared the Jesuit missions a UNESCO World Heritage Site—a location with cultural heritage of outstanding universal value.
3. Maeder and Bolsi, "La población guaraní de las misiones jesuíticas," 44.
4. For a broader discussion of mission culture, see Block, *Mission Culture*, 1–10.
5. Throughout the eighteenth century, the Guaraní mission population grew primarily through natural increase, and the missions did not rely on new converts for expansion. The Jesuits complained that they lacked the manpower for campaigns to bring in new converts. Livi-Bacci and Maeder, "The Missions of Paraguay," 204. Although the Jesuits and the Guaraní founded seven missions between 1651 and 1707, new converts accounted for a significant proportion of the population in only one (Mission Jesús). The remaining six were offshoots of previously established missions. Carbonell de Masy, *Estrategias de desarrollo rural*, 94. As of 1735, only twelve of the thirty missions registered a few inhabitants who had converted within the previous twenty years. Censuses of the thirty missions, 1735, AGN, IX 18-8-2, 18-8-3, and 18-8-4.
6. Langer, *Expecting Pears*, 7.
7. In 1745, Mission Yapeyú had 6,147 inhabitants. "Catalogo de la numeración anual de las doctrinas del Río Parana," 1745, AGN, IX 6-9-7. In 1744, Buenos Aires had approximately 10,000 inhabitants. Moreno and Díaz, "Unidades domésticas," 25.
8. In 1680–1682, the Guaraní missions had 67,561 inhabitants, while Tucumán had 20,897, Paraguay had 19,596, Buenos Aires had 11,960, and Cuyo had 5,000. Carbonell de Masy, *Estrategias de desarrollo rural*, 95. In 1759, Indians residing in the Jesuit missions accounted for 55 percent of the total population of the province of Paraguay. The thirteen Guaraní missions along the Paraná River had a population of 45,660. Census 1759, AGN, ACAL, leg. 6, 2609. Bishop Manuel Antonio de la Torre tallied 85,088 inhabitants in the Paraguayan diocese. Aguerre Core, *Una caída anunciada*, 84–85.

9. "The Jesuit reductions (*reducciones*) in Paraguay were also the most prolific mission art enterprise ever undertaken by the Society of Jesus." Bailey, *Art on the Jesuit Missions*, 144. See also Gutiérrez, *Evolución urbanística*; and Levinton, *La arquitectura jesuítico-guaraní*. By the mid-eighteenth century, many Guaraní houses were made of stone, brick, or adobe, and most missions had a cathedral-sized church that was built of stone, divided into three to five naves, and decorated profusely with sculptures. Furlong, *Misiones y sus pueblos*, 203–250.

10. Jesuit priests Pablo Hernández and Guillermo Furlong provide valuable information about the Guaraní missions, albeit from a Jesuit perspective. Hernández, *Misiones del Paraguay*; Furlong, *Misiones y sus pueblos*. Studies by Alberto Armani and Maxime Haubert provide a more condensed and less biased overview of the missions. Armani, *Ciudad de Dios y Ciudad del Sol*; Haubert, *La vida cotidiana de los indios y jesuitas*. The two volumes by Aurelio Porto focus primarily on information gleaned from the *Coleção de Angelis* at the Biblioteca Nacional in Rio de Janeiro. Porto, *História das missões orientais do Uruguai*. For an ethnohistorical approach, see Wilde, *Religión y poder*; and Ganson, *The Guaraní under Spanish Rule*.

11. For New Spain, see Radding, *Wandering Peoples*; Deeds, *Defiance and Deference*; Hackel, *Children of Coyote*; Mann, *The Power of Song*; and Yetman, *Conflict in Colonial Sonora*. For South America, see Block, *Mission Culture*; Saeger, *The Chaco Mission Frontier*; and Langer, *Expecting Pears*. For comparative work, see Langer and Jackson, *The New Latin American Mission History*; Reff, "The Jesuit Mission Frontier"; and Radding, *Landscapes of Power and Identity*.

12. Neumann, "Prácticas letradas guaraníes"; Neumann, "'Mientras volaban correos'"; Neumann, "A lança e as cartas"; Wilde, *Religón y poder*; Ganson, *The Guaraní under Spanish Rule*.

13. Anthropological and archaeological studies have greatly expanded our understanding of the Guaraní both before and during the mission period. Branislava Susnik was formative in this movement. Susnik, *El indio colonial*; Susnik, *El rol de los indígenas*; Susnik, *Los aborígenes*. In recent years, Brazilian scholars have used archaeology as a tool for exploring such diverse topics as occupation of space, social organization, geographic expansion, economics, and identity. Barcelos, *Espaço e arqueologia*; Soares, *Guarani*; Noelli, "La distribución geográfica de las evidencias arqueológicas guaraní"; Souza, "O sistema econômico nas sociedades indígenas guarani pré-coloniais"; Schiavetto, *A arqueologia guarani*. For cultural change, see Wilde, *Religón y poder*; and Ganson, *The Guaraní under Spanish Rule*. For Guaraní religion, see Chamorro, *Teología guaraní*; H. Clastres, *The Land-without-Evil*; Shapiro, "From Tupã to the Land without Evil"; and Tuer, "Old Bones and Beautiful Words."

14. Magnus Mörner and Regina Gadelha focus on the founding and early years of the missions. Mörner, *The Political and Economic Activities of the Jesuits*; Gadelha, *As missões jesuíticas do Itatim*. Arno Alvarez Kern studies the missions' role within the Spanish colonial state and the internal power structures and relationships between the missionaries and the Indians. Kern, *Missões*. Mercedes Avellaneda studies alliances formed between the Jesuits and the Guaraní, while Wilde focuses on the power dynamics among Guaraní elite. Avellaneda,

"Orígenes de la alianza jesuita-guaraní"; Avellaneda, "La alianza defensiva jesu-ita-guaraní"; Avellaneda and Quarleri, "Las milicias guaraníes"; Wilde, *Relión y poder*; Wilde, "Prestigio indígena y nobleza peninsular"; Wilde, "Los guaraníes después de la expulsión de los jesuitas."

15. Thomas Whigham and Barbara Ganson do not acknowledge such empow-erment of the cabildo in the post-Jesuit period. Whigham, "Paraguay's *Pueblos de Indios*"; Ganson, *The Guaraní under Spanish Rule*. Maeder does not even men-tion the cabildo's leadership role when discussing management at the individual mission level. Maeder, *Misiones del Paraguay*. While Edgar and Alfredo Poenitz acknowledge that post-Jesuit reforms tried to involve the cabildo in a system of control of mission management, they claim that the Guaraní were incapable of maintaining the mission economy. Edgar and Alfredo Poenitz, *Misiones, provincia guaranítica*, 20, 37.

16. By exploring Guaraní concepts of economics before European contact, José Souza and Bartomeu Melià and Dominique Temple enrich our understand-ing of the changes experienced by the Guaraní in the missions. Souza, "O sistema econômico"; Melià and Temple, *El don, la venganza y otras formas de economía guaraní*. Oreste Popescu studies the missions with respect to twentieth-century eco-nomic theory and concludes that the mission economy was an economic theocracy. Popescu, *El sistema económico en las misiones jesuitas*. More concretely, Teresa Blumers provides a useful description of Jesuit accounting practices and reprints accounting documents, but fails to analyze their importance. Blumers, *La contabi-lidad en las reducciones guaraníes*. Rafael Carbonell de Masy incorporates Blum-ers's work, but as the title of his work implies, he is not critical of the Jesuits or his sources. Carbonell de Masy, *Estrategias de desarrollo rural*. John Crocitti similarly relies heavily on Jesuit sources without critically analyzing them. Crocitti, "The In-ternal Economic Organization of the Jesuit Missions." Juan Carlos Garavaglia takes a much more critical view of the missions and highlights their regional economic importance during the Jesuit period. Garavaglia, *Economía, sociedad y regiones*.

17. Livi-Bacci and Maeder, "The Missions of Paraguay"; Maeder, "La po-blación de las misiones de guaraníes"; Maeder and Bolsi, "La población guaraní de las misiones jesuíticas"; Maeder and Bolsi, "La población guaraní de la pro-vincia de Misiones"; Jackson, "Demographic Patterns in the Jesuit Missions"; Jackson, "The Population and Vital Rates."

18. Katz, *El tratado hispano-portugués de limites de 1750*; Neumann, "A lança e as cartas"; Quarleri, *Rebelión y guerra*; Quarleri, "El territorio jesuítico-guaraní"; Quarleri, "Gobierno y liderazgo jesuítico-guaraní"; Martínez Martín, "Datos estadísticos de población."

19. José Mariluz Urquijo—one of the first scholars to focus solely on the post-Jesuit period—shows that many Guaraní who fled the missions went to cities and the countryside and did not return to their precontact lifestyle. Mariluz Urquijo, "Los guaraníes después de la expulsión." Wilde and Ganson include the post-Jesuit period in their broader studies of the Guaraní missions. Wilde, *Religión y poder*; Ganson, *The Guaraní under Spanish Rule*. Two books focus solely on the post-Jesuit period: Maeder, *Misiones del Paraguay*; and Poenitz and Poenitz, *Misiones, provincia guaranítica*.

20. James Schofield Saeger and David J. Weber primarily blame corruption by the Jesuits' replacements. Saeger, "Warfare, Reorganization, and Readaptation at the Margins of Spanish Rule," 280; Weber, *Bárbaros,* 112–113. In addition, John Lynch blames poor administration. Lynch, *Spanish Colonial Administration,* 187–188. Thomas Whigham claims that the new administrators looted the missions and "reduced the Guaraní population to little better than slaves." Whigham, *The Politics of River Trade,* 111. Ganson blames the decline on a variety of factors but especially highlights the incompetence and corruption of the officials who replaced the Jesuits, Guaraní flight, and Spanish and Portuguese incursions into mission territory. Ganson, *The Guaraní under Spanish Rule,* 137. In addition to poor administration, Maeder underscores the end of the missions' protective isolation. Maeder, *Misiones del Paraguay,* 13–15. Edgar and Alfredo Poenitz highlight the lack of social control and the inability of Indian leaders. Poenitz, *Misiones, provincia guaranítica,* 37.

21. Amateur historians such as William F. Jaenike and Frederick J. Reiter praise the Jesuits and the missions. Jaenike, *Black Robes in Paraguay*; Reiter, *They Built Utopia.*

22. In their studies of the Guaraní missions, Ganson, Whigham, and Robert H. Jackson focus on conflict between the Guaraní and the Jesuits. Their analysis revolves around Guaraní agency and resistance to and manipulation of the Jesuits and the missions. Ganson, *The Guaraní under Spanish Rule*; Jackson, *Missions and the Frontiers*; Whigham, "Paraguay's *Pueblos de Indios.*"

23. For discussion of the demographic collapse, see Cook, *Born to Die*; and Crosby, *The Columbian Exchange.*

24. Radding, *Wandering Peoples*; Deeds, *Defiance and Deference*; de la Torre Curiel, *Twilight of the Mission Frontier*; Hackel, *Children of Coyote.*

25. See, for example, Cunninghame Graham, *A Vanished Arcadia*; Baudin, *Une théocratie socialiste*; Popescu, *El sistema económico*; Sweet, "The Ibero-American Frontier Mission," 38; Nonneman, "On the Economics of the Socialist Theocracy"; Lacouture, *Jesuits: A Multibiography*; Hoerder, *Cultures in Contact.*

26. Chevalier, *Land and Society,* esp. 246; Konrad, *A Jesuit Hacienda,* esp. 124–125; Cushner, *Jesuit Ranches,* esp. 157; Cushner, *Farm and Factory*; Cushner, *Lords of the Land.*

27. While such documents have yet to be found by scholars, Neumann argues that mayordomos played an important role compiling written records related to the mission economy. Neumann, "A lança e as cartas," 164.

28. For 1770 accounting data, see 1768–1770 mission accounting data, AGN, IX 17-4-1; 1770–1772 mission accounting data, AGN, IX 17-4-2 and 17-4-4.

29. Ganson argues that the economic history of the missions during the post-Jesuit period was not simply one of deterioration but rather that there were some periods of economic recovery followed by decline. Ganson, *The Guaraní under Spanish Rule,* 137.

30. Maeder asserts that the missions maintained high levels of trade between 1768 and 1781, but acknowledges that expenses consistently exceeded revenues. Maeder, *Misiones del Paraguay*, 105, 107.

31. Ganson highlights that yerba maté production tripled during the post-Jesuit period; Maeder also points out that yerba maté production increased during the post-Jesuit period. Both authors acknowledge that most of the yerba maté was of inferior quality and suggest maintenance or reinvestment problems. Ganson, *The Guaraní under Spanish Rule*, 130; Maeder, *Misiones del Paraguay*, 162.

32. Disinvestment is the running down of capital by either selling or not replacing capacity as assets reach the end of their useful lives. Moles and Terry, *Handbook of International Financial Terms*, 165–166.

33. See, for example, Prescott, *History of the Conquest of Mexico*; Prescott, *History of the Conquest of Peru*; Bolton, "The Mission as a Frontier Institution"; and Ricard, *The Spiritual Conquest of Mexico*.

34. See, for example, Hemming, *Red Gold*; Spalding, *Huarochirí*; Ramírez, *The World Upside Down*; and Jones, *The Conquest of the Last Maya Kingdom*.

35. See, for example, Farriss, *Maya Society under Colonial Rule*.

36. See, for example, Serulnikov, *Subverting Colonial Authority*; Graubart, *With Our Labor and Sweat*; and Owensby, *Empire of Law and Indian Justice*.

37. See, for example, Stern, *Peru's Indian Peoples*; Ramírez, *The World Upside Down*; and Graubart, *With Our Labor and Sweat*.

38. See, for example, Yannakakis, *The Art of Being In-Between*.

39. Among others, see Carbonell de Masy, *Estrategias de desarrollo rural*; Furlong, *Misiones y sus pueblos*; Hernández, *Misiones del Paraguay*; and Kern, *Missões*.

40. Both sets of missions had the same goals, but Guaraní in the Franciscan missions had to provide labor service to Spanish settlers, and their missions were located much closer to the colonial center of Asunción. As a result of these differences, the Jesuit missions followed a different trajectory and experienced greater prosperity. While the Guaraní population of the Jesuit missions constantly increased except during periods of crisis, the number of Guaraní in the Franciscan missions declined or remained stable. The Franciscan missions were also generally established earlier than the Jesuit missions. With one exception, the Franciscan missions were founded between 1580 and 1611, while the Jesuits founded their first mission in 1609. Necker, *Indios guaraníes y chamanes franciscanos*; Durán Estragó, *Presencia franciscana en el Paraguay*; Maeder, "Asimetría demográfica."

41. Located well north of the thirty Guaraní missions and founded in 1746 and 1750, San Joaquín and San Estanislao did not have time to mature and declined much faster after the Jesuit expulsion. Ganson, *The Guaraní under Spanish Rule*, 118.

42. Unlike the post-Jesuit period, no detailed and comprehensive accounting records from the individual missions have been located. Teresa Blumers mentions *libros de cuentas*, *libros de procuradores y estancias*, and *libros de alhajas* at the individual mission level, but she does not refer to the existence of any of these books in the archives. Blumers, *La contabilidad en las reducciones*, 108.

CHAPTER 1

1. Noelli, "La distribución geográfica," 17; Quarleri, *Rebelión y guerra*, 28–29.

2. For a description of how the Guaraní prepared new agricultural plots every three years or less, see the report by an anonymous Jesuit, Dec. 1, 1620, in Cortesão, *Jesuítas e bandeirantes*, 166.

3. Susnik, *Los aborígenes*, 4:70–74.

4. Ibid., 4:63.

5. Carbonell de Masy, *Estrategias de desarrollo rural*, 68–69; Susnik, *El indio colonial*, 2:121.

6. Souza, "O sistema econômico," 228–229.

7. Ganson, *The Guaraní under Spanish Rule*, 18; Métraux, "The Guaraní"; Quarleri, *Rebelión y guerra*, 31–34; Susnik, *Los aborígenes*, 4:59–69. The Guaraní buried their dead in pottery urns. Susnik, *Los aborígenes*, 5:66–69.

8. For more description of Guaraní hunting and fishing practices, see José Sanchez Labrador, as quoted in Furlong, *Misiones y sus pueblos*, 287.

9. Quarleri, *Rebelión y guerra*, 31.

10. Sahlins, *Stone Age Economics*.

11. Kern, "O processo histórico"; Souza, "O sistema econômico," 242–243.

12. Shapiro, "From Tupã to the Land without Evil," 130–132; H. Clastres, *The Land-without-Evil*.

13. Susnik, *Los aborígenes*, 2:18–20.

14. Levinton, *La arquitectura jesuítico-guaraní*, 13–16.

15. Souza, "O sistema econômico," 229; Kern, "O processo histórico," 32–35.

16. Soares, *Guarani*; Susnik, *Los aborígenes*, 5:96–98, 127–134.

17. Some scholars omit the term *teÿy-ru* and use *tuvichá* instead. I follow André Luis R. Soares's use of *teÿy-ru* (*Guarani*, 122).

18. Souza, "O sistema econômico," 229; Kern, "O processo histórico," 34.

19. Susnik, *Los aborígenes*, 5:127–131; Soares, *Guarani*.

20. The Guaraní also practiced sororate marriage (when sisters marry the same man), levirate marriage (when a man marries his brother's widow), and marriages when a man marries both the mother and her daughter.

21. Susnik, *Los aborígenes*, 5:83–84.

22. For a broad discussion of chieftain leadership qualities, see Earle, *How Chiefs Come to Power*.

23. Susnik, *Los aborígenes*, 5:127.

24. Wilde, "Prestigio indígena," 127–137.

25. Ruiz de Montoya, *The Spiritual Conquest*, 48.

26. Wilde, *Religión y poder*, 120–121. For more information about shamans and Guaraní religion, see H. Clastres, *The Land-without-Evil*.

27. Gott, *Land without Evil*, 14–17.

28. Quarleri, *Rebelión y guerra*, 52–53.

29. Ganson, *The Guaraní under Spanish Rule*, 24.

30. Garavaglia, "The Crises and Transformations," 8–9.

31. Ganson, *The Guaraní under Spanish Rule*, 25.

32. Ibid., 24.
33. Service, "The Encomienda in Paraguay," 239.
34. Ibid., 242.
35. Caciques were also exempt from encomienda labor.
36. Ibid., 239, 247.
37. Carbonell de Masy, *Estrategias de desarrollo rural*, 45–46.
38. In 1628 the governor of Paraguay, Luís de Céspedes Jeria, reported seeing the mobilization of four bandeirante gangs in São Paulo with at least nine hundred bandeirantes and two thousand Tupí Indians. Mörner, *Political and Economic Activities*, 89. The Indians of the Paranapanema valley, close to São Paulo, were both the members and the victims of such raiding parties. Quarleri, *Rebelión y guerra*, 80.
39. A royal cedula first stated that Paulistas took 30,000 Indians from three Spanish cities and the Guaraní missions, then later stated that Paulistas had taken 300,000 souls from Paraguay. "Real cédula al gobernador del Río de la Plata," Madrid, Sept. 16, 1639, in Pastells, *Historia de la Compañía de Jesús*, 2:34–35.
40. Monteiro, *Negros da terra*.
41. For a more detailed discussion of how native peoples responded to such pressures, see J. C. Scott, *The Art of Not Being Governed*.
42. Reff, "The Jesuit Mission Frontier," 21.
43. Service, "The Encomienda in Paraguay," 242–243.
44. Riley, "Smallpox and American Indians Revisited," 458.
45. Members of religious orders were called regular clergy. They took the particular vows associated with their order, and the order sustained them financially. Secular priests were not members of religious orders. They made up the ecclesiastical hierarchy from parish priests to bishops and archbishops.
46. "No sphere of religious activity is held in greater esteem among the Jesuits than that of the foreign missions"; "History of the Jesuits before the 1773 Suppression," New Advent, Catholic Encyclopedia, http://www.newadvent.org/cathen/14086a.htm.
47. John O'Malley argues that the Protestant Reformation had little to do with Jesuit missionary endeavors. The first Jesuits wanted to advance Catholicism among Catholics and heathens rather than reform the church; they rarely spoke of reform. Rather, O'Malley argues, "the help of souls" best captures the self-definition of the first Jesuits. Given its strong foundation in Italy and the Iberian Peninsula, the order directed more of its efforts for "the help of souls" to the Americas, India, and Japan than to countering Protestantism in Europe. Ultimately, O'Malley concludes, the missionary enterprise would have gone forward even without the Protestant Reformation. O'Malley, "Was Ignatius Loyola a Church Reformer?"
48. *Autobiography of Ignatius of Loyola*, as quoted in O'Malley, *The First Jesuits*, 29.
49. For more information about the formula of the Institute, see O'Malley et al., *The Jesuits II*, xxiii–xxxvi.
50. Ibid., xxxv.
51. Ibid., xxxvi.

52. O'Malley, *The First Jesuits*, 6.
53. O'Malley et al., *The Jesuits II*, xxxvi.
54. Ibid., xxix.
55. O'Malley, *The First Jesuits*, 18.
56. Cushner, *Why Have You Come Here?*, 23.
57. Cohen, "Why the Jesuits Joined 1540–1600."
58. Ibid., 249.
59. The opportunity to see other parts of the world and the exotic appealed to some. Clossey, *Salvation and Globalization*, 129–130. Only 10 of the 695 Iberian Jesuits said they joined the order "to go to the Indies." Another 9 said they joined after "reading *Cartas de las Indias*" from the missions. Cohen, "Why the Jesuits Joined," 249.
60. Ibid., 250–251.
61. Clossey, *Salvation and Globalization*, 121–123.
62. Ibid., 125–126.
63. Cohen, "Why the Jesuits Joined," 249.
64. Ganson, *The Guaraní under Spanish Rule*, 31.
65. Of the remaining sixty-seven Jesuits, forty-one were born in Spain, thirteen in Germany, nine in Italy, two in Hungary, one in Austria, and one in France. Brabo, *Colección de documentos*, 212–217.
66. Clossey, *Salvation and Globalization*, 115–119.
67. In the 1620s, the procurador sent to Madrid received a license to return forty new Jesuits, six of whom were foreigners; in 1640, the procurador Francisco Diaz Taño returned from Rome with new Jesuits. Mörner, *Political and Economic Activities*, 76, 95.
68. In general, the Guaraní rejected infanticide as a means of controlling fertility, but infanticide was practiced under certain circumstances. For example, the Mbyá-Guaraní killed twins and babies born with deformities. Susnik, *Los aborígenes*, 5:16.
69. Another term for a mission is reduction, or *reducción*.
70. The Crown paid each priest a *sínodo*, or a stipend, but this money did not cover the full operational costs. The missions also generated revenues and received donations and funds from their respective religious orders.
71. Bolton, "The Mission as a Frontier Institution," 43.
72. Mörner, *Political and Economic Activities*, 53–54, 64; Carbonell de Masy, *Estrategias de desarrollo rural*, 28.
73. The Jesuit provincial Diego de Torres claimed that bandeirantes had taken more than thirty thousand Indians to work in Brazilian sugar mills. "Cópia das razões que deu o padre Diogo de Tôrres Bollo," ca. 1631, in Cortesão, *Jesuítas e bandeirantes no Guairá*, 373. The Jesuit missionary Antonio Ruiz de Montoya claimed that the bandeirantes could purchase an Indian from a Tupí middleman for two or three pesos and then sell the Indian for fifteen to twenty pesos in coastal towns or forty to fifty cruzados in Rio de Janeiro. Ruiz de Montoya, *The Spiritual Conquest*, 170.
74. Hernández, *Misiones del Paraguay*, 1:7.

75. As a result of subsequent negotiations, only Guaraní from Missions Loreto and San Ignacio Miní ever had to perform encomienda labor. Mörner, *Political and Economic Activities*, 55–73; Carbonell de Masy, *Estrategias de desarrollo rural*, 44–49.

76. Hernández, *Misiones del Paraguay*, 1:8; Carbonell de Masy, *Estrategias de desarrollo rural*, 46–48; Lozano, *Historia de la conquista del Paraguay*, 1:175–177.

77. The Indians of Guairá and Paraná practiced agriculture before European contact, which made the adaptation to mission life less abrupt for them than for the Guaycurú. Mörner, *Political and Economic Activities*, 66.

78. As quoted in the letter from Diego González to the Jesuit representative of Spain in Rome, March 13, 1612, in Pastells, *Historia de la Compañía de Jesús*, 1:240.

79. The Guaycurú maintained and defended their independence by acquiring horses, cattle, iron weapons, tools, and captives through raiding and trading. In the eighteenth century, epidemics and environmental degradation weakened the Guaycurú population. The first permanent Guaycurú mission was founded in 1743. Saeger, *The Chaco Mission Frontier*.

80. After two years, Roque González de Santa Cruz, one of the two Jesuits sent to the Chaco in 1609, left the region for Paraná, where he founded various missions.

81. Hernández, *Misiones del Paraguay*, 1:351–354.

82. In Ruiz de Montoya's opinion, Artiguaye was most disturbed by the Jesuits' prohibition of polygamy. Ruiz de Montoya, *The Spiritual Conquest*, 53–54.

83. Ibid., 56.

84. Cacique Ñezú asked Roque González to establish a mission within his territory. In response, Juan del Castillo founded Asunción del Yjuhí on August 15, 1628, and Roque González and Alonso Rodríguez founded Todos los Santos del Caaró on November 1, 1628. Two weeks later, Ñezú and his followers murdered the latter two missionaries, and two days after that killed the former. The Jesuits called Ñezú a great sorcerer (*hechicero*). Carbonell de Masy, *Estrategias de desarrollo rural*, 56–63.

85. "Certificação do padre Diogo de Tôrres," Córdoba, Mar. 5, 1614, in Cortesão, *Jesuítas e bandeirantes no Guairá*, 155.

86. Hernández, *Misiones del Paraguay*, 1:10.

87. Ibid., 1:5; Carbonell de Masy, *Estrategias de desarrollo rural*, 67.

88. Francisco de Alfaro, an inspector sent by the Audiendia of Charcas to investigate the conditions of the Indians in the Río de la Plata region, issued the decree in response to the lobbying efforts of the Jesuit provincial Diego de Torres Bollo. Mörner, *Political and Economic Activities*, 68–69.

89. Hernández, *Misiones del Paraguay*, 1:10.

90. "Cópia das razões que deu o padre Diogo de Tôrres Bollo," ca. 1631, in Cortesão, *Jesuítas e bandeirantes no Guairá*, 373.

91. Quarleri, *Rebelión y guerra*, 88.

92. Mörner, *Political and Economic Activities*, 89–90.

93. Ruiz de Montoya, *The Spiritual Conquest*, 105–111.

94. Ruiz de Montoya estimated that the overland detour added twenty-five leagues to their journey. Ibid., 109. In the 1980s, the Itaipú hydroelectric dam—one of the largest in the world—destroyed these waterfalls.

95. Ibid., 111–113.

96. Carbonell de Masy, *Estrategias de desarrollo rural*, 84.

97. Mörner, *Political and Economic Activities*, 91.

98. Hernández, *Misiones del Paraguay*, 1:12–13; Carbonell de Masy, *Estrategias de desarrollo rural*, 84–85.

99. Mörner, *Political and Economic Activities*, 94–96.

100. Quarleri, *Rebelión y guerra*, 89.

101. Ibid., 88–89; Mörner, *Political and Economic Activities*, 96–97.

102. Quarleri, *Rebelión y guerra*, 89.

103. Mörner, *Political and Economic Activities*, 119–120.

104. Officials from the royal treasury claimed, "This [tribute] rate is so low that there is not a similar [rate] in all of the kingdom. The lowest class of tributaries in the other provinces, which are composed of those named *foresteros*, contribute at least five pesos and these [tributaries] do not possess, like [the mission Guaraní] lands or goods in community." Report by Antonio de Pinedo y Antonio Carrasco, Buenos Aires, Apr. 28, 1796, AGN, IX 30-5-7.

105. Mörner, *Political and Economic Activities*, 70.

106. Quarleri, *Rebelión y guerra*, 97.

107. Ibid., 98.

108. Barbara Ganson, *The Guaraní under Spanish Rule*, 47.

109. Livi-Bacci and Maeder, "The Missions of Paraguay," 185.

110. Quarleri, *Rebelión y guerra*, 104. Starting in 1746, the Jesuits founded three more missions—San Joaquín, San Estanislao, and Belén—but these were distinct from the Paraná-Uruguay missions and did not have time to fully develop before the Jesuit expulsion in 1768. Hernández, *Misiones del Paraguay*, 1:19.

111. As quoted in Avellaneda, "Orígenes de la alianza jesuita-guaraní," 179–180. *Mita* probably refers to encomienda labor obligations.

112. Ibid., 173–200.

113. For more information about go-betweens, see Metcalf, *Go-Betweens and the Colonization of Brazil*.

114. Throughout Spanish America, missionaries deliberately used gifts to attract Indians. In Nueva Vizcaya, gifts of food attracted Indians to missions. Deeds, *Defiance and Deference*, 67, 227n. In Texas, Karankawa headmen and warriors inspected to see if food supplies and clothing were sufficient before bringing their followers to the missions. Barr, *Peace Came in the Form of a Woman*, 134. In the California missions, Franciscans reported that in the initial years, they baptized few Indians and could not keep Indians in the missions because they were unable to give them enough food. Hackel, *Children of Coyote*, 72.

115. In Ruiz de Montoya's three attempts to enter the province of Tayaoba, he brought gifts for the Indian inhabitants. Ruiz de Montoya, *The Spiritual Conquest*, 90, 93, 98. "When presented with an iron wedge worth four to six farthings in Spain, a cacique will come out of the forests, mountains, or other hidden

dwelling-places and enter the reduction with his vassals. . . . The rest [of the Indians] aspire to fishhooks, needles, pins, and beads of glass and other materials." Ibid., 131. Montoya acknowledged that a fellow missionary "won over the magician by love and with gifts which, though of slight value, are able to crack such hard rocks." Ibid., 157.

116. Ibid., 43.

117. Gutiérrez, *Evolución urbanística*, 124.

118. "Segunda instrucción del Padre Torres," 1610, published in Hernández, *Misiones del Paraguay*, 1:586.

119. The dialects spoken by different Guaraní groups were transformed and synthesized into a lingua franca that retained the basic lexical semantics (vocabulary and meanings) and grammar. Dietrich, "La importancia de los diccionarios guaraníes."

120. Tuer, "Old Bones and Beautiful Words," 79.

121. Bailey, *Art on the Jesuit Missions*, 144.

122. Ruiz de Montoya, *The Spiritual Conquest*, 43. Yerba maté was most frequently shared among a group of people. The server put a handful of yerba maté into a small cup made from a cow's horn, a gourd, or wood. Sometimes the server ground an herb or root to release its flavor and added it to a jug of water. Then the server poured a small amount of the water into the cup with the yerba maté and passed it to someone in the group, who drank the flavored water through a straw and passed it back to the server. The server repeatedly filled the cup with water and shared it among the drinkers, continuing the cycle until the brew lost its flavor.

123. "Memorial de José Arce," 1701, AGN, as quoted in Furlong, *Misiones y sus pueblos*, 415–416.

124. Ruiz de Montoya, *The Spiritual Conquest*, esp. 48–54, 99–100.

125. Rípodas Ardanaz, "Pervivencia de hechiceros en las misiones guaraníes."

126. Wilde, *Religión y poder*, 115.

127. Ibid., 258–259. As of 1784, Papá remained in Buenos Aires as a prisoner. Census, Corpus Christi, 1784, AGN, IX 18-7-2.

128. Mission fugitives practiced polygamy in the post-Jesuit era. Wilde, *Religión y poder*, 133.

129. Zavala, "Un informe del gobernador de Misiones," 167–168.

CHAPTER 2

1. While mission towns of several thousand inhabitants may not seem urban compared to present-day cities or colonial centers such as Mexico City, these densely populated, compact mission settlements were urban for their time and place. Socolow and Johnson, "Urbanization in Colonial Latin America," 42. Various other scholars discuss the urban design of mission towns; see Barcelos, *Espaço e arqueologia*, 131–133; Gutiérrez, *Evolución urbanística*; Bolcato Custódio, "Ordenamientos urbanos y arquitectónicos"; and Bailey, *Art on the Jesuit Missions*, 170.

2. Even in 1767, when the Guaraní mission population was much smaller than in earlier periods, these missions had far more Indian inhabitants than Jesuit missions elsewhere. Merino and Newson, "Jesuit Missions in Spanish America," 135–136.

3. Caciques played important leadership roles in missions throughout the Americas; see, for example, Block, *Mission Culture*, 86–89, 94; Bushnell, *Situado and Sabana*, 104–110; Langer, *Expecting Pears*, 169–186; Radding, *Landscapes of Power and Identity*, 162–195; and Saeger, *The Chaco Mission Frontier*, 122–130.

4. According to missionary José Cardiel, the Jesuits chose mission sites about a quarter of a league wide where the streets could extend approximately one mile. Furlong, *Misiones y sus pueblos*, 187.

5. Mission censuses, 1735, AGN, IX 18-8-2, 18-8-3, and 18-8-4. At their peak in 1732, an average of 4,706 Indians resided in each mission. Maeder and Bolsi, "La población guaraní de las misiones jesuíticas," 44.

6. *Plano de San Juan Bautista*, AS, Estado 7381-71.

7. Bolcato Custódio, "Ordenamientos urbanos y arquitectónicos," 217–218.

8. The image shows seventy-nine housing complexes, each accommodating five to seven separate nuclear families. In total, these units housed 446 families—2,007 individuals, assuming a family size of 4.5 individuals. According to Cardiel ("Breve relación," 168), Guaraní families generally had four to five members. Possibly as the result of upheaval associated with the Treaty of Madrid, the artist was not physically present at the mission when he made the drawing and thus did not include all of the housing units. A 1756 image of the same mission, likely drawn by the same artist, shows an additional eight housing complexes. *Pueblo de San Juan que e uno de los del Uruguay que se intentan entregar a Portugal*, n.d., BNP, GE C-2769.

9. According to the 1735 censuses, the number of families in each mission ranged from 428 to 1,564, with total populations ranging from 1,780 to 6,986 individuals. AGN, IX 18-8-2, 18-8-3, and 18-8-4.

10. The Jesuits were likely also influenced by the Franciscan missions in Paraguay, but the urban designs of the two were substantially different. Gutiérrez, *Evolución urbanistica*, 123–124.

11. Torres's first instruction (1609) included much more detail about the layout of the mission pueblo than his second instruction (1610). "Primera instrucción del P. Torres. Para el Guayrá," 1609, and "Segunda instrucción del P. Torres para todos los misioneros, de Guayrá, Paraná, y Guaycurús," 1610, in Hernández, *Misiones del Paraguay*, 1:580–589.

12. Bolcato Custódio, "Ordenamientos urbanos y arquitectónicos."

13. The plaza generally measured 150 varas on each side. Gutiérrez, *Evolución urbanística*, 125. One vara equals three feet or .8359 meters. Carbonell de Masy, *Estrategias de desarrollo rural*, 379.

14. Furlong, *Misiones y sus pueblos*, 376.

15. Hernández, *Misiones del Paraguay*, 1:186; Cardiel, "Breve relación," 140–146.

16. Cardiel, "Breve relación," 63.

17. Levinton, *La arquitectura jesuítico-guaraní*, 76.

18. Various scholars have compared the similarity between the façades of the church at Mission San Miguel, the cathedral of Buenos Aires, and the church of the Gesù (the Jesuits' mother church in Rome). Ibid., 77.

19. Bolcato Custódio, "Ordenamientos urbanos y arquitectónicos," 203, 239–240.

20. Ibid., 250–254.

21. Furlong, *Misiones y sus pueblos*, 252–253; Gutiérrez, *Evolución urbanística*, 131.

22. Bolcato Custódio, "Ordenamientos urbanos y arquitectónicos," 254–255; Furlong, *Misiones y sus pueblos*, 257–258.

23. Furlong, *Misiones y sus pueblos*, 237–251; Carbonell de Masy, *Estrategias de desarrollo rural*, 171–174; Cardiel, "Costumbres de los guaraníes," 467.

24. Carbonell de Masy, *Estrategias de desarrollo rural*, 171–175; Furlong, *Misiones y sus pueblos*, 237–238.

25. Furlong, *Misiones y sus pueblos*, 245–246; Gutiérrez, *Evolución urbanística*, 129; Barcelos, *Espaço e arqueologia*, 210; Levinton, *La arquitectura jesuítico-guaraní*, 11–12.

26. Ganson, *The Guaraní under Spanish Rule*, 72–74; Bolcato Custódio, "Ordenamientos urbanos y arquitectónicos," 256–259.

27. According to Ruiz de Montoya, Guaraní widows committed suicide: "Upon their husbands' death, wives fling themselves shrieking from a height of three yards, sometimes suffering death or crippling from the impact." Ruiz de Montoya, *The Spiritual Conquest*, 50.

28. Gaspar Rodero, "IHS Hechos de la verdad, contra los artificios de la calumnia . . . ," 1746, BANH, Jesuita: LV, 1.

29. *Recopilación de leyes de los reynos de las Indias* (Madrid: Ediciones Cultura Hispánica, 1973), bk. 6, tit. 3, laws 18, 19; tit. 17, law 6.

30. Furlong, *Misiones y sus pueblos*, 410–419.

31. According to Escandón, only seven missions had land nearby that was suitable for cultivating yerba maté; the other twenty-three missions had to send Indians to harvest it, sometimes a distance of over 350 miles. Juan de Escandón to Andrés Marcos Burriel, 1760, in Furlong, *Juan de Escandón, S.J.*, 117.

32. Cardiel, "Breve relación," 79.

33. Instructions given by the padre provincial and issued by the superior of the Guaraní missions, Bernardo Nusdorffer, Candelaria, Sept. 1, 1735, BNM, MS 6976. José Cardiel confirmed that missions frequently hired Spaniards as ranch managers. Cardiel, *Declaración de la verdad*, 215.

34. Bolcato Custódio, "Ordenamientos urbanos y arquitectónicos," 264. As of 1767, farms and ranches associated with Jesuit colleges (not including Mendoza, Jujuy, or Catamarca) in the Río de la Plata region had 3,164 slaves. Cushner, *Jesuit Ranches*, 102.

35. Cardiel, "Breve relación," 82.

36. Ibid., 62.

37. Juan de Escandón to Andrés Marcos Burriel, 108.

38. Ibid., 115.

39. The trip upstream from Buenos Aires to Mission Yapeyú (the southernmost mission) took two months for 12 Jesuits and 450 Indians in seventeen boats. Antonio Betschon to R. P. Javier Am-Rhin, Paraguay, 1719, in Mühn, "El Río de la Plata visto por viajeros alemanes," 241–242.

40. "Relación compendiosa de los servicios, que han hecho a su Majestad los Indios de las Doctrinas, que están a cargo de los PP de la Compa. de Jesus en esta Provincia del Paraguay . . . 1637 hasta Oct. 1735 assi en el distrito del Gobierno de Buenos Aires como en el del Paraguay," AGN, IX 6-9-7; Furlong, *Misiones y sus pueblos*, 383–396.

41. Furlong, *Misiones y sus pueblos*, 395–396.

42. California missions had hundreds, not thousands, of Indians. Jackson and Castillo, *Indians, Franciscans, and Spanish Colonization*, 53–56. In 1645, Nicolás de Barreda recommended combining missions in Nueva Vizcaya into larger pueblos along the lines of the larger Paraguayan missions. Deeds, *Defiance and Deference*, 67. The population in Chiquitos missions oscillated between one thousand and three thousand Indians; Sonoran missions had smaller populations. Radding, *Landscapes of Power and Identity*, 58, 144. Even in 1767, when the Guaraní mission population was much smaller than in earlier periods, these missions had far more Indian inhabitants than the other Jesuit missions. Merino and Newson, "Jesuit Missions in Spanish America," 135.

43. The average population of a mission was calculated by dividing the total population of all the missions by thirty. Maeder and Bolsi, "La población guaraní de las misiones jesuíticas," 42–44. In various censuses between 1732 and 1764, I only found three missions that recorded populations of less than one thousand— Santa María la Mayor from 1739 to 1743, San Lorenzo in 1739, and San Nicolás in 1756. Copies of mission censuses, various years, AGN, ACAL, leg. 6, 2609.

44. The Guaraní inhabitants of the missions totaled 130,000, while nonmission Guaraní numbered no more than 20,000. P. Clastres, *Society against the State*, 97.

45. Carbonell de Masy, *Estrategias de desarrollo rural*, 94–98, 267.

46. Mission censuses, 1735, AGN, IX 18-8-2, 18-8-3, and 18-8-4.

47. Memorial from Father Bartolomé Jiménez, procurador general of the province of Paraguay, to the king, October 12, 1713, in Pastells, *Historia de la Compañía de Jesús*, 5:326–328.

48. Telesca, *Tras los expulsos*, 215–220.

49. The gender and age structure provide evidence of high birth rates and robust growth. Jackson, "The Population and Vital Rates," 420.

50. Cardiel, "Breve relación," 138–140.

51. Mission censuses, 1735, AGN, IX 18-8-2, 18-8-3, and 18-8-4.

52. Cardiel, "Breve relación," 168; Livi-Bacci and Maeder, "The Missions of Paraguay," 213.

53. Male and female orphans and widows were not included in these male-head-of-household families. The censuses included these categories separately after listing all of the families. For Mission Santa Ana, 6 percent, 5 percent, and 3 percent of the total population in 1735 were male orphans, female orphans, and widows, respectively. In 1759, each of these categories accounted for 2 percent

of the total population, while 1 percent were women whose husbands were long-term fugitives. Census, Santa Ana, 1735, AGN, IX 18-8-2; 1759, AGN, IX 17-3-6.

54. Livi-Bacci and Maeder, "The Missions of Paraguay," 218.

55. Livi-Bacci, "Depopulation of Hispanic America," 204–205.

56. Disease mortality varied only slightly during this period. Mortality rates were about the same for the first four generations. Cook, *Born to Die*, 207.

57. Maeder and Bolsi, "La población guaraní de las misiones jesuíticas," 17–21. For information about the Comunero Revolt, see López, *The Colonial History of Paraguay*; and Saeger, "Origins of the Rebellion of Paraguay."

58. Riley, "Smallpox and American Indians," 445–446.

59. Ibid., 451, 453. The mortality rate among a population never exposed to the virus measured between 30 and 50 percent for smallpox and 10 percent for measles. Livi-Bacci and Maeder, "The Missions of Paraguay," 209.

60. Riley, "Smallpox and American Indians," 451.

61. Ibid., 449.

62. Ibid., 458.

63. Hernández, *Misiones del Paraguay*, 1:102; Carbonell de Masy, *Estrategias de desarrollo rural*, 173.

64. Riley, "Smallpox and American Indians," 455.

65. Jackson, "The Population and Vital Rates," 409–411.

66. Livi-Bacci and Maeder, "The Missions of Paraguay," 207–209.

67. Cardiel, "Breve relación," 65. The number of cabildo members varied in practice. Wilde, *Religión y poder*, 76. See also Díaz de Zappia, "Participación indígena."

68. Cardiel, "Costumbres de los guaraníes," 471–472.

69. José Peramás, as quoted in Furlong, *Misiones y sus pueblos*, 367; Cardiel, "Breve relación," 65–66.

70. Cardiel, "Breve relación," 100.

71. Ibid., 94.

72. Alden, *The Making of an Enterprise*, 246.

73. Ibid., 308.

74. Wilde, *Religión y poder*, 75.

75. Hernández, *Misiones del Paraguay*, 1:110.

76. Alden, *The Making of an Enterprise*, 308–309.

77. Cardiel, "Breve relación," 66.

78. Juan de Escandón to Andrés Marcos Burriel, 107.

79. Ibid., 114.

80. Ibid., 96.

81. Ibid., 90.

82. Cardiel, "Breve relación," 67.

83. Juan de Escandón to Andrés Marcos Burriel, 110.

84. Cardiel called them *alcaldes* and Escandón called them *sobrestantes*. Cardiel, "Breve relación," 67; Juan de Escandón to Andrés Marcos Burriel, 88, 92, 116.

85. Guañana Indians who joined the Guaraní missions during the eighteenth century both formed their own cacicazgos in the missions and joined preexisting

Guaraní cacicazgos. Censuses of Mission Corpus Christi, 1735 and 1759, AGN, IX 18-8-2 and 17-3-6. For more discussion, see Sarreal, "Caciques as Placeholders."

86. Wilde, *Religión y poder*, 103; Juan de Escandón to Andrés Marcos Burriel, 107–108.

87. Kern, *Missões*, 38–43.

88. At the time, "Don" only referred to truly aristocratic Spaniards. Mumford, *Vertical Empire*, 57.

89. Furlong, *Misiones y sus pueblos*, 375, 367.

90. The *Recopilación de leyes de los reynos de las Indias* dedicated one of the nineteen titles pertaining to Indians solely to caciques (bk. 16, tit. 7, laws 1–17).

91. Even though a cacique sometimes brought land when he joined a mission, the mission generally absorbed this territory over time. Carbonell de Masy, *Estrategias de desarrollo rural*, 165.

92. Cardiel, "Breve relación," 68.

93. Gutiérrez, *Evolución urbanística*, 127.

94. Juan de Escandón to Andrés Marcos Burriel, 107–108; Cardiel, "Breve relación," 68; Cardiel, "Costumbres de los guaraníes," 474.

95. Juan de Escandón to Andrés Marcos Burriel, 94.

96. Ibid., 112; Cardiel, "Breve relación," 68; Cardiel, "Costumbres de los guaraníes," 484.

97. See note 43 above for calculation method and sources.

98. Wilde, "Prestigio indígena," 137–144.

99. The following discussion of cacique leadership in 1735 is based on the censuses of the thirty missions, 1735, AGN, IX 18-8-2, 18-8-3, and 18-8-4.

100. *Recopilación de leyes de los reynos de las Indias*, bk. 6, tit. 3, laws 18, 19; tit. 17, law 6.

101. Maeder and Bolsi, "La población guaraní de las misiones jesuíticas," 17.

102. *Recopilación de leyes de los reynos de las Indias*, bk. 6, tit. 3, law 21.

103. According to Cardiel, "Knowing how to read and write, he became, almost continuously, the mayordomo of the priests' house, in other words, of the pueblo." Cardiel also reported that the unnamed mulatto raised his own herd of cows, grew his own tobacco and sugarcane, and sent goods that he produced to Buenos Aires for sale. Cardiel, "Costumbres de los guaraníes," 470, 490.

104. Cardiel described thirty, forty, or more vassals per cacicazgo. Cardiel, "Breve relación," 68. Furlong claims that caciques oversaw up to five hundred individuals. Furlong, *Misiones y sus pueblos*, 367. Kazuhisa Takeda also found wide variations in the number of members in a particular cacicazgo. Takeda, "Estudio preliminar," 7.

105. Cardiel, "Breve relación," 67–88; Cardiel, *Declaración de la verdad*, 292–293. Elsewhere, Cardiel called these groupings tribes (*tribus*) instead of parcialidades. Cardiel, "Costumbres de los guaraníes," 473. In contrast to Cardiel, Juan de Escandón did not distinguish between parcialidades and cacicazgos. Juan de Escandón to Andrés Marcos Burriel, 107–108. Despite this discrepancy, cacicazgos were likely grouped into larger organizational levels. Other documents,

including one written by Pedro Comentale in 1657, refer to groups of cacicazgos in separate neighborhoods; Furlong, *Misiones y sus pueblos*, 268–270.

106. Sepp, "Algunas advertencies," 116.

107. "Memorial de Padre Provincial Antonio Machoni al Padre Superior," Yapeyú, March 7, 1742, BNM, MS 6976, 297–298.

108. Quarleri, *Rebelión y guerra*, 253.

109. Cardiel, "Costumbres de los guaraníes," 500. The 1735 census exempts twelve individuals—frequently listed as church officials and corregidor—in each mission from tribute.

110. Ibid., 471.

111. Juan de Escandón to Andrés Marcos Burriel, 107.

112. Cardiel, "Costumbres de los guaraníes," 511–512.

113. As quoted in Salinas and Svriz Wucherer, "Liderazgo guaraní," 144.

CHAPTER 3

1. Miguel Ximenez, witness, "Información y certificación acerca de varios puntos pertenecientes a los yndios guaranís . . . ," 1735, in Cortesão, *Tratado de Madrid. Antecedentes*, 294.

2. Cardiel, "Breve relación," 63–114; Cardiel, "Costumbres de los guaraníes," 470–500; Cardiel, *Declaración de la verdad*, 268–307; Juan de Escandón to Andrés Marcos Burriel, 1760, in Furlong, *Juan de Escandón, S.J.*, 87–119; Jaime Oliver, "Breve noticia de la numerosa y florida cristiandad Guaraní" (written after 1768), ARSI, Paraguay 14, doc. 4, 17–25; Sepp, "Algunas advertencias," 111–127.

3. Cardiel arrived in Buenos Aires in 1729 and was expelled from Mission Concepción; Escandón arrived in Buenos Aires in 1734, was expelled from Córdoba, Argentina, and died one year before the suppression of the order; Oliver was born in Spain, entered the Jesuit order in Paraguay in 1751, and was expelled from Mission Santa María de Fe. Storni, *Catálogo de los jesuitas*, 52, 91, 203.

4. Cardiel, *Declaración de la verdad*, 288, 291, 293.

5. Juan de Escandón to Andrés Marcos Burriel, 106.

6. Cardiel, *Declaración de la verdad*, 274.

7. Cardiel, Escandón, and Oliver did not mention the Guaraní returning to work after the afternoon religious ceremonies. In contrast, Furlong claims that the Guaraní returned to work from two or three in the afternoon until seven or eight in the evening. Furlong, *Misiones y sus pueblos*, 266.

8. Aguerre Core, *Una caída anunciada*, 88.

9. Cardiel, "Breve relación," 69, 71; Cardiel, "Costumbres de los guaraníes," 475.

10. Cardiel, "Carta y relación," 141–142.

11. According to Cardiel, the Guaraní worked on tupambaé plots on Mondays and Saturdays during the six months allotted to agriculture. Cardiel, "Breve relación," 72; Cardiel, "Costumbres de los guaraníes," 479. According to Escandón, the men worked on the tupambaé plots two or three days a week during the agricultural season. Juan de Escandón to Andrés Marcos Burriel, 108.

12. Antonio Betschon to R. P. Javier Am-Rhin, Paraguay, 1719, in Mühn, "El Río de la Plata visto por viajeros alemanes," 245.

13. Cardiel estimated that this labor should easily take only four or five hours. Cardiel, "Costumbres de los guaraníes," 482.

14. Ganson, *The Guaraní under Spanish Rule*, 62–63, 73–74. According to Artur H. F. Barcelos, the transformation of men into horticulturalists was one of the two main changes instituted in agricultural production. Barcelos, *Espaço e arqueologia*, 310–311.

15. Between 1637 and 1735, Guaraní militias assisted the Crown fifty-eight times and called more than 45,000 Indians into service. "Relación compendiosa de los servicios, que han hecho a su Majestad los Indios de las Doctrinas," AGN, IX 6-9-7. Furlong, *Misiones y sus pueblos*, 383–396.

16. Furlong, *Misiones y sus pueblos*, 395–396.

17. Between 1690 and 1767 a smallpox epidemic struck every fifteen years on average. Livi-Bacci and Maeder, "The Missions of Paraguay," 207–209. With only about a third of the population immune, smallpox had devastating consequences; catastrophic mortality rates of over 25 percent of the total population were not rare in the missions. Livi-Bacci, *Conquest*, 213. In addition to smallpox, the mission population were also subject to measles and other diseases such as scarlet fever and typhus. Livi-Bacci and Maeder, "The Missions of Paraguay," 208–209.

18. Droughts generally occurred every three or four years, and the harvest barely fed the Indians for half of the year. Cardiel, "Breve relación," 76. Sometimes there were three or four years in a row without enough rain. Cardiel, "Costumbres de los guaraníes," 483–484.

19. Ganson, *The Guaraní under Spanish Rule*, 76; Wilde, *Religión y poder*, 82. Antonio Betschon provided a brief but vivid description of the festivities and celebrations when he visited mission pueblos. Antonio Betschon to R. P. Javier Am-Rhin, 242–243.

20. Sepp, "Algunas advertencias," 125.

21. Juan de Escandón to Andrés Marcos Burriel, 116.

22. Ganson, *The Guaraní under Spanish Rule*, 63.

23. Cardiel, "Costumbres de los guaraníes," 484, 496–497; Cardiel, "Breve retlación," 72, 94; Juan de Escandón to Andrés Marcos Burriel, 109.

24. Cardiel, *Declaración de la verdad*, 293–294.

25. Cardiel, "Costumbres de los guaraníes," 476.

26. Wilde convincingly argues that the Jesuits attempted to make notions of time and work synonymous in the missions and that work, religious activities, and military exercises dominated daily life. Wilde, *Religión y poder*, 69–73, 79–82.

27. Juan de Escandón to Andrés Marcos Burriel, 94.

28. Oliver, "Breve noticia," 21.

29. Cardiel, "Costumbres de los guaraníes," 477.

30. For this reason the economic management of the missions did not lead to coercion but rather simulated productivity. Kern, *Missões*, 75.

31. Gonzalo de Doblas, "Memoria histórica, geográfica, política y económica sobre la Provincia de Misiones de Indios Guaraníes," Concepción, Sept. 27, 1785, in *Los escritos de D. Gonzalo de Doblas*, 72–73.

32. Cardiel, "Breve relación," 69; Cardiel, "Costumbres de los guaraníes," 476. It is unlikely that any soil is this fertile.

33. Report by Joseph Peralta, Jan. 8, 1743, BANH, Jesuita: LVIII, 116–120.

34. Juan Joseph Rico, "Reparos que se han hecho contra la buena conducta y govierno civil de los treinta pueblos . . . ," BNM, MS 12966-9, 12–16.

35. Antonio Betschon to R. P. Javier Am-Rhin, 248.

36. Juan de Escandón to Andrés Marcos Burriel, 103. According to Cardiel, other than a few chickens and the fruit of individual production, "all the rest [of the goods] belong to the community and is at the disposition of the priest." Cardiel, "Breve relación," 69.

37. Cardiel, *Declaración de la verdad*, 287, 289, 293.

38. Ibid., 290.

39. Juan de Escandón to Andrés Marcos Burriel, 108.

40. Rico, "Reparos que se han hecho . . . ," 12–16.

41. According to Sepp, the oxen were given to the caciques, who then distributed the animals to the Indians in their cacicazgos. Sepp, "Algunas advertencias," 116. Cardiel did not mention a role for the caciques in the distribution of oxen to the Indians. Cardiel, "Breve relación," 77.

42. Cardiel, "Costumbres de los guaraníes," 480.

43. In the nineteenth and twentieth centuries, scholars hotly contested the Guaraní missions' socialist and communist characteristics. R. B. Cunninghame Graham suggested that the Jesuits anticipated socialism. Cunninghame Graham, *A Vanished Arcadia*, 193. The title of Louis Baudin's work (*Une théocratie socialiste*) reveals his opinion. Oreste Popescu argued that while collective property was prevalent, the efforts to foster private property prevented the Guaraní missions from truly being socialist. Popescu, *El sistema económico*. Even though most mission scholars now find such labels to be inappropriate, the Guaraní missions' reputation as models of socialism continued into the late twentieth and early twenty-first centuries. Sweet, "The Ibero-American Frontier Mission," 38; Nonneman, "On the Economics of the Socialist Theocracy"; Lacouture, *Jesuits*, 243; Hoerder, *Cultures in Contact*, 190.

44. Cardiel, "Costumbres de los guaraníes," 511–512; Cardiel, "Breve relación," 117.

45. Cardiel, "Breve relación," 115, 130, 141–146. Whigham acknowledges that cabildo members and their families lived marginally better lives but gives no further description. Whigham, "Paraguay's *Pueblos de Indios*," 162.

46. Cardiel, "Costumbres de los guaraníes," 484; Cardiel, "Breve relación," 78.

47. Juan de Escandón to Andrés Marcos Burriel, 109; Cardiel, "Costumbres de los guaraníes," 481–482.

48. Cardiel, "Breve relación," 72.

49. Cardiel, "Costumbres de los guaraníes," 496–497.

50. José Cardiel, "Carta y relación," 143.

51. Cardiel, "Breve relación," 76.

52. Juan de Escandón to Andrés Marcos Burriel, 110; Cardiel, "Costumbres de los guaraníes," 484.

53. A mission of one thousand families killed ten cows to provide a ration of four pounds for each family of four to five people. Cardiel, "Breve relación," 168.

54. USDA estimate based on the 1994–1996 and 1998 Continuing Survey of Food Intakes by Individuals (CSFII). It is important to note that this beef consumption comparison does not include fish, poultry, or other meat consumption. Christopher G. Davis and Biin-Hwan Lin, "Factors Affecting U.S. Beef Consumption," *Electronic Outlook Report from the Economic Research Service, United States Department of Agriculture* LDPM13502 (Oct. 2005), http://www.ers.usda.gov/publications/ldp/Oct05/ldpm13502/ldpm13502.pdf. In 2010, Americans consumed 60.1 pounds (retail weight) per capita of beef and veal. "USDA Long-Term Projections," Feb. 2012, 83, http://www.ers.usda.gov/media/273335/oce121e_1_.pdf.

55. Ruiz de Montoya, *The Spiritual Conquest*, 106.

56. Ibid., 111.

57. Ibid., 112.

58. Cardiel, "Costumbres de los guaraníes," 483–484.

59. Assuming each family had four to five members. Cardiel, "Breve relación," 168. The thirty missions had 88,774 Guaraní inhabitants in 1768.

60. Dobrizhoffer, *An Account of the Abipones*, 1:222.

61. Escandón explained that a mission generally killed twelve, twenty, or thirty head three times a week for beef rations. The quantity and frequency varied depending on the abundance and the need. Juan de Escandón to Andrés Marcos Burriel, 110. Historian María Inés Moraes Vázquez estimates that the missions slaughtered approximately 44,500 cattle for beef rations at the time of the expulsion and that the number of cattle slaughtered for beef rations reached a high of 59,737 per year in the 1720s. Moraes Vázquez, "Crecimiento del litoral rioplantese colonial," 33.

62. Report of *visita*, Francisco Vázquez Trujillo to the general of the Society of Jesuits, Itapúa, Oct. 30, 1629, in Pastells, *Historia de la Compañía de Jesús*, 1:450.

63. Cardiel, "Breve relación," 80. Cardiel also stated, "If there is meat in abundance, above all beef, the Indian is satisfied." Cardiel, "Costumbres de los guaraníes," 487.

64. Dobrizhoffer, *An Account of the Abipones*, 1:223.

65. Ganson, *The Guaraní under Spanish Rule*, 65.

66. Cardiel, "Breve relación," 79.

67. Cardiel, *Declaración de la verdad*, 291. Betschon likewise asserted, "If in the future the Indians should lack the beef without which they cannot live, there is the danger that they would abandon the missions and would go to the forests to live by hunting." Antonio Betschon to R. P. Javier Am-Rhin, 248.

68. Cardiel, "Breve relación," 76.

69. "Memorial de Padre Provincial Antonio Machoni al Padre Superior," San Ignacio Guazú, June 28, 1740, BNM, MS 6976, 291.

70. Carbonell de Masy, *Estrategias de desarrollo rural*, 123; Porto, *História das missões orientais*, 1:181–223.

71. Cardiel, "Costumbres de los guaraníes," 483–484.

72. González Rissotto and Rodríguez Varese de González, *Contribución al studio de la influencia guaraní*, 291.

73. For a description of how the Guaraní trained the oxen for labor, see Cardiel, "Costumbres de los guaraníes," 484–485.

74. Nusdorffer permitted the hiring of Spaniards or other people who were knowledgeable and careful to work in mission estancias. "Memorial del Padre Superior, Bernardo Nusdorffer," Candelaria, Jan. 1, 1735, BNM, MS 6976, 259. Five years later, Antonio Machoni confirmed that the missions could bring some Spaniards to care for the pasturage and increase the stock of cattle. "Memorial del Padre Provincial Antonio Machoni," June 28, 1740, BNM, MS 6976, 291.

75. Mission inventories, 1768, AGN, IX 22-6-3 and 22-6-4.

76. While such Guaraní "cowboys" rode horses, the agricultural Guaraní generally did not adopt a horse culture as a strategy for resisting the Spanish, as did the nonsedentary Guaycuruans of the Chaco and the Mapuche of Chile. Ganson, *The Guaraní under Spanish Rule*, 65.

77. Cardiel, "Costumbres de los guaraníes," 486–487; Cardiel, "Breve relación," 79.

78. Carbonell de Masy, "La génesis de las vaquerías," 22.

79. Cardiel, "Costumbres de los guaraníes," 487–488.

80. Antonio Betschon to R. P. Javier Am-Rhin, 247. After describing how the Guaraní consumed great quantities of beef, Jesuit missionary Martin Dobrizhoffer wrote, "Such being the voracity of the inhabitants, and so continual the slaughters of innumerable oxen, you will agree with me that Paraguay may be called the devouring grave, as well as the seminary of cattle." Dobrizhoffer, *An Account of the Abipones*, 1:223.

81. Rodero Gaspar, "IHS Hechos de la verdad, contra los artificios de la calumnia . . . ," BANH, Jesuita: LV, 1, c. 1746, 3.

82. The Jesuits also attempted to form another cattle reserve, Vaquería de Río Negro. Carbonell de Masy, "La génesis de las vaquerías," 24–35.

83. Mörner, *Actividades políticas y económicas*, 122–123; Carbonell de Masy, "La génesis de las vaquerías"; Cardiel, "Breve relación," 79–82.

84. Cardiel, "Breve relación," 82–83.

85. Aguilar likely intended for each reserve to support 200,000 cattle—the offspring of the original 40,000 cattle. Ibid., 82.

86. "Memorial del Padre Provincial Jayme de Aguilar para el Padre Superior," Santiago, Sept. 13, 1737, AGN, IX 6-9-7.

87. Carbonell de Masy, "La génesis de las vaquerías," 44; Barcelos, *Espaço e arqueologia*, 3331.

88. "Memorial del Padre Provincial Jayme de Aguilar para el Padre Superior," Santiago, Sept. 13, 1737, AGN, IX 6-9-7; Cardiel, "Breve relación," 82–84.

89. For a more detailed discussion of the Jesuits' failed efforts to fully transition the Guaraní into domesticating livestock and practicing cultivated

agriculture, see Sarreal, "Revisiting Cultivated Agriculture, Animal Husbandry, and Daily Life in the Guaraní Missions."

90. "Memorial del Padre Provincial Antonio Machoni para el Padre Superior," Yapeyú, Mar. 7, 1742, BNM, MS 6976, 297–302.

91. Ganson, *The Guaraní under Spanish Rule*, 92, 109–110.

92. Cardiel, "Breve relación," 84.

93. Cardiel did not distinguish between San Ignacio Guazú and San Ignacio Miní. Carbonell de Masy, *Estrategias de desarrollo rural*, 278.

94. Cardiel, "Breve relación," 76.

95. Souza, "O sistema econômico," 243.

96. Cardiel, "Costumbres de los guaraníes," 483; Cardiel, "Breve relación," 75–76.

97. Antonio Betschon to R. P. Javier Am-Rhin, 246.

98. Haubert, *La vida cotidiana*, 219.

99. Based on a summary table of domesticated and undomesticated cattle compiled in 1784 by a post-Jesuit administrator, Moraes Vázquez estimates that the missions had 749,608 domesticated and 384,985 undomesticated cattle at the time of the Jesuit expulsion. Moraes Vázquez, "Crecimiento del litoral rioplantese colonial." Moraes Vázquez's source overstated the number of domesticated cattle; the 1784 summary table registers almost 100,000 more domesticated cattle than the sum of each of the missions' 1768 inventory. Summary of the missions' livestock inventory in 1768 compiled by Juan Ángel de Lazcano, AGN, IX 18-7-6; inventories of the thirty missions in 1768, AGN, IX 22-6-3 and 22-6-4.

100. Antonio Betschon to R. P. Javier Am-Rhin, 247.

101. Decades later, wild cattle disappeared and cattle-raising estancias developed in response to the booming export market for cattle products. Amaral, *The Rise of Capitalism on the Pampas*, 4; Garavaglia and Gelman, "Rural History of the Río de la Plata," 80.

102. Ruiz Montoya, *The Spiritual Conquest*, 42–43.

103. Cardiel, "Breve relación," 89.

104. "Relación de las misiones guaraníes," in Hernández, *Misiones del Paraguay*, 1:264.

105. While most contemporaries used the term "caaminí" solely to refer to this particular production process, Jesuit missionary José Sánchez Labrador wrote that "caaminí" referred to both the production process and a particular species of yerba maté. Sánchez Labrador, *El Paraguay católico*, 2:211, 245.

106. Cardiel, "Breve relación," 89; Cardiel, "Costumbres de los guaraníes," 492.

107. Cardiel, "Carta y relación," 147–148; Cardiel, "Breve relación," 89–90; Juan de Escandón to Andrés Marcos Burriel, 117–118.

108. Cardiel, "Breve relación," 90.

109. Growing the yerba maté tree from seed was difficult. Outside of the missions, Paraguayans primarily extracted yerba maté from wild yerbales until after the Triple Alliance War (1864–1870), when it was increasingly cultivated on large plantations. Whigham, *The Politics of River Trade*, 131.

110. "Memorial de José Arce," 1701, AGN, as quoted in Furlong, *Misiones y sus pueblos*, 415–416.

111. Cardiel, "Breve relación," 90.

112. Juan de Escandón to Andrés Marcos Burriel, 117.

113. Mission inventories at the date of the Jesuit expulsion, AGN, IX 22-6-3 and 22-6-4.

114. Cardiel, "Breve relación," 92; Cardiel, *Declaración de la verdad*, 292.

115. Juan de Escandón to Andrés Marcos Burriel, 96.

116. Cardiel, "Costumbres de los guaraníes," 474–475.

117. Juan de Escandón to Andrés Marcos Burriel, 109.

118. The mother of a family gave a weaver the cotton that the family had produced in its familial plot; the quantity generally yielded some ten varas of cloth. Cardiel, "Costumbres de los guaraníes," 482. One vara equals three feet.

119. A mission with six hundred families used more than 4,500 varas of wool cloth and 15,300 varas of cotton cloth. "Relación de las misiones guaraníes," in Hernández, *Misiones del Paraguay*, 1:266. Between 1702 and 1767, average family size was 4.4 individuals. Maeder and Bolsi, "La población guaraní de las misiones jesuíticas," 14.

120. Cardiel, "Breve relación," 78.

121. Ibid., 78.

122. Ibid., 70–71; Cardiel, "Costumbres de los guaraníes," 478; Juan de Escandón to Andrés Marcos Burriel, 108, 116.

123. Initially, the king offered the Jesuits a sínodo of 933 pesos 2 reales for each mission—the same amount received by priests in Peru. The Jesuits declined the king's offer, claiming that half this amount would suffice. Cardiel, "Breve relación," 102–103.

124. Elsewhere in Spanish America, mission Indians did not pay taxes; instead, the Crown provided annual funds from its own coffers to offset mission expenses and provide a stipend for the missionaries. Missionaries in Sonora, Mexico, and Moxos, Bolivia, annually received stipends of three hundred pesos and two hundred pesos, respectively, without the Indian residents paying tribute. Torre Curiel, "Conquering the Frontier," xvi; Block, *Mission Culture*, 67.

125. "Copia . . . el arreglo de tributes de los pueblos en tiempo de los Regulares expulsos," AGN, XIII 47-3-17.

126. Cardiel, "Costumbres de los guaraníes," 493.

127. The oficios appear to have served as savings bank for many non-Jesuit individuals. Mörner, *Actividades políticas y económicas de los jesuitas*, 127.

128. Crocitti, "The Internal Economic Organization of the Jesuit Missions," 7.

129. Cardiel, "Carta y relación," 149–150.

130. Cardiel, "Costumbres de los guaraníes," 495.

131. Garavaglia, *Economía, sociedad y regiones*, 161–165.

132. TePaske and Klein, *The Royal Treasuries of the Spanish Empire*, 3:172–174.

133. Garavaglia, *Mercado interno*, 68–72.

134. Prices fell overall: short periods of increasing prices (less than ten years) occurred during trade disruptions followed by extended periods of declining prices (more than twenty-five years). Tandeter and Wachtel, "Precios y producción agraria," 209–211.

135. Cardiel, "Breve relación," 89. Calculations based on mission sales at the oficios confirm Cardiel's claim. AGN, IX 47-3-5 and 47-3-7.

136. "Oficio de Santa Fe, 1730–1745," in "Misiones cuentas con los pueblos, colegios y oficios . . . ," AGN, XIII 47-3-5; "Oficio de Buenos Aires, Libro de las visitas que hacen los padres provincials . . . ," 1731–1767, AGN, XIII 47-3-7.

137. Mission oficio account books, AGN, XIII 47-3-5 and 47-3-7; "Razón de las Partidas de los efectos que han bajado de los pueblos . . . a este oficio de misiones de Santa Fe desde el día quince de marzo del año de 1750," AGN, IX 16-8-5.

138. Cardiel, "Breve relación," 168.

139. Ibid.

140. The sales price for yerba maté averaged four pesos per arroba in the account book and was confirmed by Cardiel ("Breve relación," 91–92).

141. Ibid., 93.

142. "Oficio de Buenos Aires, Libro de las visitas que hacen los padres provincials . . . ," 1731–1767, AGN, XIII 47-3-7.

143. Manuel Antonio de la Torre, "Rázon de la visita," 1761, as quoted in Aguerre Core, *Una caída anunciada*, 89.

CHAPTER 4

1. Scott, "Religion and Realpolitik," 37.

2. Bireley, *The Jesuits and the Thirty Years War*, 18.

3. O'Malley et al., *The Jesuits II*, xxix–xxxvi.

4. Letter to Antonio de Araoz from Juan Alfonso de Polanco in Ignatius's name, Dec. 1, 1551, as quoted in ibid., xxix.

5. Callahan, *Church, Politics, and Society*, 28.

6. Cushner, *Soldiers of God*, 107–108, 203, 206; Furlong, *Historia social y cultural*, 239.

7. Kendall W. Brown argues that scholars have overstated the economic importance of the Jesuits in southern Peru: while the Jesuit rural estates in southern Peru were prosperous, they did not dominate the regional economy. K. Brown, "Jesuit Wealth and Economic Activity," 25.

8. Ibid., 34.

9. Chevalier, *Land and Society*, 239; Konrad, *A Jesuit Hacienda*; Cushner, *Lords of the Land*; Cushner, *Farm and Factory*; Cushner, *Jesuit Ranches*.

10. Cushner, *Soldiers of God*, 186–191.

11. The forty-four transactions ranged from as small as the 5 pesos 5 reales that remained of the larger payment in cows that don Martín de Sayas had contracted with the oficio to as large as the 4,800 pesos 1 real that don Francisco de Vieyra borrowed from the oficio in the previous year. Summary of the debits and credits of the missions' oficio in Buenos Aires, May 1, 1739, AGN, IX 6-9-7.

12. For more about the Comunero Revolt, see Saeger, "Origins of the Rebellion of Paraguay"; Avellaneda, "La alianza defensiva jesuita-guaraní"; and López, *The Colonial History of Paraguay*.

13. Smidt, "Bourbon Regalism," 26.

14. The Jesuits generally interpreted their vow of poverty to mean not seeking financial recompense. O'Malley, *The First Jesuits*, 85, 347.

15. Smidt, "Bourbon Regalism," 32.

16. Alden, "The Gang of Four," 707; Prado, *Côlonia do Sacramento*.

17. Boxer, *The Golden Age of Brazil*, 293–296; Maxwell, *Pombal*, 52–53.

18. Quarleri, *Rebelión y guerra*, 228.

19. Ibid., 125–126.

20. Tratado firmado en Madrid, Jan. 13, 1750, in Kratz, *El tratado hispano-portugués*, 251–252.

21. Quarleri, *Rebelión y guerra*, 158.

22. Ibid., 205–206.

23. Alden, "The Gang of Four," 708–709.

24. Carvalho e Melo was granted the title of marquês de Pombal in 1769.

25. Alden, *Royal Government in Colonial Brazil*, 90.

26. Kratz, *El tratado hispano-portugués*, 45.

27. Pedro de Logu never reached Madrid. Upon his arriving in Rio de Janeiro, the governor prohibited the continuation of his journey and ordered him to return to Buenos Aires. When Logu arrived in Buenos Aires, the commission sent from Spain to implement the terms of the treaty had already landed in Buenos Aires and ordered submission. Thus, Quesada canceled Logu's trip. Ibid., 49–51.

28. Quarleri, "El territorio jesuítico-guaraní," 179.

29. Ganson, *The Guaraní under Spanish Rule*, 91–93.

30. Letter from Luis Altamirano to the priests of the Guaraní missions, Dec. 15, 1752, AGN, ACAL, leg. 6, 2609.

31. Kratz, *El tratado hispano-portugués*, 25.

32. Ibid., 45–49; Quarleri, *Rebelión y guerra*, 144, 181.

33. Cardiel showed Altamirano maps and papers in a failed attempt to convince him of the damage that would be caused by the treaty. Quarleri, *Rebelión y guerra*, 181.

34. Quarleri, "El territorio jesuítico-guaraní," 180; Quarleri, "Gobierno y liderazgo jesuítico-guaraní," 98n23, 99; Kratz, *El tratado hispano-portugués*, 65–66.

35. As quoted in da Silva e Orta and Ennes, "Teresa Margarida da Silva e Orta," 425.

36. Furlong, *Misiones y sus pueblos*, 659.

37. Before crossing the Paraná River, the Indians from San Juan Bautista left the priest who accompanied them and returned to their original mission site. The Indians from San Ángel did the same even though they had already constructed temporary housing. The Guaraní from San Lorenzo either returned to their original mission site or joined other missions in Spanish territory. The Guaraní from San Luis returned to their original site after being attacked by Charrúas. Quarleri, *Rebelión y guerra*, 157–158.

38. Ibid., 153.

39. Ibid., 167–168.

40. Ibid., 171.

41. Quarleri, "Gobierno y liderazgo jesuítico-guaraní," 99–100.

42. Quarleri, *Rebelión y guerra*, 175.

43. Ibid., 182–183.

44. Ganson, *The Guaraní under Spanish Rule*, 97; Quarleri, *Rebelión y guerra*, 184–185.

45. Ganson, *The Guaraní under Spanish Rule*, 98–102; Neumann, "A lança e as cartas," 163; Neumann, "'Mientras volaban correos,'" 105–106; Quarleri, *Rebelión y guerra*, 187–188.

46. Ganson, *The Guaraní under Spanish Rule*, 102.

47. Quarleri, *Rebelión y guerra*, 233–234.

48. Ibid., 229, 231–232.

49. Neumann, "'Mientras volaban correos,'" 104–105.

50. Neumann, "A lança e as cartas"; Neumann, "'Mientras volaban correos.'"

51. Altamirano complained that messengers were not prompt or secure. Neumann, "'Mientras volaban correos,'" 100–101.

52. Quarleri, *Rebelión y guerra*, 253, 269.

53. Quarleri, *Rebelión y guerra*; Neumann, "'Mientras volaban correos,'" 110.

54. Quarleri, *Rebelión y guerra*, 218.

55. Alden, "The Gang of Four," 711.

56. Ganson, *The Guaraní under Spanish Rule*, 108.

57. Quarleri, *Rebelión y guerra*, 272.

58. Ganson, *The Guaraní under Spanish Rule*, 108.

59. Quarleri, *Rebelión y guerra*, 281.

60. Ibid., 276.

61. Ganson, *The Guaraní under Spanish Rule*, 109–110.

62. Pedro de Cevallos to Ricardo Wall, October 7, 1758, in Pastells, *Historia de la Compañía de Jesús*, 8.1:396.

63. Quarleri, "Gobierno y liderazgo jesuítico-guaraní," 98–99.

64. Ibid., 98n22.

65. Quarleri, *Rebelión y guerra*, 293–333.

66. Cardiel, *Declaración de la verdad*, 286.

67. Domingo Muriel, "Recurso de la Provincia del Paraguay . . . ," written after 1759, ARSI, Paraguay 13, Paraguay Historia Tomo III, 28–29.

68. Ganson, *The Guaraní under Spanish Rule*, 110–112. Of the 29,191 inhabitants of the seven missions in 1751, 14,018 had returned by the end of 1762. Furlong, *Misiones y sus pueblos*, 674.

69. Maeder and Bolsi, "La población guaraní de las misiones jesuíticas," 44.

70. Quarleri, *Rebelión y guerra*, 214.

71. Alden, "The Gang of Four," 711, 719.

72. Ibid., 719–720; Maxwell, *Pombal*, 19–20.

73. Maxwell, *Pombal*, 79–86.

74. Voltaire's opinion of Jesuit activities in the Guaraní missions sharply conflicts with the writings of Montesquieu. Montesquieu praised the Jesuits for creating a model republic that joined religion and concern for humanity. His enthusiasm about the Guaraní missions can, in part, be explained by timing; Montesquieu wrote before the Guaraní War and the surge in anti-Jesuit propaganda. Ganson, *The Guaraní under Spanish Rule*, 6.

75. "The Jesuits have indeed made use of religion to deprive the inhabitants of Paraguay of their liberties"; ". . . those of Paraguay have no slaves to till their lands, or hew their timber, as the Spartans had; but are themselves slaves to the Jesuits." Voltaire, *Short Studies*, 269, 272.

76. Ibid., 277, 272.

77. "This [payment of tribute] is the only mark of vassalage which the Spanish government has thought requisite to demand of them. But the governor of Buenos Ayres cannot appoint any person to any office, either military or civil, in the Jesuits' country; nor can the bishop send so much as a parish priest thither." "It is certain that the Jesuits have already formed to themselves an empire in Paraguay, of about four hundred leagues in circumference, and that they have it in their power to add to its extent. Though vassals, in all appearance, to the crown of Spain, they are in effect kings, and perhaps the best obeyed of any kings on earth." Ibid., 272–273, 276.

78. Voltaire, *Candide*, 59.

79. First and foremost, Jansenists were proponents of predestination, while the Jesuits defended free will. Jansenists also opposed papal supremacy, one of the basic Jesuit tenets. Furthermore, Jansenists complained about the Jesuits' moral laxity in accommodating Christianity to potential converts.

80. Van Kley, *The Jansenists*; Herr, *The Eighteenth-Century Revolution in Spain*, 14–18.

81. Wright, "The Suppression and Restoration," 265–272.

82. Smidt, "Bourbon Regalism," 37; Mörner, "The Expulsion of the Jesuits," 161–162.

83. Stein and Stein, *Apogee of Empire*, 89.

84. Stelio Cro points out similarities between Campomanes's *Dictamen fiscal* and Voltaire's *Essai sur les moeurs*. Cro, *The Noble Savage*, 71–75.

85. Campomanes, *Dictamen fiscal*, 130.

86. Ibid., 129.

87. Ibid., 131.

88. Herr, *The Eighteenth-Century Revolution in Spain*, 20–22; "Colección del Real Decreto de 27 de Febrero de 1767 para la ejecución del Estrañamiento de los Regulares de la Compañía . . . ," BNM, MS 11024.

89. Mörner, *The Expulsion of the Jesuits*, 16.

90. Wright, "The Suppression and Restoration," 272.

CHAPTER 5

1. Between 1767 and 1768, Crown officials removed 2,200 Jesuits from the Americas and 2,800 from Spain. Weber, *Bárbaros*, 109–110.

2. Merino and Newson, "Jesuit Missions in Spanish America," 135.

3. Brabo, *Colección de documentos*, 212–217; Maeder and Bolsi, "La población guaraní de las misiones jesuíticas," 44.

4. Similarly, in 1758 the Portuguese issued the *Diretório que se deve observer nas Povoações dos Indios do Pará e Maranhão* to missions among the Indians in Brazil. Sommer, "Negotiated Settlements," 70–90.

5. Condé de Aranda, "Adición a la instrucción sobre el extrañamiento de los Jesuitas," Madrid, Mar. 1, 1767, in Brabo, *Colección de documentos*, 12–15.

6. Ibid., no. 6, 13.

7. Ibid.

8. Ibid., no. 5, 13.

9. An exception was the northernmost Sonoran missions, where the Franciscans partially preserved the economic administration as it had been under the Jesuits. De la Torre Curiel, *Twilight of the Mission Frontier*, 194–195; Radding, *Wandering Peoples*, 96. Even when Spain founded new missions as a way of securing Alta California, the Crown wanted a greater role. Hackel, *Children of Coyote*, 42–64. After overseeing the Jesuit expulsion in New Spain, Inspector General José de Gálvez entrusted the Franciscan order with the establishment of new missions among native peoples north along the Pacific coast in California. Gálvez's successors unsuccessfully tried to limit the missionaries' powers to religious matters. Weber, *Bárbaros*, 120–126.

10. Weber, *Bárbaros*, 102–120.

11. Campomanes, *Dictamen fiscal*, 132.

12. Ibid., 135.

13. Weber, *Bárbaros*, 4–8, 102–104.

14. Ringrose, *Spain, Europe and the "Spanish Miracle,"* 169–173; Adelman, *Republic of Capital*.

15. Wait, "Mariano Moreno," 373–374.

16. Fisher, *Economic Aspects*, 4.

17. Marquis of Esquilache's Special Junta, "Consulta original," Feb. 14, 1765, AHN, Estado 2314/1, quoted in Stein and Stein, *Apogee of Empire*, 70.

18. Aranda, "Adición a la instrucción," no. 5, 13.

19. Bucareli issued his first instructions about mission management on August 23, 1768. Francisco Bucareli y Ursúa, "Instrucción á que se deberán arreglar los gobernadores interinos que dejo nombrados en los pueblos de indios guaranís del Uruguay y Paranaá, no habiendo disposición contraria de S. M.," Candelaria, Aug. 23, 1768, in Brabo, *Colección de documentos*, 200–210. On January 15, 1770, Bucareli gave further instructions. Francisco Bucareli y Ursúa, "Adición á mi Instrucción de 23 de agosto de 1768 . . . ," Buenos Aires, Jan. 15, 1770, in Brabo, *Colección de documentos*, 300–324. On June 1, 1770, Bucareli gave detailed instructions for managing the mission economy. Francisco Bucareli y Ursúa, "Ordenanzas para regular el comercio de los españoles con los pueblos de indios tapes y guaranís, del Paraná y Uruguay," Buenos Aires, June 1, 1770, in Brabo, *Colección de documentos*, 324–347.

20. Furlong, *Misiones y sus pueblos*, 676–677.

21. Weber, *Bárbaros*, 113.

22. Bucareli, "Ordenanzas para regular el comercio," 332–333. Francisco Bucareli y Ursúa to Juan José de Vértiz, Aug. 15, 1770, in Brabo, *Colección de documentos*, 297–300.

23. Maeder, *Misiones del Paraguay*, 20–29.

24. Bucareli, "Instrucción á que se deberán arreglar los gobernadores interinos," 200.

25. While the Jesuits clearly prioritized evangelization over temporal matters, they seemingly worked toward the same goals mentioned by both Aranda and Bucareli. Introducing the Catholic faith was of primary importance to the Jesuits, but the Guaraní forced the Jesuits to attend to their temporal welfare before paying attention to religious affairs. The difference in the post-Jesuit period is that the Indians' temporal well-being was pursued as a goal in and of itself and not merely as a means of pursuing spiritual objectives.

26. Bucareli, "Instrucción á que se deberán arreglar los gobernadores interinos," 200.

27. Ibid.

28. Bucareli, "Ordenanzas para regular el comercio," 324–347.

29. Section 2 outlines the duties and obligations of the general administrator. Ibid., 332–341.

30. Bucareli, "Instrucción á que se deberán arreglar los gobernadores interinos," 203–207. Section 3 outlines the duties and obligations of these administrators. Bucareli, "Ordenanzas para regular el comercio," 341–345.

31. Marquis of Esquilache's Special Junta, "Consulta original"; Bucareli, "Ordenanzas para regular el comercio," 324.

32. Bucareli, "Ordenanzas para regular el comercio," 324.

33. Ibid., 206.

34. *Diretório que se deve observer nas Povoações dos Indios do Pará e Maranhão*, as quoted in Sommer, "Negotiated Settlements," 71.

35. As quoted in Popescu, *Studies in the History of Latin American Economic Thought*, 165, 170.

36. Bucareli, "Ordenanzas para regular el comercio," 324, 326.

37. Bucareli, "Instrucción á que se deberán arreglar los gobernadores interinos," 201.

38. Ibid., 206.

39. Ibid., 208.

40. Ibid., 203.

41. Cardiel, "Carta y relación," 131.

42. Maeder discusses the post-Jesuit political structures for governing both the missions and the mission economy, as well as addressing how these structures changed over time and the mission officials' effectiveness. Maeder, *Misiones del Paraguay*, 17–46, 77–120.

43. Royal Cedula, San Ildefonso, Oct. 5, 1778, AGN, IX 17-6-3.

44. Azara, *Descripción general*, 157.

45. Francisco Bruno de Zavala to Francisco de San Gines, Cruz, Mar. 3, 1769, AGN, IX 18-5-1.

46. Ganson, *The Guaraní under Spanish Rule*, 76–77.

47. Whigham says that whenever friction arose among the priest, administrator, and cabildo, two of the parties would ally against the third, but he does not explain how the Guaraní used this to their advantage. Whigham, "Paraguay's *Pueblos de Indios*," 175.

48. Francisco Bruno de Zavala to Francisco de San Gines, Cruz, Mar. 3, 1769, AGN, IX 18-5-1.

49. Gonzalo de Doblas, "Memoria histórica, geográfica, política y económica sobre la Provincia de Misiones de Indios Guaraníes," Concepción, Sept. 27, 1785, in *Los escritos de D. Gonzalo de Doblas*, 63.

50. Ganson, *The Guaraní under Spanish Rule*, 142–143.

51. For conflict with Lazcano, see AGN, CBN, 4411, 23 and AGN, IX 17-3-4; with lieutenant gobernadors Juan Valiente and Francisco Faijo y Noguera, see various letters, AGN, IX 17-6-3; with lieutenant gobernador Doblas, see "Expediente sobre lo ocurrido con el gobernador de Misiones Don Francisco Bruno de Zavala y el teniente gobernador de dicho Departamento . . . ," 1788, AGN, IX 22-8-2; and with priests, see Francisco Bruno de Zavala to Francisco de San Gines, Cruz, Mar. 3, 1769, AGN, IX 18-5-1.

52. Maeder, *Misiones del Paraguay*, 29.

53. Juan Valiente to señor Gobernador y Capitán General, Concepción, Aug. 6, 1776, AGN, IX 17-6-3.

54. Bucareli, "Ordenanza para regular el comercio," 324.

55. Bucareli, "Instrucción á que se deberán arreglar los gobernadores interinos," 208.

56. Juan Valiente to señor Gobernador y Capitán General, Candelaria, July 14, 1775, AGN, IX 17-6-1.

57. Azara, *Descripción general*, 157.

58. For details about the mission-oficio relationships, see "Libro de quentas del Oficio de Santa Fe en la comodidad, pueblos de las Doctrinas, Colegios, Oficios . . . ," AGN, XIII 47-3-5; "Libro de los Generos que se remitieron del Oficio de Missiones de Buenos Aires . . . ," AGN, XIII 47-3-6; Carbonell de Masy, *Estrategias de desarrollo rural*, 215–222, 304–306; and Cushner, *Jesuit Ranches*, 146–151.

59. Bucareli's instructions included plans for administrators to conduct trade on behalf of the missions and reside in Asunción, Corrientes, and Santa Fe. Such centralized trade did not develop outside of Buenos Aires.

60. Various documents in AGN, IX 6-9-7.

61. Mörner, *Actividades políticas y económicas*, 209–213.

62. Maeder, *Misiones del Paraguay*, 195. The marqués de Loreto (1784–1789), Nicolás de Arredondo (1789–1795), and the marqués de Avilés (1799–1801) either barely mention the missions or leave them out entirely in their memorias. Pedro de Melo (1795–1797) and Antonio Alaguer Feliú (1797–17999) did not leave memorias for their successors. González, *Memorias de los virreyes*, 203–536.

63. Cardiel, "Breve relación," 102.

64. Temporal coadjutor was the lowest of the four grades of Jesuits; such individuals would not attain full incorporation as a solemnly professed member of the Jesuit order.

65. "Pie de lista de los Regulares de la Compañáa recogidos en los pueblos del Uruguay y Paraná," in Brabo, *Colección de documentos*, 212–222.

66. Cardiel, "Breve relación," 102–103.

67. Except where indicated, the following discussion about mission employees and salaries is based on "Estado general de los pueblos . . . ," [1773], AGN, IX 18-7-6.

68. "Administración General cuentas corrientes con los pueblos, 1772–1773," AGN, IX 17-5-1.

69. Azara, "Informe sobre el gobierno y libertad de los Indios Guaranís y Tapis de la Provincia del Paraguay, Madrid, Jan. 1, 1806," in *Escritos fronterizos*, 206; Maeder, *Misiones del Paraguay*, 172.

70. Aguirre, "Diario del Capitán de Fragata D. Juan Francisco Aguirre, 1793," 359.

71. Hernández, *Misiones del Paraguay*, 2:231.

72. Juan José de Vértiz y Salcedo, "Memoria de Vértiz, Buenos Aires, Mar. 12, 1784," in González, *Memorias de los virreyes*, 114–115.

73. In 1773, all of the administrators except for one earned 300 pesos per year. The other administrator, who was assigned to San Juan Bautista, earned 400.

74. "Carta de Francisco Bruno de Zavala," Candelaria, Nov. 24, 1786, AGN, IX 18-4-4.

75. Doblas estimated an additional 9,000 pesos to maintain the colegio and seminary in Mission Candelaria; 9,000 pesos for emergencies; 15,000 pesos to rent church facilities; and 54,000 pesos to maintain an alms house, pay the school and music teachers, repair infrastructure, feed those sent to the colegio and orphanage in Candelaria, and pay bonuses, tribute, tithes, and every other expense. Also included in the 54,000 pesos is compensation for school and music teachers. Doblas, "Memoria histórica," 173–175.

76. Bucareli, "Ordenanzas para regular el comercio," 335.

77. Entrada y venta records, 1772–1773, AGN, IX 17-5-1 and 18-6-6.

78. "Estado general de los pueblos . . . ," Dec. 21, 1776, AGN, IX 17-6-3.

79. Bucareli, "Instrucción á que se deberán arreglar los gobernadores interinos," 201.

80. Maeder, *Misiones del Paraguay*, 176.

81. In addition to the nine missions employing maestros de primeras letras in 1776, Santa María la Mayor, Santo Tomé, Apóstoles, San Carlos, San José, San Luis, and San Xavier had Spanish teachers as of the mid-1780s according to various documents in AGN, IX 18-4-4.

82. "Instancia de don Pablo Tompson, administrador de Apóstoles sobre que se le aumente el sueldo, y en caso de no haver lugar a el, se le releve de su empleo," 1788, AGN, IX 17-8-4.

83. Report by Francisco Bruno de Zavala, Candelaria, Nov. 24, 1786, in "Liquidación de las cuentas del Pueblo de Concepción . . . ," AGN, IX 18-4-4.

84. "Expediente promovido a instancia de Gonzalo de Doblas . . . ," AGN, IX 33-3-6.

85. According to testimony by general administrator Diego Casero, Buenos Aires, Feb. 14, 1788, submitted as part of Doblas's request for a 1,000-peso salary advance. AGN, IX 22-8-2.

86. Bucareli, "Instrucción á que deberán arreglar los gobernadores interinos," 207.

87. Bucareli, "Ordenanza para regular el comercio," 332–333.

88. "Copia de la Real Cedula," San Ildefonso, Oct. 5, 1778, AGN, IX 17-6-3.

89. The following discussion of mission sales revenue is based on accounting data found in three separate account books—*Entrada y venta*, *Cuenta corriente*, and *Relación jurada*. The account books cover the thirty-seven-year period from 1770 to 1806, with the exception of 1789–1790. They provide very detailed information about the mission complex's revenues and expenditures. The general administrator, who managed centralized trade on behalf of the thirty missions, composed these account records every two years. *Entrada y venta*: Records for Jan. 25, 1789, to Jan. 24, 1791, have not been found; Jan. 1, 1770, to Dec. 31, 1771, in AGN, Sala XIII 47-3-30; Jan. 1, 1772, to Dec. 31, 1773, in AGN, IX 17-5-1 and 18-6-6; Jan. 1, 1774, to Dec. 31, 1775, in AGN, IX 25-7-6, but much of it is illegible, so the net sales revenue figures from *Cuenta corriente* in AGN, IX 17-5-3 are used instead; Jan. 1, 1776, to Dec. 31, 1777, in AGN, IX 17-6-4; Jan. 1, 1778, to Dec. 31, 1779, in AGN, IX 17-7-1; Jan. 1, 1780, to Dec. 31, 1781, in AGN, XIII 47-2-56; Jan. 1, 1782, to Dec. 31, 1784, in AGN, IX 17-5-2; Jan. 25, 1785, to Jan. 24, 1787, in AGN, IX 12-4-1; Jan. 25, 1787, to Jan. 24, 1789, in AGN, IX 18-7-5; Jan. 25, 1791, to Jan. 24, 1793, in AGN, IX 17-8-2; Jan. 25, 1793, to Oct. 18, 1794, in AGN, IX 17-7-4; Oct. 19, 1794, to July 19, 1796, in AGN, IX 18-1-6; July 20, 1796, to July 20, 1798, in AGN, IX 27-2-7; July 21, 1798, to July 20, 1800, in AGN, IX 18-5-7; July 21, 1800, to July 20, 1802, in AGN, XIII 47-2-58; July 21, 1802, to July 20, 1804, in AGN, IX 17-8-3; July 21, 1804, to July 20, 1806, in AGN, IX 18-3-5. *Cuenta corriente*: Records for Jan. 1, 1770, to Dec. 31, 1771, Jan. 1, 1778, to Dec. 31, 1779, and Jan. 25, 1789, to Jan. 24, 1791, have not been found; Jan. 1, 1772, to Dec. 31, 1773, in AGN, IX 17-5-1; Jan. 1, 1774, to Dec. 31, 1775, in AGN, IX 17-5-3; Jan. 1, 1776, to Dec. 31, 1777, in AGN, IX 18-5-6; Jan. 1, 1780, to Dec. 31, 1781, in AGN, IX 17-7-3; Jan. 1, 1782, to Dec. 31, 1784, in AGN, IX 17-5-4; Jan. 25, 1785, to Jan. 24, 1787, in AGN, IX 12-4-1 and 18-6-1; Jan. 25, 1787, to Jan. 24, 1789, in AGN, IX 18-7-5; Jan. 25, 1791, to Jan. 24, 1793, in AGN, IX 17-8-2; Jan. 25, 1793, to Oct. 18, 1794, in AGN, IX 17-7-4; Oct. 19, 1794, to July 19, 1796, in AGN, IX 18-2-1; July 20, 1796, to July 20, 1798, in AGN, IX 27-2-7; July 21, 1798, to July 20, 1800, in AGN, IX 18-5-7; July 21, 1800, to July 20, 1802, in AGN, IX 18-4-1 and AGN, XIII 47-2-58; July 21, 1802, to July 20, 1804, in AGN, IX 17-8-3 and 20-7-2; July 21, 1804, to July 20, 1806, in AGN, IX 18-3-5. *Relación jurada*: Records for the period ending Jan. 24, 1791, have not been found; ending Jan. 3, 1770, in AGN, IX 17-4-1; ending Dec. 31, 1771, in AGN, IX 17-4-2 and 17-3-4; ending Dec. 31, 1773, in AGN, IX 17-5-1; ending Dec. 31, 1775, and Dec. 31, 1777, in AGN, IX 37-2-3; ending Dec. 31, 1779, calculated on the basis of previous year and yearly balances listed in AGN, IX 17-7-4; ending Dec. 31, 1781, in AGN, IX 33-1-6; ending Dec. 31, 1784, in AGN, IX 17-7-4; ending Jan. 24, 1787, in AGN, IX 18-6-1 and 12-4-1; ending Jan. 24, 1789, in AGN, 18-7-5; ending Jan. 24, 1793, in AGN, IX 17-8-2; ending Oct. 18, 1794, in AGN, IX 17-7-4; ending July 19, 1796, in AGN, IX 7-7-7; ending July 20, 1798, in AGN, IX 27-2-7; ending July 20, 1800, in AGN 18-5-7; ending July 20, 1802, in AGN, IX 18-5-4; ending July 20, 1804, in AGN, IX 17-8-3; ending July 20, 1806, in AGN, IX 18-3-6.

90. Juan Ángel de Lazcano to señor Gobernador y Capitán General, Buenos Aires, Apr. 28, 1773, AGN, IX 17-4-6.

91. Report by Lucas Cano, corregidor Isidro Yaguarlaga, lieutenant corregidor Carlos Taguacu, alcalde segundo voto Lorenzo Sanday, and the rest of the cabildo, Jesús, Nov. 30, 1776, AGN, IX 17-6-3.

92. This investigation resulted in part from the conflicts between Lazcano and gobernador Zavala discussed earlier in this chapter.

93. "Nombramento de Apoderado general interino de los Pueblos de Misiones," Buenos Aires, Jan. 7, 1785, and "Carta orden noticeandole que a don Juan Ángel de Lazcano se le a mandado cesar en la Administración General . . . ," Buenos Aires, Jan. 25, 1785, AGN, IX 17-7-2; "Copia de la Orden Circular que le comunicado a estos treinta pueblos de este Govierno de Misiones," Itapúa, June 23, 1796, AGN, IX 18-6-3; "Vista al señor Protector General de Naturales," Buenos Aires, May 26, 1803, AGN, IX 20-5-7.

94. Report by Francisco Bruno de Zavala, Candelaria, Nov. 24, 1786, in "Liquidación de las cuentas del Pueblo de Concepción . . . ," AGN, IX 18-4-4.

95. Ibid.

96. This includes the 42,871 pesos for the priests, administrators, and other employees as of 1776 plus the 8 percent commission on sales awarded to the general administrator; the 2 percent commission on purchases is not included in the calculation.

97. Based on a census conducted by Colonel Marcos José de Larrazabal, the thirty missions owed 17,611 pesos per year in tribute between 1772 and 1795. In addition, the missions paid 3,000 pesos in tithes. "Expediente obrada sobre si se hacer los enteros correspondientes por los pueblos de Misiones Guaranís al ramo de mayor servicio . . . ," 1796, AGN, IX 30-5-7.

98. "Expediente promovida a instancia de Gonzalo de Doblas, teniente gobernador sobre la cobranza de sus sueldos," 1786, AGN, IX 33-3-6.

99. For example, Pedro Herrera, administrator of San Ignacio, 1784, AGN, IX 33-2-6; Ponciano de Silva, teacher, San Lorenzo, 1795, AGN, IX 31-6-6 and 31-5-7; Miguel Ignacio Perisena, administrator of Apostóles, 1800, AGN, IX 34-2-6; Manuel de Bustamante, administrator of Loreto, AGN, IX 18-3-4.

100. "Expediente obrada sobre si se hacer los enteros correspondientes por los pueblos de Misiones Guaranís al ramo de mayor servicio . . . ," 1796, AGN, IX 30-5-7.

CHAPTER 6

1. Caciques of San Juan Bautista to señor Gobernador y Capitán General, Jan. 30, 1773, AGN, IX 17-4-6.

2. Gaspar de la Plaza, Buenos Aires, May 17, 1773, AGN, IX 17-4-6. Underlined in original text.

3. Alcalde de primer voto, regidor, and caciques of San Juan Bautista to señor Gobernador y Capitán General, Oct. 7, 1773, AGN, IX 22-2-7.

4. Maeder and Bolsi, "La población guaraní de la provincia de Misiones."

5. 1772 census, AGN, IX 18-8-5, 18-8-6, and 18-8-7; 1801 census, AGN, IX 18-2-6; the remaining census data are from Maeder and Bolsi, "La población guaraní de la provincia de Misiones," 89–92.

6. Maeder and Bolsi, "La población guaraní de las misiones jesuíticas," 44.

7. Gonzalo de Doblas, "Memoria histórica, geográfica, política y económica sobre la Provincia de Misiones de Indios Guaraníes," Concepción, Sept. 27, 1785, in *Los escritos de D. Gonzalo de Doblas*, 42.

8. Maeder, *Misiones del Paraguay*, 57.

9. Jackson, "The Post-Jesuit Expulsion Population," 137. In contrast, Ernesto Maeder claims higher mortality rates for the post-Jesuit period than the Jesuit period. But Maeder's data is problematic: he does not include any data between 1769 and 1791. Maeder, *Misiones del Paraguay*, 58.

10. "Relación de la fatal ruina, que cayó la peste de viruelas . . . ," Feb. 1770, AGN, IX 18-5-1.

11. Yapeyú 1772 padrón, AGN, IX 18-8-7.

12. Jackson, "The Post-Jesuit Expulsion Population," 137.

13. José Barbosa to Juan José de Vértiz, Santiago, Sept. 13, 1778, AGN, IX 17-6-3.

14. Census, Nuestra Señora de Fe, Jan. 30, 1779, AGN, IX 17-7-2.

15. Manuel de Lazarte y Esquivel, "Razon del numero de naturales a que saltó la epidemia de viruela," Oct. 10, 1786, AGN, IX 17-8-1.

16. Maeder, *Misiones del Paraguay*, 57. Population figure as of January 1, 1797, calculated from "Annua numeración de los individuos . . . ," Mission San Borja, Jan. 1, 1798, AGN, IX 18-6-5.

17. Lieutenant gobernador Doblas traced a smallpox epidemic in Mission Apóstoles to an infected Indian from Mission San Borja who passed through and later died in Apóstoles. From the time Doblas became aware of the epidemic, he tried to stop its spread by prohibiting communication between missions infected with smallpox and those that the epidemic had not yet reached. Gonzalo de Doblas to Francisco de Paula Sanz, Nov. 15, 1786, AGN, IX 22-8-2.

18. Manuel de Lazarte y Esquivel, "Razon del numero de naturales a que saltó la epidemia de viruela," Oct. 10, 1786, AGN, IX 17-8-1.

19. Smallpox inoculation was introduced into Europe at the beginning of the eighteenth century, but according to Charles-Marie de la Condamine, it had been practiced since ancient times by many peoples around the world. Schiebinger, *Plants and Empire*, 101–103.

20. Mark and Rigau-Pérez, "Spanish Smallpox Vaccine Expedition," 65–66; Maeder, *Misiones del Paraguay*, 180–181. Inoculation differed from vaccination (injecting a person with liquid from a cowpox lesion) in that a person gained immunity to smallpox without falling seriously ill. Edward Jenner first injected a young boy with liquid from a dairymaid's cowpox lesions in 1796; hence, this important advance did not reach the missions until after the period studied here. Riedel, "Edward Jenner," 21–25.

21. Manuel de Lazarte y Esquivel, "Razon del numero de naturales a que saltó la epidemia de viruela," Oct. 10, 1786, AGN, IX 17-8-1.

22. Ganson, *The Guaraní under Spanish Rule*, 129.

23. Maeder and Bolsi claim that high mortality rates played a bigger role than flight. Maeder and Bolsi, "La población guaraní de la provincia de Misiones," 87; Maeder, *Misiones del Paraguay*, 64. Livi-Bacci and Maeder claim the opposite. Livi-Bacci and Maeder, "The Missions of Paraguay," 199.

24. Yapeyú lost five thousand Indians to this epidemic; the thirty missions combined lost approximately eight thousand Indians over the period. 1772 census, AGN, IX 18-8-7, 18-8-5, and 18-8-6. The 1768 census is from Maeder and Bolsi, "La población guaraní de la provincia de Misiones," 89.

25. "Estado que manifiesta el numero de Indios . . . ," Department of Candelaria, 1772–1777, AGN, IX 17-6-3.

26. Censuses for missions in Santiago department, 1781, AGN, IX 7-9-2.

27. The data include all thirty missions except the thirteen from the departments of Candelaria and Santiago in 1797, 1798, and 1799 and Mission La Cruz in 1798 and 1799. Data for 1797, AGN, IX 18-6-5; 1798, AGN, IX 18-2-4; and 1799, AGN, IX 18-2-5.

28. Ganson discusses Guaraní flight from the missions and provides various illustrative examples of individual cases. Ganson, *The Guaraní under Spanish Rule*, 125–136.

29. Cardiel estimated that less than 1 percent of the Guaraní fled the missions during the Jesuit period. Cardiel, "Breve relación," 96.

30. Livi-Bacci and Maeder, "The Missions of Paraguay," 197.

31. Gobernador of Buenos Aires to condé de Aranda, Buenos Aires, Sept. 4, 1767, in Brabo, *Colección de documentos*, 31.

32. "Yo les dije que no tenían más Rey que al Sr. D. Cárlos III; que se retirasen á cuidar de sus pueblos y familias y á trabajar sus tierras, cuyo fruto les pertenecía, porque no eran esclavos de los padres Jesuitas" [I told them that they did not have any other King than Señor Don Charles III; that they should return to their pueblos and families to work their fields whose fruits pertained to them because they were no longer slaves of the Jesuit fathers]. Francisco Bucareli to condé de Aranda, Buenos Aires, Sept. 14, 1767, in Brabo, *Colección de documentos*, 82. Even after carrying out the expulsion, Bucareli continued to promote the idea that the new regime would empower the Guaraní and improve their lives. In the addition to his original instructions for managing the missions, he wrote, "Up until this time the Indians were made to suffer effectively in slavery, violating their natural and divine rights, and almost innumerable royal decrees, licenses, and laws." Bucareli, "Adición a mi instrucción," Buenos Aires, Jan. 15, 1770, in Brabo, *Colección de documentos*, 303.

33. Wilde, *Religión y poder*, 187–188.

34. Ibid., 185.

35. Ganson, *The Guaraní under Spanish Rule*, 200–201.

36. Wilde, *Religión y poder*, 192.

37. Mission San Luis to the governor of Buenos Aires, Feb. 28, 1768, in Ganson, *The Guaraní under Spanish Rule*, 198–199.

38. Joseph de Añasco to the corregidors, cabildos and caciques, and administrators of the twenty Paraná missions, Apr. 6, 1769, AGN, IX 18-5-1.

39. Joseph de Añasco to the governor of Buenos Aires, Apr. 6, 1769, AGN, IX 18-5-1.

40. Letters from the Guaraní leaders of San José, Santa María la Mayor, Concepción, San Ignacio Guazú, San Xavier, San Cosme, and Yapeyú, AGN, IX 18-5-1.

41. For example, the leaders of Concepción also asked for permission to buy livestock and to sell eight carretas of cloth. Corregidor Pedro Curimande and the twelve cabildo members and caciques of Concepción to Carlos Joseph Añasco, Apr. 13, 1769, AGN, IX 18-5-1.

42. Cabildo of San Ignacio Guazú, Apr. 25, 1769, AGN, IX 18-5-1.

43. Yapeyú cabildo to Governor Bucareli, Nov. 28, 1769, AGN, IX 18-5-1.

44. Maeder, *Misiones del Paraguay*, 101–102.

45. The priest's assistant, Josef Gaona, was replaced after being accused of attacking and punching corregidor Cipriano of San Nicolás. Various documents, AGN, IX 17-6-3. The Indians of San Carlos requested the removal of their priest, Bernabé Antonio Romero, for setting a bad example with little religion, bad language, and other vices. Juan Valiente to señor Gobernador y Capitán General, Aug. 27, 1776, AGN, IX 17-6-3. The cabildo of San Cosme accused their priest, Baltasar Acosta, of splitting the head of the teacher (Santiago Saguari) in two without informing them of Saguari's having committed any offense. San Cosme cabildo to the lieutenant gobernador, Nov. 4, 1778, AGN, IX 17-6-3. In response to the complaint of the San Cosme cabildo, José Barbosa ordered the priest's replacement. Dec. 13, 1778, AGN, IX 17-6-3.

46. Lynch, *Spanish Colonial Administration*, 18.

47. Moutoukias, "El crecimiento en una economía colonial," 803.

48. Socolow, *The Merchants of Buenos Aires*, 12–13.

49. Schávelzon, *The Historical Archeology of Buenos Aires*, 42.

50. Johnson and Seibert, "Estimaciones de la población de Buenos Aires," 115. Population growth resulted from natural increase, the importation of slaves from Africa and Brazil, and immigration from Europe, the viceroyalty's interior, and other parts of the Spanish Empire. The Indian and mestizo contribution was significantly less: according to censuses, the Indian and mestizo population in Buenos Aires was quite small—less than 5 percent in 1778. Johnson and Socolow, "Population and Space," 345. The poor nonwhite population was more fluid and poorly recorded by the censuses; thus, the Indian population was probably larger than the amount recorded in the censuses. Johnson and Seibert, "Estimaciones de la población de Buenos Aires," 117.

51. Surviving evidence suggests that a majority of the slaves arriving in Buenos Aires after 1778 stayed in the city or nearby countryside. Johnson, "The Competition of Slave and Free Labor," 414, 418.

52. Ibid., 423.

53. Various sources estimate exports of cattle hides from Buenos Aires and Montevideo, including Moutoukias, *Contrabando y control colonial en el siglo XVII*; Moutoukias, "El crecimiento en una economía colonial," 804–805; Cuenca Esteban, "Statistics of Spain's Colonial Trade," 418; and Silva, *El comercio entre España y el Río de la Plata*, 51.

54. Carlos Joseph de Añasco to Francisco Bruno de Zavala, Rosario, Mar. 13, 1772, AGN, IX 17-4-4.

55. Various documents in "Diego Casero Apoderado General de los Pueblos de Indios Guaraníes solicitando se vuelven los Indios a sus distritos," AGN, IX 38-9-2.

56. Saguier, "El mercado del cuero," 115.

57. Virrey Avilés argued that more Indians deserted the thirteen Paraguayan missions in part because these missions were closer to Spanish towns. "Avilés al Rey," June 8, 1799, AGI, Audiencia de Buenos Aires, 85, as cited in White, "The Political Economy of Paraguay," 430.

58. Report by Martín Joseph de Aramburu and Juan Joseph Gonzales, Asunción, July 16, 1798, AGI, 292–294.

59. The data include all thirty missions except the thirteen from the departments of Candelaria and Santiago in 1797, 1798, and 1799 and Mission La Cruz in 1798 and 1799. Data for 1797, AGN, IX 18-6-5; 1798, AGN, IX 18-2-4; and 1799, AGN, IX 18-2-5.

60. Maeder and Bolsi, "La población guaraní de la provincia de Misiones," 81–85.

61. Ganson, *The Guaraní under Spanish Rule*, 132.

62. Zavala, "Un informe del gobernador de Misiones," 169.

63. José Barbosa to Francisco Bruno de Zavala, Santiago, Mar. 16, 1773, AGN, IX 17-4-6.

64. Susnik, *El indio colonial*, 2:209–222.

65. Report by Lázaro de Rivera about the missions, 1798, ANA, SH, 172, folios 5, 44.

66. Census, Corpus Christi, 1772, AGN, IX 18-8-7; census, Santa Ana, 1772, AGN, IX 18-8-6.

67. Censuses, Corpus Christi and Santa Ana, 1784, AGN, IX 18-7-2.

68. Censuses, Corpus Christi and Santa Ana, 1799, AGN, IX 18-2-2.

69. According to lieutenant gobernador Gonzalo de Doblas, mission Guaraní helped hide fugitives in their mission's *chacras* (agricultural fields). Doblas, "Memoria histórica," 74–75.

70. Report by Francisco Bruno de Zavala, Itapúa, Dec. 5, 1771, AGN, IX 22-2-7.

71. Gonzalo de Doblas to Francisco de Paula Sanz, Concepción, Aug. 15, 1787, AGN, IX 22-8-2, as cited in Ganson, *The Guaraní under Spanish Rule*, 130.

72. Susnik, *El indio colonial*, 2:51.

73. Zavala, "Un informe del gobernador de Misiones," 167–168.

74. Mariluz Urquijo, "Los guaraníes después de la expulsión."

75. Report by Diego Casero about returning mission Indians to their pueblos, Buenos Aires, Mar. 29, 1790, AGN, IX 17-3-6.

76. Mission Guaraní could be found in the jurisdictions of Montevideo, Santa Fe, Bajada, Gualeguay, Arroyo de la China, Yapeyú territory, Corrientes, and Paraguay. Doblas, "Memoria histórica," 74–75.

77. Lieutenant treasurer of the Royal Treasury of Corrientes to royal officials in Buenos Aires, Jan. 14, 1773, quoted in Maeder, *Historia económica de Corrientes*, 133.

78. Juan Valiente to Juan José de Vértiz, Oct. 13, 1778, AGN, IX 17-6-3.

79. González Rissotto and Rodríguez Varese de González, *Contribución al estudio*, 277, 288.

80. Josef de Urquiza to Tomas Antonio Lavin, Concepción de Uruguay, Dec. 29, 1800, AGN, IX 30-6-7.

81. Report by Francisco Bruno de Zavala, Mission San Miguel, Nov. 18, 1773, AGN, IX 17-4-6.

82. Francisco Bruno de Zavala to Agustín Fernando de Pinedo, Mission San Nicolás, Apr. 2, 1774, AGN, IX 17-4-6.

83. José Barbosa to Juan José de Vértiz, Santiago, Sept. 29, 1774.

84. Ganson, *The Guaraní under Spanish Rule*, 151–153.

85. Letter from the corregidor, administrator, and other deputies of Yapeyú, 1778, AGN, IX 39-5-5.

86. Doblas, "Memoria histórica," 100.

87. Realizing that massive Portuguese immigration to the region was impossible, Pombal wanted to Europeanize the Indians through miscegenation. Maxwell, *Pombal*, 53–54.

88. García, "'Ser índio' na fronteira."

89. Some Guaraní militias unsuccessfully tried to defend the territory in 1801; at least fifty-two Portuguese soldiers died during these minor skirmishes. Ganson, *The Guaraní under Spanish Rule*, 155–160. The Guaraní helped Portuguese troops. Hemming, *Amazon Frontier*, 109.

90. "Representacão do administrador geral dos 7 povos durante os anos de 1755 e 1784," in Cortesão, *Do tratado de Madri*, 440.

91. List of Guaraní militia members in 1800 census reports, AGN, IX 18-2-5; Ganson, *The Guaraní under Spanish Rule*, 153.

92. González Rissotto and Rodríguez Varese de González, *Contribución al estudio*, 294–299; Ganson, *The Guaraní under Spanish Rule*, 131–132.

93. Juan de San Martín to Juan José de Vértiz, Yapeyú, Jan. 8, 1776, AGN, IX 17-6-3.

94. Zavala, "Un informe del gobernador de Misiones," 176.

95. According to a 1796 report, "The caciques, abandoning their obligation, allow [their fellow Indians] to live where they want." Quoted in Wilde, *Religión y poder*, 282.

96. Ganson, *The Guaraní under Spanish Rule*, 127.

97. "Bando del Virrey Vértiz ordenando que nadie admita á su servicio los indios de las misiones . . . ," Buenos Aires, Aug. 17, 1780, in *Documentos para la historia del virreinato del Río de la Plata*, 302–303.

98. "Orden Circular del marqués de Loreto," Buenos Aires, Apr. 25, 1786, AGN, IX 17-3-6; "Copia del Orden de Nicolás de Arredondo," Buenos Aires, Mar. 16, 1790, AGN, IX 17-3-6.

99. José Barbosa to Juan José de Vértiz, Santiago, June 27, 1776, AGN, IX 17-6-3.

100. Lorenzo de Ugarte to Governor José de Vértiz, Loreto, Aug. 20, 1776, AGN, IX 17-6-3.

101. Doblas, "Memoria histórica," 74.

102. Juan Antonio Ysasviribil and the corregidor, cabildo, and caciques of San Juan Bautista, Oct. 13, 1772, AGN, IX 22-2-7.

103. Letters to the corregidor, cabildo, and caciques, priest, and administrator of San Juan Bautista, Oct. 17, 1772, AGN, IX 22-2-7.

104. Juan Antonio Ysasviribil to Francisco Bruno de Zavala, San Juan Bautista, Nov. 11, 1772, AGN, IX 22-2-7.

105. Letters to the corregidor, cabildo and caciques, and administrator of San Juan Bautista, Nov. 19 and 21, 1772, AGN, IX 22-2-7.

106. Governor Zavala, Nov. 18, 1772, AGN, IX 22-2-7.

107. Francisco de la Colina, San Juan Bautista, Nov. 24, 1772, AGN, IX 22-2-7.

108. Six caciques of San Juan Bautista to señor Gobernador y Capitán General, Jan. 30, 1773, AGN, IX 17-4-6.

109. Gaspar de la Plaza, Buenos Aires, May 17, 1773, AGN, IX 17-4-6.

110. Alcalde de primer voto, regidor, and caciques of San Juan Bautista to señor Gobernador y Capitán General, Oct. 7, 1773, AGN, IX 22-2-7.

111. "Cuenta general que presenta don Juan Antonio Ysasviribil . . . ," Aug. 4, 1787, AGN, IX 33-6-2.

112. Although the document is not dated, it must be from early 1774 because it includes unpaid tribute amounts from 1773 but not the salary of the lieutenant gobernador for Candelaria, a position established on December 12, 1774. "Estado General de los Pueblos, y de los medios que se conceptúan oportunos para su fomento," n.d., AGN, IX 18-7-6.

113. Corregidor, lieutenant corregidor, and other cabildo members of Concepción to Gonzalo de Doblas, Feb. 15, 1788, AGN, IX 22-8-2.

114. Gonzalo de Doblas to Francisco de Paula Sanz, San Carlos, Feb. 16, 1788, AGN, IX 22-8-2.

115. Francisco de Paula Sanz to Gonzalo de Doblas, Buenos Aires, March 13, 1788, AGN, IX 22-8-2.

116. "Liquidación de cuentas de los años 1789 y 1790 de este Pueblo de Concepción," AGN, IX 18-1-1.

117. "Cuentas de Concepción desde 29 de octubre de 1791 hasta 9 de septiembre de 1795," AGN, IX 17-9-5; "Inventario de Santa María la Mayor," Oct. 29, 1796, AGN, XIII 47-2-14.

118. Thomas Whigham describes how the cabildo of Santa Ana accused their mission's administrator of gross malfeasance in a letter to the interim gobernador. Whigham, "Paraguay's *Pueblos de Indios*," 172. Barbara Ganson also provides several examples of Guaraní leaders complaining about their mission's administrator and/or recommending someone for the position. Ganson, *The Guaraní under Spanish Rule*, 144–146.

119. Juan Valiente to señor Gobernador y Capitán General, Candelaria, July 14, 1775, AGN, IX 17-6-1.

120. Letter by Vicente Ximénez, Sr., Alcalde de la Villa, Apr. 21, 1790, AGN, IX 17-3-6, cited by Ganson, *The Guaraní under Spanish Rule*, 131.

121. José Barbosa to Juan José de Vértiz, Santiago, Oct. 29, 1776, AGN, IX 17-6-3.

122. Viceroy Pedro Melo de Portugal to the commander of Entre Rios, 1796, cited by Mariluz Urquijo, "Los guaraníes después de la expulsión," 327–328.

123. Doblas, "Memoria histórica," 82–83.

124. Ibid., 72–73.

125. Juan Valiente to Juan José de Vértiz y Salzedo, Santa María la Mayor, Sept. 23, 1776, AGN, IX 17-6-3.

126. Bucareli, "Adición a mi instrucción," 303.

127. Ibid., 306.

128. Corregidors and caciques of the thirty pueblos to the king, Buenos Aires, Mar. 10, 1768, in Brabo, *Colección de documentos*, 103.

129. As quoted in Ganson, *The Guaraní under Spanish Rule*, 126.

130. José Barbosa to Juan José de Vértiz, Santiago, Jan. 2, 1771, AGN, IX 17-4-4.

131. Juan Valiente to Pedro de Cevallos, San Joseph, Apr. 22, 1777, AGN, IX 17-6-3.

CHAPTER 7

1. While the Guaraní did not trade directly with their missions, they were not completely isolated from commerce during the Jesuit period. Guaraní who left the mission to work in the yerbales, hunt cattle, render militia service, transport trade goods, or communicate with another mission could barter with nonmission individuals whom they encountered.

2. Production, purchases, sales, and consumption figures related to communal property that are used throughout this chapter are found in the *Cuenta* books for San Juan Bautista: May 14, 1771, to May 16, 1787, in AGN, IX 33-6-2; Apr. 1, 1787, to Dec. 31, 1790, Jan. 1, 1794, to Dec. 31, 1794, Jan. 1, 1795, to Dec. 31, 1795, Jan. 1, 1796, to Dec. 31, 1796, and Jan. 1, 1797, to Dec. 31, 1797, in AGN, IX 17-9-1; Jan. 1, 1791, to Dec. 31, 1791, and Jan. 1, 1791, to Dec. 31, 1792, in AGN, IX 17-3-6; Dec. 16, 1798, to Dec. 31, 1799, and Jan. 1, 1800, to Dec. 31, 1800, in AGN, IX 17-9-2. Concepción: Nov. 9, 1778, to Dec. 31, 1785, in AGN, IX 18-4-4; Dec. 26, 1786, to Dec. 31, 1788, Oct. 29, 1791, to Sept. 9, 1795, Jan. 14, 1796, to May 31, 1798, June 1, 1798, to Dec. 31, 1798, Jan. 1, 1799, to Dec. 31, 1799, Jan. 1, 1800, to Dec. 31, 1800, Jan. 1, 1800, to Dec. 31, 1801, and Jan. 1, 1802, to Dec. 31, 1802, in AGN, IX 17-9-5; Jan. 1, 1789, to Dec. 31, 1790, and Jan. 1, 1791, to Dec. 31, 1791, in AGN, IX 18-1-1. La Cruz: Feb. 21, 1786, to Dec. 31, 1789, Jan. 1, 1798, to Dec. 31, 1798, Jan. 1, 1799, to Dec. 31, 1799, Jan. 1, 1800, to Dec. 31, 1800, Jan. 1, 1801, to Dec. 31, 1801, Jan. 1, 1802, to Dec. 31, 1802, Jan. 1, 1803, to Dec. 31, 1803, Jan. 1, 1804, to Dec. 31, 1804, and Jan. 1, 1805, to Dec. 31, 1805, in AGN, IX 22-9-2. Account records from the 1770s exist for San Juan Bautista and Concepción, but they consolidate all of the data for sixteen and seven years, respectively, and do not include any detail other than total inflows and outflows. Earlier account records have not been located for these or any other missions.

3. Some Guaraní elite were literate and certainly engaged in written communication, but to date scholars have not found documents written by Guaraní cabildos that pre-date the second half of the eighteenth century. Morinigo, *Raíz y destino del guaraní*, 143; Díaz de Zappia, "Participación indígena," 97.

4. Francisco Bucareli y Ursúa, "Instrucción á que se deberán arreglar los gobernadores interinos que dejo nombrados en los pueblos de indios guaranís del Uruguay y Paranaá, no habiendo disposición contraria de S. M.," Candelaria, Aug. 23, 1768, in Brabo, *Colección de documentos*, 205–206.

5. He dedicated one of three main sections in the addition to his original instructions for managing the missions to commerce. Francisco Bucareli y Ursúa, "Adición á mi instrucción de 23 de agosto de 1768 . . . ," Buenos Aires, Jan. 15, 1770, in Brabo, *Colección de documentos*, 300–324.

6. Bucareli referred to *Recopilación de leyes de los reynos de las Indias*, 1680, bk. 6, tit. 1, laws 24, 25; in Bucareli, "Instrucción á que se deberán arreglar los gobernadores interinos," 206.

7. Francisco Bucareli y Ursúa, "Ordenanzas para regular el comercio de los españoles con los pueblos de indios tapes y guaranís," Buenos Aires, June 1, 1770, in Brabo, *Colección de documentos*, 330.

8. Ibid.

9. Ibid., 342.

10. Ibid., 336–337, 339–340.

11. Cardiel, "Breve relación," 66. Amy Bushnell notes that keys served both a practical and a symbolic purpose; in Spanish Florida, several officials held keys to the treasury. Bushnell, *The King's Coffer*, 45.

12. Bucareli, "Ordenanzas para regular el comercio," 343.

13. Ibid., 344.

14. Francisco Bucareli y Ursúa, "Instrucción que deberán observer los administradores particulares de los pueblos de indios guaranís del Uruguay y Paraná en el de su destino," in Brabo, *Colección de documentos*, 297.

15. Bucareli, "Instrucción á que se deberán arreglar los gobernadores interinos," 206.

16. Bucareli, "Adición á mi instrucción," 315–316.

17. Gonzalo de Doblas, "Memoria histórica, geográfica, política y económica sobre la Provincia de Misiones de Indios Guaraníes," Concepción, Sept. 27, 1785, in *Los escritos de D. Gonzalo de Doblas*, 53.

18. Bucareli, "Instrucción á que se deberán arreglar los gobernadores interinos," 201.

19. Ibid., 202. Fruit from mission orchards was to be distributed among Spanish officials, the priests, the caciques, the corregidors, and other employed Indians, with a portion reserved for the rest of the population during festival days. Bucareli, "Adición á mi instrucción," 314–315.

20. Bucareli, "Instrucción á que se deberán arreglar los gobernadores interinos," 201.

21. "Guaraní letter to King Charles III," Buenos Aires, Mar. 10, 1768, in Ganson, *The Guaraní under Spanish Rule*, app. 4, 200–201. Bucareli had ulterior motives for his respectful treatment of the Guaraní leaders; he admitted to the

condé de Aranda that he called the corregidors and caciques to Buenos Aires in order to avoid a native uprising against the expulsion. Francisco Bucareli y Ursúa to condé de Aranda, Oct. 14, 1768, in Brabo, *Colección de documentos*, 186.

22. Wilde, *Religión y poder*, 183–198.

23. "Ordenes para todas las reducciones aprobados por N.P. General Paulo Oliva," ARSI, Paraquariae 12, Historia Paraguaya tomo II, 235.

24. Yapeyú slaughtered thirty to forty head per day to feed a population of 7,974; San Miguel consumed about the same amount. In the other missions, ten head were killed three days a week or less to feed a population of one thousand families. Cardiel used Yapeyú's 1719 population figures. He arrived in Buenos Aires in 1729 and left the region at the time of the Jesuits' expulsion. Cardiel, "Breve relación," 76, 82–83, 168–169. According to Cardiel's calculations, a Guaraní residing in Yapeyú or San Miguel consumed an average of 1.6 head of cattle per year, while Indians residing in missions that slaughtered cattle only three times a week consumed an average of .4 head of cattle per year. Forty oxen were slaughtered in a day to feed seven thousand Guaraní. Dobrizhoffer, *An Account of the Abipones*, 1:222. Dobrizhoffer's estimate corresponds to each Indian consuming .9 head of cattle per year based on distributions three times a week. The average of Dobrizhoffer's and Cardiel's estimates for three-times-a-week consumption of beef is .6 head of cattle per person per year.

25. Mission estancias had to maintain huge herds in order to feed mission Indians. Concepción, La Cruz, and San Juan Bautista killed an average of 5,026 head per year. And the estancias had to have cattle far in excess of those needed to feed mission Indians. The estancias lost a large number of cattle without their ever being of use to the missions: about a quarter of the cattle stock died from disease or jaguar attacks, disappeared, or were stolen.

26. A mission of three hundred working Indians could regularly consume two thousand cattle per year. Doblas, "Memoria histórica," 61. Between 1702 and 1767, average family size was 4.4 individuals. Maeder and Bolsi, "La población guaraní de las misiones jesuíticas," 14. Assuming that the each working-age male represented one family, each person would consume 1.5 head of cattle per year.

27. One mission with 528 Indians and 16,000 domesticated cattle consumed 4,000 cattle, while another mission with 1,727 Indians and 22,000 domesticated cattle consumed only 1,690 cattle. Report by Martín Joseph de Aramburu and Juan Joseph González, Asunción, July 16, 1798, AGI, Buenos Aires 292, 4.

28. Doblas, "Memoria histórica," 61.

29. Juan de Escandón to Andrés Marcos Burriel, 1760, in Furlong, *Juan de Escandón, S.J.*, 96.

30. "Reglamento de Lázaro de Rivera sobre las misiones, Asunción," Asunción, Oct. 18, 1798, ANA, SH, 172, 16.

31. A mission with five hundred families consumed five hundred arrobas of yerba maté per year. "Relación de las misiones guaraníes," in Hernández, *Misiones del Paraguay*, 1:264. One arroba equals 25 pounds. Between 1702 and 1767, average family size was 4.4 individuals. Maeder and Bolsi, "La población guaraní de las misiones jesuíticas," 14. This estimate is equivalent to 5.7 pounds of yerba maté per person per year. The thirty missions consumed 29,000–30,000 arrobas

per year. Juan de Escandón to Andrés Marcos Burriel, 118. Escandón wrote the letter in 1760, when almost 100,000 Guaraní resided in the missions. This estimate is equivalent to 7.4 pounds of yerba maté per person per year. The average of the two estimates is 6.5 pounds per person per year.

32. According to Doblas, three hundred arrobas of yerba maté a year was sufficient to meet the consumption needs of a mission with three hundred working adults. Doblas, "Memoria histórica," 61. Between 1702 and 1767, average family size was 4.4 individuals. Maeder and Bolsi, "La población guaraní de las misiones jesuíticas," 14. One arroba equals 25 pounds; assuming that each working-age male represented one family, each person would receive 5.7 pounds of yerba maté per year.

33. Given that children likely did not consume yerba maté, mission adults probably received about 14.6 pounds per year (double the 7.3 pounds per mission inhabitant). Peons producing hides in the Banda Oriental during the second half of the eighteenth century received 1 pound of yerba maté per month (or 12 pounds per year) in rations. Saguier, "El mercado del cuero," 121.

34. A mission with six hundred families used more than 4,500 varas of wool cloth and 15,300 varas of cotton cloth. "Relación de las misiones guaraníes," in Hernández, *Misiones del Paraguay*, 1:266. Between 1702 and 1767, average family size was 4.4 individuals. Maeder and Bolsi, "La población guaraní de las misiones jesuíticas," 14. One vara equals 3 feet, which calculates to 5.1 feet of wool cloth and 17.4 feet of cotton cloth per person.

35. According to Doblas, four thousand varas per year was needed for a mission with three hundred working males. Doblas, "Memoria histórica," 61. Between 1702 and 1767, average family size was 4.4 individuals. Maeder and Bolsi, "La población guaraní de las misiones jesuíticas," 14. One vara equals 3 feet; assuming that each working-age male represented one family, each person would receive 9.1 feet of cloth per year.

36. Distributions of sweeteners were similarly small—.6 pounds of honey/ molasses/sugar per mission inhabitant each year. The thirteen Paraguayan missions of the Santiago and Candelaria departments may have distributed greater quantities of sweeteners; these missions were located in warmer climates, more suitable for sugarcane. All of the nine missions that sold sugar through the general administration in Buenos Aires were part of either the Santiago or Candelaria department.

37. Peons received tobacco and yerba maté provisions as part of their salaries. Saguier, "El mercado del cuero," 121. The mission contractor did not give tobacco rations to individuals working in their storage facilities in Puerto Durazno, 1779–1785; he provided only yerba maté and salt as provisions. "Cuenta de don Domingo Ygarzabal de las faenas de cueros que corrieron a su cargo," AGN, IX 7-7-3.

38. Report by Joseph Peralta, Jan. 8, 1743, BANH, Jesuita: 58, 116–120.

39. Susnik found the same to be true for the thirteen Paraguayan missions, especially those from the department of Santiago: reports about annual harvests generally indicated the exact production of wheat but rarely mentioned the harvest of corn, legumes, or manioc. Susnik, *El indio colonial*, 2:182.

40. Doblas, "Memoria histórica," 135.
41. Bucareli, "Instrucción á que se deberán arreglar los gobernadores interinos," 203.
42. Doblas, "Memoria histórica," 60.
43. Juan de Escandón to Andrés Marcos Burriel, 96.
44. Cardiel, "Breve relación," 103.
45. José Cardiel, "Quadernillo sobre si en el estado presente pueden dar limosnas . . . ," Concepción, May 2, 1766, in Cortesão, *Do tratado de Madri*, 41.
46. The general administrator requested permission to purchase clothing for the Guaraní from Jesús, who accompanied their mission's boat; he said they were almost naked. Report by the *protector de naturales*, Buenos Aires, July 3, 1777, AGN, IX 17-6-3. The intendant of Paraguay complained about the nakedness of the Guaraní from San Cosme since the time of the Jesuit expulsion. Joaquín de Alós to the king concerning San Cosme and San Damián, 1788–1789, AGI, Audiencia de Buenos Aires, 142, quoted in White, "The Political Economy of Paraguay," 425–426.
47. Bucareli y Ursúa to condé de Aranda, 196; Bucareli, "Adición á mi instrucción," 303.
48. Bucareli y Ursúa to condé de Aranda, 196.
49. By royal prohibition, the Guaraní were not permitted to smoke tobacco. Cardiel, "Breve relación," 92.
50. Cardiel, "Costumbres de los guaraníes," 475.
51. Cardiel, "Breve relación," 69, 71; Cardiel, "Costumbres de los guaraníes," 475, 478; Ruiz de Montoya, *The Spiritual Conquest*, 31.
52. Cardiel, "Breve relación," 100; Cardiel, *Declaración de la verdad*, 289–290, 296.
53. Cardiel, "Breve relación," 98.
54. Juan Joseph Rico, "Reparos que se han hecho contra la buena conducta y govierno civil de los treinta pueblos . . . ," BNM, MS 12966-9, 12-6.
55. Jaime Oliver, "Breve noticia de la numerosa y florida cristiandad Guaraní," ARSI, Paraq. 14, doc. 4, 17–25. In the Paraguayan missions, the Guaraní collected significant amounts of honey. Susnik, *El indio colonial*, 2:183, 188.
56. "Cuentas del Pueblo de San Juan Bautista," Dec. 16, 1798, to Dec. 31, 1799, AGN, IX 17-9-2.
57. Ganson, *The Guaraní under Spanish Rule*, 151–153.
58. Mentioned in Juan Ángel de Lazcano to Agustin Casimiro de Aguirre, Buenos Aires, June 28, 1776, AGN, IX 17-6-3.
59. Bucareli, "Ordenanzas para regular el comercio," 326.
60. Doblas, "Memoria histórica," 44.
61. During the Jesuit period, the Guaraní made wheat bread for the sick two or three times a week. Cardiel, "Costumbres de los guaraníes," 475.
62. "Reglamento de Lázaro de Rivera sobre las misiones, Asunción," Oct. 13, 1798, ANA, SH, 172, 16.
63. "Liquidación de cuentas de los años 1789 and 1790" (note), Aug. 11, 1791, Concepción, AGN, IX 18-1-1.

64. "Pueblo de San Juan Bautista, Quaderno de Repartimiento de Vestuario, del año de 1794," AGN, IX 17-9-1.

65. The best Guaraní students also received prizes of glass beads and other trinkets. Ganson, *The Guaraní under Spanish Rule*, 141. Account entries also record cattle given to Indians for their participation in hunting expeditions or exercises to tame bulls.

66. In his 1785 report about how to reform the missions, one of lieutenant gobernador Doblas's biggest complaints was that mission Indians did not receive wages for collective labor projects. Doblas, "Memoria histórica."

67. Juan de Escandón to Andrés Marcos Burriel, 118–119.

68. Bucareli, "Instrucción á que se deberán arreglar los gobernadores interinos," 202.

69. Susnik, *El indio colonial*, 2:205–207.

70. "Recibos de data," Yapeyú, 1780–1781, AGN, IX 12-1-4. Mission boatmen also regularly received Spanish clothing during their trips to Buenos Aires—a pair of pants, vest, poncho, cap, and knife.

71. Doblas, "Memoria histórica," 61.

72. "Reglamento de Lázaro de Rivera sobre las misiones," Asunción, Oct. 13, 1798, ANA, SH, 172, 16.

73. Census, Santa Ana, 1772, AGN, IX 18-8-6; census, Corpus Christi, 1772, AGN, IX 18-8-7.

74. Censuses, Santa Ana and Corpus Christi, 1784, AGN, IX 18-7-2.

75. Censuses, Santa Ana and Corpus Christi, 1799, AGN, IX 18-2-2.

76. In many of the cases cited by Barbara Ganson as examples of Guaraní protesting abuses by the administrator, the petitioners also accused the cabildo members of abuse. Ganson, *The Guaraní under Spanish Rule*, 144–152; Wilde, "Los guaraníes después de la expulsión," 91–94; Wilde, *Religión y poder*, 211–229; Susnik, *El indio colonial*, 2:23–38.

77. Cacique don Juan Guirayú to señor Gobernador y Capitán General, Loreto, Dec. 17, 1770, AGN, IX 18-5-1.

78. Ibid.

79. Caciques of San Juan Bautista to señor Gobernador y Capitán General, Jan. 30, 1773, AGN, IX 17-4-6.

80. Don Isidro Ysurrey, don Ignacio Araro, don Juan Yassuta, don Pablo Arituicu, don Luis Curaye, and don Santiago Arandi of Jesús to Juan Ángel de Lazcano, Dec. 29, 1779, AGN, IX 17-4-6.

CHAPTER 8

1. From 1776 to 1786, hide exports from Río de la Plata (Buenos Aires and Montevideo combined) totaled 3,894,255 hides. Rosal and Schmit, "Las exportaciones pecuarias bonaerenses," 161. During the same years, the general administration sold 638,460 hides, which generated 821,218 pesos in sales revenues: Gregorio de Soto produced 256,273 hides, which generated 344,738 pesos in revenue. AGN, IX 17-7-1, 17-5-2, 17-6-4, 18-7-5, and 33-3-4, XIII, 47-2-56.

Castro Callorda produced 90,266 hides, which generated 74,699 pesos in revenue. AGN, IX 17-6-4. Domingo Ygarzabal produced 208,585 hides, which generated 294,285 pesos in revenue. AGN, IX 17-6-4, 17-5-2, 18-7-5, and 7-7-3. Antonio Pereyra produced 52,899 hides, which generated 79,506 pesos in revenue. AGN, IX 17-3-4, 18-6-1, and 20-5-5. Other contractors produced an additional 26,066 hides for the missions, which generated 23,718 pesos in revenue. AGN, IX 17-6-4. The missions embargoed 4,371 hides, which generated 4,272 pesos in revenue. AGN, IX 17-6-4 and 17-5-2. For more descriptive and quantitative data pertaining to the Guaraní missions' hide production, see Sarreal, "Globalization and the Guaraní." The quantitative information is from "Recibos de cargo y data," AGN, IX 17-6-4 and 18-6-6, XIII 47-3-21; *Entrada y venta*, AGN, IX 18-6-6, 17-7-1, 17-6-4, and 17-5-2, XIII 47-2-56. Additional documents in AGN, IX 7-7-3, 17-6-1, 18-6-1, 18-7-5, 17-3-4, 20-5-5, 33-3-4, 17-5-4, 17-8-1, 17-8-3, and 17-8-2.

2. "Informe sobre el arreglo de los campos de la Banda Oriental," *Revista Histórica* 18, nos. 52–54 (Feb. 1953): 518.

3. Around 1800, Argentina had income levels similar to or slightly higher than Europe and the United States. In 1913, only the United Kingdom, the United States, Australia, Canada, and New Zealand had higher incomes. Della Paolera and Taylor, introduction to *A New Economic History of Argentina*, 2–3.

4. Amaral, *The Rise of Capitalism*, 248. For export quantities, see Jumar, *Le commerce atlantique*, 1:370, 463; 2:637, 840–841, 890–897; Garavaglia, *Economía, sociedad y regiones*, 95; and Moutoukias, "El crecimiento en una economía colonial," 804–805. Hides from Buenos Aires were so prevalent in Amsterdam that N. W. Posthumus composed a price series from 1766 to 1818. Posthumus, *Inquiry into the History of Prices*, 1:856–857.

5. At the end of the eighteenth century, leather making was one of Britain's three largest industries. Davis, *The Industrial Revolution*, 30.

6. Church, "Labour Supply and Innovation," 25.

7. Dobrizhoffer, *An Account of the Abipones*, 1:223; Hernández, *Misiones del Paraguay*, 2:266.

8. Throughout most of the seventeenth century, domestic cattle supplies were generally sufficient to satisfy the European demand for hides. In North America, a New England tannery reported using West Indian hides as early as 1653, and after 1700 imported hides increasingly supplemented domestic supply. Welsh, *Tanning in the United States*, 4–5, 9.

9. Population growth led to rising grain prices in the second half of the eighteenth century, and in response, cultivated agriculture replaced rough pastureland. Compounding the problem, cattle pastureland decreased even further as horses took the place of oxen in pulling plows and carts. Ashton, *An Economic History of England*.

10. Deane and Cole, *British Economic Growth*, 74.

11. Bishko, "The Peninsular Background," 513–514.

12. In 1788, two-thirds of the 260,000 hides imported annually into Cádiz were re-exported to elsewhere in Europe. Fisher, "The Imperial Response to 'Free

Trade,'" 56. The majority of hides imported by Spain came from the Río de la Plata region, but Spain also imported hides from Cuba and Venezuela. Ibid., 52.

13. Descriptions of the huge numbers of wild cattle even reached Spain. In 1619, Philip III suggested to the governor of the Río de la Plata that, in light of the destruction to the land caused by the great number of wild horses and cattle, excess livestock should be slaughtered and the hides sent to Spain. Coni, *Historia de las vaquerías*, 13–15.

14. Moscatelli, "Los suelos de la región pampeana."

15. The Jesuit provincial of Paraguay instructed the Jesuit representatives in Madrid and Rome to solicit the Crown for rights to this land so that the missions could "have and multiply there some cattle." "Memorial o instrucción del P. Jayme Aguilar, provincial de esta Provincia del Paraguay para el Padre Diego Garcia Procurador General a Madrid y Roma . . . ," Córdoba, Apr. 5, 1738, AGN, IX 6-9-7.

16. "Noticias sobre los campos de la Banda Oriental" [Madrid, 1794], *Revista Histórica* 18, nos. 52–54 (Feb. 1953): 366.

17. Alden, *Royal Government in Colonial Brazil*, 468.

18. Maxwell, *Pombal*, 52.

19. Sarreal, "Disorder, Wild Cattle, and a New Role for the Missions."

20. Francisco Bucareli y Ursúa, "Instrucción á que se deberán arreglar los gobernadores interinos que dejo nombrados en los pueblos de indios guaranís del Uruguay y Paranaá, no habiendo disposición contraria de S. M.," Candelaria, Aug. 23, 1768, in Brabo, *Colección de documentos*, 203.

21. Visit by Juan Gregorio de Zamudio, Protector General de Naturales, Buenos Aires, June 4, 1773, AGN, IX 17-4-6; Marcos de Larrazabal to Gaspar de la Plaza Vértiz, Buenos Aires, May 17, 1773, AGN, IX 17-4-6; José Barbosa to Francisco Bruno de Zavala, San Ignacio Guazú, Jan. 28, 1774, AGN, IX 17-4-6; Gonzalo de Doblas, "Memoria histórica, geográfica, política y económica sobre la Provincia de Misiones de Indios Guaraníes," Concepción, Sept. 27, 1785, in *Los escritos de D. Gonzalo de Doblas*, 57; Marcos Joseph Larrazabal to Juan José de Vértiz y Salcedo, Buenos Aires, Aug. 11, 1773, AGN, IX 17-4-6.

22. Bucareli, "Instrucción á que se deberán arreglar los gobernadores interinos," 203.

23. Letter by Gregorio Espinosa, Nov. 15, 1770, in Pereda, *Paysandú en el siglo XVIII*, 181–184.

24. Report on the expenses incurred by each mission, Buenos Aires, Dec. 21, 1776, AGN, IX 17-6-3.

25. Letter by cacique Francisco Tarara referred to in the report "Representa el administrador general sobre la suspensión de las faenas de cueros . . . al Virrey marqués de Loreto," Buenos Aires, June 12, 1784, AGN, IX 17-7-2.

26. Francisco de Ortega to Francisco de Paula Sanz, Buenos Aires, July 27, 1784, AGN, IX 18-7-6.

27. "Relacion de la fatal ruina, que cayó la peste de viruelas . . . ," Feb. 1770, AGN, IX 18-5-1.

28. 1772 census by Mariano Ignacio de Larrazabal, AGN, IX 18-8-7.

29. Manuel de Labarden to Pedro de Cevallos, Buenos Aires, July 2, 1760, AGN, IX 21-1-7.

30. Juan Ángel de Lazcano to señor Gobernador y Capitán General, 1773, AGN, IX 17-4-6.

31. "Medios para socorrer los pueblos con prontitud por lo respectivo a ganados . . . ," Buenos Aires, Sept. 20, 1774, AGN, IX 30-3-9.

32. "Representa el administrador general sobre la suspensión de las faenas de cueros . . . al Virrey marqués de Loreto," Buenos Aires, June 12, 1784, AGN, IX 17-7-2.

33. Ibid.

34. Report by the administrator of the mission pueblos, Buenos Aires, Jan. 4, 1773, AGN, IX 17-6-3.

35. "Representa el administrador general sobre la suspensión de las faenas de cueros . . . al Virrey marqués de Loreto," Buenos Aires, June 12, 1784, AGN, IX 17-7-2.

36. Castro Callorda confiscated 4,666 undocumented hides and produced 85,600 hides; the accounting body of the thirty missions, the general administration, recorded these hides in 1776. Accounting receipts and debits and credits for Mission Yapeyú, AGN, IX 17-6-4.

37. "Representa el administrador general sobre la suspensión de las faenas de cueros . . . al Virrey marqués de Loreto," Buenos Aires, June 12, 1784, AGN, IX 17-7-2.

38. Juan Ángel de Lazcano to Francisco de Paula Sanz, Buenos Aires, Oct. 31, 1785, AGN, IX 17-8-1.

39. The salary amounts were agreed upon by Vértiz and the representatives of Yapeyú: the commander received thirty-five pesos per month and the cavalry received twelve pesos, with the condition that they be provided with their own horses, salt, and a quantity of meat required for their subsistence. Only when they went to the Portuguese frontier or some other remote place were they given tobacco and yerba maté rations, as well as hardtack or biscuits for the officials. Ibid.

40. "Memoria de Juan José de Vértiz y Salcedo a su sucesor," Buenos Aires, Mar. 12, 1784, in González, *Memorias de los virreyes del Río de la Plata*, 117.

41. Juan Ángel de Lazcano to Francisco de Paula Sanz, Buenos Aires, Oct. 31, 1785, AGN, IX 17-8-1.

42. Ibid.

43. Report by Francisco de Ortega y Monroy to Francisco de Paula Sanz, Buenos Aires, Aug. 23, 1784, AGN, IX 30-3-9.

44. Juan Ángel de Lazcano to the viceroy, Buenos Aires, Sept. 22, 1778, AGN, IX 30-3-9.

45. Report by Bernardo Sancho Larrea [procurador general of the Montevideo cabildo], Buenos Aires, Sept. 25, 1778, AGN, IX 30-3-9.

46. Report by Josef de Nabas [procurador general of the Santo Domingo Soriano cabildo], Buenos Aires, Sept. 30, 1778, AGN, IX 30-3-9.

47. Instructions from the corregidor, administrator, other deputies of Yapeyú, and general administrator of the missions to Domingo de Ygarzabal, Buenos Aires, Nov. 9, 1778, AGN, IX 7-7-3.

48. *Entrada y venta*, Yapeyú, AGN, IX 17-5-2, 18-7-5, and 17-6-4; Domingo Ygarzabal's account of the hides produced under his charge, AGN, IX 7-7-3.

49. Ygarzabal patrolled the countryside with Figueredo's troops in June 1779 and in 1780. Report on the embargos by Domingo Ygarzabal, Montevideo, Oct. 21, 1784, AGN, IX 7-7-3.

50. Although a written contract has not been located, Soto's formal duties likely included both hide production and armed patrols; several sources refer to Yapeyú's funding thirty to forty troops to assist Soto. "Pedimiento de Lazcano," AGN, IX 33-2-3; Juan de San Martín to Capitán General Juan José de Vértiz, San Borja, Aug. 26, 1776, AGN, IX 17-6-3.

51. Furlong, *Cartografía jesuítica*.

52. "Testimonio de las diligencias actuadas . . . sobre el extrañamiento de los regulares de la Compañía," AGN, IX 22-9-4. Yapeyú's estancia extended twenty leagues north of the Negro River, according to a copy of the letter from Francisco de Ortega to Francisco de Paula Sanz, Buenos Aires, July 27, 1784, AGN, IX 18-7-6.

53. *Entrada y venta*, Yapeyú, AGN, IX 17-5-2, 17-6-4, 17-7-1, 18-6-6, and 18-7-5; AGN, XIII 47-2-56 and 47-3-21; account of salary payments for hide production, Feb. 16, 1785, to July 31, 1786, AGN, IX 33-3-4. Yapeyú only benefited indirectly from Soto's last shipments of 95,278 hides during 1785 and 1786; for these hides, the general administration collected the revenue, paid the expenses, and after a delay of six years distributed only 9,845 pesos in 1792 to Yapeyú for storing the hides.

54. "Carta del cabildo y administrador de Yapeyú," Dec. 19, 1785, AGN, IX 17-8-1.

55. One vara is approximately three feet; eight reales equals one peso.

56. José Barbosa to Francisco Bruno de Zavala, San Ignacio Guazú, Jan. 28, 1774, and Francisco Bruno de Zavala to José de Vértiz, San Nicolás, Sept. 14, 1774, AGN, IX 17-4-6.

57. Juan Ángel de Lazcano to the viceroy, Montevideo, June 1783, AGN, IX 17-3-4.

58. Copy of contract signed by Juan Ángel de Lazcano and Antonio Pereyra, Montevideo, June 28, 1783, AGN, IX 20-5-5.

59. *Entrada y venta*, San Miguel, AGN, IX 17-3-4 and 18-6-1; "Documentos que exhibe don Antonio Pereira, en comprobación de la cuenta de cargo y data . . . ," AGN, IX 20-5-5.

60. See note 1 above.

61. The quantitative information is from "Recibos de cargo y data," AGN, IX 17-6-4 and 18-6-6, and XIII 47-3-21; *Entrada y venta*, AGN, IX 18-6-6, 17-7-1, 17-6-4, and 17-5-2, XIII 47-2-56. Additional documents in AGN, IX 7-7-3, 17-6-1, 18-6-1, 18-7-5, 17-3-4, 20-5-5, 33-3-4, 17-5-4, 17-8-1, 17-8-3, and 17-8-2.

62. The quality of a hide deteriorated over time; hides dried out and lost weight. Moths (*polillas*) were also a constant threat; hides could not last more than eight to ten months without becoming moth-eaten, and they were often damaged in much less time. Moths thrived on the fat of the hides as well as humid conditions and were attracted by dust. They could easily reduce the value of a hide by half or more. Coni, *Historia de las vaquerías*, 15; Diego Casero to Fran-

cisco de Paula Sanz, Buenos Aires, Jan. 25, 1785, AGN, IX 17-8-1; Dobrizhoffer, *An Account of the Abipones,* 1:220–222.

63. All hides received low prices between 1779 and 1782 because Spain's involvement in the American War of Independence limited transatlantic trade. Subsequently, relative peace between 1783 and 1796 resulted in the most vibrant period of trade between the Río de la Plata region and Spain and thus higher prices. Fisher, "The Imperial Response"; Saguier, "El mercado del cuero," 108–110; Sala de Touron, Rodríguez, and de la Torre, *Evolución económica,* 52. María-Inés Moraes and Natalia Stalla do not show hide prices recovering much after 1782, but they base their prices on the work of Zacarías Moutoukias, who admits there are inaccuracies in his price estimates and claims that prices increased with the amount of trade and demand. Moraes and Stalla, "Antes y después de 1810," 25.

64. Although the average price received by Castro Callorda in August 1776 was significantly lower than those received by other mission operations, his per-hide prices based on weight groupings coincided with the going rates from the previous month. Saguier, "El mercado del cuero," 108–110.

65. "Noticias sobre los campos de la Banda Oriental," 351.

66. Both Soto's 1769–1784 and 1785–1786 operations had production costs of one peso one real. Ygarzabal's 1777 and 1778–1784 operations had production costs of five reales and seven reales, respectively. Castro Callorda's records do not provide production costs, and unsold hides distorted Pereyra's production costs. For more information about the economics of the missions' hide operations, see Sarreal, "Globalization and the Guaraní."

67. Lazcano's replacement as general administrator, Diego Casero, implemented various reforms in an effort to increase hide revenues, but he did little to reduce expenses. He tried to get higher prices for hides by decreasing hide deterioration. His ideas for reform entailed greater complexity of operations rather than cost-cutting measures. *Barraca* purchase, in *Cuenta corriente,* AGN, IX 18-6-1; report by Diego Casero, May 30, 1785, AGN, IX 17-8-1; Diego Casero to the intendant governor, May 14, 1785, AGN, IX 21-4-8; Diego Casero to the intendant governor, Buenos Aires, Apr. 3, 1785, AGN, IX 17-8-1.

68. On November 11, 1770, general administrator Gregorio Espinosa named Juan Asencio Cabrera as *capataz* (overseer or foreman) and administrator of Paysandú. Cabrera received a salary of sixteen pesos per month. Letter by Gregorio Espinosa, Nov. 15, 1770, as printed in Pereda, *Paysandú en el siglo XVIII,* 181–184. In October 1772, Yapeyú's cabildo elected and verbally named Gregorio de Soto to replace Cabrera as administrator of Paysandú. Before this appointment, Soto had served as administrator of Yapeyú; the administrators of Paysandú and Yapeyú received the same salary, three hundred pesos per year. "Estado que manifiesta las cargas y gastos fijos que cada pueblo tiene . . . ," Buenos Aires, Dec. 21, 1776, AGN, IX 17-6-3.

69. Oct. 5, 1778, cedula concerning salaries, referred to in "Expediente promovido a instancia de Gonzalo de Doblas," 1786, AGN, IX 33-3-6.

70. Francisco Bucareli y Ursúa to condé de Aranda, Buenos Aires, Oct. 19, 1768, in Brabo, *Colección de documentos,* 193; Lynch, *Spanish Colonial Administration,* 69.

71. Maeder, *Misiones del Paraguay*, 128–140; Garavaglia, "Las actividades agropecuarias," 479–480.

72. Report by Pedro Joséf Ballesteros, May 31, 1785, AGN, IX 25-7-6.

73. Francisco Bucareli y Ursúa, "Ordenanzas para regular el comercio de los españoles con los pueblos de indios tapes y guaranís," Buenos Aires, June 1, 1770, in Brabo, *Colección de documentos*, 341.

74. "Instrucción que el corregidor, administrador y demás diputados del Pueblo de Yapeyú, administrador general de misiones entregan a don Domingo Ygarzabal . . . ," Buenos Aires, Nov. 9, 1778, AGN, IX 7-7-3.

75. Most likely the author did not reveal his name because of the controversial content of his report. "Noticias sobre los campos de la Banda Oriental," 351, 360, 374.

76. Many Crown officials engaged in contraband and other forms of corruption. Socolow, *The Bureaucrats of Buenos Aires*, 229–256.

77. Pivel Devoto, *Raíces coloniales*, 25–28; Sala de Touron, Rodríguez, and de la Torre, *Evolución económica de la Banda Oriental*, 100–102, 137–138.

78. *Cuentas corrientes*, 1770–1781, AGN, IX 17-4-2, 17-5-1, 17-5-3, 17-5-4, 17-6-1,17-7-1, 17-7-3, 18-5-6, 18-6-1, and 18-7-5.

79. Cardiel, "Breve relación," 79–80; Azara, *Descripción general del Paraguay*, 94.

80. Corregidor, cabildo, administrator, and Gregorio de Soto to the viceroy, Buenos Aires, Oct. 7, 1778, AGN, IX 39-5-5.

81. Juan Ángel de Lazcano to the intendant governor [copy], Buenos Aires, July 24, 1784, in "Expediente sobre el arreglo y resguardo de la campaña de este virreynato," AGN, IX 30-3-9.

82. Lazcano and García de Zuñiga purchased the former Jesuit estancia La Calera; García de Zuñiga managed the business until differences, disputes, and litigation arose between the two parties and the union was dissolved. AGN, IX 30-9-4.

83. Juan Ángel Lazcano, "Razon de los ganados que compró el Pueblo de Yapeyú," Buenos Aires, Sept. 1, 1784, AGN, IX 30-3-9.

84. In 1778, Yapeyú's Guaraní corregidor, alcalde de segundo voto, procurador mayor, and Spanish administrator received 4,331 cattle from Ygarzabal; in 1780, Yapeyú's Guaraní procurador mayor and Spanish administrator received an additional 6,138 cattle on behalf of the mission. "Yapeyú recibos de data 14, 15, and 16," AGN, IX 12-1-4.

85. Various documents concerning the epidemic and its effects, AGN, IX 18-5-1.

86. Census, Yapeyú, 1772, AGN, IX 18-8-7.

87. Pereda, *Paysandú en el siglo XVIII*, 25.

88. "Instrucción que el corregidor, administrador y demás diputados del Pueblo de Yapeyú, administrador general de misiones entregan a don Domingo Ygarzabal . . . ," Buenos Aires, Nov. 9, 1778, AGN, IX 7-7-3.

89. Gregorio de Soto to Ignacio Antonio Camaño, Aug. 26, 1785, quoted in Barrios Pintos, *Paysandú*, 80–81.

90. Number of tributaries according to Jesuit Jaime Aguilar's census, mentioned in "Yapeyú recibos de data," AGN, IX 17-5-1; census, Yapeyú, 1772, AGN, IX 18-8-7.

91. "Yapeyú recibos de data," AGN, IX 12-1-4; *Entrada y venta* and *Cuentas corrientes*, Yapeyú, AGN, IX, XIII.

92. *Barraca* purchase, in *Cuenta corriente*, AGN, IX 18-6-1; report by Diego Casero, May 30, 1785, AGN, IX 17-8-1; Diego Casero to the intendant governor, May 14, 1785, AGN, IX 21-4-8.

93. Cabildo and caciques of Yapeyú to Juan de San Martín, San Borja, 1779, AGN, IX 30-2-2.

94. Moraes, "Las economías agrarias del litoral rioplatense," 243.

95. Overseers earned ten pesos per month, and everyone else earned eight pesos per month. Yapeyú's salary expenses for hide production, Feb. 16, 1785, to July 31, 1786, AGN, IX 33-3-4.

96. On average, a crew brought 2,500 hides at a time. Ygarzabal paid the head of the crew a fixed amount—between 2 and 3.5 reales—per hide, as well as provided tools and rations of yerba maté, chili, and salt. At his storage facility in Paso del Durazno, Ygarzabal generally employed one overseer at 15 or 16 pesos per month, three *apiladores* (people who stack the hides) at 10 pesos per month, and thirteen to fifteen *barraqueros* (people who work at the *barraca*, or storage facility) at 9 pesos per month. He paid between 2 and close to 4 reales per hide for transportation to Montevideo. *Entrada y venta*, Yapeyú, 1782–1784, AGN, IX 17-5-2; Domingo Ygarzabal's accounting records, AGN, IX 7-7-3.

97. The report was commissioned three days after Loreto took office. Sala de Touron, Rodríguez, and de la Torre, *Evolución económica*, 84.

98. Francisco de Ortega y Monroy to Francisco de Paula Sanz, July 7, 1784, AGN, IX 18-7-6; Francisco de Ortega y Monroy to Francisco de Paula Sanz, Buenos Aires, Aug. 23, 1784, AGN, IX 30-3-9.

99. Juan Ángel de Lazcano to the intendant governor, Sept. 15, 1784, AGN, IX 21-4-8.

100. Yapeyú continued to pay salaries to those employed in hide production through July 16, 1786. Yapeyú's salary expenses for hide production, Feb. 16, 1785, to July 31, 1786, AGN, IX 33-3-4. The government also confiscated significant quantities of hides from the missions. Only after validating the missions' legal ownership were the hides sold. Owing to this delay, the missions continued to recognize hide revenues from the peak period as late as 1802–1804.

101. "Instrucción, que han de observar el administrador del lugar y puesto de Paysandú, y los diputados . . . en las recogidas y entregas, que han de hazerse a don Francisco Medina de treinta mil cavezas de ganado bacuno . . . ," Buenos Aires, Nov. 23, 1786, AGN, IX 17-3-2.

102. Francisco de Paula Sanz to the corregidor, cabildo, and administrator of Yapeyú, Buenos Aires, Nov. 23, 1786, AGN, IX 17-3-2.

103. For more information about Medina's salted beef operations, see Montoya, *Cómo evolucionó la ganadería*.

104. *Entrada y venta*, Yapeyú, AGN, IX 18-7-5; various documents in AGN, IX 17-8-5.

105. Letter from the corregidor, cabildo, and administrator of Yapeyú, Aug. 22, 1791, AGN, IX 17-3-6.

106. Corregidor, cabildo, and caciques of Yapeyú to the viceroy, Yapeyú, July 12, 1791, AGN, IX 18-1-4.

107. Aguirre, "Diario del Capitán de Fragata D. Juan Francisco Aguirre," *Revisita de la Biblioteca Nacional* 20, nos. 49–50 (1949): 350–351.

108. Hardin, "The Tragedy of the Commons," 1243–1248.

109. In 1792, 1,171,540 hides left from Buenos Aires and Montevideo, the majority of which were produced from wild cattle from the area around Yapeyú. "Noticias sobre los campos de la Banda Oriental," 363.

110. Diego Casero to señor Gobernador Intendente General, Apr. 11, 1785, AGN, IX 17-8-1.

111. Report by Diego Casero on Paysandú, Buenos Aires, Sept. 7, 1786, in Barrios Pintos, *Paysandú*, 391–396.

112. In 1784, Lazcano wrote that Yapeyú depended for subsistence solely on cattle, the majority of which were wild, undomesticated cattle. Juan Ángel de Lazcano to the intendant governor, Sept. 15, 1784, AGN, IX 21-4-8.

CHAPTER 9

1. Moles and Terry, *Handbook of International Financial Terms*, 165–166.

2. Mission Yapeyú is excluded from this analysis because its situation was unique; mission Indians generally did not produce the hundreds of thousands of cattle hides that generated huge revenues.

3. Up until the late eighteenth century, elite families in Chile and Argentine drank yerba maté as the social beverage of choice, and yerba maté still dominated Andean caffeine consumption. Public coffeehouses and cafés spread to South America in the late eighteenth century. In the 1790s, families began to serve coffee, which replaced the colonial habit of yerba maté. By the early nineteenth century, yerba maté began to be seen as a rural and lower-class drink in parts of South America; in the 1820s, only the older generations of Chileans drank yerba maté, while young people drank the more modern Chinese tea or coffee. Jamieson, "The Essence of Commodification," 286–287.

4. José Cardiel, "Quadernillo sobre si en el estado presente pueden dar limosnas . . . ," Concepción, May 2, 1766, in Cortesão, *Do tratado de Madri*, 43.

5. The missions produced many classes of textiles, including *sencilla*, *gruesa*, and *de hilo torcido*, in a variety of colors. Cardiel, "Costumbres de los guaraníes," 480.

6. Maeder, *Misiones del Paraguay*, 99.

7. Gonzalo de Doblas, "Memoria histórica, geográfica, política y económica sobre la Provincia de Misiones de Indios Guaraníes," Concepción, Sept. 27, 1785, in *Los escritos de D. Gonzalo de Doblas*, 57.

8. Ibid.

9. According to Félix de Azara, if only the leaves were harvested, a yerba maté tree could yield yerba maté for twenty years. He found, however, that since yerba maté trees were so abundant, they were not treated with such care. Modern plantations expect the tree to increase its annual production for up to thirty years

before yields decline. Azara, *Descripción general del Paraguay*, 81. There are examples of yerba trees surviving for more than sixty years of production. Ricca, *El maté*, 155. Native South American cotton plants were hardy and could live for thirty to forty years, but they seldom produced good yields for more than two or three years. Cardiel, "Breve relación," 70; Cardiel, "Costumbres de los guaraníes," 477; McBride, "Cotton Growing in South America," 46.

10. Cardiel, "Breve relación," 90.

11. Whigham, *The Politics of River Trade*, 131.

12. "Correspondencia de oficio, con el gobernador de misiones, don Francisco Bruno de Zavala," Sept. 13, 1787, ANA, SH, 152, 1.

13. Maeder, *Misiones del Paraguay*, 166.

14. "El gobernador intendente del Paraguay D. Lázaro de Rivera representando al infeliz estado a que han llegado los pueblos . . . ," 1798, ANA, SH, 172, 16.

15. Susnik, *El indio colonial*, 2:187.

16. Cardiel, "Costumbres de los guaraníes," 477.

17. José Custodio de Sá e Faria to the marqués de Loreto, Buenos Aires, July 30, 1789, AGN, IX 30-3-9.

18. Doblas, "Memoria histórica," 55.

19. "Medios para socorrer los pueblos con prontitud por lo respectivo a ganados . . . ," Buenos Aires, Sept. 20, 1774, AGN, IX 30-3-9.

20. Francisco Perez to Juan Ángel de Lazcano, Yapeyú, Dec. 18, 1772, AGN, CBN, 177; Gaspar de la Plaza to señor Gobernador y Capitán General, Buenos Aires, May 21, 1773, AGN, IX 17-4-6; Carbonell de Masy, *Estrategias de desarrollo rural*, 230–231, 365.

21. Maeder, *Historia económica de Corrientes*, 227–238.

22. Cooney, "North to the Yerbales," 141.

23. "Cuaderno de cuentas corrientes y tratos al contado perteneciente a la administración del Pueblo de Jesús desde enero de 1785 hasta diciembre de 1788 por su administrador Lucas Cano," ANA, NE, 74.

24. Feliciano Cortez to Antonio Olaguer Feliú, Apóstoles, Mar. 19, 1798, AGN, IX 18-6-5.

25. Ibid.

26. "Relación que yo, don Nicolás de Atienza, administrador de este pueblo de San Juan Bautista formó de los bienes de comunidad," Apr. 30, 1794, AGN, IX 18-2-1.

27. Juan Ángel de Lazcano to señor Gobernador y Capitán General, Buenos Aires, Jan. 8, 1773, AGN, IX 17-4-2.

28. The population figure for 1772—almost double that of 1768—is unreliable; it is highly unlikely that Concepción's population measured 1,475 in 1768, 2,935 in 1772, and 1,950 in 1783.

29. Mariluz Urquijo, *El virreinato del Río de la Plata*, 197.

30. "Memoria del marqués de Avilés a su sucesor," Buenos Aires, May 21, 1801, in González, *Memorias de los virreyes del Río de la Plata*, 508.

31. The 1801 census identified the Indians as either free or belonging to the community. 1801 census, AGN, IX 18-2-6. Guaraní letters also refer to the exemption as freedom.

32. "Memoria del marqués de Avilés a su sucesor," 506.

33. Quoted in Popescu, *Studies in the History of Latin American Economic Thought*, 166.

34. Ibid., 170.

35. Wait, "Mariano Moreno," 362.

36. Quoted in Adelman, *Republic of Capital*, 62.

37. Wait, "Mariano Moreno," 373–374.

38. Doblas, "Memoria histórica," 128.

39. Marqués de Avilés to Bruno Zavala, Buenos Aires, Aug. 17, 1799, AGN, IX 18-2-3.

40. The money was used to pay the priests' stipends and the salaries of Spanish officials. "Memoria de Viceroy Marqués de Avilés," 508–509.

41. 1801 census, AGN, IX 18-2-6.

42. Wilde, *Religión y poder*, 272.

43. "Apuntamiento de las provincias libradas por el Virrey de Buenos Ayres marqués de Avilés . . . ," in Larstarria, *Colonias orientales del Río Paraguay o de la Plata*, 58.

44. Wilde, *Religión y poder*, 269–271.

45. Corregidor and cabildo of Mission San José to the viceroy, Oct. 18, 1800, AGN, IX 18-2-3.

46. "Nuevo Gobierno de las Doctrinas," Aranjuez, May 17, 1803, in Hernández, *Misiones del Paraguay*, 2:705–708.

47. The seven missions (San Miguel, San Luís, San Juan Bautista, San Nicolás, San Lorenzo, San Ángel, and San Borja) had 12,680 inhabitants in 1801. AGN, IX 18-2-6.

48. Furlong, *Misiones y sus pueblos*, 175, 704–707.

49. Their population fell from 14,010 in 1801 to 6,385 in 1814, 2,385 in 1822, and 1,874 in 1827. Maeder, *Misiones del Paraguay*, 273.

50. Many of the other missions in Spanish America faced such competition in their early years and thus never achieved the same economic and demographic success as the Guaraní missions under the Jesuits.

51. López-Calva and Lustig, "Explaining the Decline in Inequality," 5–6; Silva, *Challenging Neoliberalism in Latin America*.

Glossary

alcalde   Overseer; a municipal officer in the context of the cabildo

algodonal   Cotton field

amambaé   Person's possession; private property

amundá   Group of *teýy*s that form a village

arroba   Twenty-five pounds

bandeirantes   Participants in Indian slave-raiding expeditions originating from Portuguese territory

cabildante   Member of the town council

cabildo   Town council

cacicazgo   Native lineage group

cacique   Leader of a native lineage group

cañaveral   Sugarcane field

cédula   Written authorization or royal decree

chacra   Farmland

cimarron   Wild cattle

colegio   Buildings attached to the mission church including workshops, storage facilities, governing offices, and the school

comercio libre   Trade reforms that allowed direct trade between specific Spanish and Spanish American ports; extended to Buenos Aires in 1778

corregidor   Magistrate; head of the cabildo

cotiguazú   Women's dormitory for widows, female orphans, and women whose husbands were absent from the pueblo

cuenta corriente   Mission account book that recorded net sales revenue and all other income and expenses incurred by the general administration on behalf of the thirty missions

cuero   Cattle hide

diezmo   Tithe

encomendero   Recipient of an encomienda

encomienda Coercive Spanish labor regime, under which Indians gave tribute or labor to Spaniards in return for introduction to the Catholic faith

entrada y venta Mission account book that recorded inflows of goods from the thirty missions and the sales of these same goods

estancia Livestock ranch

estanciero *Estancia* owner

fanega Equivalent to 140 liters; 1 *fanega* of wheat is equivalent to 225 pounds

gauderio Rural criminal

general administrator Manager, based in Buenos Aires, who oversaw trade and economic matters on behalf of the thirty missions during the post-Jesuit period

gobernador Governor who managed the political affairs of the thirty missions

guará Group of *teko'a*

lienzo grueso Rough cloth

mayordomo Manager or steward

mburuvichá Guaraní leader of a *guará*

memoria Report by the viceroy leaving office summarizing his term for his successor

oficio Trade center under Jesuit management

osco Reddish color

parcialidad Grouping of mission inhabitants

Paulista Inhabitant of São Paulo

procurador Representative or agent; office manager in the case of a Jesuit college

provincial Head of a Jesuit province

pueblo Town

relación jurada General administrator's summary account book

sínodo Priest's stipend

superior Head of the Jesuit missions

tabacal Tobacco field

teko'a Village or group of several villages; similar to an *amundá*

teýy Guaraní social unit of extended families or lineage group

teýy-ru Leader of a *teýy*

Tribunal Mayor de Cuentas Principal accounts office, where treasury departments gave accounts and summaries that were sent, in turn, to Spain

tupambaé God's possession; communally owned property

tuvichá Guaraní leader of an *amundá* or *teko'a*

vaquería An expedition to hunt wild cattle; location of a large quantity of wild cattle

vara Approximately three feet

yerba caaminí   Processed yerba maté without the stems
yerba de palos   Processed yerba maté with the stems
yerba maté   Paraguayan tea
yerbal   Collection of yerba maté trees
yerbal silvestre   Yerba maté trees in the wild

Bibliography

PRIMARY SOURCES

Aguirre, D. Juan Francisco. "Diario del Capitán de Fragata D. Juan Francisco Aguirre, 1793." *Revista de la Biblioteca Nacional* 20, nos. 49–50. Buenos Aires: Biblioteca Nacional, 1949.

Azara, Félix de. *Descripción general del Paraguay*. Edited by Andrés Galera Gómez. Madrid: Alianza Editorial, 1990.

———. *Escritos fronterizos*. Edited by Manuel Lucena Giraldo and Alberto Barrueco. Madrid: Ministerio de Agricultura, Pesca y Alimentación, ICONA, 1994.

Brabo, Francisco Javier, ed. *Colección de documentos relativos a la expulsión de los jesuitas de la República Argentina y del Paraguay en el reinado de Carlos III*. Madrid: Estudio Tipográfico José María Pérez, 1872.

Campomanes, Pedro Rodríguez de. *Dictamen fiscal de la expulsión de los jesuitas de España (1766–1767)*. Edited by Jorge Cejudo and Teófanes Egido. Madrid: Fundación Universitaria Española, 1977.

Cardiel, José. "Breve relación de las misiones del Paraguay" [1771]. In *Las misiones del Paraguay*, edited by Héctor Sáinz Ollero, 45–201. Madrid: Dastin Historia, 1989.

———. "Carta y relación de las misiones de la provincia de Paraguay (1747)." In *José Cardiel y su Carta-Relación*. Edited by Guillermo Furlong, 115–213. Buenos Aires: Librería del Plata, no date.

———. "Costumbres de los guaraníes." In *Historia del Paraguay desde 1747 hasta 1767*. Edited by Domingo Muriel [1779]. Translated by Pablo Hernández, 463–544. Madrid: Librería General de Victoriano Suárez, 1919.

———. *Declaración de la verdad*. Edited by Pablo Hernández. Buenos Aires: Juan A. Alsina, 1900.

Cortesão, Jaime, ed. *Antecedentes do tratado de Madri, jesuítas e bandeirantes no Paraguai (1703–1751)*. Manuscritos da coleção de Angelis, 6. Rio de Janeiro: Biblioteca Nacional, Divisão de Obras Raras e Publicações, 1955.

———, ed. *Do tratado de Madri á conquista dos Sete Povos (1750–1802)*. Manuscritos da coleção de Angelis, 7. Rio de Janeiro: Biblioteca Nacional, Divisão de Obras Raras e Publicações, 1969.

———, ed. *Jesuítas e bandeirantes no Guairá (1549–1640)*. Manuscritos da coleção de Angelis, 1. Rio de Janeiro: Biblioteca Nacional, Divisão de Obras Raras e Publicações, 1951.

———, ed. *Tratado de Madrid. Antecedentes. Colônia do Sacramento, 1669–1749*. Manuscritos da coleção de Angelis, 5. Rio de Janeiro: Biblioteca Nacional, Divisão de Obras Raras e Publicações, 1954.

Doblas, Gonzalo de. *Los escritos de D. Gonzalo de Doblas relativos a la Provincia de Misiones, 1785 and 1805*. Edited by Walter Rela. Montevideo: Ediciones de la Plaza, 1988.

Dobrizhoffer, Martin. *An Account of the Abipones, an Equestrian People of Paraguay*. Translated by Sara Henry Coleridge. 2 vols. London: John Murray, 1822.

Documentos para la historia del virreinato del Río de la Plata. Vol. 1, no. 78. Buenos Aires: Sección de Historia, Facultad de Filosofía y Letras, 1912–1913.

Furlong Cardiff, Guillermo. *Antonio Sepp S.J. y su "Gobierno temporal" (1732)*. Buenos Aires: Ediciones Theoria, 1962.

———, ed. *Cartografía jesuítica del Río de la Plata*. Buenos Aires: Tallares S. A. Casa Jacobo Peuser, 1936.

———, ed. *José Cardiel, S.J. y su carta-relación (1747)*. Buenos Aires: Librería del Plata, 1953.

———, ed. *Juan de Escandón S.J. y su carta a Burriel (1760)*. Buenos Aires: Ediciones Theoria, 1965.

González, Julio César, ed. *Memorias de los virreyes del Río de la Plata*. Buenos Aires: Editorial Bajel, 1945.

"Informe sobre el arreglo de los campos de la Banda Oriental." *Revista Histórica* 18, nos. 52–54 (Feb. 1953): 517–527.

Lastarria, Miguel de. *Colonias orientales del Río Paraguay o de la Plata*. Introduction by Enrique del Valle Iberlucea. Buenos Aires: Compañía Sud-Americana de Billetes de Banco, 1914.

Lozano, Pedro. *Historia de la conquista del Paraguay, Río de la Plata, y Tucumán*. 5 vols. Buenos Aires: Imprenta Popular, 1873.

Mariluz Urquijo, José M., ed. *Noticias del correo mercantil de España y sus Indias: sobre la vida económica del virreinato del Río de la Plata*. Buenos Aires: Academia Nacional de la Historia, 1977.

Mühn, Juan, ed. "El Río de la Plata visto por viajeros alemanes del siglo XVIII, según cartas traducidas por Juan Mühn." *Revista del Instituto Histórico y Geográfico del Uruguay* 7 (1930): 229–325.

Muriel, Domingo, ed. *Historia del Paraguay desde 1747 hasta 1767 [1779]*. Translated by Pablo Hernandez. Madrid: Librería General de Victoriano Suárez, 1919.

"Noticias sobre los campos de la Banda Oriental" [Madrid, 1794]. *Revista Histórica* 18, nos. 52–54 (Feb. 1953): 323–516.

Pastells, Pablo, ed. *Historia de la Compañía de Jesús en la provincia del Paraguay según los documentos originales del Archivo de las Indias, extractados y anotados*. 8 vols. Madrid: Libraría General de Victoriano Suárez, 1912–1949.

Recopilación de leyes de los reynos de las Indias. Book 6. Madrid: Ediciones Cultura Hispánica, 1973.

Ruiz de Montoya, Antonio. *The Spiritual Conquest Accomplished by the Religious of the Society of Jesus in the Provinces of Paraguay, Paraná, Uruguay, and Tape (1639).* Translated by C. J. McNaspy. St. Louis: Institute of Jesuit Sources, 1993.

Sánchez Labrador, José. *El Paraguay católico.* Vol. 2. Buenos Aires: Imprenta de Coni Hermanos, 1910.

Sepp, Antonio. "Algunas advertencias tocantes al govierno temporal de los pueblos en sus fabricas, sementeras, estancias y otras faenas." In *Antonio Sepp S.J. y su "Gobierno temporal" (1732),* edited by Guillermo Furlong, 111–127. Buenos Aires: Ediciones Theoria, 1962.

Voltaire. *Candide.* New York: Boni and Liveright, Inc., 1918.

———. *Short Studies.* In *Voltaire: A Contemporary Version,* ed. William Fleming. Akron, OH: Werner, 1901.

Zavala, Francisco Bruno de. "Un informe del gobernador de Misiones, don Francisco Bruno de Zavala (1784)." *Boletín del Instituto de Investigaciones Históricas* (Buenos Aires) 15 (1941): 159–187.

SECONDARY SOURCES

Adelman, Jeremy. *Republic of Capital: Buenos Aires and the Legal Transformation of the Atlantic World.* Stanford, CA: Stanford University Press, 1999.

Aguerre Core, Fernando. *Una caída anunciada: el Obispo Torre y los jesuitas del Río de la Plata (1757–1773).* Montevideo: Librería Linardi y Risso, 2007.

Alden, Dauril. "The Gang of Four and the Campaign against the Jesuits in Eighteenth-Century Brazil." In *The Jesuits II: Cultures, Sciences, and the Arts, 1540–1773,* edited by John W. O'Malley, S.J., Guavin Alexander Bailey, Steven J. Harris, and T. Frank Kennedy, S.J., 707–724. Toronto: University of Toronto Press, 2006.

———. *The Making of an Enterprise: The Society of Jesus in Portugal, Its Empire, and Beyond, 1540–1750.* Stanford, CA: Stanford University Press, 1996.

———. *Royal Government in Colonial Brazil: With Special Reference to the Administration of the Marquis of Lavradio, Viceroy, 1769–1779.* Berkeley: University of California Press, 1968.

Amaral, Samuel. *The Rise of Capitalism on the Pampas: The Estancias of Buenos Aires, 1785–1870.* Cambridge: Cambridge University Press, 1998.

Armani, Alberto. *Ciudad de Dios y Ciudad del Sol: el "Estado" jesuita de los guaraníes (1609–1768).* Mexico City: Fondo de Cultura Económica, 1982.

Ashton, T. S. *An Economic History of England: The 18th Century.* London: Methuen, 1972.

Avellaneda, Mercedes. "La alianza defensiva jesuita-guaraní y los conflictos suscitados en la primera parte de la revolución de los comuneros." *Historia Paraguaya: Anuario del Instituto Paraguayo de Investigaciones Históricas* 44 (2004): 337–404.

———. "Orígenes de la alianza jesuita-guaraní y su consolidación en el siglo XVII." *Memoria Americana* 8 (1999): 173–200.

Avellaneda, Mercedes, and Lía Quarleri. "Las milicias guaraníes en el Paraguay y Río de la Plata: alcances y limitaciones, 1649–1756." *Estudos Ibero-Americanos* 33, no. 1 (2007): 109–132.

Bailey, Gauvin Alexander. *Art on the Jesuit Missions in Asia and Latin America, 1542–1773.* Toronto: University of Toronto Press, 1999.

Barcelos, Artur H. F. *Espaço e arqueologia nas missões jesuíticas: o caso de São João Batista.* Porto Alegre, Brazil: Pontifícia Universidade Católica do Rio Grande do Sul, 2000.

Barr, Juliana. *Peace Came in the Form of a Woman: Indians and Spaniards in the Texas Borderlands.* Chapel Hill: University of North Carolina Press, 2007.

Barrios Pintos, Aníbal. *Historia de la ganadería en el Uruguay, 1574–1971.* Montevideo: Biblioteca Nacional, 1973.

———. *Historia de los pueblos orientales: sus orígenes, procesos fundacionales, sus primeros años.* Montevideo: Ediciones de la Banda Oriental, 1971.

———. *Paysandú: historia general.* Montevideo: Intendencia Municipal de Paysandú, 1989.

Baudin, Louis. *Une théocratie socialiste: l'État jésuite du Paraguay.* Paris: M. Th. Génin, 1962.

Bauss, Rudy. "Rio Grande do Sul in the Portuguese Empire: The Formative Years, 1777–1808." *The Americas* 39, no. 4 (April 1983): 519–535.

Bireley, Robert. *The Jesuits and the Thirty Years War: Kings, Courts, and Confessors.* Cambridge: Cambridge University Press, 2003.

Bishko, Charles Julian. "The Peninsular Background of Latin American Cattle Ranching." *Hispanic American Historical Review* 32, no. 4 (Nov. 1952): 491–515.

Block, David. *Mission Culture on the Upper Amazon: Native Tradition, Jesuit Enterprise, and Secular Policy in Moxos, 1660–1880.* Lincoln: University of Nebraska Press, 1994.

Blumers, Teresa. *La contabilidad en las reducciones guaraníes.* Asunción: Centro de Estudios Antropológicos, Universidad Católica, 1992.

Bolcato Custódio, Me. Luiz Antônio. "Ordenamientos urbanos y arquitectónicos en el sistema reduccional jesuítico guaraní de la Paracuaria: entre su normativa y su realización." PhD diss., Universidad Pablo de Olavide, 2010.

Bolton, Herbert E. "The Mission as a Frontier Institution in the Spanish-American Colonies." *American Historical Review* 23, no. 1 (Oct. 1917): 42–61.

Boxer, Charles Ralph. *The Golden Age of Brazil, 1695–1750: Growing Pains of a Colonial Society.* Berkeley: University of California Press, 1962.

Brown, Jonathan C. *A Socioeconomic History of Argentina, 1776–1860.* Cambridge: Cambridge University Press, 1979.

Brown, Kendall W. "Jesuit Wealth and Economic Activity within the Peruvian Economy: The Case of Colonial Southern Peru." *The Americas* 44, no. 1 (July 1987): 23–43.

Bruno, Cayetano. *Historia de la Iglesia en la Argentina.* 2 vols. Buenos Aires: Editorial Don Bosco, 1967.

Bushnell, Amy Turner. *The King's Coffer: Proprietors of the Spanish Florida Treasury, 1565–1702.* Gainesville: University Press of Florida, 1981.

———. *Situado and Sabana: Spain's Support System for the Presidio and Mission Provinces of Florida.* Athens: University of Georgia Press, 1994.

Callahan, William James. *Church, Politics, and Society in Spain, 1750–1874.* Cambridge, MA: Harvard University Press, 1984.

Carbonell de Masy, Rafael. *Estrategias de desarrollo rural de los pueblos guaraníes, 1609–1767.* Barcelona: Instituto de Cooperación Iberoamericana, Instituto de Estudios Fiscales, 1992.

———. "La génesis de las vaquerías de los pueblos tapes y guaraníes de la banda oriental del Uruguay a la luz de documentación inédita." *Pesquisas, Historia* 27 (1989): 13–48.

———. "Las 'reducciones' como estrategia del desarrollo rural." *Suplemento Antropológico* 21, no. 2 (1986): 41–66.

Chamorro, Graciela. *Teología guaraní.* Quito: Abya-Yala, 2004.

Chevalier, François. *Land and Society in Colonial Mexico.* Translated by Lesley Byrd Simpson. Berkeley: University of California Press, 1963.

Church, R. A. "Labour Supply and Innovation 1800–1860: The Boot and Shoe Industry." *Business History* 12, no. 1 (Jan. 1970): 25–45.

Clastres, Hélène. *The Land-without-Evil: Tupí-Guaraní Prophetism.* Translated by Jacqueline Grenez Brovender. Urbana: University of Illinois Press, 1995.

Clastres, Pierre. *Society against the State: Essays in Political Anthropology.* Translated by Robert Hurley and Abe Stein. New York: Zone Books, 1987.

Clossey, Luke. *Salvation and Globalization in the Early Jesuit Missions.* Cambridge: Cambridge University Press, 2011.

Cohen, T. V. "Why the Jesuits Joined 1540–1600." *Historical Papers* [Canadian Historical Association] 9, no. 1 (Dec. 1974): 237–258.

Coni, Emilio A. *Historia de las vaquerías de Río de la Plata, 1555–1750.* Buenos Aires: Editorial Devenir, 1956.

Cook, Noble David. *Born to Die: Disease and New World Conquest, 1492–1650.* Cambridge: Cambridge University Press, 1998.

Cooney, Jerry W. "North to the Yerbales: The Exploitation of the Paraguayan Frontier, 1776–1810." In *Contested Ground: Comparative Frontiers on the Northern and Southern Edges of the Spanish Empire,* edited by Donna J. Guy and Thomas E. Sheridan, 135–149. Tucson: University of Arizona Press, 1998.

Cro, Stelio. *The Noble Savage: Allegory of Freedom.* Waterloo, ON: Wilfrid Laurier University Press, 1990.

Crocitti, John J. "The Internal Economic Organization of the Jesuit Missions among the Guaraní." *International Social Science Review* 77, no. 1/2 (2002): 3–13.

Crosby, Alfred W. *The Columbian Exchange: Biological and Cultural Consequences of 1492.* Westport, CT: Praeger, 2003.

Cuenca Esteban, Javier. "Statistics of Spain's Colonial Trade, 1792–1820: Consular Duties, Cargo Inventories, and Balances of Trade." *Hispanic American Historical Review* 61, no. 3 (1981): 381–428.

Cunha, Manuela Carneiro da, ed. *História dos Índios no Brasil.* São Paulo: Fundação de Amparo á Pesquisa do Estado de São Paulo, 1992.

Cunninghame Graham, R. B. *A Vanished Arcadia: Being Some Account of the Jesuits in Paraguay, 1650–1767.* London: William Heinemann, 1901.

Cushner, Nicholas P. *Farm and Factory: The Jesuits and the Development of Agrarian Capitalism in Colonial Quito, 1600–1767.* Albany: State University of New York Press, 1982.

———. *Jesuit Ranches and the Agrarian Development of Colonial Argentina, 1650–1767.* Albany: State University of New York Press, 1983.

———. *Lords of the Land: Sugar, Wine, and Jesuit Estates of Coastal Peru, 1600–1767.* Albany: State University of New York Press, 1980.

———. *Soldiers of God: The Jesuits in Colonial America, 1565–1767.* Buffalo, NY: Language Communications, 2002.

———. *Why Have You Come Here? The Jesuits and the First Evangelization of Native America.* New York: Oxford University Press, 2006.

da Silva e Orta, Teresa Margarida, and Ernesto Ennes. "Teresa Margarida da Silva e Orta, a Brazilian Collaborator in the Anti-Jesuit Propaganda of Pombal." *The Americas* 2, no. 4 (April 1946): 423–430.

Davis, Ralph. *The Industrial Revolution and British Overseas Trade.* Atlantic Highlands, NJ: Humanities Press, 1979.

de la Torre Curiel, José Refuio. *Twilight of the Mission Frontier: Shifting Interethnic Alliances and Social Organization in Sonora, 1768–1855.* Stanford, CA: Stanford University Press, 2012.

Deane, Phyllis, and W. A. Cole. *British Economic Growth, 1688–1959: Trends and Structure.* 2nd ed. Cambridge: Cambridge University Press, 1980.

Deeds, Susan M. *Defiance and Deference in Mexico's Colonial North: Indians under Spanish Rule in Nueva Vizcaya.* Austin: University of Texas Press, 2003.

della Paolera, Gerardo, and Alan M. Taylor, eds. *A New Economic History of Argentina.* Cambridge: Cambridge University Press, 1998.

Díaz de Zappia, Sandra L. "Participación indígena en el gobierno de las reducciones jesuíticas de guaraníes." *Revista de Historia del Derecho* 31 (2003): 97–129.

Dietrich, Wolf. "La importancia de los diccionarios guaraníes de Montoya para el estudio comparativo de las lenguas tupí-guaraníes de hoy." *Amerindia: Revue d'Ethnolinguistique Amérindienne* 19–20 (1995): 287–299.

Durán Estragó, Margarita. *Presencia franciscana en el Paraguay (1538–1824).* Asunción: Universidad Católica, 1987.

Earle, Timothy. *How Chiefs Come to Power: The Political Economy in Prehistory.* Stanford, CA: Stanford University Press, 1997.

Egido López, Teófanes, coord. *Los jesuitas en España y en el mundo hispánico.* Madrid: Marcial Pons Historia; Fundación Carlona, Centro de Estudios Hispánicos e Iberoamericanos, 2004.

Farriss, Nancy M. *Maya Society under Colonial Rule: The Collective Enterprise of Survival.* Princeton, NJ: Princeton University Press, 1984.

Fausto, Carlos. "Fragmentos de história e cultura tupinambá: da etnologia como instrumento crítico de conhecimento etno-histórico." In *História dos Índios no*

Brasil, edited by Manuela Carneiro da Cunha, 381–396. São Paulo: Fundação de Amparo á Pesquisa do Estado de São Paulo, 1992.

———. "If God Were a Jaguar: Cannibalism and Christianity among the Guarani (16th–20th Centuries)." In *Time and Memory in Indigenous Amazonia: Anthropological Perspectives*, edited by Carlos Fausto and Michael Heckenberger, 74–105. Gainesville: University Press of Florida, 2007.

Fisher, John R. *Economic Aspects of Spanish Imperialism, 1492–1810*. Liverpool, UK: Liverpool University Press, 1997.

———. "The Imperial Response to 'Free Trade': Spanish Imports from Spanish America, 1778–1796." *Journal of Latin American Studies* 17, no. 1 (May 1985): 35–78.

Fradkin, Raúl O., T. Halperín Donghi, C. Mayo, A. Fernández, R. Salvatore, J. Brown, and J. Gelman, eds. *La historia agraria del Río de la Plata colonial: los establecimientos productivos*. 2 vols. Buenos Aires: Centro Editor América Latina, 1993.

Furlong Cardiff, Guillermo. *Historia social y cultural del Río de la Plata, 1536–1810: el trasplante social*. Buenos Aires: Tipográfica Editora Argentina, 1969.

———. *Misiones y sus pueblos de guaraníes*. Buenos Aires: Imprenta Balmes, 1962.

Gadelha, Regina A. F., ed. *Missões guarani: impacto na sociedade contemporânea*. São Paulo: EDUC, 1999.

———. *As missões jesuíticas do Itatim: estructuras socio-econômicas do Paraguai colonial seculos XVI e XVII*. Rio de Janeiro: Paz e Terra, 1980.

Ganson, Barbara. *The Guaraní under Spanish Rule in the Río de la Plata*. Stanford, CA: Stanford University Press, 2003.

———. "Our Warehouses Are Empty: Guarani Responses to the Expulsion of the Jesuits from the Río de La Plata, 1767–1800." In *Missões Guarani: impacto na sociedade contemporânea*, edited by Regina A. F. Gadelha, 41–54. São Paulo: EDUC, 1999.

Garavaglia, Juan Carlos. "Las actividades agropecuarias en el marco de la vida económica del pueblo de Indios de Nuestra Señora de Los Santos Reyes Magos de Yapeyú: 1768–1806." In *Haciendas, latifundios y plantaciones en América Latina*, edited by Enrique Florescano, 464–485. Mexico: Siglo Veintiuno Editores, 1978.

———. "The Crises and Transformations of Invaded Societies: The La Plata Basin (1535–1650)." In *The Cambridge History of the Native Peoples of the Americas*, edited by Frank Salomon and Stuart B. Schwartz, vol. 3, pt. 2, 1–58. Cambridge: Cambridge University Press, 1999.

———. "De la carne al cuero: los mercados para los productos pecuarios (Buenos Aires y su campaña, 1700–1825)." *Anuario del IEHS* 9 (1994): 61–95.

———. *Economía, sociedad y regiones*. Buenos Aires: Ediciones de la Flor, 1987.

———. *Mercado interno y economía colonial*. Mexico City: Editorial Grijalbo, 1983.

———. *Pastores y labradores de Buenos Aires: una historia agraria de la campaña bonaerense, 1700–1830*. Buenos Aires: Ediciones de la Flor, 1999.

Garavaglia, Juan Carlos, and Jorge D. Gelman. "Rural History of the Río de la Plata, 1600–1850: Results of a Historiographical Renaissance." *Latin American Research Review* 30, no. 3 (1995): 75–105.

Garavaglia, Juan Carlos, and Diane Melendez. "Economic Growth and Regional Differentiations: The River Plate Region at the End of the Eighteenth Century." *Hispanic American Historical Review* 65, no. 1 (Feb. 1985): 51–89.

García, Elisa Frühauf. "'Ser índio' na fronteira: limites e posebilidades: Rio da Prata, c. 1750–1800." *Nuevo Mundo Mundos Nuevos* (Debates) (2011): 1–13. http://nuevomundo.revues.org/60732.

García-Baquero González, Antonio. *Cádiz y el Atlántico (1717–1778): el comercio colonial Español bajo el monopolio gaditano.* 2 vols. Seville: Escuela de Estudios Hispano-Americanos, 1976.

Gelman, Jorge. *Campesinos y estancieros: una región del Río de la Plata a fines de la época colonial.* Buenos Aires: Editorial los Libros del Riel, 1998.

Giberti, Horacio C. E. *Historia económica de la ganadería Argentina.* Nueva edición actualizada y corregida. Buenos Aires: Ediciones Solar, 1970.

González Rissotto, Rodolfo, and Susana Rodríguez Varese de González. *Contribución al estudio de la influencia guaraní en la sociedad Uruguaya.* Montevideo: Imprenta Linea, 1989.

Gott. Richard. *Land without Evil: Utopian Journeys across the South American Watershed.* New York: Verso, 1993.

Graubart, Karen B. *With Our Labor and Sweat: Indigenous Women and the Formation of Colonial Society in Peru, 1550–1700.* Stanford, CA: Stanford University Press, 2007.

Gutiérrez, Ramón. *Evolución urbanística y arquitectónica del Paraguay, 1537–1911.* Corrientes, Argentina: Universidad Nacional del Nordeste, 1975.

Hackel, Steven W. *Children of Coyote, Missionaries of Saint Francis: Indian-Spanish Relations in Colonial California, 1769–1850.* Chapel Hill: Omohundro Institute of Early American History and Culture, University of North Carolina Press, 2005.

Halperín-Donghi, Tulio. *Politics, Economics, and Society in Argentina in the Revolutionary Period.* Translated by Richard Southern. Cambridge: Cambridge University Press, 1975.

Hardin, Garrett. "The Tragedy of the Commons." *Science* 162 (1968): 1243–1248.

Haubert, Maxime. *La vida cotidiana de los indios y jesuitas en las misiones del Paraguay.* Madrid: Temas de Hoy, 1991.

Hemming, John. *Amazon Frontier: The Defeat of the Brazilian Indians.* London: Macmillan, 1987.

———. *Red Gold: The Conquest of the Brazilian Indians.* Cambridge, MA: Harvard University Press, 1978.

Hernández, Pablo. *Misiones del Paraguay: organización social de las doctrinas guaraníes de la Compañía de Jesús.* 2 vols. Barcelona: Gustavo Gili, 1913.

Herr, Richard. *The Eighteenth-Century Revolution in Spain.* Princeton, NJ: Princeton University Press, 1958.

Hoerder, Dirk. *Cultures in Contact: World Migrations in the Second Millennium.* Durham, NC: Duke University Press, 2002.

Jackson, Robert H. "Demographic Patterns in the Jesuit Missions of the Río de la Plata Region: The Case of Corpus Christi Mission, 1622–1802." *Colonial Latin American Historical Review* 13, no. 4 (Fall 2004): 337–366.

———. *Missions and the Frontiers of Spanish America: A Comparative Study of the Impact of Environmental, Economic, Political, and Socio-Cultural Variations on the Missions in the Río de la Plata Region and on the Northern Frontier of New Spain.* Scottsdale, AZ: Pentacle Press, 2005.

———. "The Population and Vital Rates of the Jesuit Missions of Paraguay, 1700–1767." *Journal of Interdisciplinary History* 38, no. 3 (Winter 2008): 401–431.

———. "The Post-Jesuit Expulsion Population of the Paraguay Missions, 1768–1803." *Revista de História Regional* 13, no. 2 (Winter 2008): 134–169.

Jackson, Robert H., and Edward Castillo. *Indians, Franciscans, and Spanish Colonization: The Impact of the Mission System on California Indians.* Albuquerque: University of New Mexico Press, 1996.

Jaenike, William F. *Black Robes in Paraguay: The Success of the Guaraní Missions Hastened the Abolition of the Jesuits.* Minneapolis: Kirk House Publishing, 2008.

Jamieson, Ross W. "The Essence of Commodification: Caffeine Dependencies in the Early Modern World." *Journal of Social History* 35, no. 2 (Winter 2001): 269–294.

Johnson, Lyman L. "The Competition of Slave and Free Labor in Artisanal Production: Buenos Aires, 1770–1815." *International Review of Social History* 40 (1995): 409–424.

Johnson, Lyman L., and Sibila Seibert. "Estimaciones de la población de Buenos Aires en 1744, 1778 y 1810." *Desarrollo Económico* 19, no. 73 (Apr.–June 1979): 107–119.

Johnson, Lyman L., and Susan Midgen Socolow. "Population and Space in Eighteenth Century Buenos Aires." In *Social Fabric and Spatial Structure in Colonial Latin America*, edited by David J. Robinson, 339–368. Ann Arbor, MI: University Microfilms International, 1979.

Jones, Grant D. *The Conquest of the Last Maya Kingdom.* Stanford, CA: Stanford University Press, 1998.

Jumar, Fernando Alberto. *Le commerce atlantique au Río de la Plata, 1680–1778.* 2 vols. Villenueve-d'Ascq, France: Presses Universitaires du Septentrion, 2000.

Kennedy, T. Frank. "*Candide* and a Boat." In *The Jesuits: Cultures, Sciences, and the Arts, 1540–1773*, edited by John W. O'Malley, Gauvin Alexander Bailey, Steven J. Harris, and T. Frank Kennedy, 317–332. Toronto: University of Toronto Press, 1999.

Kern, Arno Alvarez, ed. *Arqueologia histórica missioneira.* Porto Alegre, Brazil: Pontificia Universidade Católica de Rio Grande do Sul, 1998.

———. *Missões: Uma utopia polîtica.* Porto Alegre, Brazil: Mercado Aberto, 1982.

————. "O processo histórico platino no seclo XVII: da aldeia guarani ao povoado missioneiro." *Estudos Ibero-Americanos* 15, no. 2 (1985): 21–41.

Konrad, Herman W. *A Jesuit Hacienda in Colonial Mexico: Santa Lucía, 1576–1767.* Stanford, CA: Stanford University Press, 1980.

Kratz, Guillermo. *El tratado hispano-portugués de limites de 1750 y sus consecuencias: estudio sobre la abolición de la Compañía de Jesús.* Translated by Diego Bermudez Camacho. Rome: Institutum Historicum S.I., 1954.

Lacouture, Jean. *Jesuits: A Multibiography.* Washington, DC: Counterpoint, 1995.

Langer, Erick D. *Expecting Pears from an Elm Tree: Franciscan Missions on the Chiriguano Frontier in the Heart of South America.* Durham, NC: Duke University Press, 2009.

————. "Missions and the Frontier Economy: The Case of the Franciscan Missions among the Chiriguanos, 1845–1930." In *The New Latin American Mission History,* edited by Erick Langer and Robert H. Jackson, 49–76. Lincoln: University of Nebraska Press, 1995.

Langer, Erick, and Robert H. Jackson, eds. *The New Latin American Mission History.* Lincoln: University of Nebraska Press, 1995.

Levene, Ricardo. *Investigaciones acerca de la historia económica del virreinato del Plata.* 2 vols. Buenos Aires: El Ateneo, 1952.

Levinton, Norberto. *La arquitectura jesuítico-guaraní: una experiencia de interacción cultural.* Buenos Aires: Editorial SB, 2008.

————. "Las estancias de Nuestra Señora de los Reyes de Yapeyú: tenencia de la tierra por uso cotidiano, acuerdo interétnico y derecho natural (misiones jesuíticas del Paraguay)." *Revista Complutense de Historia de América* 31 (2005): 33–51.

Livi-Bacci, Massimo. *Conquest: The Destruction of the American Indios.* Cambridge: Polity, 2008.

————. "Depopulation of Hispanic America after the Conquest." *Population and Development Review* 32, no. 2 (2006): 199–232.

Livi-Bacci, Massimo, and Ernesto J. Maeder. "The Missions of Paraguay: The Demography of an Experiment." *Journal of Interdisciplinary History* 35, no. 2 (Autumn 2004): 185–224.

López, Adalberto. *The Colonial History of Paraguay: The Revolt of the Comuneros, 1721–1735.* New Brunswick, NJ: Transaction Publishers, 2005.

————. "The Economics of Yerba Mate in Seventeenth-Century South America." *Agricultural History* 48, no. 4 (Oct. 1974): 493–509.

López-Calva, Luis F., and Nora Lustig. "Explaining the Decline in Inequality in Latin America: Technological Change, Educational Upgrading, and Democracy." In *Declining Inequality in Latin America: A Decade of Progress,* edited by Luis F. López-Calva and Nora Lustig, 1–24. Baltimore: Brookings Institution Press, 2010.

Lynch, John. *Spanish Colonial Administration, 1782–1810: The Intendant System in the Viceroyalty of the Río de la Plata.* London: Athlone Press, 1958.

Maeder, Ernesto J. A. "Asimetría demográfica entre las reducciones franciscanas y jesuíticas de guaraníes." *Revista Complutense de Historia de América* 21 (1995): 71–83.

———. *Historia económica de Corrientes en el período virreinal, 1776–1810.* Buenos Aires: Academia Nacional de la Historia, 1981.

———. *Misiones del Paraguay: Conflictos y disolución de la sociedad guaraní (1768–1850).* Madrid: Editorial MAPFRE, 1992.

———. "La población de las misiones de guaraníes (1641–1682): reubicación de los pueblos y consecuencias demográficas." *Estudos Ibero-Americanos* 15, no. 1 (1989): 49–80.

———. "La producción ganadera en misiones en la epoca post-jesuítica (1768–1810)." *Folia Histórica del Nordeste* 9 (1990): 55–105.

Maeder, Ernesto J. A., and Alfredo S. C. Bolsi. "La población guaraní de la provincia de Misiones en la época post jesuítica (1768–1809)." *Folia Histórica del Nordeste* 54 (1982): 61–106.

———. "La población guaraní de las misiones jesuíticas: evolución y características (1671–1767)." *Cuadernos de Geohistoria Regional* 4 (1980): 1–45.

Maeder, Ernesto J. A., and Ramon Gutiérrez. *Atlas histórico del nordeste argentino.* Resistencia, Argentina: Instituto de Investigaciones Geohistóricas, Conicet-Fundanord y Universidad Nacional del Nordeste, 1995.

Mann, Kristin Dutcher. *The Power of Song: Music and Dance in the Mission Communities of Northern New Spain, 1590–1810.* Stanford, CA: Stanford University Press; Berkeley, CA: Academy of American Franciscan History, 2010.

Mansuy-Diniz Silva, Andrée. "Portugal and Brazil: Imperial Re-Organization, 1750–1808." In *The Cambridge History of Latin America*, vol. 1, *Colonial Latin America*, edited by Leslie Bethell, 469–508. Cambridge: Cambridge University Press, 1984.

Mariluz Urquijo, José M. "Los guaraníes después de la expulsión de los jesuitas." *Estudios Americanos* 25 (1953): 323–330.

———. *El virreinato del Río de la Plata en la época del marqués de Avilés (1799–1801).* 2nd ed. Buenos Aires: Plus Ultra, 1987.

Mark, Catherine, and José G. Rigau-Pérez. "Spanish Smallpox Vaccine Expedition, 1803–1813." *Bulletin of the History of Medicine* 93, no. 1 (2009): 63–94.

Martínez Martín, Carmen. "Datos estadísticos de población sobre las misiones del Paraguay, durante la demarcación del Tratado de Límites de 1750." *Revista Complutense de Historia de América* 24 (1998): 249–261.

———. "El padrón de Larrazábal en las misiones del Paraguay (1772)." *Revista Complutense de Historia de América* 29 (2003): 25–50.

Maxwell, Kenneth. *Pombal: Paradox of the Enlightenment.* Cambridge: Cambridge University Press, 1995.

Mayo, Carlos A. "Landed but Not Powerful: The Colonial Estancieros of Buenos Aires (1750–1810)." *Hispanic American Historical Review* 71, no. 4 (Nov. 19991): 761–779.

McBride, George McCutcheon. "Cotton Growing in South America." *Geographical Review* 9, no. 1 (Jan. 1920): 35–50.

Melià, Bartomeu, and Dominique Temple. *El don, la venganza y otras formas de economía guaraní.* Asunción: Centro de Estudios Paraguayos "Antonio Guasch," 2004.

Merino, Olga, and Linda A. Newson. "Jesuit Missions in Spanish America: The Aftermath of the Expulsion." *Yearbook of Latin American Geographers* 21 (1995): 133–148.

Metcalf, Alida C. *Go-Betweens and the Colonization of Brazil, 1500–1600.* Austin: University of Texas Press, 2005.

Métraux, Alfred. "The Guaraní." In *Handbook of South American Indians,* edited by Julian H. Steward, 2:69–94. New York: Cooper Square, 1963.

Moles, Peter, and Nicholas Terry. *The Handbook of International Financial Terms.* Oxford: Oxford University Press, 2002.

Monteiro, John Manuel. "Os Guaraní e a história do Brasil meredional séuculos XVI–XVII." In *História dos Índios no Brasil,* edited by Manuela Carneiro da Cunha, 475–498. São Paulo: Fundação de Amparo á Pesquisa do Estado de São Paulo, 1992.

———. *Negros da terra: índios e bandeirantes nas origens de São Paulo.* São Paulo: Companhia das Letras, 1994.

Montoya, Alfredo J. *Cómo evolucionó la ganadería en la época del virreinato.* Buenos Aires: Plus Ultra, 1984.

Moraes Vázquez, María Inés. "Crecimiento del litoral rioplantese colonial y decadencia de la economía misionera: un análisis desde la ganadería." *Investigaciones de Historia Económica,* no. 9 (Autumn 2007): 11–44.

———. "Las economías agrarias del litoral rioplatense en la segunda mitad del siglo XVII: Paisajes y despempeño." PhD diss., Universidad Complutense de Madrid, 2011.

Moraes, María-Inés, and Natalia Stalla. "Antes y después de 1810: escenarios en la historia de las exportaciones rioplatenses de cueros desde 1760 hasta 1860." *Sociedad Española de Historia Agraria—Documentos de Trabajo,* no. 11-10 (2011): 1–33.

Morales, Martín. "Al ritmo de la *tain-tain*: el drama cotidiano en el mundo guaraní." In *Tradiciones y conflictos: historias de la vida cotidiana en México e Hispanoamérica,* edited by Pilar Gonzalbo Aizpuru and Mílada Bazant, 29–72. Mexico City: Colegio de México, 2007.

———. "Reducciones." In *Diccionario histórico de la compañía de Jesús,* vol. 4, *Piatti-Zwaans,* edited by Charles E. O'Neill and Joaquín Ma. Domínguez, 111–114. Rome: Institutum Historicum, S.I., 2001.

Moreno, José Luis, and Marisa M. Díaz. "Unidades domésticas, familias, mujeres y trabajo en Buenos Aires a mediados del siglo XVII." *Entrepasados* 8, no. 16 (1999): 25–42.

Morinigo, Marcos Augusto. *Raíz y destino del guaraní.* Asunción: Imprenta Salesiana, 1989.

Mörner, Magnus. *Actividades políticas y económicas de los jesuitas en el Río de la Plata: la era de los Habsburgos.* Buenos Aires: Paidós, 1968.

———. "The Expulsion of the Jesuits from Spain and Spanish America in 1767 in Light of Eighteenth-Century Regalism." *The Americas* 23, no. 2 (Oct. 1966): 156–164.

———. *The Political and Economic Activities of the Jesuits in the La Plata Region: the Habsburg Era.* Translated by Albert Read. Stockholm: Victor Pettersons Bokindustri, 1953.

Moscatelli, Gustavo N. "Los suelos de la región pampeana." In *El desarrollo agropecuario pampeano*, edited by Osvaldo Barsky, 11–76. Buenos Aires: Grupo Editor Latinoamericano, 1991.

Moutoukias, Zacarías. *Contrabando y control colonial en el siglo XVII.* Buenos Aires: Centro Editor de América Latina, 1988.

———. "El crecimiento en una economía colonial de antiguo régimen: reformismo y sector externo en el Río de la Plata, 1760–1796." *Arquivos do Centro Cultural Calouste Gulbenkian* 34 (1995): 771–813.

Mumford, Jeremy Ravi. *Vertical Empire: The General Resettlement of Indians in the Colonial Andes.* Durham, NC: Duke University Press, 2012.

Necker, Louis. *Indios guaraníes y chamanes franciscanos: las primeras reducciones del Paraguay, 1580–1800.* Asunción: Universidad Católica, 1990.

Negro, Sandra, and Manuel M. Marzal, eds. *Un reino el la frontera: las misiones jesuitas en la América colonial.* Lima: Pontificia Universidad Católica del Perú, 1999.

Neumann, Eduardo. "Fronteira e identidade: confrontos luso-guarani na Banda Oriental 1680–1757." *Revista Complutense de Historia de América* 26 (2000): 73–92.

———. "A lança e as cartas: escrita indígena e conflito nas reduções do Paraguai—século XVIII." *História Unisinos* 11, no. 2 (2007): 160–172.

———. "'Mientras volaban correos por los pueblos': autogoverno e práticas letradas nas missões Guaraní—século XVIII." *Horizontes Antropológicos* 10, no. 22 (2004): 93–119.

———. "Prácticas letradas guaraníes en las reducciones del Paraguay (siglos XVII y XVIII)." PhD diss., Universidade Federal do Rio de Janeiro, 2005.

———. *O trabalho guarani missioneiro no Rio da Prata colonial, 1640/1750.* Porto Alegre, Brazil: Martins Livreiro, 1996.

Noelli, Francisco Silva. "La distribución geográfica de las evidencias arqueológicas guaraní." *Revista de Indias* 44, no. 230 (2004): 17–34.

Nonneman, Walter. "On the Economics of the Socialist Theocracy of the Jesuits in Paraguay (1609–1767)." In *The Political Economy of Theocracy*, edited by Mario Ferrero and Ronald Wintrobe, 119–142. New York: Palgrave Macmillan, 2009.

O'Malley, John W. *The First Jesuits.* Cambridge, MA: Harvard University Press, 1993.

———. "The Society of Jesus." In *A Companion to the Reformation World*, edited by R. Po-chia Hsia, 223–236. Malden, MA: Blackwell, 2004.

———. "Was Ignatius Loyola a Church Reformer? How to Look at Early Modern Catholicism." *Catholic Historical Review* 77, no. 2 (Apr. 1991): 177–193.

O'Malley, John W., Guavin Alexander Bailey, Steven J. Harris, and T. Frank Kennedy, eds. *The Jesuits II: Cultures, Sciences, and the Arts, 1540–1773*. Toronto: University of Toronto Press, 2006.

O'Neill, Charles E., and Joaquín M. Domínguez, eds. *Diccionario histórico de la Compañía de Jesús*. 4 vols. Rome: Institutum Historicum, S.I., 2001.

Owensby, Brian P. *Empire of Law and Indian Justice in Colonial Mexico*. Stanford, CA: Stanford University Press, 2008.

Parry, J. H. *The Spanish Seaborne Empire*. Berkeley: University of California Press, 1966.

Peramás, José Manuel. *La república de Platón y los guaraníes*. Asunción: Parroquia de San Rafael, 2003.

Pereda, Setembrino E. *Paysandú en el siglo XVIII, época de su erección y origen de su nombre*. Montevideo: El Siglo Ilustrador, 1938.

Pivel Devoto, Juan E. *Colección de documentos para la historia económica y financiera de la república oriental del Uruguay*. Montevideo: Ministerio de Hacienda, 1964.

———. *Raíces coloniales de la revolución oriental de 1811*. 2nd ed. Montevideo: Editorial Medina, 1957.

Poenitz, Edgar, and Alfredo Poenitz. *Misiones, provincia guaranítica: defensa y disolución, 1768–1830*. Posadas, Argentina: Editorial Universitaria, Universidad Nacional de Misiones, 1998.

Popescu, Oreste. *El sistema económico en las misiones jesuitas*. Barcelona: Ariel, 1967.

———. *Studies in the History of Latin American Economic Thought*. London: Routledge, 1997.

Porto, Aurelio. *História das missões orientais do Uruguai*. 2 vols. Rio de Janeiro: Imprensa Nacional, 1943.

Posthumus, N. W. *Inquiry into the History of Prices in Holland*. Vol. 1. Leiden: E. J. Brill, 1946.

Prado, Fabricio. *Côlonia do Sacramento: o extreme sul da América Portuguesa no séclo XVIII*. Porto Alegre, Brazil: F. P. Prado, 2002.

Prescott, William H. *History of the Conquest of Mexico*. 3 vols. New York: Random House, 1843.

———. *History of the Conquest of Peru: With a Preliminary View of the Civilization of the Incas*. 2 vols. New York: Harper and Brothers, 1847.

Quarleri, Lía. "Gobierno y liderazgo jesuítico-guaraní en tiempos de guerra (1752–1756)." *Revista de Indias* 68, no. 243 (2008): 89–114.

———. *Rebelión y guerra en las fronteras del Plata: guaraníes, jesuitas e imperios coloniales*. Buenos Aires: Fondo de Cultura Económica, 2009.

———. "El territorio jesuítico-guaraní: del enfrentamiento de sentidos al conflict armado (1750–1761)." *História Unisinos* 11, no. 2 (Aug. 2007): 173–184.

Radding, Cynthia. *Landscapes of Power and Identity: Comparative Histories in the Sonoran Desert and the Forests of Amazonia from Colony to Republic*. Durham, NC: Duke University Press, 2005.

———. *Wandering Peoples: Colonialism, Ethnic Spaces, and Ecological Frontiers in Northwestern Mexico, 1700–1850*. Durham, NC: Duke University Press, 1997.

Ramírez, Susan Elizabeth. *The World Upside Down: Cross-Cultural Contact and Conflict in Sixteenth-Century Peru.* Stanford, CA: Stanford University Press, 1996.

Reff, Daniel T. "The Jesuit Mission Frontier in Comparative Perspectives." In *Contested Ground: Comparative Frontiers on the Northern and Southern Edges of the Spanish Empire,* edited by Donna J. Guy and Thomas E. Sheridan, 16–31. Tucson: University of Arizona Press, 1998.

Reiter, Frederick J. *They Built Utopia (The Jesuit Missions in Paraguay, 1610–1768).* Potomac, MD: Scripta Humanistica, 1995.

Ricard, Robert. *The Spiritual Conquest of Mexico: An Essay on the Apostolate and the Evangelizing Methods of the Mendicant Orders in New Spain, 1523–1572.* Berkeley: University of California Press, 1966.

Ricca, Javier. *El maté: los secretos desde la infusión: desde la cultura nativa hasta nuestros días.* Montevideo: Mandinga Editor, 2002.

Riedel, Stefan. "Edward Jenner and the History of Smallpox and Vaccination." *Baylor University Medical Center Proceedings* 18, no. 1 (Jan. 2005): 21–25.

Riley, James C. "Smallpox and American Indians Revisited." *Journal of the History of Medicine and Allied Sciences* 65, no. 4 (Oct. 2010): 445–477.

Ringrose, David R. *Spain, Europe and the "Spanish Miracle," 1700–1900.* Cambridge: Cambridge University Press, 1996.

Rípodas Ardanaz, Daisy. "Pervivencia de hechiceros en las misiones guaraníes." *Folia Histórica del Nordeste* 6 (1984): 199–217.

Rosal, Miguel A., and Roberto Schmit. "Las exportaciones pecuarias bonaerenses y el espacio mercantil rioplatense (1768–1854)." In *En busca de un tiempo perdido: la economía de Buenos Aires en el país de la abundancia, 1750–1865,* edited by Raul Fradkin and Juan Carlos Garavaglia, 159–193. Buenos Aires: Prometeo, 2004.

Roulet, Florencia. *La resistencia de los guaraní del Paraguay, a la conquista española [1537–1556].* Posadas, Argentina: Editorial Universitaria, 1993.

Saeger, James Schofield. *The Chaco Mission Frontier: The Guyacuruan Experience.* Tucson: University of Arizona Press, 2000.

———. "Origins of the Rebellion of Paraguay." *Hispanic American Historical Review* 52, no. 2 (May 1972): 215–229.

———. "Warfare, Reorganization, and Readaptation at the Margins of Spanish Rule—The Chaco and Paraguay (1573–1882)." In *The Cambridge History of the Native Peoples of the Americas,* edited by Frank Salomon and Stuart B. Schwartz, vol. 3, pt. 2, 257–286. Cambridge: Cambridge University Press, 1999.

Saguier, Eduardo R. "El mercado del cuero y su rol como fuente alternativa de empleo: el caso del trabajo a destajo en las vaquerías de la Banda Oriental durante el siglo XVIII." *Revista de Historia Económica* 9, no. 1 (1991): 103–126.

Sahlins, Marshall. *Stone Age Economics.* Chicago: Aldine-Atherton, 1972.

Sala de Touron, Lucía, Julio C. Rodríguez, and Nelson de la Torre. *Evolución económica de la Banda Oriental.* 2nd ed. Montevideo: Ediciones Pueblos Unidos, 1968.

Salinas, María Laura, and Pedro Miguel Omar Svriz Wucherer. "Liderazgo guaraní en tiempos de paz y de guerra: los caciques en las reducciones franciscanas y jesuíticas, siglo XVII y XVIII." *Revista de Historia Militar* 110 (2011): 113–152.

Salvatore, Ricardo, and Jonathan C. Brown. "Trade and Proletarianization in Late Colonial Banda Oriental: Evidence from the Estancia de Las Vacas, 1791–1805." *Hispanic American Historical Review* 67, no. 3 (Aug. 1987): 431–459.

Santiago, Myrna I. *The Ecology of Oil: Environment, Labor, and the Mexican Revolution, 1900–1938.* Cambridge: Cambridge University Press, 2006.

Sarreal, Julia. "Caciques as Placeholders in the Guaraní Missions of Eighteenth Century Paraguay." *Colonial Latin American Review* 23, no. 2 (2014).

———. "Disorder, Wild Cattle, and a New Role for the Missions: The Banda Oriental, 1776–1786." *The Americas* 67, no. 4 (April 2011): 517–545.

———. "Globalization and the Guaraní." PhD diss., Harvard University, 2009.

———. "Revisiting Cultivated Agriculture, Animal Husbandry, and Daily Life in the Guaraní Missions." *Ethnohistory* 60, no. 1 (Jan. 2013): 101–124.

Schávelzon, Daniel. *The Historical Archeology of Buenos Aires: A City at the End of the World.* New York: Kluwer Academic / Plenum Publishers, 2000.

Schiavetto, Solange Nunes de Oliveira. *A arqueologia guarani: construção e desconstrução da identidade indígena.* São Paulo: FAPESP, 2003.

Schiebinger, Londa. *Plants and Empire: Colonial Bioprospecting in the Atlantic World.* Cambridge, MA: Harvard University Press, 2004.

Scott, H. M. "Religion and Realpolitik: The Duc de Choisel, the Bourbon Family Compact, and the Attack on the Society of Jesus, 1758–1775." *International History Review* 25, no. 1 (March 2003): 37–62.

Scott, James C. *The Art of Not Being Governed: An Anarchist History of Upland Southeast Asia.* New Haven, CT: Yale University Press, 2009.

Serulnikov, Sergio. *Subverting Colonial Authority: Challenges to Spanish Rule in Eighteenth-Century Southern Andes.* Durham, NC: Duke University Press, 2003.

Service, Elman R. "The Encomienda in Paraguay." *Hispanic American Historical Review* 31, no. 2 (May 1951): 230–252.

———. *Spanish-Guarani Relations in Early Colonial Paraguay.* Westport, CT: Greenwood Press, 1971.

Shapiro, Judith. "From Tupã to the Land without Evil: The Christianization of Tupí-Guaraní Cosmology." *American Ethnologist* 14, no. 1 (Feb. 1987): 126–139.

Silva, Eduardo. *Challenging Neoliberalism in Latin America.* Cambridge: Cambridge University Press, 2009.

Silva, Hernán A. *El comercio entre España y el Río de la Plata (1778–1810).* Madrid: Banco de España, Servicio de Estudios, 1993.

Smidt, Andrea J. "Bourbon Regalism and the Importation of Gallicanismo: The Political Path for a State Religion in Eighteenth-Century Spain." *Anuario de Historia de la Iglesia* 19 (2010): 25–53.

Soares, André Luis R. *Guarani: organização social e arqueologia.* Porto Alegre, Brazil: Pontifícia Universidade Católica do Rio Grande do Sul, 1997.

Socolow, Susan M. *The Bureaucrats of Buenos Aires, 1769–1810: Amor al Real Servicio.* Durham, NC: Duke University Press, 1987.

———. *The Merchants of Buenos Aires, 1778–1810.* Cambridge: Cambridge University Press, 1978.

Socolow, Susan M., and Lyman L. Johnson. "Urbanization in Colonial Latin America." *Journal of Urban History* 8, no. 1 (1981): 27–59.

Sommer, Barbara Ann. "Negotiated Settlements: Native Amazonians and Portuguese Policy in Pará, Brazil, 1758–1798." PhD diss., University of New Mexico, 2000.

Souza, José Otávio Catafesto de. "O sistema econômico nas sociedades indígenas guarani pré-coloniais." *Horizontes Antropológicos* 8, no. 18 (2002): 211–253.

Spalding, Karen. *Huarochirí: An Andean Society under Inca and Spanish Rule.* Stanford, CA: Stanford University Press, 1984.

Stein, Stanley J., and Barbara H. Stein. *Apogee of Empire: Spain and New Spain in the Age of Charles III, 1759–1789.* Baltimore: Johns Hopkins University Press, 2003.

Stern, Steve J. *Peru's Indian Peoples and the Challenge of Spanish Conquest: Huamanga to 1640.* 2nd ed. Madison: University of Wisconsin Press, 1993.

Storni, Hugo. *Catálogo de los jesuitas de la provincia del Paraguay (Cuenca del Plata), 1585–1768.* Rome: Institutum Historicum S.I., 1980.

Susnik, Branislava. *Los aborígenes del Paraguay,* vol. 2, *Etnohistoria de los guaraníes (Epoca Colonial).* Asunción: Museo Etnográfico "Andrés Barbero," 1979–1980.

———. *Los aborígenes del Paraguay,* vol. 4, *Cultura Material.* Asunción: Museo Etnográfico "Andrés Barbero," 1982.

———. *Los aborígenes del Paraguay,* vol. 5, *Ciclo vital y estructura social.* Asunción: Museo Etnográfico "Andrés Barbero," 1983.

———. *El indio colonial del Paraguay,* vol. 2, *Los trece pueblos guaraníes de las misiones, 1767–1810.* Asunción: Museo Etnográfico "Andrés Barbero," 1966.

———. *El rol de los indígenas en la formación y en la vivencia del Paraguay.* 2 vols. Asunción: Instituto Paraguayo de Estudios Nacionales, 1982–1983.

Sweet, David. "The Ibero-American Frontier Mission in Native American History." In *The New Latin American Mission History,* edited by Erick Langer and Robert H. Jackson, 1–48. Lincoln: University of Nebraska Press, 1995.

Takeda, Kazuhisa. "Estudio preliminar sobre la estructura de los cacicazgos de indios guaraníes en las misiones jesuíticas del Río de la Plata: análisis de los padrones (1657–1801)." Paper presented at the 54th International Congress of Americanists, Vienna, 2012.

Tandeter, Enrique, and Nathan Wachtel. "Precios y producción agraria: Potosí y Charcas en el siglo XVIII." *Desarrollo Económico* 23, no. 90 (Jul.–Sep. 1983): 197–232.

Telesca, Ignacio. *Tras los expulsos: cambios demográficos y territoriales en el Paraguay después de la expulsión de los jesuitas.* Asunción: Centro de Estudios Antropológicos de la Universidad Católica "Nuestra Señora de la Asunción," 2009.

TePaske, John J., and Herbert S. Klein. *The Royal Treasuries of the Spanish Empire in America*, vol. 3, *Chile and the Río de la Plata*. Durham, NC: Duke University Press, 1982.

Torre Curiel, José Refugio de la. "Conquering the Frontier: Contests for Religion, Survival, and Profits in Northwestern Mexico, 1768–1855." PhD diss., University of California, Berkeley, 2005.

———. "Decline and Renaissance amidst the Crisis: The Transformation of Sonora's Mission Structures in the Late Colonial Period." *Colonial Latin American Review* 18, no. 1 (Apr. 2009): 51–73.

Torre Revello, José. *Yapeyú (ensayo histórico)*. Buenos Aires: Ministerio de Educación y Justicia, Instituto Nacional Sanmartiniano, 1958.

Tuer, Dot. "Old Bones and Beautiful Words: The Spiritual Contestation between Shaman and Jesuit in the Guaraní Missions." In *Colonial Saints: Discovering the Holy in the Americas, 1500–1800*, edited by Allan Greer and Jodi Bilinkoff, 77–98. New York: Routledge, 2003.

Van Kley, Dale. *The Jansenists and the Expulsion of the Jesuits from France 1757–1765*. New Haven, CT: Yale University Press, 1975.

Villegas, Juan. "Evangelización y agricultura en las reducciones jesuíticas del Paraguay." In *Missões Guarani: impacto na sociedade contemporânea*, edited by Regina A. F. Gadelha, 167–182. São Paulo: EDUC, 1999.

Wait, Eugene M. "Mariano Moreno: Promoter of Enlightenment." *Hispanic American Historical Review* 45, no. 3 (1965): 359–383.

Weber, David J. *Bárbaros: Spaniards and Their Savages in the Age of Enlightenment*. New Haven, CT: Yale University Press, 2005.

Weber, David J., and Jane M. Rausch, eds. *Where Cultures Meet: Frontiers in Latin American History*. Lanham, MD: SR Books, 1994.

Welsh, Peter C. *Tanning in the United States to 1850: A Brief History*. United States National Museum Bulletin, vol. 242. Washington, DC: Smithsonian Institution, 1964.

Whigham, Thomas. "Cattle Raising in the Argentine Northeast: Corrientes, c. 1750–1870." *Journal of Latin American Studies* 20, no. 2 (Nov. 1988): 313–335.

———. "Paraguay's *Pueblos de Indios*: Echoes of a Missionary Past." In *The New Latin American Mission History*, edited by Erick Langer and Robert H. Jackson, 157–188. Lincoln: University of Nebraska Press, 1995.

———. *The Politics of River Trade: Tradition and Development in the Upper Plata, 1780–1870*. Albuquerque: University of New Mexico Press, 1991.

White, Richard Alan. "The Political Economy of Paraguay and the Impoverishment of the Missions." *The Americas* 31, no. 4 (April 1975): 417–433.

Wilde, Guillermo. "La actitud guaraní ante la expulsión de los jesuitas: ritualidad, reciprocidad y espacio social." *Memoria Americana* 8 (1999): 141–172.

———. "Antropología histórica del liderazgo guaraní misionero (1750–1850)." PhD diss., Universidad de Buenos Aires, 2003.

———. "De las crónicas jesuíticas a las "etnografías estatales": realidades y ficciones del orden misional en las fronteras ibéricas." *Nuevo Mundo Mundos Nuevos* (Debates) (2011). http://nuevomundo.revues.org/62238.

———. "Los guaraníes después de la expulsión de los jesuitas: dinámicas políticas y transacciones simbólicas." *Revista Complutense de Historia de América* 27 (2007): 69–106.

———. "Prestigio indígena y nobleza peninsular: la invención de linajes guaraníes en las misiones del Paraguay." *Jahrbuch für Geschichte Lateinamerikas* 43 (2006): 119–145.

———. *Religión y poder en las misiones de guaraníes.* Buenos Aires: Editorial Sb, 2009.

Wright, Jonathan. "The Suppression and Restoration." In *The Cambridge Companion to the Jesuits*, edited by Thomas Worcester, 263–277. Cambridge: Cambridge University Press, 2008.

Yannakakis, Yanna. *The Art of Being In-Between: Native Intermediaries, Indian Identity, and Local Rule in Colonial Oaxaca.* Durham, NC: Duke University Press, 2008.

Yetman, David. *Conflict in Colonial Sonora: Indians, Priests, and Settlers.* Albuquerque: University of New Mexico Press, 2012.

Index

idolatry, 26, 37
Ignatius of Loyola, 23–24, 29, 94–95
inefficiency, 7, 11, 71, 122–26, 138, 179–80, 206, 222, 235–36
inequality, 7, 11, 37, 73–74, 170, 178, 184–90, 236
inoculation, 145
intermediaries, 12, 36, 39, 54, 64, 71, 107
Itapúa (mission), 58–59, 119, 142, 204, 234–35
Itatín, region of, 32, 38

Jackson, Robert H., 52, 144
Jansenism, 111–12
Jesuits: as confessors, 94–95, 98, 102, 107, 110, 112; expulsion from French territory, 6, 111–12; expulsion from Portuguese territory, 6, 109–11; expulsion from Spanish territory, 6, 112–14, 116; founding, 23–26; loss of power, 93–94; network, 27, 85–86, 90–93, 126–27, 139; obedience, 55, 98, 122–23; propaganda, 93–94, 109–14; relationship with papacy, 98, 107
Jesuits in Paraguay: as lobbyists, 33, 36, 67, 92–94, 97, 102–4, 108–9, 114, 126–27; stipend, 33, 85–86, 128–30; writings of, 66–67
Jesús (mission), 58, 119, 136, 142, 156, 190, 229, 234–35
John V (king of Portugal), 99
Joseph I (king of Portugal), 99, 110–12
Juan y Santacilia, Jorgé, 118

labor, 3–4, 7, 10–11, 17–23, 28–33, 47–48, 56, 61, 65–74, 81–84, 89, 96, 109, 136, 141–43, 150–80, 186–90, 198, 211–13, 217–20, 222–26, 229–36. *See also* productivity
La Cruz (mission), 58, 99, 119, 142, 170–71, 175–90, 225, 230–31
land, 5, 10, 18–19, 26, 56, 66, 73, 78–80, 93, 95, 101–6, 108, 122,

194–95, 198, 200–201, 213–15, 219, 227–36
language, 6, 9, 16, 27, 106, 122, 233
Larrazabal, Mariano Ignacio de, 144
Lazarte, Manuel de, 145
Lazcano, Juan Ángel de, 124, 130, 135–36, 150, 197–99, 201, 204, 209–10, 215, 228, 231
letters by the Guaraní, 4–5, 14, 105–6, 136, 140, 143, 148–49, 159–64, 167, 170, 174, 188–90, 197–98, 203, 214, 219, 233
liberty, 29, 111, 118, 125, 149–50, 166–67, 217–18, 231–35
lineage, 20, 28, 36, 39, 44, 56–57, 62–64, 173. *See also* cacicazgos; Guaraní, pre-contact
literacy, 9, 148. *See also* signatures
Livi-Bacci, Massimo, 50
López, Carlos Antonio, 235
Loreto, marqués de, 208, 213–15
Loreto (mission), 28–33, 58, 75, 119, 142, 189
Louis XV (king of France), 111
Lugo, Pedro de, 102

Machoni, Antonio, 61–62, 77, 80–81
Maeder, Ernesto J., 50, 59
manioc (mandioca or yucca), 17, 68, 181, 185
Manso de Velasco, José Antonio, 102
Maracayú, 46
María Bárbara of Portugal, 99, 112
market economy, 4, 8, 10, 15, 115–18, 138, 169–70, 182–84, 188–89, 218, 236
marriage, 19–20, 45, 49–50, 57, 155, 157. *See also* polygamy
Martínez de Irala, Domingo, 21
mayordomo, 53–54, 131, 164, 173, 185, 187–88, 208
Mbaeque, Ignacio, 160–63
measles, 50–52, 144, 146. *See also* disease; epidemics
Medina, Francisco, 214